EX·LIBRIS·SUNE·GREGERSEN

Corpus-based Approaches to Construction Grammar

Constructional Approaches to Language

ISSN 1573-594X

The series brings together research conducted within different constructional models and makes them available to scholars and students working in this and other related fields.

The topics range from descriptions of grammatical phenomena in different languages to theoretical issues concerning language acquisition, language change, and language use. The foundation of constructional research is provided by the model known as Construction Grammar (including Frame Semantics). The book series publishes studies in which this model is developed in new directions and extended through alternative approaches. Such approaches include cognitive linguistics, conceptual semantics, interaction and discourse, as well as typologically motivated alternatives, with implications both for constructional theories and for their applications in related fields such as communication studies, computational linguistics, AI, neurology, psychology, sociology, and anthropology.

This peer reviewed series is committed to innovative research and will include monographs, thematic collections of articles, and introductory textbooks.

For an overview of all books published in this series, please see
http://benjamins.com/catalog/cal

Editors

Jan-Ola Östman
University of Helsinki, Finland

Kyoko Ohara
Keio University, Japan

Advisory Board

Peter Auer
University of Freiburg, Germany

Hans C. Boas
University of Texas at Austin, USA

William Croft
University of New Mexico, USA

Charles J. Fillmore†
International Computer Science Institute, Berkeley, USA

Mirjam Fried
Charles University, Prague, Czech Republic

Adele E. Goldberg
Princeton University, USA

Seizi Iwata
Kansai University, Japan

Paul Kay
University of California, Berkeley, USA

Knud Lambrecht
University of Texas at Austin, USA

Michael Tomasello
Duke University, USA

Arnold M. Zwicky
Stanford University, USA

Volume 19

Corpus-based Approaches to Construction Grammar
Edited by Jiyoung Yoon and Stefan Th. Gries

Corpus-based Approaches to Construction Grammar

Edited by

Jiyoung Yoon
University of North Texas

Stefan Th. Gries
University of California, Santa Barbara

John Benjamins Publishing Company

Amsterdam / Philadelphia

The paper used in this publication meets the minimum requirements of the American National Standard for Information Sciences – Permanence of Paper for Printed Library Materials, ANSI z39.48-1984.

DOI 10.1075/cal.19

Cataloging-in-Publication Data available from Library of Congress

ISBN 978 90 272 0441 7 (HB)
ISBN 978 90 272 6660 6 (E-BOOK)

© 2016 – John Benjamins B.V.
No part of this book may be reproduced in any form, by print, photoprint, microfilm, or any other means, without written permission from the publisher.

John Benjamins Publishing Company · https://benjamins.com

Table of contents

CHAPTER 1
Corpus-based approaches to Construction Grammar: Introduction   1
    Jiyoung Yoon and Stefan Th. Gries

Part I. Frequencies and probabilities

CHAPTER 2
A constructional perspective on conceptual constituency:
Dutch postpositions or particles?   11
    Maaike Beliën

CHAPTER 3
Development and representation of Italian light-*fare* constructions   39
    Valeria Quochi

CHAPTER 4
Constructions with subject *vs.* object experiencers in Spanish and Italian:
A corpus-based approach   65
    Victoria Vázquez Rozas and Viola G. Miglio

Part II. Collostructional analysis

CHAPTER 5
Spanish constructions of directed motion – a quantitative study:
Typological variation and framing strategy   105
    Johan Pedersen

CHAPTER 6
A corpus-based study of infinitival and sentential complement
constructions in Spanish   145
    Jiyoung Yoon and Stefanie Wulff

CHAPTER 7
Sense-based and lexeme-based alternation biases in the Dutch
dative alternation   165
Sarah Bernolet and Timothy Colleman

Part III. Multifactorial and multivariate analysis

CHAPTER 8
A multifactorial analysis of *that*/zero alternation: The diachronic
development of the zero complementizer with *think*, *guess* and *understand*   201
C. Shank, K. Plevoets and J. Van Bogaert

CHAPTER 9
A geometric exemplar-based model of semantic structure:
The Dutch causative construction with *laten*   241
Natalia Levshina

Index   263

CHAPTER 1

Corpus-based approaches to Construction Grammar
Introduction*

Jiyoung Yoon and Stefan Th. Gries
University of North Texas / University of California, Santa Barbara

For a long period of time, generative approaches to grammar dominated the field of theoretical linguistics, and that theoretical dominance was coupled with a similar dominance of the 'method' of judgments of acceptability of (typically) decontextualized sentences to 'determine' whether a particular sentence was formed in accordance with the postulated rules of the grammar. However, during the 1980s, the field of theoretical linguistics began to change with the advent of cognitive / usage-based linguistics, and the concomitant cognitive commitment towards "providing a characterization of general principles for language that accords with what is known about the mind and brain from other disciplines" (Lakoff, 1990: 40). While early work in cognitive linguistics and Construction Grammar was characterized by methods quite similar to those of the generative approach, a first difference consisted in the fact that even some of the earliest Construction Grammar studies were already more based on observational data (even if those were often collected somewhat eclectically). Over time, the increase of usage-based linguistics on the one hand and discussions of the limits of cognitive-linguistic theorizing on the other hand led to a slow but steady increase of the (range of) methods that are being employed: Usage-based linguistics in general and Construction Grammar in particular are now brimming with experimental and observational studies, and the number of studies that also use statistical methods has been increasing to the point that there are now publications discussing the quantitative turn in cognitive linguistics (Janda, 2013).

---

* Part of this research has been supported by the University of North Texas Research and Creativity Enhancement (RCE) Grant and by the Spanish Ministry of Economy and Competitiveness, grant no. FFI2013-43593-P. We would like to thank anonymous reviewers and the series editors of Constructional Approaches to Language, Jan-Ola Östman and Kyoko Ohara, for their invaluable feedback on the earlier versions of this edited volume. We would also like to thank Francisco Ruiz de Mendoza who helped us at the initial stage of this project which was first planned for the 44th SLE conference in Rioja, Spain.

The methodological approach that has been growing most quickly in cognitive linguistics and Construction Grammar involves, arguably, the use of corpus data. The notion of *corpus* is a prototype category and the prototype of a corpus is a collection of files that contain text and/or transcribed speech that is supposed to be representative and balanced for a certain language, variety, register, or dialect; often, the files contain not just the language that has been written or spoken (often in UTF-8 encoding to cover different orthographies), but also extra annotation (often part-of-speech information, but also morphological, semantic, or other information in the form of XML annotation). Corpora differ most importantly in size (from a few narratives narrated in an underdocumented or even already extinct language to corpora of many billions of words) and in the degree of naturalness of the data they contain (from completely spontaneous dialog between two speakers to experimental highly-constrained situations).

In a recent survey of different kinds of data in Construction Grammar, Gries (2013) discusses four different kinds of quantitative uses of corpus data, which can be grouped into three different categories (in ascending order of statistical complexity):

- absolute frequencies and (conditional probabilities) of occurrence of constructions; this category would include as a limiting case studies based on the observation whether something is attested (and how) or not, but can also include cases where frequencies or probabilities are used to rank-order words in constructions etc.
- measures of association strength that quantify the degree of attraction or repulsion of two kinds of linguistic construction: if the two linguistic constructions are both words, corpus linguists have referred to these co-occurrences as *collocations*; if the two linguistic constructions are words and some other kind of construction (often, argument structure constructions or other constructions with lexically-unspecified slots), they are usually referred as *colligations* or *collostructions*;
- detailed co-occurrence data based on the annotation of many aspects of constructional uses which are then analyzed statistically using multifactorial or multivariate methods (such as regression methods/classifiers or exploratory tools such as cluster analysis/multidimensional scaling and others).

While the three kinds of quantitative uses of corpus data can be situated on a cline of statistical complexity, this does not mean that all studies should always be aiming for the highest level of complexity in the analysis: while more detailed analyses can be, all else being equal, potentially more revealing, different linguistic questions require different levels of analytical granularity (see Arppe et al., 2010). This is nicely exemplified by the studies in the present volume, which exemplify insightfully all three levels of statistical resolution in how they tackle different kinds of constructions. However, the present volume also provides another, from our point of view, welcome differentiation from much existing work: Just like in linguistics or cognitive linguistics as a whole, corpus linguistics has for a long time been dominated by studies of synchronic native-speaker English, a tendency which has been reinforced by the widespread availability of many English-language corpora and the much more slowly growing availability of both general and more specific corpora in other languages. None of the case studies in this volume is on synchronic native-speaker English – rather, they study various aspects in Dutch, Spanish, Italian (both synchronic native speaker data and L1-acquisition data), and in diachronic (Old) English on the basis of a much wider range of corpora than are typically found. In what follows, we provide a brief overview of the contributions in this volume.

The first part of this volume comprises three studies which are examples of the first kind of quantitative corpus method, namely Beliën's study of Dutch postpositions or particles, Quochi's analysis of light-*fare* ('do') verb constructions in Italian, and Vázquez Rozas & Miglio's study of subject and object experiencers in Spanish and Italian. Specifically, the main question in the study contributed by Beliën is the long-standing constituency issue of the Dutch particle constructions. Beliën points out that traditional syntactic constituency tests such as topicalization, passivization, and pronominalization did not satisfactorily provide an answer about the constituency of the Dutch particle construction. In her contribution, she employs a cognitive-grammar analysis based on Langacker (1997) in order to determine 'conceptual' constituency which is one type of constituency distinguished in a cognitive-grammar theory. A semantic analysis of the construction under study based on actually attested, rather than invented, examples suggests that Dutch particle constructions are analyzed similar to (transitive) separable complex verb constructions rather than (intransitive) preposition constructions.

Quochi's article explores the development and representation of light-*fare* verb constructions in Italian. On the basis of an analysis of language acquisition data from the CHILDES database (i.e., the Italian collection of longitudinal transcriptions of interactive sessions with eleven Italian-speaking children), she studies type-token ratios in children's and adult data as well as relative frequencies of co-occurrence data and proposes that light verb constructions in Italian can be viewed as a family of constructions or a radial category (Goldberg, 1995), which includes the central construction labelled as the Perform Intransitive Action Construction (e.g., *fare una passeggiata* 'take a walk'), the Perform/Emit Sound Construction (e.g., *fare chiasso* 'make noise'), the Perform Transitive Action Construction (e.g., *fare un colpo* 'hit'), and the Cause Emotion Construction (e.g., *fare rabbia* '(lit) do anger to someone'; 'make someone angry'). This family of constructions accounts for both the specificity of each construction and its proximity to the more general transitive construction. The findings of the study suggest that a light-*fare* 'do' (pivot) schema (that accounts for both conventional expressions and for new productive formations) may really exist, and may be taken to support the idea that light verbs act as facilitators in the learning of (argument structure) constructions (Ninio, 1999).

In the final chapter of this first part, Vázquez Rozas and Miglio provide a comparative study on constructions with subject versus object experiencers in Spanish and Italian. This study explores 'Experiencer-as-Subject' constructions (ESC) and 'Experiencer-as-Object' constructions (EOC) in Spanish and Italian using the ARTHUS corpus and the BDS/ADESSE database for Spanish, and BADIP, C-ORAL, and *La Repubblica* as corpora for Italian. In both languages, verbs that denote feeling or emotion involve two participants – an experiencer and a stimulus – but the puzzling fact is that some of these clauses construe the experiencer as a subject and the stimulus as object (e.g., *Amo esta ciudad* 'I love this city'), while others have experiencers coded as dative or accusative objects and stimuli as subjects (e.g., *Me gusta la música* 'Me-dative likes the music [I like music]'). In order to gain insight into how both constructions are used by speakers, the authors analyze the relative frequencies and distributions of a number of discourse-related properties of the arguments, such as animacy, person, and syntactic category, as well as textual genres. The results indicate that the distribution of the discourse-related properties of the arguments is not random when comparing the ESCs with the EOCs in the verbs of feeling and emotion: for instance, the use of the 1st person is more frequently found in EOCs than in ESCs, and EOCs are associated more with oral discourse than with written discourse.

The second part of this volume contains studies that are concerned with the co-occurrence of words and constructions on the basis of the family of methods that has come to be known as collostructional analysis (see Stefanowitsch & Gries, 2003; Gries & Stefanowitsch, 2004; Gries, 2015); this method quantifies the degree to which words and constructions are mutually attracted to, or repelled by, each other and what such attractions/repulsions reveal about the functional characteristics of constructions.

In the first chapter of this part, the fourth overall, on Spanish constructions of directed motion, Pedersen provides a language-specific view of Construction Grammar. Pedersen analyzes Spanish telic motion constructions with the constructional environment [V *a* 'to' NP] (e.g., **caminar a la biblioteca* 'to walk to the library') in order to revisit the Talmian typological distinction between satellite-framed languages (in which the verb encodes the manner as in English) and verb-framed languages (in which the verb encodes the path as in Spanish). To this end, the author applies collexeme analyses (see Stefanowitsch & Gries, 2003) to data extracted from the Corpus del Español, which confirm the basic encoding pattern of the Talmian typology: the verbal encoding of the path component, with the verb meaning 'path of motion leading to an end point'. Pedersen proposes that, from a Construction Grammar point of view, the constraining role of the verb is essential in Spanish while the role of the schematic construction is not as predominant as in Germanic languages such as English. In other words, the encoding of the Spanish argument structure is basically verb-driven (as opposed to construction-driven), but he cautions that 'verb-driven' is not the same as categorizing Spanish as a verb-framed language as defined in the Talmian tradition.

The second chapter of this part tackles the alternation of a complementation pattern, in this case the alternation between infinitival and sentential complement constructions in Spanish. In their contribution on infinitival and sentential complement constructions in Spanish, Yoon & Wulff analyze 561 instances of infinitival complements and 795 instances of sentential complements retrieved from a corpus of journalistic prose. Through the application of a distinctive collexeme analysis (Gries & Stefanowitsch, 2004), the authors identify the verbs most distinctively associated with either type of complementation. The results indicate that the two complementation patterns are in fact distinct constructions in the constructionist sense of the term (Goldberg, 1995, 2006): the infinitival complementation construction attracts verbs that denote 'desire' (e.g., *querer* 'want,' *intentar* 'try,' *preferir* 'prefer') whereas the sentential complementation construction is distinctively associated with verbs of 'communication' (e.g., *decir* 'say,' *explicar* 'explain,' *anunciar* 'announce') and 'mental activity' (e.g., *creer* 'believe,' *recordar* 'remember,' *reconocer* 'recognize'). At the same time, Yoon & Wulff stress the importance of the usage-based constructionist approaches in the sense that verbs do not fall into two mutually exclusive classes with each class licensing either type of complementation only, but are rather distributed probabilistically.

The final chapter of this second part is Bernolet & Colleman's contribution on sense-based and lexeme-based alternation biases in the Dutch dative alternation. This study raises the issue of whether the subcategorization probabilities of Dutch verbs partaking in the dative alternation are biased by the verbal lexeme or by the verb senses. In order to answer this question, the authors run a sense-based distinctive collexeme analysis (Gries & Stefanowitsch, 2004) on corpus data supplemented by a syntactic priming experiment. A total of 15 polysemous ditransitive verbs with two senses (i.e., sense 1: 'concrete', sense 2: 'figurative') were selected and analyzed for their association strengths with the double object (DO) construction and the prepositional dative (PD) construction with *aan*. The authors find that the distinct senses of the same verb display markedly different alternation biases toward either DO or PD constructions, showing that sense-based data in a collostructional analysis, and also in other kinds of analyses, provide a more precise picture of the Dutch dative alternation than the standard lexeme-based analysis. The additional psycholinguistic experiment involving the participation of twenty-five native speakers of Dutch, on the other hand, shows no effect of the lexeme-based or sense-based biases of prime verbs, but the results still support the position that language users are sensitive to sense-based verb biases and that they store such information in memory.

The final part of this volume contains two studies that involve very detailed case-by-case annotation of concordance results and, consequently, more advanced statistical methods. In the first chapter of this part, Shank, Plevoets, & Van Bogaert provide a multifactorial analysis of *that*/zero alternation and discuss the diachronic development of the zero complementizer with *think, guess* and *understand*. This study uses stepwise logistic regression analysis in order to evaluate the effects of eleven structural features such as length of the complement clause subject, presence versus absence of additional material in the matrix clause, matrix clause tense, etc. on complementizer realization with three verbs of cognition: *think, guess,* and *understand*. After analyzing a total of nearly 19,000 tokens from both spoken and written corpora from 1560–2012, the authors challenge the long-standing assumption of a diachronic trend towards a preference of the zero complementizer. Their finding indicates that *guess* is the only verb exhibiting such a diachronic increase. At the same time, the authors suggest that among many other factors, the lack of matrix internal elements and also the written or spoken mode are good conditioning factors for the presence or the absence of complementizers.

Last but not least, Levshina's contribution investigates a geometric exemplar-based model of semantic structure in her analysis of the Dutch causative construction with *laten* 'let'. Her innovative approach questions the commonly assumed notion of 'prototypical senses' of a construction in Construction Grammar, and presents a corpus-based bottom-up approach that can be used to model semantic structures. A sample of 731 occurrences of the causative *laten* randomly selected from the Corpus of Spoken Dutch as well as newspaper register is analyzed by visualizing semantic similarities between the exemplars of a construction in a semantic map computed using Multidimensional Scaling. This semantic map makes it possible to see the main semantic dimensions and senses of the Dutch causative construction with the auxiliary *laten*: In the map, the more features two exemplars share, the smaller the distance between them. The result suggests that the constructional semantics is organized as a doughnut, with an empty center and extensive periphery, which means that there is not necessarily a central sense, or prototype. Levshina concludes that the exemplars of *laten* are related in a family-resemblance fashion, with the main senses not being discrete, but representing a continuum.

"These are exciting times to be a ..." is a construction and a cliché, but here it is true. Cognitive linguistics is following the same trend that has been visible in linguistics at large: an evolution towards a more rigorously empirical and quantitative discipline, and a discipline that looks more and more outside of synchronic and L1 English. The articles in this volume, which reflect these trends, also leave a mark on Construction Grammar, with data from other languages, from a wide variety of corpora, and with very different quantitative approaches (for very different questions). While the evolution of (cognitive) linguistics in general and Construction Grammar in particular is certainly not coming to an end, the increased diversity of languages studied, questions explored, and methods/techniques used is a promising sign that Construction Grammar is maturing – may its journey/evolution continue along those lines ...

References

Arppe, Antti, Gilquin, Gaëtanelle, Glynn, Dylan, Hilpert, Martin & Zeschel, Arne. (2010). Cognitive corpus linguistics: Five points of debate on current theory and methodology. *Corpora*, 5(1), 1–27. doi:10.3366/cor.2010.0001

Goldberg, Adele E. (1995). *Constructions: A construction grammar approach to argument structure*. Chicago, IL: The University of Chicago Press.

Goldberg, Adele E. (2006). *Constructions at work: The nature of generalization in language*. Oxford: Oxford University Press.

Gries, Stefan Th. (2013). Data in construction grammar. In Graham Trousdale & Thomas Hoffmann (Eds.), *The Oxford handbook of construction grammar* (pp. 93–108). Oxford: Oxford University Press. doi:10.1093/oxfordhb/9780195396683.013.0006

Gries, Stefan Th. (2015). More (old and new) misunderstandings of collostructional analysis: On Schmid & Küchenhoff (2013). *Cognitive Linguistics*, 26(3), 505–536. doi:10.1515/cog-2014-0092

Gries, Stefan Th. & Stefanowitsch, Anatol. (2004). Extending collostructional analysis: A corpus-based perspective on 'alternations'. *International Journal of Corpus Linguistics*, 9, 97–129. doi:10.1075/ijcl.9.1.06gri

Janda, Laura A. (Ed.). (2013). *Cognitive linguistics – The quantitative turn*. Berlin & Boston: De Gruyter Mouton. doi:10.1515/9783110335255

Langacker, Ronald W. (1997). Constituency, dependency, and conceptual grouping. *Cognitive Linguistics*, 8(1), 1–32. doi:10.1515/cogl.1997.8.1.1

Lakoff, George. (1990). The invariance hypothesis: Is abstract reason based on image schemas? *Cognitive Linguistics*, 1(1), 39–74. doi:10.1515/cogl.1990.1.1.39

Ninio, Anat. (1999). Pathbreaking Verbs in Syntactic Development and the Question of Prototypical Transitivity. *Journal of Child Language* 26, 619–653.

Stefanowitsch, Anatol & Gries, Stefan Th. (2003). Collostructions: Investigating the interaction between words and constructions. *International Journal of Corpus Linguistics*, 8(2), 209–243. doi:10.1075/ijcl.8.2.03ste

PART I

Frequencies and probabilities

CHAPTER 2

A constructional perspective on conceptual constituency
Dutch postpositions or particles?

Maaike Beliën
Delft University of Technology

Cognitive Grammar distinguishes three types of constituents: phonological, conceptual, and grammatical constituents. This study argues that this distinction offers a new and promising perspective on constructions whose constituent structure, or 'constituency', has seemed to defy analysis in the past. In particular, the study proposes a method to analyze conceptual constituency, which crucially relies on semantic considerations. The method is applied to constructions from Dutch with adpositions whose syntactic status has been unclear: they have been analyzed as postpositions by some, yet as particles by others. Using corpus data rather than constructed data with grammaticality judgments, the study concludes that the method provides new arguments for a 'particle analysis'.

1. Introduction

Constituent structure, a central notion in the generative tradition to language, has received little attention in constructional approaches. A notable exception is Langacker (1995, 1997), who describes how the Cognitive Grammar view on constituent structure (or 'constituency') contrasts with the notion in the generative tradition. Essentially, Cognitive Grammar does not consider constituency to comprise "a separate, purely 'syntactic' level of representation" (Langacker, 1995: 162), but rather regards it as emergent from "our capacity for grouping on the basis of similarity and contiguity" (Langacker, 1997: 1). In particular, constituency in Cognitive Grammar is understood to be "merely the order in which simpler symbolic structures combine to form progressively larger ones" (Langacker, 1995: 162). As different kinds of structures can be combined, Cognitive Grammar distinguishes three types of constituents: phonological, conceptual and grammatical constituents.

This paper argues that the Cognitive Grammar view of constituency offers a new perspective on constructions whose constituent structure has been notoriously hard to analyze, such as (1) from Dutch. Relying on well-known constituency tests such as topicalization, passivization, and pronominalization, earlier studies have not been able to reach a consensus on how to analyze the structure of such examples.

(1) hun   fietspontje   [vaart] het kanaal over   (jgdapr95)[1]
    their bicycle-ferry sails   the canal   over
    'Their bicycle ferry sails across the canal'

Some studies consider their constituency to be similar to that of constructions such as (2), which consist of a subject, an intransitive verb, and a prepositional phrase, and which will be referred to as 'Preposition Constructions' (PreCs) in this study. Based on perceived syntactic similarities between (1) and (2), these studies analyze constructions such as (1) in terms of a subject, an intransitive verb and a postpositional phrase (Helmantel, 2002; Paardekooper, 1959).

(2) We varen over het Haren-Rüttenbrockkanaal   (wk199212)
    we sail   over the Haren-Rüttenbrock-canal
    'We are sailing along the Haren-Rüttenbrock Canal'

Other studies have proposed that (1) is syntactically similar to constructions such as (3), which consist of a subject, a separable complex verb, and a direct object. Separable complex verbs (SCVs, cf. e.g. Blom, 2005; Booij, 1998) are 'complex' because they consist of two elements, i.e. a verb and a particle (*haalt* 'pulls' and *over* 'over' in (3)). And they are 'separable' because the particle occurs separate from the verb in some syntactic contexts, cf. (3), yet prefixed to the verb in other contexts, e.g. *overgehaald* 'over-pulled' in the subordinate clause in (4). Constructions such as (3) and (4) will be referred to as SCV Constructions (SCVCs) in this study. Based on perceived syntactic similarities between constructions such as (1) and SCVCs, some studies have proposed that (1) consists of a subject, a separable complex verb and a direct object (Beeken, 1993; Verkuyl & Zwarts, 1992).

(3) de   gevangene haalt de   trekker over   (jnlfeb93)
    the prisoner   pulls the trigger over
    'The prisoner pulls the trigger'

(4) [...] dat het slachtoffer [...] de   trekker heeft overgehaald (mcfeb93ove)
         that the victim   the trigger has   over-pulled
    'that the victim has pulled the trigger'

---

1. The examples followed by this type of code in brackets are from the 38 million word corpus of the Institute for Dutch Lexicology (www.inl.nl).

The majority of the studies, however, allow both types of analysis, because they consider constructions such as (1) to be syntactically similar to PreCs in some respects, yet similar to SCVCs in others. Under this type of analysis, (1) is considered to be structurally ambiguous: it essentially consists of a subject, an intransitive verb and a postpositional phrase, but the postposition may be 'reanalyzed' as a particle (Blom, 2005; de Haas & Trommelen, 1993; de Schutter, 1974; Hoekstra, 1984; Luif, 1992; van Riemsdijk, 1978).

The cognitive-grammar view of constituency can shed new light on this old constituency issue, because it distinguishes between phonological, semantic, and grammatical constituency. Inspired by this view, the present paper proposes a constructional method for determining constituency, which is based on the analysis of constructions such as (1) in Beliën (2008). As the conclusion there was that such constructions have a similar constituency to that of SCVCs, constructions such as (1) will be referred to as 'Particle Constructions' (ParCs) here.

The method proposed in this paper differs fundamentally from one that uses constituency tests such as topicalization and passivization. In accordance with the cognitive-grammar view that "symbolic considerations are critical to the determination of grammatical constituency" (Langacker, 1987: 366), the method focuses first and foremost on the semantics of the constructions involved, which earlier studies have largely ignored. A second difference is that the method is applied to corpus data, because they show what types of structures are actually produced by speakers, and in which contexts. Earlier studies, on the other hand, relied on isolated, constructed sentences, with diverging grammaticality (or acceptability) judgments as a result. The authentic data presented here were collected from the 38 million word corpus of the Institute for Dutch Lexicology (cf. fn. 1), and from the Internet.

The article is organized as follows. Section 2 shows how the method of constituency tests as used in the generative approach to language has resulted in a lack of consensus. Section 3 proposes a constructional method for determining conceptual constituency, which consists of three steps, which are illustrated in the sections that follow: (i) a semantic analysis of the construction under study (Section 4); (ii) a semantic comparison of that construction with relevant other constructions, i.e. constructions whose constituency may be similar (Section 5); and (iii) an account of semantic differences and similarities in terms of constituency (Section 6). Section 7 explores how the presented method can be extended to a full constructional analysis of constituency, which includes an evaluation of the relevance of the data from the constituency tests. Section 8 concludes that the constructional method for determining constituency yields new insights into the semantics of the construction from Dutch, which in turn offer a new type of argumentation for an analysis of their constituency as well as that of other long-standing constituency issues.

2. Constituency tests: Lack of consensus

To determine the constituency of ParCs, previous studies have compared the construction's 'syntactic behavior' with that of PreCs and SCVCs. By applying such constituency tests as topicalization, passivization, coordination, auxiliary choice and pronominalization (see Beliën, 2008: Ch. 2 for a complete overview), the studies have tried to decide whether ParCs are more similar to PreCs or to SCVCs. The present section illustrates, by focusing on two such tests, how this use of constituency tests has not led to a consensus about the constituency of ParCs.

The first test to be discussed is topicalization. The test is based on the assumption that a string of words that occurs in sentence-initial position of a main clause, i.e. in the slot before the finite verb, is a constituent. It is presented in some studies as an argument for the structural ambiguity of ParCs, cf. Examples (5)–(7) below (from Haeseryn et al., 1997: 508–509). (6) is regarded as evidence that the NP-P combination (*de garage in*, lit. 'the garage in') is a constituent, i.e. unlike the direct object and particle of an SCV. (7), on the other hand, is considered to indicate that the NP is similar to a direct object of an SCV and not part of a postpositional phrase.

(5) *Hij rijdt de garage in*
he drives the garage in
'He is driving into the garage'

(6) *De garage in rijdt hij altijd zelf*
the garage in drives he always himself
'Into the garage he always drives himself'

(7) *De garage rijdt hij altijd heel voorzichtig in*
the garage drives he always very carefully in
'The garage he always drives into very carefully'

Other studies that use the topicalization test come to different conclusions. Verkuyl and Zwarts (1992) and Beeken (1993), for example, use the test as an argument for analyzing ParCs as similar to SCVCs. This is because they have different intuitions about the 'topicalizability' of NP-P combinations than Haeseryn et al. (1997), cf. the asterisk and question mark in Example (8) from Verkuyl and Zwarts (1992: 395).

(8) *?*Het bos in is zij ondanks mijn advies toch gelopen*
the wood in is she despite my advice nevertheless walked
*?'Into the wood she has walked despite my advice'

Blom (2005), conversely, uses topicalization as an argument for considering ParCs to be different from SCVCs. Focusing on the topicalization of P-V combinations, she argues that while such combinations can occur in topicalized position in the case of SCVCs, they cannot do so in the case of ParCs, cf. her example in (9) (from Blom, 2005:119). Luif (1992), on the other hand, does consider this type of topicalization to be possible in some cases, cf. his example in (10) (from Luif, 1992:163), which is presented as evidence that ParCs are in some cases similar to SCVCs.

(9) *In gereden heeft hij de garage niet
    in driven has he the garage not
    'He has not driven into the garage'

(10) Voorbijlopen mag jij je buurman niet
     past-walk must you your neighbor not
     'You must not walk past your neighbor'

The topicalization test, in other words, has led to different results in different studies, because linguists have diverging grammaticality judgments about the examples, and different studies use the test in different ways.

The second test discussed here is passivization, which is based on the assumption that the direct object of an active construction can occur as the subject of a corresponding passive construction. Many studies consider passivization to be impossible with ParCs (e.g., Blom, 2005; de Haas & Trommelen, 1993; Paardekooper, 1966), cf. (11) from Blom (2005:119), which is taken as evidence that ParCs consist of a subject, an intransitive verb and a postpositional phrase.

(11) *De garage werd in gereden
     the garage was in driven
     'The garage was driven into'

Other studies, however, consider passivization to be possible in some cases, cf. (12) from Hoekstra (1984:172; see also de Vries, 1975), which is taken as evidence that they do not contain a postpositional phrase.

(12) Dat kanaal is nog nooit door iemand over gezwommen
     that canal is so-far never by anyone over swum
     'That channel has so far never been swum across by anyone'

Yet others agree with the grammaticality judgment in (11), but question the validity of using passivization as a constituency test (cf. de Schutter, 1974; Verkuyl & Zwarts, 1992). These studies refer to other 'two-place predicates' that, according to them, do not passivize for semantic reasons, such as *naderen* 'approach' (see also Section 7).

These constituency tests have, in other words, led to different conclusions about the constituency of ParCs. Different studies have used different sets of tests, different linguists have different intuitions about the grammaticality of the examples, and some tests have been considered to yield conflicting results. In addition, some studies have questioned the validity of some of the constituency tests. This situation warrants a different approach, which is described in the following section. The types of constructions involved in the topicalization and passivization tests are checked against authentic data in Section 7, which evaluates their relevance for determining the constituency from a constructional perspective.

3. A constructional method for determining conceptual constituency

Semantics has hardly played a role in previous studies that have sought to determine the constituency of ParCs.[2] The constituency tests that they have used are mainly concerned with whether a certain string of words is grammatical or not. According to Cognitive Grammar, however, "symbolic considerations are critical to the determination of grammatical constituency" (Langacker, 1987: 366). The present section explores how this framework can offer a method to determine constituency, in particular, conceptual constituency.

Cognitive Grammar is a construction grammar (cf. Langacker, 2005) and shares a number of basic assumptions with other construction grammars (Construction Grammar, Goldberg, 1995; Radical Construction Grammar, Croft, 2001). A number of these are listed below (selected from Langacker, 2005: 102; presented here in a different order):

- Linguistic knowledge comprises vast numbers of constructions, a large proportion of which are 'idiosyncratic' in relation to 'normal', productive grammatical patterns.
- Constructions (rather than 'rules') are the primary objects of description.
- Constructions are form-meaning pairings ('assemblies of symbolic structures').
- Composition is effected by 'unification' ('integration').
- Regularities (rules, patterns) take the form of constructions that are schematic relative to instantiating expressions.
- Constructions are linked in networks of inheritance ('categorization').

---

[2]. The study by Verkuyl and Zwarts (1992) is an exception: it argues for an SCVC-type analysis of ParCs on the basis of aspectual similarities between ParCs and SCVCs as well as constituency tests. Note also that they, like de Schutter (1974), question the validity of using the passivization test on the basis of semantic grounds.

In Cognitive Grammar, the term 'construction' is reserved for a complex expression, i.e. one that consists of component structures that combine to form a composite structure. For Dutch, for example, we can assume that speakers know the specific construction *op de grond* 'on the ground', which consists of the component structures *op* 'on' and *de grond* 'the ground'.[3] Figure 1 is a (simplified) cognitive-grammar representation of this construction, with the component structures at the bottom and the composite structure at the top.

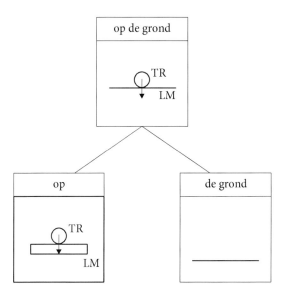

Figure 1. The construction *op de grond* 'on the ground'

The component structures as well as the composite structure are form-meaning pairings, i.e. symbolic structures: they consist of phonological structure, semantic structure and a symbolizing relationship between these structures. Each box in Figure 1 represents the phonological structure at the top, in lower case letters, and the semantic structure at the bottom, by means of a pictorial representation (in accordance with cognitive-grammar conventions, capital letters between square brackets will also be used below to represent semantic structures). The semantic structure in the case of *op* 'on', for example, consists in a spatial relation between two entities, i.e. a trajector (TR) and a landmark (LM, cf. e.g., Langacker, 1987: 217), in which the TR is in contact with a surface of the LM and there is a force pointing from the TR to the LM (cf. Beliën, 2008: 156–157).

---

3. *De grond* 'the ground' is a composite structure too, consisting of the component structures *de* 'the' and *grond* 'ground'.

Component structures can combine "by virtue of having certain substructures in common" (Langacker, 1987: 278). The semantic structures [OP] and [DE GROND], for example, can combine because [DE GROND] can be understood to be identical to a substructure of [OP], i.e., its LM. The result of their integration is represented by the upper box in Figure 1: the LM is no longer schematic, as it was in the structure of *op*, but specified in more detail, i.e. understood as [DE GROND]. The phonological structures involved are also integrated: the phonological structure [de grond], symbolizing the LM, directly follows the phonological structure [op], symbolizing the spatial relation.

Constituency is regarded in Cognitive Grammar not as autonomous, but as emergent from "our capacity for grouping on the basis of similarity and contiguity" (Langacker, 1997: 1; cf. for a similar view Beckner & Bybee, 2009; Bybee, 2002). Quite crucially, Cognitive Grammar distinguishes three types of constituents, which are illustrated in Figure 1: phonological, conceptual and grammatical constituents. The phonological structures [op] and [de grond] together form a *phonological constituent*, which is defined "as arising when two phonological structures form a group on the basis of temporal contiguity" (Langacker, 1995: 166, cf. the notion of 'chunking' in Beckner & Bybee, 2009; Bybee, 2002). The semantic structures [OP] and [DE GROND] form a *conceptual constituent*, because there is a 'valence link' between them: they "show substantial conceptual overlap[, …] which permits their integration to form a coherent composite conceptualization" (Langacker, 1995: 165). The composite structure *op de grond* 'on the ground', finally, is a *grammatical constituent*, because it represents a case in which "a conceptual constituent is symbolized by a phonological constituent" (Langacker, 1995: 166; cf. Bybee's notion of a 'traditional constituent', 2002: 130).

Distinguishing these three types of constituents opens up new and promising ways to analyze constructions whose constituency has so far seemed to defy analysis. This is because a conceptual constituent need not necessarily be symbolized by a phonological constituent, and a phonological constituent need not necessarily symbolize a conceptual constituent. Langacker (1995: 168–169) gives the example of *The package arrived that you were expecting*, in which *the package* and its relative clause are not a phonological constituent, but their semantics do form a conceptual constituent. Bybee (2002), conversely, discusses automated 'chunks' of language like English pronoun-auxiliary contraction (*I'm, I've, I'd*) or Spanish preposition-determiner combinations (*al* 'to the', *del* 'from the): they are phonological constituents, but not conceptual constituents ("they do not meet the criterion of semantic relevance", Bybee, 2002: 130). These examples are, in other words, not grammatical constituents, but either conceptual or phonological constituents.

From specific constructions, i.e. those with fully specified phonological and semantic content, language users will abstract generalizations, i.e. constructional schemas. Such schemas allow speakers to produce and understand expressions that they have not heard before. Knowing specific constructions such as *op de grond* 'on the ground', *op tafel* 'on the table', *op je bord* 'on your plate', and *op het dak* 'on the roof'", a language user may notice similarities between them. These similarities then constitute a schematic construction: the symbolic structure *op* combines with a more schematic symbolic structure, i.e. with schematic phonological structure and a [THING] as its semantic structure (see Langacker, 1987, Ch. 5 on the notional characterization of word classes in Cognitive Grammar). The constructional schema will also include the similarities in phonological, conceptual and grammatical constituency across the specific constructions, i.e. it "reflect[s] in abstract terms the symbolic compositionality observable across arrays of complex expressions" (Langacker, 1995: 152).

To shed light on the constituency of ParCs, this paper focuses mainly on conceptual constituency, i.e. the question of how the component semantic structures combine to form the composite semantic structure. The constructional method for determining conceptual constituency proposed here consists of the following steps:

1. a semantic analysis of the problematic construction,
2. a semantic comparison of the problematic constructions and relevant other constructions, i.e. constructions whose constituency may be similar, and
3. an account of the observed semantic differences and similarities in terms of constituency.

These steps are illustrated in the following three sections using Dutch ParCs as a case study, which will be compared to PreCs and SCVCs in Section 5.

4. A semantic analysis of the construction

As a first step in the method, it is necessary to analyze the semantics of the construction under study. In Beliën (2008: 105), the semantics of ParCs is characterized as follows, where P stands for the adposition (and cf. Talmy, 2003: 25 for the notion 'motion event'):

(13) The Dutch ParC profiles a motion event in which a trajector *traverses* a landmark so that *result* P is achieved: the trajector moves from where it is *not* P to where it is *completely* P.

This is, in other words, a description of the composite semantic structure of the constructional schema representing the commonalities across such specific ParCs as (1) with *over* 'over', (14) with *op* 'up, on', and (15) with *af* 'off'.[4]

---

[4] In addition to these three adpositions, eight other adpositions can occur in ParCs: *binnen* 'inside', *door* 'through', *in* 'in, into', *langs* 'along', *om* 'around', *rond* 'around', *uit* 'out, out of', and *voorbij* 'past'. Except for *af* 'off', all of these can also function as prepositions.

(1) hun   fietspontje   [vaart] het kanaal   over   (jgdapr95)
     their bicycle-ferry sails   the canal   over
     'Their bicycle ferry sails across the canal'

(14) Johan Cruijff sprintte   het veld   op   (jgdmay92)
     Johan Cruijff sprinted   the field on/up
     'Johan Cruijff sprinted onto the field'

(15) [Hij] huppelde [...] het Piazza Navona af[5]
     he   skipped   the Piazza Navona off
     'He hopped and skipped off the Piazza Navona'

As the adposition (P) is understood as the result of the motion event, the path that the TR follows with respect to the LM differs depending on which adposition is used. Figures 2–4 schematically represent the TRs' paths with respect to the LMs for these examples, which are described in more detail below. In each figure, the TR is represented by a circle, the LM by a rectangle, and the TR's path by an arrow.

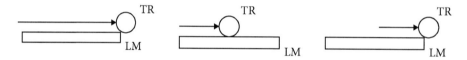

Figure 2. ParCs with *over*   **Figure 3.** ParCs with *op*   **Figure 4.** ParCs with *af*

Before turning to these, I should note that 'traversal' in (13), i.e. "a trajector *traverses* a landmark", has a broader definition than its common usage. In its normal usage, *to traverse* means moving from one side to the other of some LM, cf. the arrow in Figure 2. In this study, however, it is also used for 'partial traversal', in which case a TR traverses only part of the LM, cf. the arrows in Figures 3 and 4.[6] This broader definition of 'traversal' is meant to capture the idea that throughout the event designated by a ParC, the TR is closely involved with the LM: the TR may be in contact with the LM, in close proximity to the LM, or drawn to the LM by some force.[7]

---

5. From the novel *Kaplan* by Leon de Winter (Amsterdam: De Bezige Bij, 1989: 305).

6. In Beliën (2008: 113–114), it is also used for 'perimeter traversal' (cf. Langacker, 1991: 402) to characterize ParCs with *langs* 'along', *om* 'around' and *voorbij* 'past'.

7. The examples in the present section illustrate the first type of involvement, i.e. contact. For an illustration of the second type, i.e. proximity, see Example (20) in Section 5.1. An example of the third type of involvement can be found in (i) below. When the TR *dit meisje* 'this girl' flies across the LM *Amerika* 'America', there will be a force-dynamic relationship between her and the LM: as she flies, she will experience the force of gravity pulling her towards the LM (cf. also Beliën, 2008: 109–110).

The ParC in (1), repeated below, designates a motion event that has *over* as its result, see Figure 2. At the start of the event, the TR (*hun fietspontje* 'their bicycle ferry') is on one side of the LM (*het kanaal* 'the canal'), i.e. where the TR is not *over* the LM. At the end of the event, the TR is completely *over* the LM, i.e. on the opposite side of it.[8] The TR crosses, in other words, the breadth of the canal. Throughout the event, the TR is closely involved with the LM: the bottom of the ferry is in the water of the canal from start to finish.

(1) hun   fietspontje   [vaart]   het   kanaal   over   (jgdapr95)
    their   bicycle-ferry   sails   the   canal   over
    'Their bicycle ferry sails across the canal'

The ParC in (14) designates a motion event that has *op* 'up, on' as its result, see Figure 3. For the TR (football coach *Johan Cruijff*) to achieve this result, he must move from where he is not *op* the LM (*het veld* 'the field') to where he is completely *op* the LM, i.e. no longer supported by anything else but the field. As the construction also requires that the TR traverses the LM (be it completely or partially), *Johan Cruijff* needs to start running minimally from a boundary of the LM, i.e. where he

(i) Dit meisje [...] heeft al   aangekondigd dat zij volgend jaar gaat
    this girl   has   already   announced   that she next   year goes
    proberen om ook Amerika   over te   vliegen   (jgdsep93)
    try   to also America   over to   fly
    'This girl has already announced that next year she will try to fly across America as well'

8. It could be that the event is at some point interrupted, in which case the TR does not reach the result 'completely P', cf. (i) as an example of such an interrupted event. Certain modifiers can also be used to specify that the TR carries out only part of the event, such as *een stukje* 'a little bit, a short way' in (ii). Even in such cases, however, the language user needs to think of the complete event, i.e. from *not* P to *completely* P, to understand that only a part of it was actually achieved. In cognitive-grammar terms, each time a ParC is used, it evokes the conceptualization of the complete motion event as its 'base'; in certain cases, only part of this motion event may actually be 'profiled' (cf. Beliën, 2008: 123–132 for more discussion and examples).

(i) De Schaijkenaar   was bezig de breedste kant van de plas over te
    the man-from-Schaijk   was busy   the broadest side of   the lake over to
    zwemmen, toen hij door nog onbekende oorzaak verdronk.
    swim   when he by yet unknown   cause   drowned
    'The man from Schaijk was swimming across the broadest side of the lake, when he drowned by a yet unknown cause.'
              (Http://www.deomroeper.nl/nieuws/17-jarige-jongen-uit-schaijk-verdronken-
                          de-recreatieplas-bij-camping-de-maashorst/, December 2012)

(ii) We [...] lopen [...] een stukje de markt over
     we   walk   a   bit   the market over
     'We are walking a short way across the market'
                          (Http://www.landenweb.net/zuid-afrika/reisverhalen/reisverslagzuidafrika, May 2008)

is not yet on the field, so that he (partially) traverses the field to a position where he is completely *op* the field. From start to finish, in other words, the TR is closely involved with the LM, by being in contact with it. In a ParC with *op*, a TR can continue to traverse the LM as long as it is 'construed' as headed towards the result 'completely *op*' (cf. Beliën, 2008: 119–122). At some point his path may have continued for too long, so that a speaker will construe the path as no longer leading towards a result *op*, but rather as leading towards the result *af* 'off', cf. Example (15) below.

(14) *Johan Cruijff sprintte het veld op* (jgdmay92)
Johan Cruijff sprinted the field on/up
'Johan Cruijff sprinted onto the field'

The ParC in (15), finally, designates a motion event with *af* 'off' as its result, see Figure 4. The TR, in other words, traverses the LM from a position where *hij* 'he' is not *af* 'off', i.e. somewhere on the LM, *Piazza Navona*, to where he is completely *af* 'off', i.e. no longer supported by the LM, so just across a boundary of the square. Here too, the TR is in contact with the LM throughout the motion event.

(15) *[Hij] huppelde [...] het Piazza Navona af*[9]
he skipped the Piazza Navona off
'He hopped and skipped off the Piazza Navona'

This section has illustrated how the proposed (composite) semantic structure of the schematic ParC described in (13) is a generalization over specific instances of the construction. They describe motion events with the following characteristics: the motion event is resultative; it involves a TR that moves with respect to a LM from a position where the TR is *not* P to where it is *completely* P; and throughout the event, the TR is in contact with, or close to the LM, or in a force-dynamic relation with it.

5. A semantic comparison with relevant other constructions

The second step in the constructional method for determining constituency consists in a semantic comparison between the construction under study and relevant other constructions, i.e. constructions whose constituency may be similar. This section therefore compares the semantics of ParCs, described in the previous section, with that of PreCs (in subsection 5.1) and SCVCs (in subsection 5.2). It argues that while at first sight ParCs appear to be semantically more similar to

---

9. From the novel *Kaplan* by Leon de Winter (Amsterdam: De Bezige Bij, 1989: 305).

PreCs than to SCVCs, they differ from PreCs and resemble SCVCs in three crucial respects, i.e. the italicized notions in (13): resultativity, change from *not* P to *completely* P, and traversal.

5.1 Comparing ParCs and PreCs

ParCs are similar to PreCs in that both types of constructions describe motion events. In such an event, a TR (designated by the subject) moves in the manner described by the verb with respect to a LM (designated by the other noun phrase (NP) in the construction). In fact, for some pairs of ParCs and PreCs, native speakers find it very hard to formulate a meaning difference at all. The constructions are, however, not synonymous, as this subsection will show.

First of all, unlike ParCs, PreCs are not necessarily resultative. In (16), for example, the prepositional phrase (PP) is a modifier rather than a complement (Beliën, 2012; for these notions in Cognitive Grammar, cf. e.g. Langacker, 2008: 202–203): the atelic motion event designated by *reed* 'was driving' is understood as the TR of the PP (*op de Prinsenstraat* 'on Prince Street'). The construction does not describe a change of state; instead, it describes the atelic process that the subject is engaged in, all the while being *op de Prinsenstraat* 'on Prince Street'.

(16) *De man reed op de Prinsenstraat* (mcfeb93ove)
'The man was driving on Prince Street'

A second difference between PreCs and ParCs is that PreCs that do describe a change of state do not necessarily require that at the end of the event, the TR is *completely* P. In a PreC, the TR may end up being only *partially* P. This contrast is illustrated in (1) and (2). The ParC in (1), discussed in Section 4, designates a motion event in which the TR (*hun fietspontje* 'their bicycle ferry') moves from one side of the LM (*het kanaal* 'the canal') to the opposite side of the LM, i.e. from where it is not *over* to where it is completely *over*. The PreC in (2), on the other hand, requires only that the TR sails along some path with respect to the canal, while following its surface: the path can have any length or direction. In the context in which (2) occurs, it is clear that the people referred to by *we* follow the canal lengthwise; when they stop sailing, they are not *completely* over the canal.[10]

(1) hun   fietspontje   [vaart] het kanaal over   (jgdapr95)
    their bicycle-ferry   sails   the canal   over
    'Their bicycle ferry sails across the canal'

---

10. Unlike ParCs, in other words, PreCs do not necessarily evoke the conceptualization of a motion event from *not* P to *completely* P, cf. the discussion in fn. 8.

(2) *We varen over het Haren-Rüttenbrockkanaal* (wk199212)
we sail over the Haren-Rüttenbrock-canal
'We are sailing along the Haren-Rüttenbrock Canal'

A similar contrast can be found in (14) and (17). As described in Section 4, the ParC in (14) requires that the TR ends up completely *op* the LM: at the end of the motion event, the TR is supported only by the LM. The PreC in (17), on the other hand, does not impose this requirement. The LM, *een mijn* 'a mine', is much smaller than the TR, *het legervoertuig* 'the army vehicle', so the TR could not possibly be completely *op* 'on' it. Instead, at the end of the event, the TR is only partially *op* the LM: it is very likely that only one of the vehicle's wheels comes into contact with the mine. Turning this PreC into a ParC has a very awkward result: the ParC in (18) evokes the idea of a mine that is big enough for the army vehicle to drive onto it so that it is completely supported by it.

(14) *Johan Cruijff sprintte het veld op* (jgdmay92)
Johan Cruijff sprinted the field on/up
'Johan Cruijff sprinted onto the field'

(17) *Het legervoertuig [...] reed [...] op een mijn* (jgdoct93)
'The army vehicle drove on a mine'

(18) ??*Het legervoertuig reed een mijn op*
the army vehicle drove a mine on/up
??'The army vehicle drove up a mine'

A third semantic difference between ParCs and PreCs is that PreCs do not require that the TR traverses the LM. The PreC in (19), for example, designates a motion event in which the TR is in contact with the LM only at the very end. The TR need not traverse the LM in any way. In the context of (19), in fact, the TR, *Japie*, jumps from a tree down to the ground, see Figure 5.

(19) *Japie [sprong] op de grond* (gp94-2)
'Japie jumped on the ground'

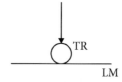

Figure 5. A PreC with *op*: no traversal required

The ParC in (20), for example, cannot receive an interpretation such as represented Figure 5, i.e. without traversal. The TR, *de fanatieke fan* 'the fanatical fan', is understood to jump from one side of the field, i.e. where he is not yet *op* 'on' the field, to a position *op* 'on' the field, cf. Figure 6. With his jump, he traverses part of the LM, i.e. moves with respect to, in the case of *op*, the surface of the LM while constantly being close to that surface and drawn towards it by gravity.

(20) De fanatieke fan sprong het veld op[11]
      the fanatical fan jumped the field on/up
      'The fanatical fan jumped onto the field'

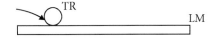

Figure 6. ParC with *op*: traversal required

Despite their obvious similarities, then, ParCs differ semantically from PreCs in that PreCs are not necessarily resultative, do not require that the TR ends up completely P, and do not require that the TR traverses the LM. As we shall see in the following subsection, these are exactly the respects in which ParCs are similar to SCVCs.

5.2 Comparing ParCs and SCVCs

At first sight, ParCs and SCVCs appear to be semantically quite different, cf. e.g. the SCVCs in (3), (21), and (22). A clear difference between ParCs and SCVCs concerns the entity that undergoes a change of state. In ParCs, it is the referent of the *subject* (it changes location), while in SCVCs, it is the referent of the *direct object* (i.e. the 'affected Theme', Blom, 2005: 124–125).[12] This subsection, however,

---

11. Http://www.voetbalzone.nl/doc.asp?uid=44197, November 2007.

12. This generalization holds only for ParCs and SCVCs as defined in Section 1 above, i.e. constructions that consist of a verb, an adposition and two noun phrases. It does not, in other words, apply to constructions such as (i) and (ii), which fall outside the scope of the present paper.

(i) Ik   reed mijn motor   […] de   boot op
     I   rode my   motorcycle   the boat on/up
     'I rode my motorcycle onto the boat'
                    (http://www.motorclubschoonebeek.nl/reisverslag.htm, August 2008)

identifies three semantic similarities between ParCs and SCVCs, which are, in fact, those respects in which ParCs differ from PreCs.

(3) de gevangene haalt de trekker over (jnlfeb93)
the prisoner pulls the trigger over
'The prisoner pulls the trigger'

(21) Iedereen dronk zijn drankje op (mcmar95ove)
everyone drank his drink up
'Everyone finished their drinks'

(22) hij [...] maakte de compositie af (mcdec92ove)
he made the composition off
'He finished the composition'

In both ParCs and SCVCs, the adposition is understood as the *result* of the event, with the event being finished when the relation *completely* P has been established. The motion event designated by a ParC, see Section 4, results in the TR, i.e. the subject referent, being *completely* P (*over* 'over', *op* 'on', *af* 'off'). With SCVCs too, the event is finished when the relation *completely* P has been achieved. The trigger in (3), for example, needs to be pulled towards a critical point; then the gun will fire. It therefore needs to be pulled over to that point completely. The drinks in (21) and the composition in (22) need to be completely *op* 'finished' and *af* 'finished' for the event to be completed. If they are just partially *op* or *af* 'finished', the event is not yet complete.

A further similarity between ParCs and SCVCs is the close connection between the participants throughout the event: from start to finish, the subject referent is engaged with the referent of the other NP in the construction. For ParCs, this was described in Section 4 in terms of 'traversal': throughout the motion event, the TR is in contact with, or somehow closely involved with, the LM. Similarly in an SCVC, the subject referent engages with the direct object referent throughout the event, i.e. pulling the trigger, finishing a drink, or finishing a

---

(ii) *het frietvet kookte over*
'the frying fat boiled over'
(http://www.bloggen.be/ruiselede8755/archief.php?ID=1860060, December 2012)

The construction in (i) expresses caused motion and consists of three nominals. In this type of construction, it is the referent of the second nominal (*mijn motor* 'my motorcycle') that undergoes a change of state (cf. also Beliën, 2008: 25–26, 177–178, on the role of this construction in the debate about the constituency of ParCs). The construction in (ii) contains an intransitive separable complex verb, *overkoken* 'to boil over', which requires only one nominal, the subject, whose referent undergoes a change of state (cf. also Blom, 2005: 128).

composition (cf. Tenny's 1994 description of eating an apple in terms of the event "progress[ing] through the internal argument", 1994: 15).

On the basis of this semantic comparison between ParCs, PreCs and SCVCs, we can draw the following conclusion: ParCs and SCVCs are similar in exactly those respects in which ParCs differ from PreCs. Unlike PreCs, both ParCs and SCVCs are necessarily resultative, they describe a change of state from *not* P to *completely* P, and their participants are in a close relationship throughout the event.

6. Accounting for semantic similarities and differences in terms of constituency

This section illustrates the third and final step in the proposed constructional method, i.e. accounting for the observed semantic similarities and differences between the construction under study and relevant other constructions in terms of conceptual constituency. In this particular case, I propose that the semantic similarities between ParCs and SCVCs can be accounted for in terms of similar constituency: ParCs, like SCVCs, consist of a subject, a separable complex verb, and a direct object. The semantic differences between ParCs and PreCs can then be accounted for in terms of their differences in constituency, as PreCs consist of a subject, an intransitive verb, and a prepositional phrase. The present section provides arguments for this proposal (see also Beliën, 2008: 154–163).

One of the constituents in the PreC is a prepositional phrase (PP): the adposition combines with the NP that follows it (cf. the description of *op de grond* 'on the ground' in Section 3). The semantic integration of P and NP in a PP has, I propose, a specific semantic effect that is not found in ParCs: the NP elaborates the LM of P, which makes the spatial relation designated by P more specific: some 'portion' of the LM is selected for involvement with the TR (cf. van der Leek's 1996 analysis of the semantic contribution of *at*-phrases in English conative constructions).[13]

This aspect of the conceptual constituency of PreCs can explain why they do not require traversal, resultativity, or the TR being 'completely P'. With a preposition such as *op* 'on', for example, the 'portion' of the LM that is selected is a point. When *op* 'on' combines with *de grond* 'the ground', for example, we know that

---

13. The holistic/partitive effect observed for pairs such as (i) and (ii) (from Beavers, 2006: 64) is accounted for by van der Leek (1996) as follows: "the *at*-phrase, by merely asserting a *point* of contact between the ingester's mouth/teeth etc. and the entity subjected to ingestion, explicitly leaves it open how much of this entity is, in fact, ingested" (1996: 371).

  (i) *The forlorn diner ate his sandwich.*
  (ii) *The forlorn diner ate at his sandwich.*

there is a point on the surface of *de grond* 'the ground' where the TR is or will be involved with LM, i.e. be in contact with the LM. Such a point can be construed as the location of the motion described by the intransitive verb, as with the PP *op de Prinsenstraat* 'on Prince Street' in (16). In such a case, then, there is no resultativity.

(16) *De man reed op de Prinsenstraat* (mcfeb93ove)
'The man was driving on Prince Street'

The point of contact inherent in the semantics of a PP with *op* may also be construed as the end point of the motion described by the intransitive verb, as with *op de grond* 'on the ground' in (19). In that case, no traversal of the LM is required: the moving TR only ends up in contact with the LM.

(19) *Japie [sprong] op de grond* (gp94-2)
'Japie jumped on the ground'

A point of contact does not specify to what extent the TR is supported by the LM. Dutch *op* has been defined above in terms of a force-dynamic relation of contact between TR and LM. This in itself leaves unspecified whether the TR is completely supported by the LM, cf. (16) and (19), or only partially so, cf. (17).

(17) *Het legervoertuig [...] reed [...] op een mijn* (jgdoct93)
'The army vehicle drove on a mine'

With a preposition such as *over* 'over', the 'portion' of the LM that is selected is not a point, but a path. The semantics of Dutch *over* 'over' (see Beliën, 2008: Ch. 4) includes a path that follows a surface of the LM. The path is unspecified for length; there is no requirement that the path stretches from one end of the LM to the other end. This explains why the TR in (2) need not be *completely over* the LM after the motion event: the verb of motion *varen* integrates with the PP *over het Haren-Rüttenbrockkanaal*, which results in a semantic structure involving motion along a path (with unspecified length) following the surface of the canal.

(2) We varen over het Haren-Rüttenbrockkanaal (wk199212)
   we sail over the Haren-Rüttenbrock-canal
   'We are sailing along the Haren-Rüttenbrock Canal'

For both ParCs and SCVCs, on the other hand, I propose that the adposition forms a conceptual constituent with the verb. The process designated by the verb integrates with the relation designated by the adposition in such a way that the relation is understood as the result of the event. So, in the ParC in (1) as well as in the SCVC in (3), *over* 'over' is the result of the event designated by the complex verb. The event progresses from a state that can be described as *not over* to a state that can be described as *completely over*.

(1) hun fietspontje   [vaart] het kanaal over   (jgdapr95)
    their bicycle-ferry sails the canal over
    'Their bicycle ferry sails across the canal'

(3) de gevangene haalt de trekker over   (jnlfeb93)
    the prisoner pulls the trigger over
    'The prisoner pulls the trigger'

The close connection between the two participants in both ParCs and SCVCs can be explained as follows. The complex verb in a ParC requires two participants, just as a complex verb in an SCVC does. A motion verb like *varen* 'sail' itself is intransitive: it designates a process that requires just one participant, a moving TR. When it combines with an adposition in a ParC, however, the verb and the adposition together designate a process that requires *two* participants. The complex verb *overvaren* 'sail over' in (1), for example, designates a motion event that has the spatial relation *over* as its result. For this spatial relation to be achieved, two participants are required: one participant, a TR, which moves with respect to a second participant, a LM. Throughout the event, the TR engages with the LM in such a way that result P is achieved.

In summary, then, the semantic differences between PreCs, on the one hand, and ParCs and SCVCs, on the other, can be accounted for in terms of different patterns of semantic integration, i.e. their different conceptual constituency. In a PreC, a motion verb and a prepositional phrase, i.e. a spatial relation with an elaborated LM, together designate a process that requires just one participant, a TR, expressed by the subject. In ParCs and SCVCs, on the other hand, the verb and the adposition together designate a resultative process that requires two participants.

7. Towards a full constructional analysis of the constituency of ParCs

The analysis of the conceptual constituency of ParCs provided in the previous section is based on a new, semantic type of argumentation which assumes the cognitive-grammar distinction between three types of constituents: phonological, conceptual, and grammatical. This distinction has made it possible to analyze the verb and the adposition in a ParC as a *conceptual* constituent, even when they do not form a *phonological* constituent.

The paper has focused on ParCs of a particular type, i.e. active main clauses with a finite verb of motion and the word order [NP_{Subj} V_{Motion} NP P], see e.g. (14), repeated here. In such examples, the verb and the adposition are not adjacent and therefore do not form a phonological constituent. By definition, then, they do not form a grammatical constituent either, because a grammatical constituent only arises when a conceptual constituent is symbolized by a phonological constituent. In a subordinate clause such as in (23), however, the verb and the adposition are adjacent to one another. In that case, they lend themselves to an analysis in which they form a phonological as well as a conceptual constituent, thereby forming a grammatical constituent too.[14]

(14) *Johan Cruijff sprintte het veld op* (jgdmay92)
Johan Cruijff sprinted the field on/up
'Johan Cruijff sprinted onto the field'

(23) *het leek [...] of ze de berg opsprintte*[15]
it seemed as-if she the mountain up-sprinted
'It seemed as if she sprinted up the mountain'

With its focus on the conceptual constituency of one particular type of ParC, the presented analysis is a first step towards a full constructional analysis of the constituency of ParCs. A full analysis would examine the phonological (and possibly grammatical) constituency involved in more detail, as well as take into account a wider range of data. In particular, such an analysis would evaluate whether the proposed conceptual constituency can be extended to the types of constructions that played a role in the argumentation of earlier studies, such as passives and topicalization constructions (see Section 2). A full constructional analysis is beyond the scope of this paper, but this section provides some suggestions as to what it would look like. As grammaticality (or acceptability) judgments diverged, the section checks the relevant types of constructions against authentic data.

From a constructional perspective, the types of examples that figured in the constituency tests, such as passivization and topicalization, are constructions in their own right, with their own semantics. In that sense, they do not affect the analysis of the type of ParCs whose conceptual constituency was determined in the previous section on independent, i.e. semantic, grounds. There may, however, be other constructions that share their conceptual constituency, i.e. in which the adposition and the verb form a conceptual constituent that requires two participants. To establish that, such constructions first need to be analyzed semantically.

As we saw in Section 2, many studies argue against an SCV analysis of ParCs because they consider examples such as (14) to be 'unpassivizable'. While some other studies agree with these intuitions, they do not draw the same conclusion,

---

14. In this example, the adposition and the verb are written together as one word, an orthographic indication that they are felt to form a unit. For a discussion of the variation and conflicting advice in this respect, see Cappelle (2013).

15. Http://martijnkoelewijn.waarbenjij.nu/, June 2015.

arguing that there are more 'two-place predicates' which do not passivize for semantic reasons, such as *naderen* 'approach' (cf. de Schutter, 1974; Verkuyl & Zwarts, 1992). Rice (1987) takes the same position in her cognitive-grammar account of English passive constructions, when she says that "a verb bearing two arguments does not guarantee that the finite clause it governs will have a passive version nor does it assure that it will *always* have a passive version" (1987: 64).

Some studies claimed that passive versions of ParCs are possible. And indeed, when we look on the Internet, authentic passive constructions can be found. (24), for example, is one of the 111 Google hits for the string *"werd voorbijgereden door"* (accessed on January 17, 2013), which translates as 'was overtaken by' ('was past-driven/ridden by'). A simplified, constructed active counterpart is given in (25).

(24) *De Fransman   Sylvain   Chavanel   ging   als   eerste   de*
the Frenchman Sylvain Chavanel went as the-first the
Knokteberg   op   maar werd voorbijgereden door zijn
Knokte-mountain on/up but was past-ridden by his
ploegmakker   Boonen.[16]
team-mate Boonen
'Frenchman Sylvain Chavanel went up the Knokteberg first but was overtaken by his team mate Boonen.'

(25) *Boonen   reed   Chavanel   voorbij*
Boonen rode Chavanel past
'Boonen overtook (cycled past) Chavanel'

Interestingly, Examples (24) and (25) are different from the constructions that we have considered so far, because the LM, *Sylvain Chavanel*, is not an inanimate reference object, but a human being that is affected by the TR's action. Both the TR and the LM are cyclists competing in the race: the result of the motion event is that the TR, *Boonen*, is completely *voorbij* 'past' the LM, *Sylvain Chavanel*. This affects a change in the LM: being overtaken by the TR, the LM is now in a less advantageous position in the race.

Rice (1987) has argued for English passive constructions that their naturalness depends on the semantics involved, in particular, the degree of 'transitivity'. In her analysis, transitivity is a semantic notion which involves affectedness: "the *canonical* transitive event is a physical world event in which an active participant makes contact with a passive participant and affects or effects a change in the latter" (1987: 154). In most of the ParCs discussed in this paper so far, the second participant, i.e. the LM, does not undergo a change: the TR's motion does not

---

16. Http://www.hln.be/hln/nl/2444/Ronde-Van-Vlaanderen/article/detail/799634/2009/03/28/Pozzato-wint-E3-Prijs-voor-Boonen.dhtml, January 2013.

affect the LM in any way. The unnaturalness of the corresponding passives, as apparent in the grammatical judgments in many earlier studies, could therefore well have a semantic reason rather than provide evidence for a certain constituency. The affectedness of the LM as illustrated in (24) could explain the relatively high number of hits for *werd voorbijgereden door* ('was overtaken by').

Affectedness of the LM, however, is not a necessary aspect of Dutch passives (cf. for semantic analyses of Dutch passives, Cornelis, 1997; Vandenbosch, 1992). Other authentic examples of passives can be explained as a means to background the TR of the motion event. The passage in (26), for example, comes from a three-page description of a cycling trip that is full of constructions that do not mention the actual cyclists (cf. e.g. the nominalization *de volgende klim* 'the next climb' in the second line of Example (26)). In keeping with this style, the passive in (26), in bold, allows the motion event (*opsprinten* 'sprint up') to be conveyed without explicitly mentioning the movers. Note that the subject of this passive, a hill, is unlikely to be affected by the motion event.

(26) *De route ging verder door het centrum van Rhenen*
 'The route went on through the center of Rhenen'
 waar de volgende klim zich alweer snel aandiende.
 'where the next climb soon presented itself.'
 De koerheuvel werd opgesprint
 the Koer-hill was up/on-sprinted
 'Koer Hill was climbed (sprinted up)'
 en een eerste indruk van de krachtsverhoudingen werd duidelijk[17]
 'and a first impression of the power relationships became clear'

In terms of their semantics, the passives in (24) and (26) appear to be quite similar to the active ParCs in (14) and (25). In both (14) and (26), for example, the TR (*Johan Cruijff*/a group of cyclists) moves from where it is not yet *op* 'on' the LM (*het veld* 'the field'/*de koerheuvel* 'Koer Hill') to where it is completely *op* the LM, i.e. no longer supported by anything else. It therefore makes sense to assume the same conceptual constituency for the active in (14) and the passive in (26): the semantic structures of the verb *sprinten* and the adposition *op* form a conceptual constituent, i.e. a motion event which has *op* as its result. This motion event requires two participants: a TR and a LM. In the active construction (14), the TR is expressed as the subject and the LM as a direct object; in the passive construction (26), the LM is expressed as the subject and the TR is understood, but not

---

17. Http://www.hcdevechtstreek.nl/doorlopr/uitgvs/2008dl5.pdf, January 2013.

expressed.[18] It seems, in other words, that we can posit a more schematic ParC that can be instantiated as an active construction with a subject and a direct object, but also, in certain cases, as a passive construction.[19]

This discussion of passives has shown that the ungrammaticality judgments found for passive ParCs in earlier studies can be explained in terms of a semantic incompatibility between constructions. Authentic data have proven crucial, because they show that passive constructions in fact do occur, i.e. that passives and ParCs do not always conflict semantically. On the basis of an initial semantic analysis, these passive constructions appear to be sufficiently semantically similar to active ParCs. They can therefore be argued to have the same conceptual constituency.

Authentic examples of the topicalization examples are harder to find, but all types do occur: see the 'topicalization' of P and V in (27), of a non-subject NP in (28), and of an NP-P combination in (29).

(27) *Inrijden mag je die weg niet,*
in-drive may you that road not,
maar dat stukje lopen was geen probleem[20]
but that bit walk was no problem
'You cannot drive into that road, but the short walk was no problem'

(28) *drie rivieren moest ie overzwemmen* (jgdsep95)
three rivers had-to he over-swim
'three rivers he had to swim across'

(29) *De stad in moeten we over een volle driebaans autoweg*
the town in must we over a full three-lane highway
zonder vluchtstroken rijden, best eng[21]
without emergency-lanes ride quite scary
'Into town we have to ride along a busy three-lane highway without emergency lanes, quite scary'

---

18. Note furthermore that in the passive, the verb and the adposition form not only a conceptual constituent, but a phonological one as well, which means that they are a grammatical constituent.

19. Cf. in this respect Goldberg (2006: 10) on the combination of constructions:

> An actual expression typically involves the combination of at least half a dozen different constructions. [...] Constructions are combined freely to form actual expressions as long as they are not in conflict. Unresolved conflicts result in judgments of ill-formedness.

20. Http://www.flitsservice.nl, January 2007.

21. Http://www.velomobiel.nl/nl/nieuws_body_0204_nl, December 2006.

In earlier analyses, the first two types are presented as evidence for an SCV analysis of ParCs, while the third type is presented as evidence for a postposition analysis. The constructional method proposed in this paper, however, emphasizes the importance of providing a semantic analysis of such topicalization examples before it can be assessed whether a similar conceptual constituency is involved.

While (27) and (28) might very well involve a similar conceptual constituency to the one proposed for ParCs with the more ordinary word order [NP$_{Subj}$ – V$_{Motion}$ – NP – P], I have suggested elsewhere that constructions in (29) do not, because they are semantically different (see Beliën, 2008: 190–193). The NP-P combination in sentence-initial position in (29), *de stad in* 'the town in', seems to evoke, all by itself, a complete 'ParC-type' motion event, i.e. without the presence of a motion verb. Just reading the NP-P combination evokes the idea of a motion event in which some TR moves from where it is not in the town to where it is completely in the town, i.e. no longer contained by anything else. In this particular example, the rest of the construction does contain a motion verb, but that seems to form a PreC with *we* 'we' as the subject and a prepositional phrase headed by *over* as the motion verb's complement.[22] This PreC makes explicit what happens during the motion event evoked independently by the NP-P combination.

Earlier analyses have not concerned themselves with the semantics of the examples that figured in their constituency tests. If the suggestions given here about the complex semantics of (29) are on the right track, it seems unwarranted to draw conclusions about the constituency of a 'simple' ParC of the type [NP$_{Subj}$ – V$_{Motion}$ – NP – P] on the basis of a construction such as (29). The semantics of (29) needs to be further examined before any conclusions about its conceptual constituency can be drawn.

This section has explored in what ways the analysis of the conceptual constituency of a particular type of ParCs can be extended to a full constructional analysis. Such an analysis would include an analysis of the phonological (and possibly grammatical) constituency involved. It would also include an analysis of the constructions deemed relevant to the constituency question in earlier studies. For

---

22. NP-P combinations also occur in sentence-initial position in constructions without any motion verb at all. The combination in (i), for example, evokes a fictive motion event in which a TR, presumably understood as the reader of the novel, mentally goes from the start of the book to practically the end, where the TR would be completely *door* 'through'.

(i) *Vrijwel   het hele   boek door   zien we hoe Mayling zich   zorgen*
    Practically the whole book through see we how Mayling herself worries
    maakte   over   haar gezondheid.
    made   about   her health
    'Practically throughout the whole book, we see how Mayling is worried about her health.'
    (http://www.ezzulia.nl/interviews/lucaszandberg2012.html, January 2013)

passives as well as topicalization cases with P-V or the non-subject NP in sentence-initial position, the section has suggested that they could well have the same conceptual constituency as the ParCs discussed in Sections 4–6. For constructions with NP-P in sentence-initial position, on the other hand, it was argued that they could be semantically different from such ParCs.

8. Conclusion

The constructional method for determining conceptual constituency presented in this paper has provided a new way of analyzing Dutch ParCs, whose constituency has proven elusive in the past. The method, based on the cognitive-grammar distinction between phonological, conceptual and grammatical constituents, has yielded semantic arguments for analyzing ParC as similar to (transitive) SCVCs and different from (intransitive) PreCs: the adposition in the ParC forms a constituent with the motion verb, and together, the adposition and the verb require two participants, expressed as the subject and the direct object in active ParCs. The method consists of three steps: (i) a semantic analysis of the construction under study, (ii) a semantic comparison of the construction with other relevant constructions, i.e. constructions whose constituency may be similar, and (iii) an account of their semantic similarities and differences in terms of constituency.

Using constituency tests such as passivization and topicalization, earlier studies had not come to a consensus, partly because of diverging grammaticality judgments. The present study therefore used authentic data, which revealed that all types of constructions that figured in earlier studies do indeed occur. From the perspective of the method of the constituency tests as used in the generative tradition, such 'conflicting' results make it difficult to reach a conclusion about the constituency of the ParC. From the perspective of the constructional method presented here, however, the sheer existence of one construction, for example, with NP-P in sentence-initial (topicalized) position, does not warrant any immediate conclusion about the constituency of another construction. As the method crucially relies on semantics of the constructions involved, it first needs to be established whether the same semantics are involved, on the basis of which the same 'symbolic compositionality' can be inferred. With this focus on semantics and the distinction between phonological, conceptual, and grammatical constituents, the method is expected to open up new ways for studying other long-standing constituency issues as well.

References

Beavers, J. (2006). *Argument/oblique alternations and the structure of lexical meaning*. Ph.D. dissertation, Stanford University.

Beckner, C., & Bybee, J. (2009). A usage-based account of constituency and reanalysis. *Language Learning*, 59(Suppl. 1), 27–46. doi:10.1111/j.1467-9922.2009.00534.x

Beeken, J. (1993). *Spiegelstructuur en variabiliteit: Pre- en postposities in het Nederlands* [Mirror structure and variability: Prepositions and postpositions in Dutch]. Leuven: Peeters.

Beliën, M. (2008). *Constructions, constraints, and construal: Adpositions in Dutch*. Ph.D. dissertation, VU Amsterdam. Utrecht: LOT.

Beliën, M. (2012). Dutch manner of motion verbs: Disentangling auxiliary choice, telicity and syntactic function. *Cognitive Linguistics*, 23(1), 1–26. doi:10.1515/cog-2012-0001

Blom, C. (2005). *Complex predicates in Dutch: Synchrony and diachrony*. Ph.D. dissertation, VU Amsterdam. Utrecht: LOT.

Booij, G. (1998). Samenkoppelingen en grammaticalisatie [Separable complex verbs and grammaticalization]. In E. Hoekstra & C. Smits (Eds.), *Morfologiedagen 1996* (pp. 6–20). Amsterdam: Meertens Institute.

Bybee, J. (2002). Sequentiality as the basis of constituent structure. In T. Givón & B. F. Malle (Eds.), *The evolution of language out of pre-language* (pp. 109–132). Amsterdam: John Benjamins. doi:10.1075/tsl.53.07byb

Cappelle, B. (2013). De aaneenschrijfregels de prullenmand *in gooien of ingooien* [Throwing orthographic rules into the bin]? *Over Taal*, 52(3), 66–67.

Cornelis, L. H. (1997). *Passives and perspective*. Amsterdam: Rodopi.

Croft, W. (2001). *Radical construction grammar: Syntactic theory in typological perspective*. Oxford: Oxford University Press. doi:10.1093/acprof:oso/9780198299554.001.0001

de Haas, W., & Trommelen, M. (1993). *Morfologisch handboek van het Nederlands: Een overzicht van de woordvorming* [Morphological handbook of Dutch: An overview of word formation]. The Hague: SDU.

de Schutter, G. (1974). *De Nederlandse zin: Poging tot beschrijving van zijn structuur* [The Dutch sentence: An attempt to describe its structure]. Brugge: De Tempel.

de Vries, J. W. (1975). *Lexicale morfologie van het werkwoord in modern Nederlands* [Lexical morphology of the verb in modern Dutch]. Leiden: Universitaire Pers Leiden.

Goldberg, A. E. (1995). *A construction grammar approach to argument structure*. Chicago, IL: The University of Chicago Press.

Goldberg, A. E. (2006). *Constructions at work: The nature of generalization in language*. Oxford: Oxford University Press.

Haeseryn, W., Romijn, K., Geerts, G., de Rooij, J., & van den Toorn, M. C. (1997). *Algemene Nederlandse spraakkunst* [General Dutch grammar]. Groningen: Nijhoff.

Helmantel, M. (2002). *Interactions in the Dutch adpositional domain*. Ph.D. dissertation, Leiden University. Utrecht: LOT.

Hoekstra, T. (1984). *Transitivity: Grammatical relations in government-binding theory*. Dordrecht: Foris.

Langacker, R. W. (1987). *Foundations of cognitive grammar, vol. I: Theoretical prerequisites*. Stanford, CA: Stanford University Press.

Langacker, R. W. (1991). *Foundations of cognitive grammar, vol. II: Descriptive application*. Stanford, CA: Stanford University Press.

Langacker, R. W. (1995). Conceptual grouping and constituency in cognitive grammar. In I.-H. Leek (Ed.), *Linguistics in the morning Calm* 3 (pp. 149–172). Seoul: Hanshin.

Langacker, R. W. (1997). Constituency, dependency, and conceptual grouping. *Cognitive Linguistics*, 8(1), 1–32. doi:10.1515/cogl.1997.8.1.1

Langacker, R. W. (2005). Construction grammars: Cognitive, radical, and less so. In F. J. Ruiz de Mendoza Ibáñez & M. Sandra Peña Carvel (Eds.), *Cognitive linguistics: Internal dynamics and interdisciplinary interaction* (pp. 101–162). Berlin: Mouton de Gruyter.

Langacker, R. W. (2008). *Cognitive grammar: A basic introduction*. New York, NY: Oxford University Press. doi:10.1093/acprof:oso/9780195331967.001.0001

Luif, J. (1992). Over richtingsbepalingen [On directional phrases]. In E. C. Schermer-Vermeer, W. G. Klooster, & A. F. Florijn (Eds.), *De kunst van de grammatica* [The art of grammar] (pp. 157–167). Amsterdam: Vakgroep Nederlandse Taalkunde, University of Amsterdam.

Paardekooper, P. C. (1959). Voor- en achterzetsels [Prepositions and postpositions]. *De Nieuwe Taalgids*, 52, 310–320.

Paardekooper, P. C. (1966). *Beknopte ABN-syntaksis*. Den Bosch: Malmberg.

Rice, S. (1987). Towards a cognitive model of transitivity. Ph.D. dissertation, University of California, San Diego.

Talmy, L. (2003). *Toward a cognitive semantics, vol. II: Typology and process in concept structuring*. Cambridge, MA: The MIT Press.

Tenny, C. L. (1994). *Aspectual roles and the syntax-semantics interface*. Dordrecht: Kluwer. doi:10.1007/978-94-011-1150-8

Vandenbosch, L. (1992). *Aspekten van passiefvorming in het Nederlands: Een kognitief-pragmatische benadering* [Aspects of passive formation in Dutch: a cognitive-pragmatic approach]. Ph.D. dissertation, University of Antwerp.

van der Leek, F. C. (1996). The English conative construction: A compositional account. *Chicago Linguistics Society*, 32, 363–378.

van Riemsdijk, H. C. (1978). *A case study in syntactic markedness: The binding nature of prepositional phrases*. Lisse: De Ridder.

Verkuyl, H., & Zwarts, F. (1992). Postpositie, incorporatie en terminativiteit [Postposition, incorporation, and terminativity]. In: H. J. Bennis & J. W. de Vries (Eds.), *De binnenbouw van het Nederlands* [The inner structure of Dutch] (pp. 383–400). Dordrecht: Foris.

CHAPTER 3

Development and representation of Italian light-*fare* constructions

Valeria Quochi
Consiglio Nazionale delle Ricerche, Istituto di Linguistica Computazionale

This contribution analyzes the development and use of light *fare* 'do' constructions in Child-directed Speech and in Child Language with the twofold goal of showing that a Construction Grammar approach is viable, and of providing support to usage-based, functional predictions on language acquisition. The analysis of naturalistic data derived from the CHILDES database lead to two main findings: first, a representation of *fare* Light Verb Constructions as a family of constructions organized like a radial category is possible, second, there exists a *fare* pivot schema that children generalize at an early stage because it serves the purpose of naming new events, activities or situations.

1. Introduction

Light, or Support, Verb Constructions (LVCs) have received extensive attention in the literature and have been studied from different theoretical backgrounds: generative grammar, relational grammar, lexico-semantics, lexical-collocational approaches (Grimshaw & Mester, 1988; Myiagawa, 1989; Namer, 1998; La Fauci & Mirto, 2003; Alba-Salas, 2002; Giry-Schneider, 1987; D'Agostino & Elia, 1997; Cantarini, 2004; Sinclair, 1991; Moon, 1998; to mention just a few). Typical examples of LVCs are *give a talk, take a walk* or *tenere una conferenza* (lit. hold a conference 'make a speech'), *fare una passeggiata* (lit. do a walk). The mainstream position is to consider them as kinds of multi-word units, (semi-)fixed idioms or collocations; a view that reflects the bias of theories based on a neat separation between grammar and lexicon. Yet, they constitute a conspicuous class of constructs across even typologically different languages. Similar structures have been observed and investigated in various world languages: English, French, Dutch, Japanese, and many others (see Alba-Salas, 2002 for a review of the languages investigated).

Although there is some variation depending on the theoretical approaches, the definition of LVCs is generally based on 3 main assumptions: (1) the subjects of the noun and of the verb/clause need to be co-referential, (2) the verb is semantically light or bleached, (3) the noun is the semantic nucleus of the sentence: it determines argument structure and assigns the semantic roles to the sentential arguments. By a strict definition usually adopted by generative approaches, only verbal nominalizations are allowed as the semantic heads of the constructs. A looser definition, common in relational grammar and lexico-syntactic approaches, requires the noun to be predicative, argument-taking, no matter its morphological status.

According to the stricter definition, thus, only expressions like *fare un salto* as in (1) would be true LVCs because *salto* 'jump.N' is a nominalization, while *fare una serenata* and *fare rumore* as in (2) and (3) would be LVCs only by the broader definition.

(1) Marco   fa   un   salto
     Marco   does   a   jump
     'Marco jumps'

(2) Romeo   fa   una   serenata   a   Giulietta   da   sotto   il   balcone
     Romeo   makes   a   serenade   to   Juliet   from   under   the   balcony
     'Romeo serenades Juliet from under the balcony'

(3) Il   motore   dell'   aeroplano   fa   un   rumore   assordante
     The   engine   of.the   plane   makes   a   noise   deafening
     'The plane engine makes a deafening noise'

In any case, LVCs constitute a challenge for syntactic theories, esp. those based on the centrality of verbs in determining syntactic and semantic structures, because it is not the verb that determines the number and kind of arguments at sentence level, but the noun. In many languages LVCs behave like lexical verbs at sentence level, but at the same time show a certain degree of syntactic freedom, semantic transparency and productivity, which makes it difficult to treat them purely at the lexical level. This is also the case in Italian.

Moreover, by both definitions, expressions like *fare le carte* 'to shuffle the cards' and *fare paura* 'to scare sb' would be considered as fixed idioms bearing no relationship to LVCs, because the noun is not (intrinsically) predicative (4), or the subjects are not co-referential (5) (cfr. Giry-Schneider, 1987).

(4) Ora   faccio   io   le   carte
     Now   do   I   the   cards
     'I am shuffling the cards now'

(5) Mi   hai   fatto   tanta   paura
     To-me   do.2SG   done   very much   fear
     'You scared me very much'

Although it is true that (4) can be considered idiomatic and (5) presents some important (argument structure) differences from typical LVCs, they also share both structural and semantic similarities that get lost in these accounts.

Focusing mainly on structural or formal properties, the traditional approaches to LVCs, as we have briefly seen, show important limitations. In particular, they fail to account for the productivity and semantic relatedness of (some of) these constructs.

On the contrary, cognitive, usage-based theories of language, and in particular Construction Grammar (Goldberg, 1995 and 2006; Croft, 2001; Fried & Östman, 2004), provide an interesting alternative for the investigation of these types of expressions especially for seeking an explanation of their productivity and relatedness. While not specifically addressing the issue of Light Verb Constructions, they seem to offer interesting tools to account for (local) regularities and to explain their partial productivity.[1] The notion of family, or network, of constructions (Goldberg, 1995; Croft, 2001) inspired the present analysis as well as the attention given to acquisitional issues. Investigations of language development are, in fact, fundamental for cognitive-functional approaches to language, because their main and common assumption is that language is learned from the ambient language. Thus, if language is not innate and not hardwired in the brain, then we need to understand how children arrive at acquiring the linguistic structures and competence of adults, from their first rudimental attempts.

The ultimate goal of this contribution is thus twofold: first, I try to show that LVCs are better accounted for as a network of related constructions organized as a radial category; and second I intend to provide support to a functional, usage-based hypothesis of language acquisition and claim that there exists a LVC pivot schema that children learn at an early stage because it serves the purpose of naming new events, activities or situations for which they do not have a single lexical word yet.

To achieve these goals I make use of naturalistic data and study the distribution and development of constructs with the Italian light verb *fare* 'do' in Child Language and in Child Directed Speech. First, the dataset is thoroughly analyzed focusing on the properties of the nouns in the LVCs and then on the constructions as a whole. In particular, I will advocate that an account of LVCs in terms of family of constructions (Goldberg, 1995) is more appropriate and explicative than traditional approaches. So, a set of Constructions will be identified and coarsely defined based on the data. Finally, the study of the distribution and evolution in Child Language of the constructions identified will bring us to sketch a possible development pattern of the LVCs in child language, which is in line with functional hypotheses of language acquisition and in particular with Tomasello's verb island hypothesis (1992, 2003).

---

[1]. To the best of my knowledge, very few studies within the framework of Construction Grammar specifically addressed support/light verb constructions (Palancar, 2003; Family, 2009; Doğruöz and Backus, 2009).

2. A developmental study of *fare* LVCs using naturalistic data

The main focus of the research described here is to study the use of the light-*fare* + direct object constructs in early childhood and in Child Directed Speech (CDS hereafter) with the aim of exploring the nature of Light Verb Constructions broadly defined on a basis of spontaneous language production. A dataset of developmental data was semi-automatically created starting from the corpus of transcriptions of communicative interactions contained in the CHILDES database (MacWhinney, 2000, and web site).

I have first approached the analysis of the data assuming the perspective of traditional views of LVCs, and thus expected that, being Light Verb Constructions (LVCs) close to lexical units (semi-fixed idioms in the traditional sense), they are stored, unrelated, rote-learned items both in adult and child language. This, in fact, is not the case, as it becomes clear from the observations made and the problematic cases found. The analysis of the data thus will lend support to a different explanation, i.e. to a functional-constructionist approach to language acquisition.

The CHILDES database consists of a set of transcripts of "spontaneous" child-adult conversational interactions. Each transcription file represents one recording session. The Italian collection used in this study consists of longitudinal transcriptions of interactive sessions with eleven, non-impaired, Italian-speaking children. For the present study, 4 corpora are used, which collectively cover an age span between 16 and 40 months and consist of a total of 117 transcriptions:

The Antelmi corpus is a longitudinal study of one girl observed from the age of 26 months to 40 months.
The Calambrone corpus contains both longitudinal and cross-sectional data from six normal and 11 language-disordered children. Only the data of the 6 non-impaired children, 4 girls and 2 boys, which cover an age span from 19 to 39 months, is used in this study.
The Roma corpus is a longitudinal study of one boy observed from the age of 16 months to 20 months.
The Tonelli corpus is a longitudinal study of three children, one girl and two boys, and covers an age-span from 17 to 26 months.
The transcriptions were semi-automatically analyzed and all utterances that contain a verb were stored in a database.

At this point, a first analysis of the distribution of light verbs and of utterance types is performed in order to assess the general properties and trends of both CDS and child language (CL). It turns out that CDS is richer in questions than in declaratives or imperative utterances and that *fare* is more frequently used in questions than in other utterance types. This is interesting as it might constitute a kind of priming for LVCs. Children, not surprisingly, use mostly declarative utterances.

Notice that a similar trend has been observed in English by Cameron-Faulkner and colleagues (2003). After observing the general trends, for each session all CDS and CL utterances in which an instance of the verb *fare* 'do' co-occurs with a noun in direct object position were annotated and extracted. This constitutes the main data for the study discussed here. In the rest of the paper, we shall refer to this data as the *fare* dataset, or simply dataset. We shall also refer to "*fare* + N in apparent direct object position" as *fare* + noun combinations, constructs or expressions alternatively with a theory neutral attitude. The use of "construction" will always have to be intended as theory specific in Construction Grammar terms.[2]

A simple statistical analysis of the dataset shows that, overall, *fare* + noun combinations produced by children account for 41% of all their uses of the verb *fare*, while for adults they account for 48% of their uses of the verb, as shown in Table 1.[3]

Table 1. *Fare* dataset composition

Constructs	Child's production	Adults' production
Fare + noun	250 (41%)	1848 (48%)
All *fare* contexts	611	3855

Looking more qualitatively at *fare* constructs in CDS, one striking albeit not surprising observation is that the verb *fare* very frequently has a generic semantics: it often occurs with no "heavy" argument or no argument at all, especially in questions. Examples are given in (6) below.

(6) a. Cosa   fai?
       What   do?
       'What are you doing'?
    b. Come   fai   a?
       How   do.2SG to?
       'How do you …?'
    c. Fai   così
       do.2SG so
       'Do it like this'

Qualitatively, it is also worthy of note that *fare* in such contexts seems to elicit descriptions or mentions of actions, events or situations in response, and that children usually start answering by repeating the verb itself (which is also phonologically salient in

---

2. I.e. a Construction is a pairing of form and meaning.

3. In a preliminary analysis of the general characteristics of the dataset it was observed that there is no consistent qualitative difference between verb production in mothers and other adults, and therefore both have been used as representative of Child Directed Speech (Quochi 2007).

the speech stream) and add other words that evoke the situation or action prompted by the adult, although not necessarily in a syntactically adult-like utterance.

3. *Fare* constructs. Three macro categories

As mentioned above, most studies on LVCs are based on three main assumptions: (1) the subject is coreferential, (2) the verb is semantically light or bleached, (3) the noun determines argument structure. As such, traditional approaches require that the noun be predicative: i.e derived from a verb, or argument taking (which admits some abstract nouns).

Assuming these assumptions as correct, I started by analyzing our dataset on the basis of the types of nouns occurring in direct object position of the verb *fare*. In this exercise, thus, the utterances are annotated according to the supposedly "inherent" formal (lexical semantic or morphological) properties of the nouns, as if out of context.[4]

I thus distinguished three basic types of nouns: nouns morphologically related to verbs, abstract (thus potentially predicative) nouns, and concrete nouns (Table 2 below gives their distribution in the dataset). Now, if we think in terms of the traditional approaches to LVCs the expectation is to find (most) LVCs in the group of constructs with nouns morphologically related to verbs, some LVCs among the constructs with abstract nouns and no LVCs among constructs with concrete nouns. As will become clear in the following subsections, this is not the case. Although certainly few in number, there are expressions in the concrete noun group that bear no literal meaning but rather interesting similarities to classical LVCs. As such they would be treated as isolated idiomatic expressions in traditional, formal approaches, while in construction grammar their similarity to a wider class of expressions could be accounted for.

Table 2. Noun types in the *fare* dataset (token frequency)

	Concrete nouns	Verb-related nouns	Abstract nouns	All nouns
Adults	1006 (54%)	302 (16%)	540 (30%)	1848
Children	146 (58%)	35 (14%)	69 (28%)	250

But let us proceed step by step and analyze the constructs by noun groups.

---

4. This is clearly controversial. In fact, the objections and problems arising from this analysis contribute to support a constructionist approach to LVCs.

3.1 *Fare* + nouns morphologically related to verbs

This class groups together nouns that are morphologically (or perceptually) related to common verbs, no matter the direction of derivation since it is not easy to determine the direction of the derivation, especially in the case of zero derivation, and in any case it seems to be more a matter for linguistic description than for the speaker's consciousness (cfr. Iacobini, 2000).

For this task I had to make some other decisions as to what to classify as verb-related nouns, which may not be uncontroversial. So, for example, nouns like *fotografia* 'picture' are included in this group because the corresponding verb *fotografare* 'to take a picture' is quite commonly used in everyday language, while *triangolo* 'triangle' is not included although it corresponds to the verb *triangolare* 'to triangulate', because the verb is a technical term.

Within this group I included all types of derivation: zero derived nouns (further separating forms altered by diminutive or augmentative suffixes), *-ata* nominals, *-ione* nominals, and nouns derived by means of other suffixes. The most interesting quantitatively are the first two.

Zero Derived Nouns are derived by conversion directly from one form of the base verb (e.g. *salto* 'jump', *gioco* 'game', *ballo* 'dance') and are considered to be highly conservative of the properties of the base verb. However, they are for the most part countable and therefore are cognitively closer to nouns than verbs (cfr. Gaeta, 2002). If we take their semantics into account, they generally denote some type of action, and thus belong to the traditional class of Nomina Actionis, or to the Process/ Result alternation classes.

-ata Nominals are formed from the past participle of the base verb and always in in feminine form (e.g. *passeggiata* 'walk', *girata* 'stroll'). The *-ata* derivation from regular verbs is highly productive and transparent. Semantically, they denote single occurrences of the action or event denoted by the base verb; they cannot normally be used in a generic sense, but only as individuated instances, and are generally not compatible with definite determiners, except in marked contexts where the deverbal is closer to an entity-denoting noun. Their characteristics are highly compatible with "classic" LVCs.

In general and in line with our expectations, the constructs in this group appear to be cases of canonical LVCs: e.g. *fare un salto* 'do a jump', *fare la spesa* 'go shopping' as in Examples (7) and (8). As is conventional in the CHILDES database, in the transcripts CHI always refer to the child, MOT to the mother and ADU to other adults.

(7) CHI: oa   io   faccio i   satti   dice Ila.
         Now   I   do   the jumps   says Ila
         'Now I jump, says Ilaria' [Rosa, 2:11]

(8) MOT: questa è   la   nonna   che   va   a   fare la   spesa.
         This   is the grandma who   goes to do   the expenditure
         'This is the grandma who goes shopping' [Rosa, 2:5]

These can be considered classic examples of LVCs with the noun contributing most of the semantics to the clause and the verb being semantically "light". The schematic abstract semantics of such constructs appears to be something like DO ACTION, provisionally labelled: 'Perform Action'.

In Table 2 we saw that *fare* constructs containing nouns morphologically related to verbs account for the 16% of all adult *fare* + nouns constructs, and 14% of children's, that is: the production of *fare* + verb-related nouns in children is proportionally very similar to adults', which suggests that children do not creatively produce such expressions, but rather imitate what they hear in their environment. This is in fact corroborated by further inspection of the data.

Table 3 reports the frequency distribution of the two main derivation types considered.

Table 3. Distribution of various subtypes of verb-related nouns in the dataset. Both type and token frequency is given as well as TTR

	Adult			Child		
	Types	Tokens	Ratio	Types	Tokens	Ratio
Zero-derived nouns	33	159	0.21	13	19	0.68
ata-nominals	17	60	0.28	3	8	0.38
Other deverbals	21	83	0.25	3	8	0.38
Total	71	302	0.24	19	35	0.54

As we see, children mostly use zero derived nouns, while adults pool from a wider range of types. Still adults seem to show little variability, with a low type/token ratio that indicates the repeated use of relatively few lexicalized constructs, which is confirmed by qualitative analysis.

Overall, however, we observe a similar trend both in CDS and in child language in terms of token production: children's production of zero derived nouns account for 7% of their *fare* + noun combinations and for 54% of their combinations with a verb-related noun, against the 9% and 53% in adults.

Children produce fewer types and relatively more tokens than adults of constructs with -*ata*, e.g. (9), and nouns derived by means of other suffixes.[5] Again, this is not surprising since they are morphologically more complex and thus expected to be learnt at later stages.

(9) CHI: perché si va a fare una girata, allora devono stare pronti
because we go to do a turned, then must.3PL stay ready
'because we are going to take a stroll, so they must be ready'
[Camilla, 3:01]

The relatively low type-token ratio (TTS) with nouns derived by suffixation also suggests that these productions are rote-learned, which is in fact supported by an inspection of the data: in all cases the constructs used are conventional and entrenched.

Still, even though they are conventional or lexicalized nominalizations, these nouns always keep a process meaning similar to their base verb, and this meaning may be what licenses the LVCs in the first place. For example, *spesa* lit. spent, expenditure 'shopping' is lexicalized, but may still refer to an activity which is metonymically related to the meaning of *spendere* 'to spend'.

In order to get a clearer idea of the evolution of the use of such constructs, we now look at the distribution of *fare* constructs with verb-related nouns in children across age groups in Figure 1. In the figures of the rest of the paper you will find, on the x axis, the age of children expressed in months; on the y axis the frequency. The dark line represents CL, the light one CDS. The same graphic applies to the dotted lines that indicate the linear trends.

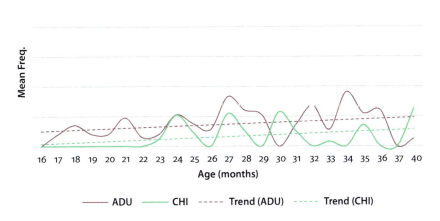

Figure 1. *Fare* + verb related nouns across age

---

5. The constructs are: *fare* + *passeggiata* 'do + walk', *fare* + *girata* 'do + stroll', *fare* + *spesa* 'do + shopping', *fare* + *carezza* 'do + caress', *fare* + *foto* 'do + picture'.

Here, children start producing *fare* + V-related noun constructs around 24 months and tend to increase their production in the following periods, though not dramatically. However, such a growth in production is likely dependent on the general vocabulary growth which takes place in the time span covered by this research and on the fundamental role of the input on the child's language, as predicted by usage-based, functional theories of language acquisition. The distribution of the same constructs in CDS shows a similar tendency. Vocabulary growth, moreover, is generally considered an important factor that encourages a process of abstraction into more general classes (see Bates & Goodman, 1997; Ninio, 1999).

Around 30–31 months of age we observe a counter-tendency: while adults do not produce virtually any combination with verb-related nouns, children are productive. The constructs uttered by children in those sessions contain the nouns *bagno, foto, carezza, disegno* 'bath, picture, caress, drawing'. As observed above, however, these are lexicalized nominalizations, the constructs are rather conventional and all types observed are also used by adults in previous sessions. Also, in most cases it is the same child that produces the same construct type with a relatively high token frequency. All these observations favor the assumption that *fare* constructs with verb-related nouns are rote-learned and meet the expectation to see imitative, not creative child production.

3.2   *Fare* + (physical) entity-denoting nouns

This group of nouns co-occurring with *fare* contains typical (physical) entity-denoting nouns like *casa* 'house/home', *balena* 'whale', *sedia* 'chair'. As such, they are found mostly in canonical transitive syntax, in which the verb is used as a fully lexical verb of creation. Consider for example (10) where the verb can be paraphrased with *disegnare* 'draw' as in (10a), or *costruire* 'build/make', *decorare* 'decorate' as in (10b).

(10) a. CHI: faccio   una   balena grossa!
             Do.1SG   a   whale   big
             'I'm making/drawing a big whale'   [Raffaello, 2;7]

     b. MOT: chi   l'   ha   fatto   l'   albero di   Natale?
              Who   it   has   done   the   tree   of   Christmas?
              'Who made/decorated the Christmas tree?'   [Marco, 2;0]

Looking at the distribution of *fare* + Concrete Nouns across age groups for both children and adults (Figure 2), in spite of the great variability, we observe a constant growth in CL (as indicated by the trend line), whereas adults show a more constant behavior.

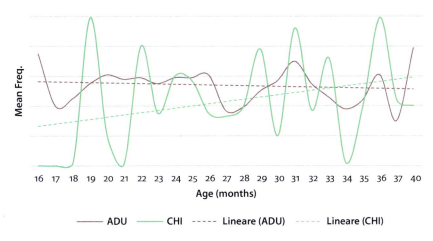

Figure 2. *Fare* + (physical) entity-denoting nouns across age

Children, not surprisingly, prove to be productive in this group of constructs and the trend observed is in line with our knowledge of the development of the lexicon and syntax in early childhood: productive transitive constructs appear after the one-word utterance phase, and after the first noun-noun and noun-verb combinations (Camaioni, 2001; Tomasello, 2003; Lust, 2006).

In the literature on LVCs, constructs with such nouns are generally excluded *apriori* from the analyses. In this study I decided to take them into consideration, given the possibility that, in combination with *fare,* they give rise to lexically filled LVCs, and therefore instances, albeit non-prototypical, of the general schema. If we consider for example (11), although the noun 'little horse' is intrinsically clearly entity-denoting (it is even a diminutive form), the construct does not refer to a creation event in a physical sense: there is no entity coming into being, rather the whole construct refers to an activity (i.e. the game of taking a child on ones lap and moving ones legs *as if* to be a horse).

(11) CHI: Luca si fa valluccio?
      Luca SI do.3SG horse.DIM
      'Shall we play the little horse, Luca?'   [Diana, 1:11]

While this is clearly a lexicalized expression, the strategy for evoking an activity or situation is strikingly similar to that of canonical LVCs, that is with verb-related nouns. In these cases, the semantics of the verb *fare* seems closer to PERFORM than to CREATE/MAKE.

Although most of the constructs in this group involve some sense of creation, where the verb can be paraphrased with verbs like 'drawing', 'building', 'decorating', the fact that there are some metaphorical, or idiomatic, expressions sharing strong similarities with canonical LVCs provides us with interesting support against traditional accounts of LVCs.

3.3 *Fare* + abstract nouns

Many of the verb-noun combinations in this group are expected to be LVCs according to the broad definition, since many abstract nouns are argument-taking.

Typical examples of *fare* + abstract nouns found in the dataset are: *fare bang, fare acrobazie, fare chiasso* (lit., 'make/do bang, acrobatics, noise'). Most of the combinations in this group yield expressions bearing some kind of non-literal meaning: some of them are clear examples of LVCs, in which the verb does not contribute the usual creation meaning, but a more abstract, general one (ex. *fare rumore, ginnastica, paura, blitz* 'make/do noise, gymnastics, fear, blitz'). Some are typical "motherese" expressions that are not normally used in adult conversations, but are nevertheless conventional (ex. *fare totò* 'to spank', whose noun is an entry in the De Mauro dictionary). Others are considered as (semi-)fixed idioms like *farsi una cultura* lit. make oneself a culture 'become educated', *fare (i) guai* lit. make (the) mess 'to mess up', or *fare il proprio repertorio* lit. make the own repertoire 'to do/perform one's own repertoire' as in (12).

(12) ADU: Giulio fa   tutto il   suo repertorio
             Giulio makes all   the his   repertoire
             'Giulio makes his whole repertoire'   [Viola, 2:1]

In this macro-group, two classes of expressions deserve special attention: those related to *sound emission* (e.g., *fare un verso, fare rumore, fare chiasso* 'make a cry, a noise', 'to moo'), which are LVCs in the broad sense; and those related to *gestures* (like *fare ciao, fare caro, fare totò* (lit., make hello 'say hello', do dear 'caress', do slap 'to slap'), which do not fall within the definitions of LVCs, but share formal and semantic properties with them and seem to play a role in the learning of more typical constructions. Among the similarities with expressions that, instead, meet the definitions of LVCs perfectly, I mention here that these expressions can be paraphrased using a single verb lexeme, although the nouns are neither 'intrinsically' related to such verbs, nor intrinsically argument-taking. *Caro* 'precious, dear', for example, is more commonly used as an adjective and it's relation to the noun *carezza* 'caress' and the verb *(ac)carezzare* 'to caress' is more an etymological issue than an everyday speaker awareness.

Regarding the distribution of constructs with abstract nouns, it is surprising to find high type frequency, like that with concrete nouns, among constructs with abstract types as well, since children are usually thought to acquire concrete words first, and abstract ones later. We may speculate that this is an effect of their use in the specific context *fare* + Noun and that their distribution in the overall corpus would confirm the shared knowledge about lexicon acquisition. If so, abstract nouns must play a special role in these constructs.

As for the development of such constructs, a quite different behaviour than with verb-related nouns emerges. There is a mild growing trend in children here (see Figure 3), but also a greater variability as shown by the higher type frequency. Children start producing these constructs around 20 months of age and they seem to acquire some creativity around 24–25 months. Their frequency is higher than the frequency of the constructs with verb-related nouns, and higher than in CDS.

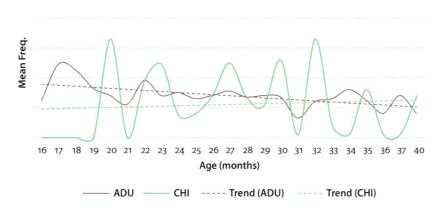

Figure 3. *Fare* + abstract nouns across age

What is also interesting here is that children produce more constructs with abstract nouns than adults from the age of 20–24 months up to 33 months. After this period, their production decreases again. Turning to a qualitative inspection of the types of noun in such constructs, we find conventional "baby-talk" expressions like *fare la nanna* 'take a nap' or *fare paura* 'scare', but also "invented" expressions with onomatopoeic words like (13) and (14).

(13) CHI: sopra una collina # abbaiando # fanno bu bu
     On   a   hill   barking   do.3PL bu bu
     'on the top of a hill # barking # they do "bow wow"'   [Raf, 2:8]

(14) CHI: no guarda uno uno sparato e   loro fanno pum!
     No look   one one shot   and they make pum
     'No, look one is shot and they shot him'   [Raf, 2:11]

Some of them turn out to be child "inventions" that do not survive in adult language, and are not even reflected in the input.

These inventions are very interesting because they share surface properties with canonical LVCs, the verb does not seem to be used in its basic lexical sense and the entire construct often evokes whole situations or denote actions and activities. For the moment, we shall call this class of expressions the *fare* + SOUND pattern.

An example of child 'misuse' or invention is *fare musica* 'make music' (15), which is used by the child to mean that some object like a radio is emitting music, and not that a volitional agent is playing an instrument, as it might be used in adult language.

(15) CHI: ma non fa musica?
     But not does music?
     'Doesn't it [the radio] make music?' [CAM, 2:6]

Since during the qualitative analysis of constructs with abstract nouns, onomatopoeic words (i.e. words indicating typical sounds of objects or cries of animals, words whose sound/phonetic iconically resembles the sound denoted) emerged as a conspicuous class, they have been further isolated as a subtype of the abstract noun category.

All onomatopoeic words used as surface direct objects of *fare* in the present analysis will be considered as nouns for reasons of consistency, given that many of the onomatopoeic words found in the corpus are also defined as nouns in traditional dictionaries (e.g., the De Mauro dictionary of contemporary Italian for example has a nominal entry for *miao* 'meow', the cry of cats).

Some of these words are sometimes used metonymically, especially in CDS, to refer to concrete entities, e.g *coccodè* 'cluck-cluck' for hen, *ciccì* for bird. Children, not surprisingly, seem to prefer these words and show early productivity. *Fare* combinations with onomatopoeic words in CDS overall account for 8% of the abstract noun group, while in children it accounts for 13%.

In our dataset, children produce various types of these combinations from quite an early age. Results from a session per session analysis show that starting from 17 months, all children produce some of these construct types without directly imitating the adults. Also interesting is the fact that, while adults use more conventional onomatopoeic words (e.g., *coccodè, chicchirichì, dindon* 'cackle, cock-a-doodle-doo, dingdong'), children are more inclined to invent them (*bumbe* 'boom', *cià cià* 'splash', *crac denk* ...).

Sound words in combination with *fare* are also often used to express events or activities, especially by children: Marco at 20 months says *fare ahm* meaning 'to eat', and Marco's mother, when he is 17 months of age, says *fare crack* meaning 'to break' in its two possible meanings, both as a causative verb (16) and as an inchoative (17).

(16) MOT: puoi   fare crac con   queste, puoi   romper-le.
         Can.2SG   do   crack with   these,   can.2SG break-them
         'you can make crack with these, you can break them'   [Mar09]

(17) MOT: la   scatola di polistirolo è   fragile e   ha   fatto crac.
         the   box   of polystyrene is   fragile and has   done crack
         'the polystyrene box is delicate and it broke'   [Mar09]

One meaning of *fare crac* implies that an agent intentionally breaks a patient object, while in the other meaning, it is the patient that *fa crac* 'breaks'. *Crack*, therefore, is metonymically related to the event implied, in that it is the "typical" sound of a breaking thing, and its combination with the verb *fare* in an iconic fashion suggests that this may be the way a child first learns LVCs.

All this seems to suggest that *fare* + N acts as a pivot for naming many "sound" and "action" events, especially in CL.[6] If we also consider that *fare* is very frequent in adults' questions, the role of this verb as a pivot for constructions naming actions and events may also be explained with a priming effect. Adults, especially mothers, appear to use *fare* in questions that aim at eliciting answers from their children about what activity or action he/she, or somebody else, is doing, or about what is happening. So, it is reasonable to assume that *fare* becomes a very general "action" word in early CL: a word that can combine with virtually any other word that activates or refers to a whole event or scene.

4. A constructionist hypothesis for *fare* + N constructs

On the basis of the observations reported in the previous sections and the properties of the nouns and constructs in the various groups, it is now clear that a traditional formal approach to LVCs does not account for similarities among expressions whereas a constructionist explanation appears more viable. In particular, I shall claim here that the *fare*-constructs found in our dataset are better accounted for as a family of constructions.[7]

Taking into account the distribution of the constructs in CDS and some semantic, denotational properties of the nouns and constructs as a whole, I provide here a tentative representation of both the schematic constructions and of

---

6. We have encountered at least one example of CDS in which the *fare* + sound pattern is used to introduce a probably new lexical verb to the child, e.g. *fare crac* 'do crack' for *rompere* 'break' in (23).

7. For the notion of family of constructions see in particular Goldberg (1995 and 2006).

the family as a whole. It is not the goal of the present work to formally establish a full specification of the constructional syntactic, semantic and pragmatic properties as well as of the specific relations among them. This is certainly an important and interesting issue for a constructional description of Italian, but is reserved for future research. The purpose of this study is, instead, to provide a tentative coarse-grained representation of the family of *fare* constructions as it emerges from the dataset, in an attempt to prove that such a representation is not only viable, but also that it can account for both the more schematic and productive types of LVCs and for the more conventional, lexicalized instances in a uniform way. I proceed, therefore, to give an informal description of these constructions, based on the exemplars found in the dataset.

Four more general, or schematic, constructions were identified that can account for several exemplars in the dataset, and tentatively assume, based on the distributional evidence discussed in Section 3, that there is one central construction. Figure 4 displays a naïve representation of the *fare*-family of constructions.

The seemingly central construction, which we shall call the *Perform Intransitive Action* construction, would have a form-meaning like in (18):

(18)   agt   <Activity/action>   (loc/goal)
     V   Subj   (Comp)
     Fare NP   predN   PP

Pragmatically, the construction embodies the "EVENTS ARE OBJECTS" metaphor, which seem to be inherited by most of the related constructions (for details on the metaphor see Lakoff & Johnson, 1980).

This construction is still quite abstract, and we may envisage that many single conventional LVC are individually stored as instances of the more general pattern, or of one of its subtypes, in the speaker's mind. Thus, *fare una passeggiata, fare una girata, fare un salto* 'take a walk, take a stroll, do a jump' would be individually stored. In addition to the higher token frequency of conventional instances of the LVC, a motivation for their storage might be that in most cases they are associated with a lexical verb expressing approximately the same content, and this synonymy link is likely to be explicitly represented.[8]

The *Perform/Emit Sound* construction roughly corresponds to the *fare* + Sound constructs discussed in Section 2: e.g. *fare chiasso, fare miao* 'make noise, to meow'. This construction can be roughly described as in (19).

---

8. There is another possibility though: in Frame Semantics terms, an action noun and the corresponding verb, if any, would be part of the same frame; their semantic relatedness, therefore, could be already established at the lexical construction level. This would save storing many instances. Unfortunately, it is outside the scope of this work to enter into the details of Frame Semantics, or of how this could be integrated in a constructional representation of LVCs.

Chapter 3. Development and representation of Italian light-*fare* constructions

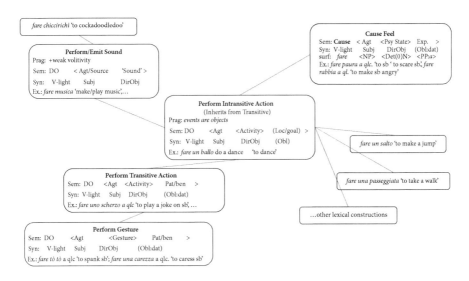

Figure 4. The *fare* LVC family of constructions

(19)   Agent/source <Emit/produce Sound>
    V   Subj
    Fare NP   predN

Examples of this constructions are *fare un fischio, fare bee* (Lit. do a whistle, do baa).

The *Perform Transitive Action* construction corresponds to constructs with nouns denoting a two argument, 'act upon' action. For example: *fare un colpo, fare una carezza, fare uno scherzo (a qualcuno)* 'hit, caress, spank, trick sb' (Lit., to do a hit, do a caress, do a joke to sb). The form and function of this construction would roughly be as in (20).

(20)   agt   <Activity> pat/ben
    V   Subj   DObj   Obl
    Fare NP   NP   PP:a

The *Cause Emotion* construction corresponds to constructs of the type *fare* + noun denoting a psychological state (e.g., *fare paura a ql.* Lit., do fear to sb, 'to scare sb.'; *fare rabbia* Lit., do anger to sb, 'make sb angry) and its form and meaning might be something like (21).

(21)   Cause   <PsyState>   Exp
    V   Subj   Obl
    Fare NP   Det(0)PredN PP:a

Even with these sketchy definitions of the properties of the constructions, the similarities among them appear evident. Treating *fare* constructs as a family of constructions, or a network of nodes organized like a radial category, allows us to capture the inheritance and similarity relation among them, as well as their differences, while maintaining the possibility of a full representation of conventional, entrenched instances, which can be stored as "peripheral" items. At the same time it allows us to represent lexicalized conventional instances as individual stored items.

Now, if we consider the predicative function of the noun as a dynamic property emerging in context, which can be explained and motivated on the bases of similarity and analogy, constructs with (apparently) concrete nouns are not excluded *apriori* from the *fare* LVC family, since they can still be forced into a predicative reading by the construction itself. This permits, for instance, relating expressions like *fare il trenino* 'do a conga line' with the LVCs "event naming" function.

5. Acquisition of the family of LVCs

After sketching a representation of the *fare* LVC family of construction as emerging from CDS, we now focus on the distribution of the constructions in CL, in order to understand how children acquire such constructions and whether they use them productively or not. The focus will be on the three most interesting constructions: the Perform Intransitive Action, the Perform Sound, and the Perform Transitive Action, and look at their distribution in the dataset and their evolution in child language. To this end, each *fare* + Noun occurrence in the dataset is further annotated as an instance of one of these three constructions, or none.

The three subsets of constructs obtained with this annotation partly overlap with the sets based on the types of nouns discussed above, but are not identical. Here, the main criterion is constructional form-meaning, as broadly defined above; therefore, in the same construction we may group abstract, verb-related and concrete nouns together. *Fare canestro* 'score a basket', for instance, is considered and counted as an instance of the Perform Intransitive Action.

5.1 The Perform Intransitive Action construction

Instances of Perform Intransitive Action are, for example: *fare il bagno* 'have a bath', *fare una scalata* 'make a climb', *fare il solletico* 'to tickle', *fare finta* 'pretend', *fare confusione* 'make noise/a mess'. This construction appears to be particularly frequent in both CL and CDS: overall it accounts for about 30% of all *fare* + Noun constructs in CL, and about 27% in CDS. If we look at the distribution in Figure 5, after 24 months we observe basically the same trend in children and adults: child production is clearly growing, but it basically reflects adults' uses.

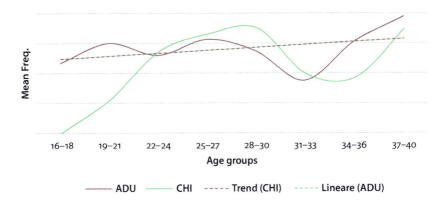

Figure 5. Development of the Perform Intransitive Action construction

This result is strikingly similar to the one found for verb-related nouns in Section 3.1 above. Given that verb-related nouns constitute a considerable subgroup of this construction, it is not very surprising. If we exclude instances with verb-related nouns from the present set, we obtain the distribution in Figure 6, which shows a quite different situation. Instances of this construction with abstract nouns are: *fare canestro, fare patatrak* 'score a basket, make a damage' as in (22) and (23).

(22) CHI: fatto   canetro   ho   fatto   canetro
         done   basket   have.1SG   done   basket
         'I scored a basket, I scored a basket'   [Mar26, 2:1]

(23) CHI: ho   fatto   una   patatrack   io
         Have.1SG   done   a   patatrak   I
         'I've made a mess'   [Mar24, 2:0]

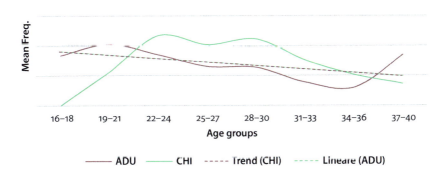

Figure 6. Development of the Perform Intransitive Action construction with abstract nouns only

Child production starts quite early, but until around 23–24 months children produce only highly conventional expressions like *fare (la) nanna* 'go to bye-bye'. At 24, instead they start to produce proportionally more instances than adults, which shows that the pattern has been, or is being, acquired. Interestingly, children's production of the Perform Intransitive Action construction with abstract nouns progressively decreases after 29–30 month of age, as if they had experimented enough with it. Moreover, around 34–36 months of age, when the proportion of constructs with abstract nouns is quite low, we register an increase in the production of instances of the same construction, but with verb-related nouns (see Figure 7). This latter observation is again in line with common knowledge of language acquisition. Verb-related nouns, being more complex, are expected to be acquired later than other nouns. It is however interesting to observe a sort of mutually exclusive usage pattern between abstract and verb-related nouns.

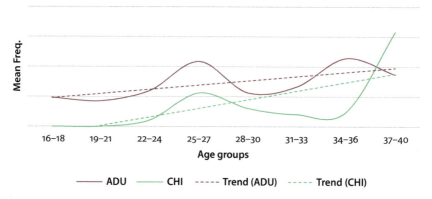

Figure 7. Development of the Perform Intransitive Action construction (verb-related nouns)

5.2 The Perform Sound construction

The *Perform Sound* construction is a more specific construction that inherits most of its properties from the central one (the Perform Intransitive Action construction). Its distribution overlaps mostly with the class of constructs that we called Perform Sound in Section 3.3. Typical examples of this construction are: *fare* + onomatopoeic noun combinations like *fare muh, fare pum* 'to Moo, to shoot'; and other combinations with abstract nouns like *fare musica, fare rumore* 'make music, make noise'.

As we can see in Figure 8, children start to produce the *Perform Sound* construction quite early in development, around 21 months and seem to be quite productive from around 23 months of age. Around 33 months we see a significant decrease in production. Interestingly, adults show the opposite tendency: they produce a high percentage of instances when their children are very young, and progressively decrease their number as they grow. This trend in part explains why children start producing these types of constructs earlier than others and the fact that they seem to apply the *fare* ACTION generalization by using this type, as will be discussed later.

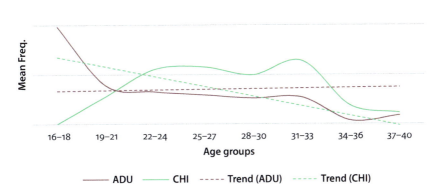

Figure 8. Development of the Perform Sound construction

5.3 The Perform Transitive Action construction

Typical instances of this construction are: *fare la bua, fare caro/a, fare il solletico, fare paura* 'to hurt sb., to caress, to tickle, to scare'. In Figure 9 we see that while adults' production is quite constant, children's is rather discontinuous, which does not permit identification of a clear trend.

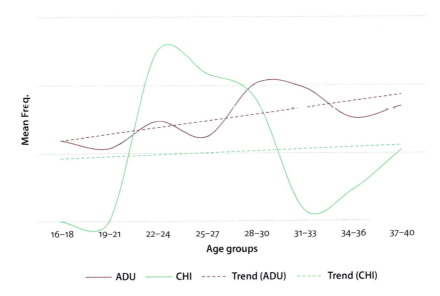

Figure 9. Distribution of the Perform Transitive Action construction

Children produce a few types of this construction with a relatively high token frequency, which indicates that they are rote-learned, entrenched items. This is not surprising, given that the syntax-semantics of this construction is more complex: it involves at least two participants and a causative predicative meaning.

5.4 The pattern of acquisition

After studying the distributional trends of the constructions and inspecting the data more deeply, I will now proceed to delineate a tentative general pattern of acquisition for Italian *fare* LVCs.

Clearly, at first children start by imitatively producing those instances that have a relative high frequency in their ambient language: i.e. lexicalized, conventional LVCs. Then, they begin with forming a *fare*-pivot schema in which the free slot is filled with various sound words and is first used to refer to actual sound emission events. Starting from about 24 months of age this schema is then generalized to refer to actions where a volitional agent performs some kind of (intransitive) action. Children indeed seem to use the Perform Sound construction productively to refer to some event or action. (e.g., from *fa pum* 'it emits a pum sound' to *fa pum* 'to shoot at somebody'). Therefore, initially, the schema is applied to refer to simple events with only one participant, which leads to the acquisition of a more general *fare*-ACTION schema (Perform Intransitive Action construction). It is likely that this latter constriction is further extended later to encompass more complex, transitive, actions, leading to the establishment of the Perform Transitive Action construction.[9] Unfortunately the data is insufficient to make a strong claim to this. A dataset covering a longer age period would be needed. Still, given the observation and the trend observed in the data, this is a reasonable hypothesis.

6. Conclusion

This paper focused on the study of the development and use of Italian *fare* LVCs in Child Language and Child-directed Speech as emerging from the analysis of a corpus of naturalistic data.

---

9. It is possible that in adult language only one of the more abstract constructions survives, i.e., that the Perform Intransitive and Transitive constructions converge to one abstract *fare* + EVENT construction. As said above, in order to define the extent, scope and properties of LVCs from a construction grammar perspective precisely, a more extensive and dedicated analysis is needed.

First, the data was approached assuming the perspective of traditional, formal approaches to LVCs with the objective of showing their weaknesses. The results show that, indeed, there are expressions that bear similarities to typical LVCs, which will not be accounted for according to the traditional definitions. Consequently, I have claimed that they are better accounted for by a constructionist approach to language and specifically as a family of constructions represented as a radial category. To support this claim, I sketched a potential representation both of the individual constructions and of the whole family. A full specification of the properties of the constructions and their relations in the network is outside the scope of this research and is left for future investigation.

Finally, the analysis of the development of the three most represented *fare* Constructions identified in Child Language led, perhaps, to the most interesting findings of this research: Children's very first productions are indeed rote-learned instances, or fully lexical constructions. The situation is different for each child, of course, but, in general, they use very few types with a relatively high token frequency. Later, they start showing some creativity in their usage. Their first type of LVC is the Perform Sound construction. From 23 months, the increased type variability, in the form of *fare* + onomatopoeic words (e.g., *fare clic* 'make click' for *fare una fotografia* 'take a picture' or *scattare* 'go-off'), can be taken as the first manifestation of a '*fare* + Action/event/situation' pivot schema that enables later combinations with abstract nouns. The use of such a pivot-schema is motivated by the need to name events or situations for which they have no lexical verb yet.

This pattern of development is in line with the predictions and findings of usage-based theories of language acquisition and, in particular, with Tomasello's verb-island hypothesis (1992, 2003): from lexical, item based constructions, a pivot schema is generalized with the function of naming new events, actions or situations. The open slot can be filled first with sound words, then with (abstract) nouns. Interestingly, children seem to learn the general schema starting from a peripheral *fare* construction in adult language: the *Perform Sound* construction.

In spite of some limitations due to the size and density of the corpus, I believe that the results constitute a step toward a full understanding of the development of grammatical constructions in Italian. Far from being simply rote-learned expressions (as they could be if they were unmotivated and fixed or restricted collocations), Light Verb Constructions may instead have an important role in the acquisition of the more general and abstract transitive construction. Still, many more pieces need to be added to the puzzle.

Future work should be directed towards the analysis of the behavior and acquisition of other light verbs, which would provide us with more information both on the generality/specificity of these constructions and on the way the transitive construction(s) is gradually formed. Secondly, to reach a more comprehensive picture of the acquisition of both LVCs and the transitive construction, a fundamental step appears to be the enlargement of the corpus, possibly with new data based on a denser sampling technique (cfr. Tomasello & Stahl, 2004), and certainly with data from older children. Finally, since any naturalistic observation study bears the intrinsic limitations of studying what there is in the data (cfr. also Theakston et al., 2004), experimental studies along the same line are most welcome.

Acknowledgements

I am grateful to the editors of this volume who first organized the very interesting workshop at SLE 2011 and then made this volume possible. Since this paper is a revision of the heart of my PhD research, I would like to offer my special thanks to Alessandro Lenci for his supervision and for the precious advices on the original manuscript. Without him this research would not have been possible. Finally, I am thankful to the anonymous reviewers of the draft and Michele Carolyne Carlucci, who helped me improve the paper considerably with their comments and corrections. Responsibility for the content and for any errors that remain is of course mine alone.

References

Alba-Salas, J. (2002). *Light verb constructions in romance: A syntactic analysis*. Cornell University. Unpublished PhD Dissertation.
Bates, E., & Goodman, J. C. (1997). On the inseperability of grammar and the lexicon: Evidence from acquisition, aphasia and real time processing. *Language and Cognitive Processes*, 12, 507–586. doi:10.1080/016909697386628
Camaioni, L. (2001). *Psicologia dello sviluppo del linguaggio*. Bologna: Il Mulino.
Cameron-Faulkner, T., Lieven, E., & Tomasello, M. (2003). A Construction based analysis of child directed speech. *Cognitive Science*, 27, 843–873. doi:10.1207/s15516709cog2706_2
Cantarini, S. (2004). *Costrutti con Verbo Supporto: Una Descrizione contrastiva Italiano – Tedesco*. Ferrara: PhD Dissertation. (published as Costrutti con verbo supporto: italiano e tedesco a confronto. Bologna: Pàtron).
Croft, W. (2001). *Radical construction grammar: Syntactic theory in typological perspective*. Oxford: OUP. doi:10.1093/acprof:oso/9780198299554.001.0001
D'Agostino, E., & Elia, A. (1997). Il significato delle frasi: un continuo dalle frasi semplici alle forme polirematiche. In F. A. Leoni, D. Gamabarara, S. Gensini, F. Lo Piparo, & R. Simone (Eds). *Ai limiti del linguaggio* (pp. 287–310). Bari: Laterza.
De Mauro, T. (2000) *De Mauro. Il dizionario della Lingua Italiana*. Milano: Paravia.
Doğruöz, S. A., & Backus, A. D. (2009). Innovative constructions in Dutch Turkish: An assessment of ongoing contact-induced change. *Bilingualism: Language and Cognition*, 12(1), 41–63. doi:10.1017/S1366728908003441
Family, N. (2009). Mapping semantic spaces: A constructionist account of the "light verb" eat in Persian. In M. Vanhove (Ed.), *From polysemy to semantic change: Towards a typology of lexical semantic associations* (pp. 139–161). Amsterdam: John Benjamins. doi:10.1075/slcs.106.08fam

Fried, M., & Östman, J-O. (2004). Construction grammar: A thumbnail sketch. In M. Fried & J-O. Östman (Eds.), *Construction grammar in a cross-language perspective* (pp. 11–86). Amsterdam: John Benjamins. doi:10.1075/cal.2.02fri

Gaeta, L. (2002). *Quando I verbi compaiono come nomi*. Milano: FrancoAngeli Editore.

Giry-Schneider, J. (1987). *Les Prédicats Nominaux en Français. Les Phrases Simples à Verbe Support*. Geneva: Droz.

Goldberg, A. E. (2006). *Constructions at work*. New York: OUP.

Goldberg, A. E. (1995). *Constructions: A construction grammar approach to argument structure*. Chicago: Chicago University Press.

Grimshaw, J., & Mester, A. (1988). Light verbs and μ-Marking. *Linguistic Inquiry*, 19, 205–231.

Iacobini, C. (2000). Base and direction of derivation. In G. Booij, C. Lehmann, & J. Mugdan (Eds.) *Morphology. An international handbook on inflection and word formation*, Vol. 1 (pp. 865–876). Berlin & New York: De Gruyter.

La Fauci, N., & Mirto, I. (2003). *Fare: Elementi di sintassi*. Pisa: Edizioni ETS.

Lakoff, G., & Johnson, M. (1980). *Metaphors we live by*. Chicago: The University of Chicago Press. (2nd ed. 2008).

Lust, B. (2006). *Child language: Acquisition and growth*. New York: CUP. doi:10.1017/CBO9780511803413

MacWhinney, B. (2000). *The CHILDES project: Tools for analyzing talk* (3rd ed.). Hillsdale, NJ: Lawrence Erlbaum.

Miyagawa, S. (1989). Light verbs and the ergative hypothesis. *Linguistic Inquiry*, 20, 659–668.

Moon, R. (1998). *Fixed expressions and idioms in English: A corpus-based approach*. Oxford: Oxford University Press.

Namer, F. (1998). Support verb constructions. In F. van Eynde & P. Schmidt (Eds.), *Linguistic specifications for typed feature structure formalisms* (Studies in MT and NLP). Brussels: CEC.

Ninio, A. (1999). Pathbreaking verbs in syntactic development and the question of prototypical transitivity. *Journal of Child Language*, 26, 619–653. doi:10.1017/S0305000999003931

Palancar, E. L. (2003). La polisemia dei verbi dar, pegar e meter in spagnolo. In L. Gaeta & S. Nuraghi (Eds.), *Introduzione alla Linguistica Cognitiva* (pp. 197–211). Roma: Carocci.

Quochi, V. (2007). *A usage-based approach to light verb constructions in Italian: Development and use*. University of Pisa. Unpublished Dissertation.

Sinclair, J. (1991). *Corpus, concordance, collocation*. Oxford: Oxford University Press.

Theakston, A. L., Lieven, E. V. M., Pine, J. M., & Rowland, C. F. (2004). Semantic generality, input frequency and the acquisition of syntax. *Journal of Child Language*, 31, 61–99. doi:10.1017/S0305000903005956

Tomasello, M. (2003). *Constructing a language: A usage-based theory of language acquisition*. Cambridge, MA: Harvard University Press.

Tomasello, M. (1992). *First verbs: A case study of early grammatical development*. Cambridge: CUP. doi:10.1017/CBO9780511527678

Tomasello, M., & Stahl, D. (2004). Sampling children's spontaneous speech: How much is enough? *Journal of Child Language*, 31, 101–121. doi:10.1017/S0305000903005944

CHAPTER 4

Constructions with subject *vs.* object experiencers in Spanish and Italian
A corpus-based approach

Victoria Vázquez Rozas and Viola G. Miglio
University of Santiago de Compostela / University of California, Santa Barbara

This study analyzes Spanish and Italian clauses that denote processes or states of feeling or emotion involving two participants, an experiencer and a stimulus. Some of these clauses construe the experiencer as Subject and the stimulus as Object, while others have experiencers coded as dative or accusative Objects and stimuli as Subjects.

Using corpus data, we track the frequency and distribution of a number of discourse-related properties of the arguments, such as animacy, person, and syntactic category, in order to gain insight into how both constructions are really used and conceived of by speakers. The results point to a non-random distribution of these properties when comparing the 'Experiencer-as-Subject' with the 'Experiencer-as-Object' constructions, and reveal striking differences in their frequency across textual genres.

1. The constructions: Experiencer as Subject (ESC) *vs.* Experiencer as Object (EOC)*

1.1 The constructions

We analyze Spanish and Italian clauses that denote processes or states of feeling or emotion involving two participants, an experiencer and a stimulus.

The examples in (1) show a syntactic-semantic pattern different from the pattern exemplified in the examples in (2). In (1), the clauses encode the experiencer

---

* We wish to thank Stefan Gries for his invaluable help with the statistical analysis for this paper, and two anonymous reviewers for their comments, which helped us improve the paper. All remaining errors are of course our own. Part of this research has received financial support from the Spanish Ministry of Economy and Competitiveness (projects FFI2010-17417 and FFI2014-52287-P).

as a subject – 'I' in Spanish and 'he' in Italian – and the stimulus as a direct object – 'haughty men' (Sp.) and 'society' (It.) –, whereas in (2) the experiencer – 'He' (Sp. and It.) – is cast as an indirect object and the stimulus – 'long and noisy parties' (Sp.), 'grandiose schemes' (It.) – as the syntactic subject that triggers verb agreement:

(1) a. Yo   detestaba   a   los   hombres   altaneros
       I.NOM.1SG detest.PST.1SG to the.M.PL man.PL   haughty.M.PL
       'I detested haughty men'   (CRÓN: 35, 6)
    b. Egli   detestava   la   società   (della sua epoca)
       He.NOM.1SG detest.PST.3SG the.F.SG society.SG (of   his time)
       'He detested the society of his time'   (LaRep, 03.17.92, 'Cultura')

(2) a. Le gustaban   las   fiestas   ruidosas   y   largas
       3SG.OBJ=like.PST.3PL the.F.PL parties.F.PL noisy.F.PL & long.F.PL
       'He liked long and noisy parties'   (CRÓN: 32, 20)
    b. Gli piacevano [...]   i   grandi   disegni
       3SG.M.DAT=like.PST.3PL the.M.PL schemes.M.PL grandiose.PL
       'He liked grandiose schemes'   (LaRep, 02.12.92, 'Affari & Finanza')

Similar contrasts have been described in a number of languages that have both an 'Experiencer as Subject' construction (henceforth called ESC) and an 'Experiencer as Object' construction (henceforth called EOC), both historically and synchronically, including English.[1] The study of these alternative patterns has mostly focused on the formal properties of the constructions and on their semantic motivation, particularly the meanings behind the various valency options like state *vs.* action, differences in causation, control, and volition, among others. However, little attention has hitherto been paid to the real frequencies of these patterns in running texts and little is known about their function in discourse.

Well-known articles on so-called psych-verbs[2] tend to concentrate on the structure of constructions with non-nominative experiencers, especially those written in the generative paradigm (Belletti & Rizzi, 1988; Masullo, 1993). They continue the tradition of research started in the sixties and seventies by Fillmore, Lakoff and Postal (Fillmore, 1968; Lakoff, 1970; Postal, 1971). These authors attribute the same semantic role of experiencer both to the subject of a transitive construction (such as the *Yo*, 'I-NOM' in 1a above), as to the object of an 'inverse construction' (such as the *le* 'he-DAT' in 2a above) and argue that the semantic structure of the clause is the same. Their efforts are mostly aimed at ascertaining whether the experiencer has

---

1. The bibliography on this subject is very extensive, for a number of languages including English, Icelandic, Italian, and Spanish see, among others, Lightfoot (1981), Fischer and Van der Leek (1983), Allen (1986), Sigurðsson (1989), Whitley (1998), Shibatani (1999), Haspelmath (2001), Barðdal & Eyþórsson (2003, 2009), Bentley (2006), Gutiérrez Bravo (2006), Melis & Flores (2007).

2. Psych verbs are verbs expressing mental processes, as the ones analyzed in this paper.

all the necessary features of a subject. Instead of using corpus data, however, they use constructed examples. This allows the researchers to control for specific factors that would otherwise invalidate the tests used to establish whether the experiencer behaves indeed as a syntactic subject. Moreover, they do not evaluate the frequency of use of the different structures, or their communicative value.[3]

1.2 Case marking and pronominal syncretism in ESCs and EOCs

Cross-linguistically, experiential predicates tend to be cast as EOCs[4] rather than ESCs more frequently than with other verb types (Bossong, 1998; Shibatani, 1999; Bauer, 2000; Haspelmath, 2001). The constructions we analyze in this paper fall into this semantic class. The present study explores the supposed identity between dative experiencers of verbs such as *gustar* (Sp.)/*piacere* (It.) 'to like', and the nominative experiencers of verbs such as *amar*/*amare* 'to love', using data from actual usage. EOCs are found to be very lively in both Romance languages, and they are especially productive in Spanish.

Because of considerable syncretism between the dative and accusative forms of the experiencer pronouns, as well as the frequent dative-accusative pronominal alternations found in Spanish (see below), we propose to classify all of the non-nominative experiencers as 'objects' in one category, hence the use of 'EOC,' i.e. 'experiencer as object' construction. This point requires the discussion of some examples and previous literature to justify the data treatment in this study.

Sentences (3)–(5) below are examples of ESC clauses in the Spanish corpus, and (6)–(8) are their equivalent Italian constructions:

(3) Pero no *aguanto* sus ideas, su falta de fe en
    but not stand.PRS.1SG her/his ideas his/her lack of faith in
    un mundo nuevo
    a world new
    'But I can't stand his/her ideas, his/her lack of faith in a new world'
    (CAR:156.21)

(4) todos los jugadores le *temen* al árbitro único
    all the players 3SG.DAT=fear.PRS.3PL to.the referee only
    del encuentro
    of-the game
    'All the players are afraid of the only referee for the game' (1VO:010-1.2-57)

---

3. See for instance Belletti & Rizzi, 1988; Sigurðsson, 1989; Masullo, 1993; Gutiérrez Bravo, 2006. A discussion of subjecthood tests for Icelandic and their value can also be found in Barðdahl, 2001, which otherwise advocates for a CxG analysis of quirky subjects in Icelandic.

4. EOCs are also called *inverse* or *reverse* constructions, and the experiencer is often referred to as an *oblique* or *quirky* subject. ESCs may be referred to simply as transitive constructions.

(5) El sí   *amaba*   esa   ciudad
    he yes love.PST.3SG that town
    'He did love that town'   (MIRADA: 93, 32)

These are all constructions that have their equivalent in Italian too and are frequently used in common speech:

(6) Non *sopporto*   i   miei coetanei
    not stand.PRS.1SG   the my   contemporaries
    'I can't stand my contemporaries'   (LaRep, 09.07.91, 'Extra')

(7) Gli altri politici [...] *temono*   le   reazioni   delle femministe
    the other politicians   fear.PRS.3PL   the reactions   of.the feminists
    'The other politicians are afraid of the feminists' reactions'
                                                (LaRep, 03.24.91, 'Cronaca')

(8) Cendrars *amava*   il   cinema di un amore non ricambiato.
    Cendrars love.PST.3SG   the cinema of a   love   not requited
    'Cendrars loved cinema with unrequited love'
                                       (LaRep, 06.24.89, 'Mercurio-Scaffale')

The examples below, on the other hand, depict EOC constructions both in Spanish and in Italian, where objects can be marked both in dative (9a, 13a and 13b, 15a and 15b), accusative (9b, 12a and 14b), or an ambiguous syncretic form that could be either (10a and 10b, 11a and 11b, 14a) in order to show the similarity between the two languages, as well as the existing syncretism:[5]

(9) a. hacer   música les *entretiene*   mucho más   que jugar
        make.INF   music   3PL.DAT=amuse.PRS.3SG   much   more   than play
        al   fútbol
        to.the   soccer
        'Playing music amuses them much more than playing soccer'
                                                         (2VO:072-2.2-09)

    b. Chiacchierare di politica li *diverte*
        talk.INF   of politics 3PL.M.ACC=amuse.PRS.3SG
        'Talking about politics amuses them'   (LaRep, 03.22.92, 'Extra')

(10) a. francamente   la   televisión a   mí   me *aburre*
        frankly   the   television to   me   1SG.OBJ=bore.PRS.3SG
        'Frankly television bores me'   (SEV:094.08)

---

5. Moreover, Spanish allows for dative-accusative alternations with the same verb (see Vázquez Rozas, 2006b; Miglio et al. 2013), such that (9a) and (12a) would be grammatical in Spanish also as *hacer música los(ACC) entretiene mucho más que jugar al fútbol* and *la música de Los Bandidos le(DAT) entristecía* with no substantial change in meaning.

b. Il   teatro, sono   sincera,   mi *annoia*
    the theater be.PRS.1SG sincere.F 1SG.OBJ=bore.PRS.3SG
    'I admit it: theater bores me'   (LaRep, 02.06.92, 'Spettacoli')

(11) a. A mí me *asusta*,   me *desagrada*
         to me 1SG.OBJ=scare.PRS.3SG 1SG.OBJ=disgust.PRS.3SG
         este Madrid ruidoso
         this Madrid noisy
         'The noise of Madrid scares and disgusts me'   (MAD:103.17)
     b. Non mi *spaventa*,   ma non lo ritengo   corretto
         not 1SG.OBJ=scare.PRS.3SG but not it consider.PRS.1SG fair
         '[It] does not scare me, but I do not think it's fair'
                                               (LaRep, 03.01.92, 'Extra')

(12) a. La música de Los bandidos lo *entristecía*
         the music of Los Bandidos 3SG.M.ACC=sadden.PST.3SG
         'The music of Los Bandidos made him feel sad'   (HIS:055.03)
     b. questo è   il sospetto che *rattristava*   l'umore
         this be.PRS.3SG the suspicion that sadden.PST.3SG the-mood
         del   presidente
         of.the president
         'this was the suspicion that saddened the president's mood'
                                               (LaRep, 06.15.91, 'Extra')

(13) a. lo que   le *interesa*   al   Ayuntamiento
         it which 3SG.DAT=interest.PRS.3SG to.the Council
         de Vigo es poder   seguir   otorgando licencias.
         of Vigo is can.INF keep.INF issuing   licenses
         'What the Council of Vigo is interested in is being able to keep on issuing
         licenses'   (1VO:026-4.1-11)
     b. quello che   gli *interessa*⁶   è   una Padania unita
         that   which 3SG.M.DAT=interest.PRS.3SG is a   Padania unified
         attorno a Milano
         around to Milan
         'what interests him is a Padania region unified around Milan'
                                               (LaRep, 03.26.92, 'Commenti')

(14) a. La suavidad de la manita   *conmueve*   al   viejo
         the softness of the small hand move.PRS.3SG to.the old man
         'The softness of the small hand moves the old man'   (SON:235.16)

---

6. *Interessare* in Italian is problematic, because it can be constructed as a EOC with the meaning of 'to interest', but also as a ESC with the meaning of 'to affect', and this latter is typical of formal or journalistic style, hence common in the *La Repubblica* database.

    b. lo *commuove* con la perfezione della bellezza
       3SG.M.ACC=move.PRS.3SG with the perfection of.the beauty
       'it moves it [the audience] with the perfection of beauty'
                                               (LaRep, 11.24.91, 'Spettacoli')

(15) a. Le *gustaban* las fiestas ruidosas y largas
       3SG.DAT=like.PST.3PL the.F.PL parties.F.PL noisy.F.PL & long.F.PL
       'He liked long and noisy parties'   (CRÓN: 32, 20)
    b. E non *piace* invece ai reazionari, agli
       and not like.PRS.3SG conversely to.the reactionaries to.the
       incolti, ai provinciali
       uncultivated to.the country bumpkins
       'Reactionaries, uncultivated people, and country bumpkins, on the other hand, do not like it'   (LaRep, 03.26.92, 'Politica Estera')

Syntactic descriptions of Spanish and Italian usually distinguish two types of objects, direct and indirect. Direct objects are often represented by non-prepositional constituents (*sus ideas, su falta de fe en un mundo nuevo* in 3, *i miei coetanei* in 6) or accusative clitics (Sp. *lo* in 12a; It. *lo* in 14b). Only in Spanish, however, they are quite frequently introduced by the preposition *a* 'to', particularly if they are animate and definite (*a los hombres altaneros* in 1). Indirect objects, which are mainly animate and definite, are invariably marked by the preposition *a* if represented by a NP both in Spanish (see Example 16 below) and in Italian (*ai reazionari, agli incolti, ai provinciali* in 15b):

(16) Se rumorea que el negocio interesa asimismo
      REFL rumor.PRS.3SG that the business interest.PRS.3SG also
      a los ejecutivos de una poderosa multinacional
      to the executives of a powerful multinational
      'It is rumored that the business also interests the executives of a powerful multinational'   (PAI:113.20)

The prepositional phrase introduced by *a* is frequently found in combination with a co-referent dative clitic in Spanish[7] (*le* in 13a), or the dative clitic can otherwise stand on its own (*le* in 2a for Sp., *gli* in 13b for It.).

In addition to the use of the same preposition for both indirect objects and some direct objects, other factors contribute to blur the contrast between these two functions especially in Spanish. In some Spanish varieties the dative clitics *le, les* are also used as direct objects ("leísmo"), mainly, but not exclusively,

---

7. Clitic doubling is ungrammatical in standard Italian and would not be found in formal written texts, although there are examples of non-standard reduplication in the oral BAdIP corpus.

with masculine human referents as in (4), while accusative clitics *lo, la, los, las*, also represent indirect objects in a few dialects (the "laísta" and "loísta" varieties[8]). More relevant still is that there is no formal distinction between direct and indirect object for first and second person clitics, which are syncretic forms (Examples 10 and 11), both in Spanish and Italian, and this should be considered also in the light of usage data.[9]

The tendency of Spanish direct and indirect objects to conflate into one category is noticeable precisely in EOC clauses, as their object usually refers to animate and definite participants, which is typical for the semantic role of the experiencer.[10] This is true also for the examples we analyzed for Italian, although an exact parallel with the Spanish data cannot be drawn because we did not have a comparable database to ADESSE for Italian. From Examples (9)–(16) above, it is clear that the syncretism between direct and indirect object forms may have been resolved in favor of direct object constructions in Italian, since among those examples only *interessare* – with the meaning of 'to be interesting to' – and *piacere* are constructed with dative objects.

In Italian, the tendency towards EOCs with direct objects may be a historical evolution, confirmed by some archaic forms found for instance in the 1612 *Vocabolario degli Accademici della Crusca*:[11] here we find examples such as *Ciascuno gl' infastidisce, e fugge* 'Everyone annoys him-DAT and he runs away', where *infastidire* is constructed as and EOC with dative object, whereas in contemporary standard Italian it can only participate in an EOC construction with a direct object.

High animacy and definiteness of the objects in EOC are not the only features that result in similar coding properties of direct and indirect objects in these constructions. The aforementioned syncretism of first and second person clitic objects is prominent in EOC clauses, when compared to the general frequency data of the objects in two-argument clauses with the same Subject-Object syntactic pattern. Figures in Table 1 below show that 62.47% of the EOC clauses in the corpus ARTHUS do not make any coding distinction between two types of object.

---

8. NGLE (2009: 2591ff., 2655ff.).

9. Note that 3rd person non-doubled lexical objects can be seen as syncretic too (compare 14a and 16 above).

10. In ARTHUS 95,6% of the objects in EOCs are animate and 97.7% are definite.

11. Available online at: http://vocabolario.signum.sns.it/. The corresponding Spanish verb, *molestar* 'to annoy', is constructed with an EOC that can take both dative and accusative object, depending on the semantic interpretation and dialect.

Table 1. Syncretic object clitics in EOC and all Subject-Object constructions in Spanish

Construction	EOC	Subject-Object
Total number	2953	65103
1st person object clitics	1495 (50.62%)	4151 (6.37%)
2nd person object clitics	350 (11.85%)	1459 (2.24%)
Sum of syncretic clitic forms	1845 (**62.47%**)	5610 (**8.62%**)

Usage data support, therefore, the combination of all the Experiencers of EOCs into a single category of Object, without distinguishing between direct or indirect objects, at least in a broad analysis of the data. This does not preclude the usefulness of a more fine-grained distinction for a more specific analysis. By conflating the two types of object, our proposal is based on a more realistic and unbiased empirical evidence and overcomes the aforementioned drawbacks caused by the existence of syncretic forms.

The structure of the paper is as follows: in Section 1.3 below we discuss relevant previous literature on the relation between case marking of the experiencers and verb types participating in the EOC/ESC 'alternation'; in Section 2 we lay out the methodology and the corpora used for this study; the results of the study are to be found in Section 3, including discourse properties of experiencers and stimuli and their interactions with genre; the discussion of results is in Section 4 and our conclusions in Section 5.

1.3 The object experiencer in Di Tullio (2004) and Melis (1999)

Since the issue of the accusative *vs.* dative status of the object experiencer with verbs of feeling has been exhaustively discussed in the literature, it should be further assessed here by addressing two important contributions to the topic. We will first consider the formal approach taken in Di Tullio (2004) and then comment on the corpus-based analysis presented by Melis (1999).

Di Tullio (2004) adopts Belletti and Rizzi's (1988) tripartite analysis of psych-verbs. The first type (*temer* 'fear', *respetar* 'respect') chooses to cast the experiencer as a subject. The other two types choose to cast the experiencer as an object, which is assigned accusative case by the second one (*preocupar* 'worry', *asustar* 'frighten') and dative case by the third one (It. *piacere*, Sp. *gustar* 'like'). However, Di Tullio, who takes a lexicalist approach, observes that 'in Spanish the boundaries between the second and the third group are blurry' (*en español los límites entre segundo [grupo] y tercero se desdibujan*, p. 23).

Chapter 4. Constructions with subject vs. object experiencers in Spanish and Italian 73

Her analysis focuses on the second type of verbs, 'verbs of emotional reaction' (*verbos de reacción emotiva*), characterized by the possibility of alternating accusative object structures with dative object structures.[12] Di Tullio attributes a different aspectual meaning to each construction: the accusative one depicts an event while the dative one depicts a state. Di Tullio adduces constructed clauses like (1b) and (28b) below as instances of the -eventive- accusative pattern, and examples like (2a) and (29b) below as instances of the -stative- dative one [we keep her numbering in the examples below]:

(17) Di Tullio's examples:

(1b) Los problemas de seguridad intimidan   a los turistas
      the problems of safety   intimidate.PRS.3PL to the tourists
      'Safety problems intimidate tourists'

(28b) El cine   italiano lo aburre   a Juan, pero
      the cinema Italian 3SG.M.ACC=bore.PRS.3SG to Juan but
      últimamente no.[13]
      lately   not
      'Italian cinema bores Juan, but lately not [so much]'

(2a) A los turistas *(les) intimidan   los problemas de seguridad
      to the tourists *(3PL.DAT)=intimidate the problems of safety
      'Tourists are intimidated by safety problems'

(29b) A Luis le aburre / fascina / interesa
      to Luis 3SG.DAT=bore.PRS.3SG / fascinate.PRS.3SG / interest.PRS.3SG
      el cine   italiano
      the cinema Italian
      'Luis is bored by / fascinated by / interested in Italian cinema'

Di Tullio claims that the constructions with dative objects (2a) and (29b) denote a 'derived state' as opposed to the 'inherent states' denoted by the first type (*temer*) and third type – with dative object too – (*gustar*), but the tests she adduces do not confirm this distinction empirically (the progressive with *estar* + GERUND, the interpretation of the simple present, among other tests, produce ambiguous

---

12. This alternation is not possible in Italian, where EOC constructions have arguments either cast in the accusative or the dative depending on verb choice.

13. We wish to thank a reviewer for pointing out that the clitic doubling of a direct object is typical of and widely accepted in Argentinian Spanish, in light of which we can make better sense of the acceptability of Di Tullio's example, which at first seemed odd to us.

results; cf. ibid.: 34).[14] Therefore, there are no convincing grammatical arguments that support a distinction between clauses like (29b) *A Luis le aburre/ fascina / interesa el cine italiano*, and clauses with third type verbs like *A Luis le gusta / encanta el cine italiano*. The consequence for our corpus analysis is that we find justifiable to combine 'dative object' patterns of second type verbs in the same category (EOCs) in Di Tullio's proposal with patterns of the third type in her classification.

The possibility of distinguishing two subtypes of structures for the second type verbs – accusative marked experiencer object plus eventive reading as in Di Tullio's (1b) and (28b) *vs.* dative marked experiencer object plus stative reading as in her (2a) and (29b) also warrants some discussion. As stated above, because of the frequent syncretism, in these clauses the coding properties alone seem too weak to justify a clear-cut distinction between the direct and the indirect object. To overcome this difficulty, the contrast between the two functions has been based on some behavioral properties of the constructions such as passive alternation (passivization), the substitution of the lexical objects by clitics (pronominalization), or the preposing of the lexical object to check if it entails either accusative or dative clitic doubling (thematization). But these tests are not really useful: the sequences are manipulated by the analyst and most of the resulting expressions can hardly be interpreted unambiguously (cf. Di Tullio *passim*, main text and footnotes). Furthermore, the difficulties in making a distinction between direct and indirect objects through behavioral criteria are even greater in the case of the 1st and 2nd person clitics. Despite these shortcomings, Di Tullio also draws interesting conclusions about the semantic make-up of the structures she analyzes.

Melis (1999), on the other hand, carries out a thorough empirically-based analysis of the syntax and semantics of causative emotional verbs (*causativos emocionales*). She defines this verb class by stipulating that the verbs can be used in all the three following constructions [we keep her numbering in the examples below]:

(18) Melis's examples:

(i) the 'basic transitive' construction, with a preverbal subject and a direct object:
(1a) Pedro la había desilusionado
Pedro 3SG.F.ACC=disappoint.PST.PRF.3SG
'Pedro had disappointed her';

---

14. We also have reservations about the use of this type of tests as heuristic tools in analyzing real linguistic data.

Chapter 4. Constructions with subject vs. object experiencers in Spanish and Italian 75

(ii) the 'inverse voice' construction,[15] with an 'initial' direct or indirect object and a postverbal subject:[16]

(2a) lo irritaban varias cosas de su agenda
3SG.M.ACC=annoy.PST.3PL various things of his schedule
'Various things about his schedule annoyed him'

(2b) le desesperaba el tránsito de la Ciudad de México;
3SG.DAT=infuriate.PST.3SG the traffic of the City of Mexico
'The traffic in Mexico City infuriated him'

(iii) the middle voice construction, which takes pronominal *se* and a prepositional phrase:

(3a) qué tal si se horrorizaba con la sangre.
What if REFL freak.PST.3SG with the blood
'what would happen if s/he freaked out at the sight of blood?'
(cf. Melis, 1999: 50)

The distinction between classes (i) and (ii) poses problems partly similar to those we have seen in Di Tullio's account. Besides, particular criticisms can be raised against the mixing of two different parameters in the classification: the sequential order of subject and object relative to the verb, and the presence of a direct object in (i) versus a direct or indirect object in (ii). Even if it were possible to discriminate between direct and indirect objects in all cases – which is not the case when the forms are syncretic –, one wonders which of the two constructions is represented by a clause like (19) below: it has a preverbal subject, as (i) constructions are expected to have, but also has an indirect object, as required in (ii) constructions.

(19) El texto que acaba de redactar no le satisface
the text that finish.PRS.3SG of write.INF not 3SG.DAT=satisfy.PRS.3SG
en absoluto
at all
'The text s/he has just written doesn't satisfy her/him at all' (PAI:181.10)

---

15. "The inverse construction is formally distinguished from the transitive construction in the order of its arguments: the object-experimenter appears in preverbal position, whereas the subject-stimulus moves to a post-verbal position" (ibid.: 51) (or *La construcción inversa se diferencia formalmente de la transitiva en el orden de colocación de los argumentos: el experimentante-objeto aparece en posición preverbal, mientras que el estímulo-sujeto se desplaza hacia el lugar posverbal* (ibid.).

16. The clauses Melis gives as examples are actually not good illustrations of the 'initial' position of the object, as they are clitics, and their position is therefore obligatorily proclitic to the verb form.

An additional consequence of the criteria proposed for distinguishing the 'basic transitive' construction from the 'inverse' construction is shown through Examples (20) and (21) below, which will be classified differently – (20) as basic transitive (i), and (21) as inverse (ii) –, though there is no apparent syntactic or semantic difference between them. The difference in the sequential order of subject and verb, it could be argued, affects the information-structural level, but not the grammar:

(20) la   actitud de mi amigo   me sorprendió   y
     the attitude of my friend 1SG.OBJ=surprise.PST.3SG and
     me entristeció
     1SG.OBJ=sadden.PST.3SG
     'My friend's attitude surprised and saddened me'   (HIS:132.09)

(21) Me ha sorprendido   la   negación y   la   pasividad de un
     1SG.OBJ=surprise.PRF.3SG the denial   and the passiveness of a
     pequeño sector
     small   sector
     'The denial and passiveness of a small sector has surprised me' (JOV:144.16)

Then, as far as the direct *vs.* indirect object distinction is concerned, the analysis of Melis (1999) does not provide operational criteria to maintain the two categories separate.

As convincing evidence for establishing separate functions is lacking, the figures corresponding to EOCs in this paper were calculated on the basis of a single object category – combining direct objects and indirect objects in an all-encompassing object function.

The study by Melis (1999) is based on a sample of 839 clauses from a corpus of Mexican Spanish texts from the 1980s and 1990s, from which she elaborates a penetrating analysis of the semantics and syntax of causative emotional verbs. She does, however, not include ESCs in her paper.[17] Nevertheless, Melis (1999) provides interesting data and remarks to further understand the relationships between the syntactic form and the semantic and discourse-functional meanings of the constructions we are studying.

Melis examines the 'inverse voice' clauses (ii) as compared to middle voice clauses (iii), focusing her attention on two factors associated with the stimulus – its form, NP *vs.* clause, and its cataphoric persistence (Givón, 1983) – and a third factor associated with the affectedness of the experiencer. Melis claims that the object experiencers of (ii) are affected while the subject experiencers of (iii) are not. Such a semantic difference is related to the person of the participant. Melis

---

[17] Nor the non-causative EOC verbs, such as *gustar*, or other verbs that do not enter in all three above-mentioned constructions; cf. her footnote on p. 50.

bases this relationship on the notion of 'empathy' (Kuno and Kaburaki, 1977) and assumes that the speaker tends to identify or empathize more easily with entities more similar to him/herself. In this particular case,

> The concept of empathy allows us to understand why it is easier for a speaker to evaluate the state of affectedness of the experiencers cast in first and second person, as they are much closer to him than those in the third person[18]
>
> (Melis, 1999: 56)

The data provided by Melis (1999: 58) show a greater number of 1st and 2nd person experiencers in inverse voice constructions as compared to the experiencers in middle voice constructions, which are mostly 3rd person participants.[19] The relationship between affectedness and empathy suggested by Melis is certainly useful for us to analyze the contrast between EOCs and ESCs.

The use of textual corpora for this study provided relevant data to fill the gap in the analyses of EOCs that take actual usage into account. We used the ARTHUS corpus and BDS/ADESSE database for Spanish and the BADIP, C-ORAL (Cresti & Moneglia, 2005), and *La Repubblica* corpora for Italian, to track the frequency and distribution of a number of discourse-related properties of the arguments, such as animacy, person, and syntactic category. Ultimately, this study provides some insight into how both ESC and EOC constructions are used and conceived of by speakers in actual discourse. Our analysis of these constructions is couched in Construction Grammar terms, because CxG offers the ideal framework to integrate semantic (such as animacy of participants or level of agentivity of the clause), syntactic (speakers' choice of EOC or ESC constructions), and discourse properties (such as topic continuity or salience) in the study of grammar.

2. Methods

We analyzed the features of EOCs and ESCs in two Romance languages, Italian and Spanish, where the usage and vitality of non-nominative subjects showed certain parallels. In order to work with naturalistic data, we used corpora comprising both written and spoken usage for both languages.

---

[18]. "El concepto de empatía nos permite entender por qué le resulta más fácil al hablante valorar el estado de afectación de los experimentantes de primera y segunda persona que le son mucho más próximos que los de tercera."

[19]. Notice though that Melis's 'inverse construction' is not strictly comparable to our EOC, because her 'basic transitive' construction (i) (e.g., *Pedro la había desilusionado*) sets the class apart from the 'inverse voice' construction (ii), whereas our EOC is a broader class that includes all the constructions with object experiencers, therefore our EOCs subsume (i) and (ii).

The analysis of the Spanish data is based on the ARTHUS corpus, which comprises American and Peninsular samples for a variety of genres. ARTHUS is not simply a corpus of 'raw data'. Syntactic and semantic features for each clause, numbering 159,000, are recorded in a complex database (BDS/ADESSE) for further detailed syntactic and semantic studies of Spanish (García Miguel, 2005; Vaamonde et al., 2010). The database allows for general searches and counts of clausal schemata and subschemata, as well as for automatic counts of syntactic and semantic features including verbal semantic classification. Each clause in the corpus was annotated for syntactic functions of the arguments (subject, direct object, etc.), syntactic categories (NP, pronoun, etc.), semantic roles, verb semantic class, etc. With the ADESSE/BDS database, it is also possible to have forms tallied by textual genres. Its drawbacks are however, that it is mostly comprised of written language texts (only about 20% of its contents are oral), and that contents are limited in size to 1,449,005 words. Table 2 below, shows the distribution of the number of words in the ADESSE database across textual genres and broad dialectal areas for Spanish.

Table 2. Number of words in the ARTHUS corpus according to text types and regions

# of words	Spanish (totals)	Spain	Latin America[20]
Fiction	538,906 (37.19%)	385,661	153,245
Press	166,804 (11.51%)	166,804	0
Theater	212,507 (14.66%)	212,507	0
Essay	257,718 (17.78%)	168,511	89,207
Oral	273,070 (18.85%)	207,948	65,122
Total	1,449,005	1,141,431	307,574

The situation is more problematic for Italian, since there are no publicly available, automatically searchable, tagged corpora. We therefore had to compound the contents of the following databases: BADIP, C-ORAL, and an excerpt from *La Repubblica*. BADIP[21] is a database that contains the totality of the Spoken Italian Lexical Frequency Corpus (LIP). The corpus is made up of different oral text types: informal conversations (face to face or on the phone), transcripts from meetings, oral exams, interviews, conferences, classes (K-12 to university level), homilies, TV programs not based on a written screenplay (De Mauro et al. 1993). The LIP corpus contains 490,000 words. The second corpus used was the Italian

---

20. http://adesse.uvigo.es/data/corpus.php.

21. http://badip.uni-graz.at.

section of the C-ORAL-ROM[22] corpus (approximately 300,000 words), which comprises spontaneous conversation from unscripted sources including informal conversations in private and in public, formal speeches in natural contexts (political speeches and debates, preaching, conferences), formal spoken discourse in the media (talk shows, interviews, political debate), and formal and informal telephone calls.

Finally, for the press section of the analysis, we used an excerpt of about 500,000 words from the *La Repubblica* newspaper archives to make the comparison between the two languages numerically more balanced. The texts analyzed from *La Repubblica* were taken from two randomly chosen weeks in 1991 and 1992 to make the language comparable to that gathered in the other corpora, which are also from the beginning of the 1990s, except for the LABLITA corpus (part of C-ORAL-ROM), which spans 1965–2000. It was only possible to distinguish between oral *vs.* press textual genres in the Italian corpora, and the number of searches was limited by the fact that they had to be performed manually. Table 3 below shows the distribution of the number of words in the Italian databases across textual genres. Dialectal areas were not recoverable for Italian, although the sources are from different regions.[23]

Table 3. Number of words used for the Italian analysis according to text types and corpus

# of words	Italian (totals)	Corpus
Press	500,000 (38.8%)	500,000 – La Repubblica
Oral	790,000 (61.2%)	300,000 – C-Oral
		490,000 – BAdIP
Total	1,290,000	

Because we were forced to conduct manual searches of non-tagged corpora for Italian, the analysis of those data is more limited and less sophisticated than the detailed analysis of the ARTHUS corpus data. We can, however, point to similar tendencies between the two languages, even if EOCs – especially those with dative experiencers – seem to be more productive in Spanish than in Italian.

---

22. http://www.elda.org/en/proj/coralrom.html

23. LABLITA is multidialectal, but many of the speakers are not classified by provenance (http://lablita.dit.unifi.it/corpora/descriptions/lablita/), BAdIP is made up of texts from Florence, Naples, Rome and Milan, and the texts in *La Repubblica* have no clear dialectal bias, since they are mostly written in formal standard Italian.

2.1 Data selection

Previous studies on experiential predicates, such as those mentioned in Section 1, underline that non-nominative subjects tend to be found in constructions with verbs expressing mental processes and feelings in a variety of languages. Mental processes and feelings can however also be expressed through regular transitive constructions: these verbs thus offer a good testing ground for the distribution of EOC and ESC constructions. Corpus analysis provides a solid empirical foundation to identify the differences between ESCs and EOCs with verbs of feeling at the discourse level and to determine if the relative distribution of the two constructions in usage is random or not. To address the issue, we have carried out a quantitative analysis of the following features of the experiencer and stimulus: animacy, syntactic class, and grammatical person in both ESCs and EOCs. We have also examined the frequency of the constructions according to textual genre.

Data from the Spanish ARTHUS corpus were restricted to clauses (and their verbs) that met the following conditions, and the same was done in the choice of constructions for Italian:

a. Verbs must belong to the semantic class of 'feeling' (Sp. *sensación* in ADESSE), except the 'volition' subclass, which is always encoded by ESC without alternate EOC pattern.

In ADESSE, clauses are categorized into six main types according to their conceptual meaning: mental, relational, material, verbal, existential and directive.[24] In this study we focus on the mental process category, which involves two basic participants, the experiencer and the phenomenon causing the mental process (stimulus). Mental processes represent a 23.67% of the clauses in the corpus (37,636 items) and comprise four classes: feeling, perception, cognition and choice. Feeling and cognition classes are in turn divided into two subclasses: 'volition' is a subdivision of 'feeling,' while 'knowledge' and 'belief' are subsets of the cognition category.

As the paper analyzes the distribution of ESC *vs.* EOC, only subclasses that display both types of constructions can be taken into account. Therefore, perception (e.g., *ver* 'see', *mostrar* 'show'), choice (e.g. *decidir* 'decide', *elegir* 'choose'), the cognition general class (e.g. *pensar* 'think', *entender* 'understand'), and the volition subclass of feeling (e.g. *querer* 'want')[25] were excluded from our sample, since all

---

24. Some clauses are ascribed to more than one class. The reader is referred to http://adesse.uvigo.es/data/clases.php for further information. See also Albertuz (2007), Vaamonde et al. (2010). The ADESSE typology of verbal processes goes back to the one proposed by Halliday (1985).

25. It is worth noticing that the verb *querer* belongs to the volition subclass when it has the sense of "to wish for something, to want something, or to want something to happen" (ADESSE),

the clauses in these categories are ESCs. The 'belief' and 'knowledge' subclasses were also excluded from the study. These subclasses display very unbalanced distributions of the two constructions examined: EOC represent just a 0.8% of the total of clauses in the knowledge subclass (46 vs. 5599 of ESC),[26] and a mere 16.5% in the belief subclass (483 vs. 2436 of ESC).[27] In contrast, the general class of feeling provides us with a more balanced number of occurrences of both constructions and a wider range of verb lexemes.

b. Clauses must have just two arguments that fill either ESC or EOC conditions.

Table 4. Criteria for data searches in *ADESSE*

	Argument 1	Argument 2
ESC	Experiencer = Subject	Stimulus = Object
EOC	Experiencer = Object	Stimulus = Subject

c. Clauses must be in the active voice. Passive and middle (reflexive) constructions were avoided in this study; as a consequence, expressions like *interesarse por algo/ interessarsi di qualcosa* 'be interested in something', *asustarse con algo/ spaventarsi per/di qualcosa* 'be afraid of something' etc., were not included in the counts.

The total number of verb forms analyzed for Spanish was 4,114. Similar criteria were followed for Italian, but only six lemmas were analyzed, three participating in ESC constructions and three in EOC constructions, for a total of 689 forms. Despite the disparity in size, the Italian forms analyzed offer a comparable picture to that of the Spanish verbs, corroborated by statistical analysis provided by the classification and regression tree in Section 3. The Italian verb forms were chosen with the same selection criteria as the Spanish ones, so as to parallel some of the most common verbal lemmas in the ARTHUS corpus participating in the EOC/ESC alternation; we made sure that the chosen verbal forms for Italian were also used frequently both in the oral and written genre, in both EOC and ESC constructions (see results below).

---

which is by and large its most frequent meaning in the corpus (1040 clauses); ex.: *Erni, ¿quieres apagar las luces?* (CIN:063,12) 'Erni, do you want to turn off the lights?'. In other contexts (183 clauses), *querer* means "to feel or show affection towards someone" (ibid.), so it is not a volition verb, but a verb of the general feelings class, and as such it is included in the analysis.

26. Tally carried out on Dec. 8, 2012.

27. These figures represent the clauses that fulfill condition b: all of them are constructions with two participants, experiencer and stimulus, cast respectively as subject and object in ESCs, and *vice versa* in EOCs.

3. Results

In BDS/ADESSE there are 1161 ESC clauses that fulfill criteria a–c above. The more frequent verbs in this construction are those included in Table 5 below, along with their figures:

Table 5. Verb lemmas participating in ESC constructions and their quantity in the Spanish corpus used

Verb	Quantity	Verb	Quantity
querer 2 'love'	165	*adorar* 'adore'	28
temer 'fear'	113	*experimentar 2* 'feel'	20
vivir 2 'live'	103	*despreciar* 'despise' 'scorn'	20
sufrir 'suffer'	101	*desdeñar* 'scorn'	19
amar 'love'	73	*gozar* 'enjoy'	16
sentir 2 'feel'	68	*apreciar 1* 'be fond of'	15
odiar 'hate'	67	*paladear* 'relish'	14
respetar 'respect'	51	*detestar* 'detest'	12
admirar 'admire'	40	*extrañar* 'miss'	12
aguantar 'stand'	39	*añorar* 'long or yearn for'	12
padecer 'suffer'	38	*acusar 2* 'show signs of'	10
lamentar 'regret'	34	*compadecer* 'feel sorry for'	8
celebrar 2	28	Other	55
		Total**	1161

* Numbers next to the verbs mark the specific verb meaning in the construction (cf. ADESSE).
** There are 43 different verb lexemes in ESCs in our sample.

As for EOCs, the more frequent Spanish verbs in our corpus are listed in Table 6.

These verbs all have common equivalents in Italian, which can be rendered by EOC constructions, sometimes they are periphrases with verbs such as *dare* 'to give', or *fare* 'to do/make': *gustar – piacere* 'like', *importar – importare* 'matter', *interesar – interessare* 'interest', *sorprender – sorprendere* 'surprise', *encantar – affascinare* 'like a lot, charm', *doler – far(e) male* 'hurt', *atraer – attrarre* 'attract', *extrañar – sorprendere* 'surprise',[28] *molestar – dar(e) fastidio* 'bother', *asustar – spaventare/far(e) paura* 'frighten', *divertir – divertire* 'amuse', *calmar – calmare* 'calm', *alegrar – far(e) piacere* 'to be happy'. *Apetecer* 'feel like' in Italian can be translated by an equivalent EOC construction *far(e) gola*, but it is most commonly translated by an ESC construction: *aver(e) voglia (di qualcosa)*.

---

28. The relevant meaning of *extrañar* here is 'to surprise' as in *ya son las ocho, me extraña que no haya llegado* 'it's already 8 o'clock, I am surprised that s/he hasn't arrived yet,' which is constructed as an EOC, not *extrañar* as in 'to miss (someone),' which is constructed as an ESC.

Table 6. Verb lemmas participating in EOC constructions and their quantity in the Spanish corpus used

Verb	Nr	Verb	Nr
gustar 'like'	1219	*impresionar* 'strike'	29
interesar 1 'interest'	167	*tranquilizar* 'calm down'	25
importar 1 'matter'	153	*calmar* 'calm'	23
encantar 'love'	98	*animar 1* 'cheer up'	23
sorprender 1 'surprise'	77	*conmover 1* 'move'	22
doler 'hurt'	54	*ofender* 'offend / be ofended)	22
molestar 1 'bother'	54	*asombrar* 'amaze / be amazed'	22
atraer 2 'attract'	45	*entusiasmar* 'to be enthusiastic'	21
apetecer 'feel like'	44	*divertir* 'amuse'	20
extrañar 'surprise'	43	*fascinar* 'love / be mad about'	19
asustar 'frighten'	37	*alegrar* 'to be happy'	17
satisfacer 'satisfy'	36	*irritar* 'annoy / get annoyed'	16
preocupar 'worry'	32	Other*	635
		Total	2953

* Our whole Spanish corpus includes 174 verbs in EOC clauses.

The Italian equivalent verbs could not all be included in our study, but all of the verbs in Tables 5 and 6 were analyzed for Spanish, while the manual searches for all verbal forms in Italian limited the number of lemmas we could analyze for the present study to the six mentioned in Table 7 below. The same criteria, however, were followed in the Italian searches as those used in the automatic searches for the Spanish corpus through ADESSE; but in practice, only 689 Italian forms were analyzed, comprising 6 verb types corresponding to frequent Spanish verbs found in ADESSE, covering similar semantic fields and paired in ESC-EOC constructions: *amare* 'to love' vs. *piacere* 'to like', *avere paura* 'to be afraid' vs. *fare paura* 'to scare', *ammirare* 'to admire' vs. *affascinare* 'to fascinate,' as laid out in Table 7. Nevertheless, we trust that the frequency of use of these forms in Italian across genres (oral vs press) and the sizable Italian sample make the comparison between Italian and Spanish EOCs and ESCs still viable.

Table 7. Verb lemmas participating in ESC&EOC constructions and their quantity in the Italian corpus used

ESC verbs	Quantity	EOC verbs	Quantity
amare 'to love'	104	*piacere* 'to like'	408
avere paura 'to be afraid'	10	*fare paura* 'to scare'	70
ammirare 'to admire'	74	*affascinare* 'to fascinate'	23

The EOC type of construction is very productive in Spanish, especially with dative pronominal marking, as attested by non-standard expressions such as EOC *molar* 'to like', *latir* 'to surmise' that are very typical of non-standard, oral, youth Spanish, both in Spain and in Latin America. As can be gleaned from the equivalent forms in Italian in the examples above, EOCs are also commonly found in this other Romance language, even if the objects tend not to be marked with dative as often and as productively as in Spanish.

3.1 Discourse-related and semantic features of EOCs and ESCs

In this section we lay out quantitative results concerning some semantic and discourse-related properties of the constructions under examination. The data analysis is aimed at getting a better understanding of the EOCs' and ESCs' communicative function.

3.1.1 *Properties of the experiencer*

To begin with, if we compare the animate character of the experiencer in both constructions, a clear (and expected) semantic parallel between the subject of ESC and the object of EOC appears, i.e. the fact that they are predominantly animate in both languages:

Table 8. Experiencer's Animacy in ESCs and EOCs in Spanish and Italian

		ESC		EOC	
		N.	%	N.	%
Spanish	Experiencer + Animate	1110	95.6%	2802	94.8%
	Total	1161		2953	
Italian	Experiencer + Animate	223	99%	454	98%
	Total	225		464	

However some differences appear when we examine the syntactic categories that codify the experiencer in each construction (subject *vs.* object) (see Table 9).

The object experiencer (EOC) is represented by a clitic or a personal pronoun in 82.78% of the cases, while the subject experiencer (ESC) is expressed by verbal agreement alone or personal pronouns 76.64% of the times. These differences are slight, but present both in Spanish and Italian (see Table 10 below), and they could be related to the fact that, in discourse, the object experiencer is more accessible or more continuous as a topic than the subject experiencer. About topic continuity, the literature generally agrees that there is a relation between speakers' accessibility to a referent and the linguistic encoding it requires (cf. Givón, 1983, 1992; Ariel,

Table 9. Experiencer's syntactic categories in ESCs and EOCs in Spanish

	ESC		EOC	
	N.	%	N.	%
Stressed personal pronoun	95	8.37%	305	10.32%
Verbal agreement alone (ESC) / clitic alone (EOC)	776	**68.37%**	2140	**72.46%**
Other (NPs, relative prons.)	264	23.36%	508	17.20%
Total*	1135		2953	

* As generic infinitives and gerunds were excluded from the figures pertaining to the ESC, the total of ESC cases is lower than in Table 5. The slight discrepancies in the ADESSE figures – if queried now – result from corrections operated on the database in the last year since we carried out our analysis.

1990). In fact, if a referent is *more accessible*, it will typically be expressed by *less* semantic and phonetic content (Vázquez & García, 2012).

However, the similarities in frequency of occurrence of the experiencer in each construction point to the fact that an experiencer in general is usually highly salient, recoverable, and does not need to be mentioned again by a fully fledged noun phrase.

Table 10. Experiencer's syntactic categories in ESC and EOC in Italian

	ESC		EOC	
	N.	%	N.	%
Stressed personal pronoun	24	10.66%	64	13.85%
Verbal agreement alone (ESC) / clitic alone (EOC)	130	**57.77%**	322	**69.39%**
Other (NPs, relative prons.)	71	31.55%	78	16.88%
Total	225		464	

Incidentally, the low ratio of full-fledged experiencers in usage should be noticed: these are less than a third in both ESCs and EOCs (the sum of stressed pronouns and "other") in Spanish and 42% in ESCs and 30% in EOCs respectively in Italian. However, the order of constituents has often been employed in literature as a means for supporting functional distinctions in EOC constructions (Melis, 1999: 50–51; Di Tullio, 2004: 33; Gutiérrez-Bravo, 2006), but this should be reconsidered in view of the actual usage of such constructions. The experiencer, in fact, is often expressed by agreement only or by a clitic, whose position is obligatorily determined. Thus, the low frequency of lexical experiencers undermines the criterion of the pre- or post-verbal 'experiencer position' to classify the constructions.

As for the person and number of the experiencer, Table 11 below shows a remarkable contrast between ESCs and EOCs: object experiencers (EOCs) are mostly 1st person sg. participants (47%), while subject experiencers (ESCs) are represented by 3rd person in 38.6% of the cases, and only 29.7% are 1st pers. sg.

Table 11. Person/number distribution of the experiencer in ESC and EOC clauses in Spanish

Experiencer's person & number	ESC	%	EOC	%
1ª sg	345	29.7	1389	47
2ª sg	83	7.1	333	11.3
3ª sg	449	**38.6**	597	20.2
Vd sg	10	0.8	71	2.4
1ª pl	83	7.1	106	3.6
2ª pl	8	0.6	17	0.6
3ª pl	154	13.2	114	3.9
Vd pl	3	0.2	3	0.1
Generic inference / No clitic*	26	2.2	323	10.9
Total	1161		2953	

* EOC data are classified by the person and number of the clitic experiencer. The 323 units marked as 'no clitic' in EOCs with verbs of feeling correspond to 3rd person object experiencer with no clitic-doubling, as in Example (14a) above. Since ADESSE does not allow to distinguish between singular and plural in this case, we opted to consider them as an independent set, even if they belong with the third person (sg. or pl. as the case may be).

This is paralleled in Italian too, as can be seen in Table 12 below:

Table 12. Person/number distribution of the experiencer in ESC and EOC clauses in Italian

Experiencer's person & number	ESC	%	EOC	%
1ª sg	49	26.63	198	42.67
2ª sg	4	2.17	53	11.42
3ª sg	74	**40.20**	137	29.52
Vd sg	2	1.08	7	1.50
1ª pl	13	7.06	19	4.09
2ª pl	11	5.97	6	1.29
3ª pl	31	16.84	44	9.48
Vd pl	0		0	
Total personal forms	184		464	

The relationship between mental process clauses and the person of the experiencer has captivated the attention of (discourse-functional) linguists since at least 1958 with the seminal work of Benveniste (cf. also Lyons, 1994; Bentivoglio & Weber, 1999; Scheibman, 2001, 2002; Travis, 2006). These studies pointed out the tendency of the clauses of mental process – and especially those of the cognition subclass – to be associated with a first person singular subject. Benveniste called attention to the function of mental process verbs ("propositional attitude verbs" in particular) in the first person and the present tense, since with first person subjects, these verbs do not describe mental states or processes as they do with third person subjects (*she believes that ...; he supposes that ...*), but they express instead the epistemic attitude of the speaker towards the proposition that follows (*I believe that ...; I suppose that ...*), which makes them 'markers of subjectivity' (cf. Benveniste, 1958: 185).

The recurrent use of this function in discourse has provoked the formal freezing of elements such as (*yo) creo / creo yo* 'I believe, I think', *me parece* 'it seems to me', *supongo* 'I suppose', etc., and the consequent weakening of their argument structure as they little by little lost their event-codifying function as a result of their progression towards becoming subjective experience markers (cf. Weber & Bentivoglio, 1991; Bentivoglio & Weber, 1999; Vázquez Rozas, 2006a; Travis, 2006).

If we return to Tables 11 and 12, we see that corpus data show the preference of EOC for 1st person experiencer in both Spanish and Italian, as in Examples (10a–b) and (11a) (repeated here):

(10) a. francamente la   televisión   a   mí   me *aburre*
         frankly   the television to   me   1SG.OBJ=bore.PRS.3SG
         'Frankly television bores me'   (SEV:094.08)
     b. Il teatro, sono   sincera,   mi annoia
         the theater be.PRS.1SG sincere.F 1SG.OBJ=bore.PRS.3SG
         'I admit it: theater bores me'   (LaRep, 02.06.92, 'Spettacoli')

(11) a. A mí   me asusta,   me desagrada   este
         to me 1SG.OBJ=scare.PRS.3SG 1SG.OBJ=disgust.PRS.3SG   this
         Madrid   ruidoso
         Madrid   noisy
         'The noise of Madrid scares and disgusts me'   (MAD:103.17)

As for ESC, third person experiencers outnumber first person experiencers, so the more frequent uses can be illustrated through examples like (5) for Sp. and (8) for It. above, repeated here:

(5) Él   sí   amaba   esa   ciudad
    he   yes love.PST.3SG   that town
    'He did love that town'   (MIRADA: 93, 32)

(8) Cendrars   amava   il   cinema di un   amore non ricambiato.
    Cendrars   love.PST.3SG   the cinema of a   love   not requited
    'Cendrars loved cinema with unrequited love'
                                              (LaRep, 06.24.89, 'Mercurio-Scaffale')

Interestingly, the association between the object experiencer and the first person singular in the ARTHUS corpus mirrors the tendency detected by Melis (1999) in her Mexican corpus, as the object experiencer of her 'inverse voice' construction is also more often a Speech Act Participant (SAP) than the subject experiencer of middle constructions (cf. footnote nr. 19).

Melis relates the different person choices of the experiencer to the notions of empathy and affectedness and quotes Mithun (1991:522) when she states that "Speakers do not claim to feel what another individual is feeling" (cf. Melis, 1999:58). And feelings, emotions, affectedness and other mental states are expected to be more often expressed by the person who experiences or feels them. Corpus data confirm that EOCs meet this expectation, but the data of ESCs show a different picture.

Why do the experiencers of ESCs fail to meet the expected preference for 1st person referents, then? As they are syntactic subjects, these experiencers are candidates to be conceptualized as potentially endowed with agency, volition and control.

> Even with symmetric predicates, the participant assigned to subject position is interpreted as the more controlling participant or at least the more empathized-with participant (Kuno and Kaburaki, 1977). This is a general tendency of the interpretation of arguments assigned to subject position (cf. DeLancey, 1984).
> (Croft, 1993:61)

Subjects are initiators of causal events and in ESC, being typically animate and human, they are assigned a certain degree of responsibility in the process, as they have to direct attention to the object stimulus.

Actually, the control and agency of the experiencer over the state of affairs have been identified in instances of ESCs with the usual tests of agency and control (imperative, compatibility with adjuncts of purpose, etc.).

(22) ¡quiéreme!   Tú   aún no lo sabes,   pero
     love.IMP.2SG=1SG.OBJ you yet not 3SG.OBJ=know.PRS.2SG but
     te   queda   poco tiempo de abuelo.
     2SG.OBJ=remain.PRS.3SG little time as grandfather.
     'Love me! You don't know it yet, but you only have a short time left as grandfather'   (SON:281.14)

In contrast, object experiencers do not display any trace of activity or control over the situation.

Usage data suggest, therefore, that a higher agency potential of the experiencer associates more with 3rd person (ESC), while a lower agency potential promotes the 1st person reference (EOC). However, these data run counter to what is predicted by the 'Animacy Hierarchy,' which assigns the top position to the 1st person pronoun and is defined in Silverstein (1976) as a scale of "likelihood of functioning as transitive agents" (*apud* Dixon, 1979: 85).

According to the hierarchy, the speaker occupies the position of highest agentivity, as Dixon maintains (1994: 84):

> [...] a speaker will think in terms of doing things to other people to a much greater extent than in terms of things being done to him. In the speaker's view of the world, as it impinges on him and as he describes it in language, he will be the quintessential agent.

The clauses with verbs of feeling analyzed here suggest, however, a different interpretation: it is the 3rd person that is conceptualized more frequently as an agent, since it is more often cast as a syntactic subject than the 1st person, which prefers the function of object, and whose role is, as a consequence, less active.

Several researchers have maintained that agentivity does not justify the position of first person discourse participants in the upper level of the animacy hierarchy compared to 3rd person (cf. DeLancey, 1981; van der Auwera, 1981: 94 ff.; Myhill, 1992: 224 and 278, in a footnote)[29] and it has been pointed out that 1st and 2nd persons are also high in the hierarchy because of their features of empathy and topicality. These notions are found in the original formulation of the hierarchy by Hawkinson & Hyman (1974), and are also part of the proposals by Givón (1976), Kuno & Kaburaki (1977), Langacker (1991: 306–307) and Lehmann *et al.* (2000: 6 & ff.), among others.

In the constructions analyzed here, what is most surprising is that the most empathetic experiencers, 1st person experiencers, are not preeminently associated with the subject function (which happens instead in other verbal classes both in Spanish and other European languages, cf. Lehmann *et al.*, 2000), but rather with the object, whereas 3rd person experiencers, the less empathetic ones, do indeed associate with subject function.

3.1.2 *Properties of the stimulus*

The stimulus participant also displays different syntactic and semantic properties in ESC and EOC constructions.

In ESC and EOC, as reported in Table 13 and 14 below, the stimulus, which is cast as the object in ESC and as subject in EOC, is predominantly inanimate.

---

29. "Silverstein motivates his animacy hierarchy by claiming that it reflects the likelihood of different NP types serving as agents. However, as pointed out in work such as DeLancey, 1981, topicality, viewpoint, or empathy is a more likely motivation, as it is clear why these parameters would rank first and second person pronouns higher than third person pronouns, but it is not clear why first and second person pronouns should be more likely than third person pronouns to serve as agents." (Myhill, 1992: 278 in a footnote).

However, there is a considerable incidence of animate stimuli in ESC constructions. This corresponds to the referents in the construction having a more 'visible side' (public, external, objective), which is consistent with the representational (descriptive, referential) function of ESCs analyzed in the previous section.

Figures in Tables 13 and 14 show remarkable differences related to the animacy of the stimulus:

Table 13. Stimulus's animacy in Spanish

		ESC (object)	%	EOC (subject)	%	% ESC	% EOC
Animate		385	33.16	495	16.76		
Inanimate	Concrete	163	14.03	567	19.20	51.41	55.36
	Abstract	434	37.38	1068	36.16		
	Propositional	179	15.41	823	27.86		
Total		1161		2953			

These figures are also confirmed by the Italian data, which report similar percentages for animate stimuli in ESC and EOC:

Table 14. Stimulus's animacy in Italian

		ESC (object)	%	EOC (subject)	%	% ESC	% EOC
Animate		70	38.25	51	11.61		
Inanimate	Concrete	29	15.84	175	39,86	36.61	71.52
	Abstract	38	20.76	139	31.66		
	Propositional	46	25.13	74	16.85		
Total		183		439			

The large proportion of animate (mostly human) objects as stimuli is worthy of further research. This rate of animate participants in object function in Spanish, for instance, is notably higher than the percentage of animates in the total of Subject-Object clauses in ARTHUS (22.5%).

The stimulus in EOC – cast as subject – displays a lower percentage of animate referents and a higher proportion of propositional referents.

(23) yo me gusta que los chiquillos sepan por lo menos
 I 1SG.OBJ=like.PRS.3SG that the kids know at least
 nociones de música
 notions of music
 'As for me, I like the kids to have at least some notions about music'
 (MADRID: 210, 20)

This is possible in Italian too, see Example (24) below, and Italian also has a high proportion of clausal stimuli in ESC, as exemplified in both clauses below. The structure found in (25) reflects a common use of the verb 'to love' in Italian,[30] i.e. 'to like a lot' as in the generic English usage of 'to love (to do) something'; it should be noticed that Spanish differs from Italian (or English) in this usage of the verb 'to love', as Sp. *amar* would not be used for the same construction with a clausal stimulus.

(24) Cossiga ha   premesso   che non gli piace
     Cossiga have.PRS.3SG opened.PPT that not 3SG.DAT=like.PRS.3SG
     'tracciare identikit'
     draw.INF profiling
     'Cossiga opened by saying that he does not like to 'do any profiling'
                                                        (LaRep, 03.29.92, 'Extra')

(25) [Tiri da tre]   'Entrambe le   squadre amano   farne'
     [threepointers]   both   the teams   love.PRS.3PL make.INF=3SG.OBJ
     '[Threepointers] Both teams love to shoot them'   (LaRep., 05.16.91, 'Sport')

Clauses, as 'third order entities', are not conceived of as individuals, which can be acting on other individuals,[31] so the sentences of which they are a part (those with cognitive predicates, such as 'I think,' 'I believe,' 'I suppose' etc., and with evaluative predicates, such as 'I like,' 'I hope,' etc.), are not primarily directed at representing "objective" events. On the contrary, such sentences tend to refer to subjective (private, internal) states of affairs and to have an evaluative function.

Di Tullio (2004) also analyzes interpretive differences related to subject features, and observes that a 'causal subject' (which in this case could also be defined as a 'clausal' subject, unlike an actual agentive one) activates a psychological reading of predicates that also admit a physical reading (in which the subject would be an agent). She maintains, thus, that the psychological reading of the verb depends on the 'clausal' reading of the subject: 'it is not the category of the subject – noun

---

30. A sample from the *La Repubblica* corpus reveals that they account for about 30% of the occurrence of this verb in this corpus.

31. Melis (1999:53): 'The medio-passive voice is used more often with clausal stimuli, which can hardly be seen as 'participants' in the event' ("[...] la media se utiliza más con los estímulos oracionales que con dificultad se ven como "participantes" del evento [...]"). Also: 'However, even when they exhibit referential or functional affinities, nouns and clauses do not behave identically in syntax (Lehmann, 1991:203–204). According to Lehmann (1991:205), this is due to the fact that clauses, unlike nouns, cannot refer to an entity that can 'participate' in the described event and that can be characterized as having less 'prominence' and 'cognitive independence' than nouns' ("Sin embargo, aun cuando presentan afinidades referenciales y funcionales, se sabe que los nombres y las oraciones no se comportan de manera idéntica en la sintaxis (Lehmann, 1991:203–204). Esto se debe, en la opinión de Lehmann (1991:205), a que las oraciones se distinguen de los nombres en que no sugieren al igual la figura de un ente que 'participa' en el evento descrito y que se caracterizan, frente a las entidades nominales, por tener un menor grado de 'prominencia' e 'independencia cognoscitiva'") (ibid.: 57).

phrase or clause – that activates the psychological meaning, but rather the possibility of a clausal interpretation (i.e. of a 'propositional thematic role').[32] (28) – Di Tullio in fact concludes that the basic form of the subject (stimulus) in these verbs is the expression of an event, whose canonical structure is an infinitival clause or nominalization. Verbs of feeling, she maintains, select mostly clausal subjects, and only indirectly agentive ones (ibid.: 28–29).

However, although clausal stimuli do appear in considerable numbers in our data, the majority of stimuli are represented by fully-fledged NPs. This is in clear opposition to what was mentioned above for the experiencer in both ESC and EOC constructions, and points to a lower salience of the stimulus in discourse.

Table 15. Syntactic class of stimulus in Spanish

	ESC	%	EOC	%
Stressed pers. pron.	12	1.03	18	0.60
Subject Agreement / Object Clitic alone	370	31.86	820	27.76
NP	660	**56.84**	1524	**51.60**
Clause	119	10.24	564	19.09
Adverbial			1	0.03
Generic infinitives			26	0.88
Total	1161		2953	

The Italian data show that there are similar tendencies in the frequency of NPs to represent stimuli (see Table XVI below), although Spanish ESCs are more inclined to represent their object by a NP than Italian ones, and conversely Italian EOCs are fonder of NP stimuli than Spanish ones:

Table 16. Syntactic class of stimulus in Italian

	ESC	%	EOC	%
Stressed pers. pron.	1	0.53	1	0.22
Subject Agreement / Object Clitic alone	54	28.72	113	24.88
NP	87	**46.27**	267	**58.81**
Clause	46	24.46	73	16.07
Adverbial	0		0	
Total*	188		454	

* Minor discrepancies in numbers of stimuli/experiencers and total number of clauses analyzed in Italian is due to either experiencer or stimulus being omitted or only partially recoverable from the limited context offered by the database.

---

32. "No es la categoría del sujeto – sintagma nominal u oración – lo decisivo para activar el significado psicológico sino la viabilidad de una interpretación oracional (en otros términos, de un 'Papel Temático Proposicional.)'

3.2 ESCs, EOCs and text type (genre)

Last but not least, we examined the incidence of cross-genre variation in the frequency and distribution of the constructions examined.

The figures in Tables 17 and 18 clearly show the tendency of EOCs to correlate with oral discourse, although this tendency is more marked in Spanish than in Italian (where, however, admittedly the analyzed sample is much more restricted).

Table 17. Distribution of ESC and EOC according to text type in Spanish

	ESC		EOC		Total
	N	%	N	%	
Novel	579	34.15	1116	65.85	1695
Press	75	58.14	54	41.86	129
Theater	254	33.82	497	66.18	751
Essay	152	41.87	211	58.13	363
Oral	101	8.59	1075	91.41	1176
Total	1161	28.2	2953	71.8	4114

The Table 18 represents the Italian results according to genre:

Table 18. Distribution of ESC and EOC according to text type in Italian

	ESC	%	EOC	%	Total
Press	103	45.37	124	54.62	227
Oral	122	26.40	340	73.59	462
Total	225		464		689

If the distinction is not clearer for the Italian press (represented by *La Repubblica*), this may be due to interviews and reports of direct speech, where EOCs would mimic oral usage and frequencies. Nevertheless, it is to be expected that in talking about feelings, emotions, likes and dislikes, in short where the speaker offers subjective evaluations, EOCs would be preferred and that these would correlate with oral texts, rather than with the printed word. ESC constructions, which correlate with event descriptions and objectivity, are more frequently found in the detached, descriptive style of the press as would be expected, and this is indeed what happens in Spanish. Italian, however differs from Spanish in this respect, by having more EOCs even in the press section. This may be a genuine distinction between the two Romance languages or it may be the effect of a high amount of oral interviews in our random sample of Italian texts analyzed.

While percentages may give us a hint about tendencies, only statistical analysis may confirm the accuracy of conclusions based on raw data. A classification and regression tree[33] was fitted to the target variables (construction types EOCs and ESCs) using different predictors (see Figure 1).

Predictors used in the model were animacy of the stimulus (with two levels: yes/no), person of the experiencer (with three levels: 1st, 2nd, 3rd), number of the experiencer (with two levels: sg., pl.), and genre (with 5 levels: novel, press, theater, essay, oral). The model had a high classification accuracy of 87.9%, compared to a baseline of 58.9%.

As we surmised, genre is clearly a factor in the choice of construction, where a clear distinction can be found between oral, on the one hand, and the written word on the other (subsuming essay, novel, press, and theater). Person and number of the experiencer are also significant, as well as animacy of the stimulus. Moreover some language differences are also significant.

4. Discussion

As mentioned above, there is a clear distinction between oral and written texts. If a text is oral, there is a further highly significant difference between singular and plural experiencers. If the experiencer is plural or is not recoverable from the context or is just a generic entity, there is a distinction between Italian and Spanish (node 8). In Italian, if the experiencer is generic or non-recoverable, ESCs are prevalent; whereas if the experiencer is plural, EOCs are predicted to be a little over 50%, and ESCs a little more than 40%. In Spanish on the other hand, in either case EOCs are predominant.

If the experiencer is singular (node 2 > 3) in an oral genre, there is also a distinction between Italian and Spanish: in Spanish with singular number we find all EOCs, whereas in Italian it is all EOCs with first and second person, whereas we find some ESCs with third person singular. This is the same tendency discussed above (end of Section 3.3.1) that finds some of the less empathetic experiencers (3rd person experiencers) tied to the subject function of ESCs.

In the written language, first and second person (node 15 > 21) are further classified by animacy of the stimulus; however, if the experiencer is in the first person we find a majority of EOCs regardless of animacy of the stimulus (node 27, and node 22 > 23), once again establishing the importance of the association between 'private' verbs, first person experiencers and EOCs. This confirms Melis's conclusions and Mithun's intuition that "Speakers do not claim to feel what another individual is feeling" (Mithun, 1991; Melis, 1999: 58, and cf. Section 3.1.1

---

33. Our thanks to Stefan Th. Gries who ran the statistics for the classification and regression tree.

Chapter 4. Constructions with subject vs. object experiencers in Spanish and Italian

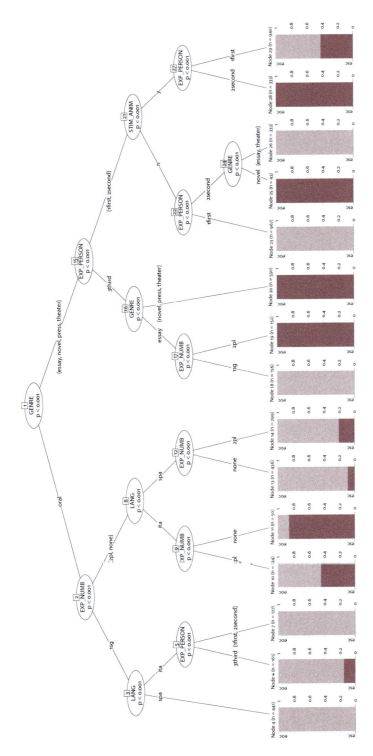

Figure 1. Classification and regression tree showing EOCs and ESCs as dependent variables and several predictors (person, number, animacy of stimulus) related to the semantic and discourse features of the constructions

above). By contrast, at least in the novel, press, and theater, if the experiencer is in the third person (node 16 > 20), the construction of choice is ESC.

We can therefore surmise that what characterizes the use of EOCs with the 1st person, then, is not their potential agency, but, as Melis, Mithun and others pointed out, it is the capability of witnessing his/her own inner mental state, as is sensed first-hand by the experiencer him/herself.

Empathy and agentivity function as alternating organizing principles within processes of feeling in Spanish and Italian. What isolates the speaker *vis à vis* other persons is his/her unique ability to perceive his/her mental state as a private and non-transferable experience. In fact, mental activity verbs have been referred to as 'private verbs' because 'they refer to activities available for perception by the speaker only" (Weber & Bentivoglio, 1991: 194, citing Palmer, 1965: 95ff.).

The fundamental difference between the first and other persons – in Melis's words – is that 'the speaker knows what he is feeling, but since he cannot avail himself of evidence as to what third parties feel, he chooses to represent them as not affected.'[34] (Melis, 1999: 58). The tendency to codify third persons as subjects in ESCs can be explained because their emotional states are not directly accessible to the speaker and therefore this is less amenable to empathy and to the understanding of others as affected experimenters.[35]

On the other hand, the relative activity of the subject experiencer contributes to his/her visibility, and as a consequence, makes it easier to infer his/her feelings and other mental states. The speaker can have – indirect – access to the inner cognitive state of a 3rd person on the basis of his/her public behavior.

Östen Dahl (2000: 48) proposes a semantic scale "private-public" or "internal-external"[36] that can be applied to the constructions examined here: the propensity of the object experiencers to be in 1st person would be related to the 'private' content conventionally associated to EOCs; and the likely tendency of subject

---

34. "El hablante sabe lo que él siente, pero al no disponer de la misma evidencia respecto a terceros opta por representarlos como no afectados."

35. The correlation between mental processes and persons in discourse can manifest itself also in combinatorial restrictions. In Japanese, for instance, certain predicates indicating 'direct experience' such as 'to be cold', 'to feel lonely' in the so-called *reportive style* can only be used in statements with a first person experiencer subject and in questions with a second person experiencer (cf. Kuroda, 1973; Tenny, 2006).

36. "That is, the propensity of a predicate to occur with egophoric subjects [and we would add "or objects"] depends primarily on the extent to which a judgment of the truth or falsity of the proposition in question involves private knowledge, i.e. knowledge that is directly accessible to one individual only." (Dahl, 2000: 48).

experiencers to refer to 3rd person would be triggered by the more 'public' or visible character of the states conceptualized by means of ESC clauses.

The differences across genres highlight the importance of taking into account all the factors producing variation in linguistic usage. Cumulative data from a broad spectrum of sources often obscure the impact of context-dependent parameters on the frequency of use of linguistic constructions (text type is just a broad factor among others). It is therefore generally advisable to undertake a more fine-grained analysis of linguistic phenomena. This, in turn, leads to methodological consequences in the design of corpora that aim at being representative of language use as a whole, and of techniques to tag and query corpora in order to establish a better picture of discourse-influenced linguistic phenomena.

5. Conclusions

Our paper explored the importance that semantic and discourse-related factors have on syntax by analyzing what features may influence the speakers' choice of EOC or ESC constructions. We have stressed the importance of analyzing the frequency and distribution of grammatical properties with naturally occurring data pertaining to actual usage, to question the usefulness of categories provided by traditional grammar (as seen for instance in the syncretism of the direct and indirect objects in actual usage). In formal approaches, in fact, the argument structure of the clause has generally been studied by analyzing contextless strings that, in many cases, were created *ad hoc* by the researcher to illustrate theoretical structural possibilities.

Our findings support the fundamental principle of CxG that grammatical constructions are non-componential, complex symbolic units pairing form and meaning. The study pays particular attention to the discourse level, conceived of as a core part of the construction intimately intertwined with the syntactic form and the semantic structure of the clause. Thus, our paper broadens the range of syntactic constructions studied by means of a usage-based functional analysis. Moreover, by analyzing constructions in Spanish and Italian, it contributes to balance the strong focus of the CxG literature on typical English constructions (ditransitive, resultative, caused-motion constructions, cf. Goldberg, 1995, 2006; Sag, 2012).

We have shown the usefulness of studying the frequency of syntactic and semantic features to gain insight into the communicative function of these constructions. With verbs of feeling, for instance, it is expected that speakers have a tendency to talk about themselves rather than about a third party, and for the same reasons there are fewer examples of third persons: speakers do not feel entitled to talk about the feelings or impressions of others, since they usually have no access to them.

In turn the high frequency of the 1st person in EOC constructions has a modal effect similar to that described in Melis and Flores (2007), whereas the 3rd person of ESC is associated to the representation of events, which influences the distribution of the constructions according to genre.

We have also shown, in fact, that text type is a crucial factor behind the variation in the distribution and frequency of the constructions examined: there is clearly an association between genre and verb class, such as spoken discourse and mental processes. However, other variation parameters are also relevant to understand the use of the construction (clausal *vs.* NP stimuli, for instance), and more fine-grained accounts should be undertaken to avoid an overgeneralization on the basis of obtained results.

For a compelling analysis of a phenomenon, it is necessary therefore to research both its quantitative and qualitative aspects, which are complementary facets of the same issue. Contextualization is clearly necessary for a qualitative analysis, and corpora are indispensable for a quantitative analysis.

As for future developments, our paper points to various avenues worth exploring, for instance expanding the Italian data analyzed. The validity of our proposal, on the other hand, i.e. that the ESC/EOC "alternation" is triggered by discourse function, would make it interesting to ascertain whether it can be applied to the whole distribution of ESCs and EOCs (not just limited to the verb class of feelings as in this paper). Our analysis, moreover, points to similarities, but also to subtle differences between the two Romance languages analyzed, and raises the need for extending parallel empirical research to other languages with the ESC/EOC alternation.

Finally, the results of a discourse and usage-based analysis such as this one may well enable us to achieve a better understanding of the evolution of these constructions, another aspect of this phenomenon that needs to be investigated.

References

ADESSE = Base de datos de verbos, alternancias de diátesis y esquemas sintáctico semánticos del español. <http://adesse.uvigo.es/>

Albertuz, F. (2007). Sintaxis, semántica y clases de verbos: Clasificación verbal en el proyecto ADESSE. In P. Cano López, et al. (Coords.), *Actas del VI Congreso de Lingüística General, Santiago de Compostela, 3–7 de mayo de 2004. Vol. 2, Tomo 2, Las lenguas y su estructura (IIb)* (pp. 2015–2030). Madrid: Arco Libros.

Allen, C. L. (1986). Reconsidering the history of *Like*. *Journal of Linguistics*, 22, 375–409. doi:10.1017/S0022226700010847

Ariel, M. (1990). *Accessing noun-phrase antecedents*. London: Routledge.

ARTHUS = Archivo de Textos Hispánicos de la Universidad de Santiago. <http://www.bds.usc.es/corpus.html>

BADIP/Lip corpus, available online at http://badip.uni-graz.at/

Barðdal, J. (2001). The perplexity of dat-nom verbs in icelandic. *Nordic Journal of Linguistics*, 24, 47–70. doi:10.1080/033258601750266187

Barðdal, J., & Eythórsson, T. (2003). The change that never happened: The story of oblique subjects. *Journal of Linguistics*, 39(3), 439–72. doi:10.1017/S002222670300207X

Barðdal, J., & Eythórsson, T. (2009). The origin of the oblique subject construction: An indo-european comparison. In V. Bubenik, J. Hewson, & S. Rose (Eds.), *Grammatical change in Indo-European languages* (pp. 179–193). Amsterdam: John Benjamins. doi:10.1075/cilt.305.19bar

Bauer, B. L. M. (2000). *Archaic syntax in indo-european. The spread of transitivity in Latin and French*. Berlin: Mouton de Gruyter. doi:10.1515/9783110825992

bds = *Base de datos sintácticos del español actual*. USC. <http://www.bds.usc.es/>

Belletti, Ad., & Rizzi, L. (1988). Psych-verbs and theta-theory. *Natural Language and Linguistic Theory*, 6, 291–352. doi:10.1007/BF00133902

Bentivoglio, P., & Weber, E. G. (1999). El perfil discursivo del verbo saber en el español hablado en Venezuela. In A. Morales et al. (Eds.), *Estudios de la lingüística hispánica: homenaje a María Vaquero* (pp. 90–109). San Juan: Editorial de la Universidad de Puerto Rico.

Bentley, D. (2006). *Split intransitivity in Italian*. Berlin: Mouton de Gruyter. doi:10.1515/9783110896053

Benveniste, É. (1958). De la subjectivité dans le langage. *Journal de Psychologie*. Reprinted in Problèmes de linguistique générale I (pp. 258–266). Paris: Gallimard, 1966.

Bossong, G. (1998). Le marquage de l'expérient dans les langues d'Europe. In J. Feuillet (Ed.), *Actance et Valence dans les Langues de l'Europe* (pp. 259–294). Berlin : Mouton de Gruyter.

Cresti, E., & Moneglia, M. (2005). *C-oral-rom: Integrated reference corpora for spoken romance languages* (Studies in Corpus Linguistics). Amsterdam: John Benjamins. doi:10.1075/scl.15

Croft, W. (1993). Case marking and the semantics of mental verbs. In J. Pustejovsky (Ed.), *Semantics and the Lexicon* (pp. 55–72). Dordrecht: Kluwer. doi:10.1007/978-94-011-1972-6_5

Dahl, Ö. (2000). Egophoricity in discourse and syntax. *Functions of Language*, 7, 33–77. doi:10.1075/fol.7.1.03dah

DeLancey, S. (1981). An interpretation of split ergativity and related patterns. *Language*, 57(3), 626–657. doi:10.2307/414343

DeLancey, S. (1984). Notes on agentivity and causation. *Studies in Language*, 8(2), 181–213. doi:10.1075/sl.8.2.05del

De Mauro, T., Mancini, F., Vedovelli, M., & Voghera, M. (1993). *Lessico di frequenza dell'italiano parlato*. Milan: Etaslibri.

Di Tullio, Á. (2004). Los verbos psicológicos y la estatividad: realizaciones del español. *Cuadernos de Lingüística del Instituto Universitario Ortega y Gasset*, 11, 23–43.

Dixon, R. M. W. (1979). Ergativity. *Language*, 55, 59–138. doi:10.2307/412519

Dixon, R. M. W. (1994). *Ergativity*. Cambridge: Cambridge University Press. doi:10.1017/CBO9780511611896

Fillmore, Ch. J. (1968). The case for case. In E. Bach & R. T. Harms (Eds.), *Universals in linguistic theory* (pp. 1–88). New York: Holt, Rinehart and Winston.

Fischer, O. C. M., & van der Leek, F. C. (1983). The Demise of the old english impersonal construction. *Journal of Linguistics*, 19, 337–368. doi:10.1017/S0022226700007775

García-Miguel, J. M., & Albertuz, F. J. (2005). Verbs, semantic classes and semantic roles in the ADESSE project. In K. Erk, A. Melinger, & S. Schulte im Walde (Eds.), *Proceedings of interdisciplinary workshop on the identification and representation of verb features and verb classes* (pp. 50–55). Saarbrücken.

Givón, T. (1976). Topic, pronoun and grammatical agreement. In C. N. Li (Ed.), *Subject and topic* (pp. 151–188). New York: Academic Press.
Givón, T. (Ed.). (1983). *Topic continuity in discourse. A quantitative cross-language study*. Amsterdam: John Benjamins. doi:10.1075/tsl.3
Givón, T. (1992). The grammar of referential coherence as mental processing instructions. *Linguistics*, 30, 2–55. doi:10.1515/ling.1992.30.1.5
Goldberg, A. E. (1995). *Constructions: A construction grammar approach to argument structure*. Chicago: Chicago University Press.
Goldberg, A. E. (2006). *Constructions at work. The nature of generalization in language*. New York: Oxford University Press.
Gutiérrez-Bravo, R. (2006). A reinterpretation of quirky subjects and related phenomena in spanish. In C. Nishida & J.-P. Y. Montreuil (Eds.), *New perspectives on romance linguistics: Vol. I: Morphology, syntax, semantics, and pragmatics. selected papers from the 35th linguistic symposium on romance languages (LSRL)* (pp. 127–142). Amsterdam: John Benjamins. doi:10.1075/cilt.275.11gut
Halliday, M. A. K. (1985). *Introduction to functional grammar*. London: Edward Arnold.
Haspelmath, M. (2001). Non-canonical marking of core arguments in european languages. In A. Y. Aikhenvald, R. M. W. Dixon, & M. Onishi (Eds.), *Non-canonical marking of subjects and objects* (pp. 53–83). Amsterdam/philadelphia: John Benjamins. doi:10.1075/tsl.46.04has
Hawkinson, A. K., & Hyman, L. M. (1974). Hierarchies of natural topic in Shona. *Studies in African Linguistics*, 5, 147–170.
Kuno, S., & Kaburaki, E. (1977). Empathy and syntax. *Linguistic Inquiry*, 8, 627–672.
Kuroda, S.-Y. (1973). Where epistemology, style, and grammar meet: A case study from Japanese". In S. R. Anderson & P. Kiparsky (Eds.), *A Festschrift for Morris Halle* (pp. 377–391). New York: Holt Rinehart and Winston.
Lakoff, G. (1970). *Irregularity in syntax*. New York: Holt, Rinehart and Winston.
Langacker, R. W. (1991). *Foundations of cognitive grammar*, vol. II. Stanford: Stanford University Press.
La Repubblica, database of past issues of the newspaper available online at: http://ricerca.repubblica.it/repubblica.
Lehmann, Ch. (1991). Predicate classes and participation. In H. Seiler & W. Premper (Eds.), *Partizipation. Das sprachliche Erfassen von Sachverhalten* (pp. 183–239). Tübingen: Gunter Narr.
Lehmann, Ch., Shin, Y.-M., & Verhoeven, E. (2000). *Person prominence and relation prominence*. München: Lincom Europa.
Lightfoot, D. (1981). The history of NP movement. In C. L. Baker & J. McCarthy (Eds.), *The logical problem of language acquisition*. Cambridge, Massachusetts: MIT Press.
Lyons, J. (1994). Subjecthood and subjectivity. In M. Yagüello (Ed.), *Subjecthood and subjectivity* (pp. 9–17). Paris: Ophrys.
Masullo, P. J. (1993). Two types of quirky subjects: Spanish versus Icelandic. Proceedings of *Nels 23* (pp. 303–317). Amherst: University of Massachusetts.
Melis, C. (1999). Variación sintáctica con los verbos de emoción. *Español Actual*, 71, 49–62.
Melis, C., & Flores, M. (2007). Los verbos seudo-impersonales del español. Una caracterización semántico-sintáctica. *Verba*, 34, 7–57.
Miglio, V., Gries, S. Th., Harris, M. J., Wheeler, E. M., & Santana-Paixão, R. (2013). Spanish *lo(s)-le(s)* clitic alternations in psych verbs: A multifactorial corpus-based analysis". In J. C. Amaro, G. Lord, A. De Prada Pérez, & Aaron (Eds.), *Selected proceedings of the 16th hispanic linguistics symposium* (pp. 268–78). Somerville, MA: Cascadilla.

Mithun, M. (1991). Active / agentive case marking and its motivations. *Language*, 67, 510–546. doi:10.1353/lan.1991.0015

Myhill, J. (1992). *Typological discourse analysis. Quantitative approaches to the study of linguistic function*. Oxford: Blackwell.

NGLE = Real Academia Española & Asociación De Academias de la Lengua Española. 2009. *Nueva gramática de la lengua española*. Madrid: Espasa Libros.

Palmer, F. R. (1965). *A linguistic study of the English verb*. London: Longmans.

Postal, P. (1971). *Crossover phenomena*. New York: Holt, Reinhart and Winston.

Sag, I. A. (2012). Sign-based construction grammar: An informal synopsis. In H. C. Boas & I. A. Sag (Eds.), *Sign-based construction grammar* (pp. 69–202). Stanford: CSLI Publications.

Scheibman, J. (2001). Local patterns of subjectivity in person and verb type in American English conversation. In J. Bybee & P. Hopper (Eds.), *Frequency and the emergence of linguistic structure* (pp. 61–89). Amsterdam: John Benjamins. doi:10.1075/tsl.45.04sch

Scheibman, J. (2002). *Point of view and grammar: Structural patterns of subjectivity in American English conversation*. Amsterdam/philadelphia: John Benjamins. doi:10.1075/sidag.11

Shibatani, M. (1999). Dative subject constructions twenty-two years later. *Studies in the Linguistic Sciences*, 29(2), 45–76.

Sigurðsson, H. A. (1989). *Verbal syntax and case in Icelandic*. Ph. D. dissertation, Lund University.

Silverstein, M. (1976). Hierarchy of features and ergativity. In R. M. W. Dixon (Ed.), *Grammatical categories in australian languages* (pp. 112–171). Canberra: Australian Institute of Aboriginal Studies.

Tenny, C. L. (2006). Evidentiality, experiencers, and the syntax of sentience in Japanese. *Journal of East Asian Linguistics*, 15, 245–288. doi:10.1007/s10831-006-0002-x

Travis, C. E. (2006). Subjetivización de construcciones: los verbos 'cognitivos' en el español conversacional. In R. M. Ortiz Ciscomani (Ed.), *Serie Memorias del VIII Encuentro Internacional de Lingüística en el Noroeste*, vol. 2 (pp. 85–109). Hermosillo, Sonora: UniSon.

Vaamonde, G., González Domínguez, F., & García-Miguel, J. M. (2010). ADESSE. A database with syntactic and semantic annotation of a corpus of Spanish. Proceedings of the *seventh international conference on language resources and evaluation (LREC'10)*. Valletta, Malta: European Language Resources Association (ELRA).

van der Auwera, J. (1981). *What do we talk when we talk. Speculative grammar and the semantics and pragmatics of focus*. Amsterdam: John Benjamins. doi:10.1075/pb.ii.3

Vázquez Rozas, V. (2006a). Construcción gramatical y valor epistémico. El caso de *supongo*. In M. Villayandre Llamazares (Ed.), *Actas del XXXV Simposio Internacional de la Sociedad Española de Lingüística*. León: Universidad de León, 1888–1900. <http://www3.unileon.es/dp/dfh/SEL/actas.htm>

Vázquez Rozas, V. (2006b). *Gustar*-type verbs. In J. C. Clements & J. Yoon (Eds.), *Functional approaches to Spanish syntax. Lexical semantics, discourse and transitivity* (pp. 80–114). Hampshire/New York: Palgrave MacMillan.

Vázquez Rozas, V., & García Salido, M. (2012). A discourse-based analysis of object clitic doubling in Spanish. In K. Davidse, T. Breban, L. Brems, & T. Mortelmans (Eds.), *Grammaticalization and language change: New reflections* (pp. 271–297). Amsterdam/philadelphia: John Benjamins. doi:10.1075/slcs.130.11vaz

Weber, E. G., & Bentivoglio, P. (1991). Verbs of cognition in spoken Spanish: A discourse profile. In S. Fleishman & L. R. Waugh (Eds.), *Discourse-pragmatics and the verb. The evidence from Romance* (pp. 194–213). London and New York: Routledge.

Whitley, M. S. (1998). Psych verbs: Transitivity adrift. *Hispanic Linguistics*, 10, 115–153.

PART II

Collostructional analysis

CHAPTER 5

Spanish constructions of directed motion – a quantitative study
Typological variation and framing strategy*

Johan Pedersen
University of Copenhagen

In typological studies of expressions of motion events, there is a need for a quantitative methodology that assesses and qualifies inter- and intra-linguistic variation. The article reports on a large corpus study of the use of Spanish motion verbs in constructions of telic motion. Verb associations with the constructional V-slot were measured by using collostructional methodology (Stefanowitsch & Gries, 2003). Six categories of construction-specific variation were identified. The corpus data and broad evidence from other semantic domains suggest that the encoding of Spanish argument structure is verb-driven and that verb constraints versus schematicity is a typological parameter. The study concludes that Spanish is a *verb-framing* language rather than a verb-framed language (cf. Talmy, 2000), which explains the substantial variation observed.

1. Introduction

Over the past several decades, a constant flow of interesting data and new insights has emerged from research based on the influential Talmian typology of motion events. Nevertheless, important typological variation remains unaccounted for – and unexplained – in recent elaborations of the typology. This is reflected in the fact that substantial amounts of evidence that do not fit the proposed models of lexicalization can be found in almost all languages. For instance, the Romance languages are generally regarded as verb-framed languages (i.e., in expressions of directional motion, they code path of motion in the verb and manner of motion optionally outside the verb), while Germanic languages are classified as

---

* I am grateful to several anonymous reviewers for valuable comments and suggestions on an earlier version of this article. I would also like to thank the editors of this volume.

DOI 10.1075/cal.19.05ped
© 2016 John Benjamins Publishing Company

satellite-framed (i.e., they code path of motion in a satellite and manner of motion in the verb). Nevertheless, in Spanish, some manner-of-motion verbs actually occur in expressions of directional motion, even when the motion event is telic. Italian is a Romance language and, just like Spanish, it is characterized as verb-framed. However, Italian is also characterized by high-frequency verb-particle constructions; and, if we focus on this aspect, it appears more like a Germanic language (e.g., Masini, 2005, 2008; Simone, 1996).

In these typological studies, there is a need for a quantitative methodology that assesses and qualifies *inter- and intra-linguistic variation*. It is important to be able to test the validity of hypotheses on typological differences and take into account the observed patterns of variation. In short, it is important to anchor the typological assessment in both inter- and intra-linguistic variation. Such an approach allows theoretical interpretations to be grounded in real usage.

In this study, I suggest a usage-based methodology that enables a quantitatively-based assessment of the variation. The purpose is to qualify the variation and to be able to test and elaborate typological theories and hypotheses. The basic idea is that, instead of taking a universal componential approach to the study of motion events (cf. Talmy's work and followers of this line of research), the collostructional methodology that quantitatively associates lexical types with a specific syntactic environment (e.g., Stefanowitsch & Gries, 2003, 2005) allows for determining specific categories of variation. In previous research, the collostructional methodology has typically been used to determine the association of top-ranked verbs with the objective of determining prototypical constructional meaning (Gries, 2012; Stefanowitsch & Gries, 2003). In this study, however, the focus is equally on low-ranked verbs with very little or no association with the constructional environment. Specific Spanish expressions of directional motion and their typological features will be analyzed on the basis of such assessments.

Focus will be on the verb and the encoding of path and manner of motion. The reason is that the encoding of path and manner has been at the center of the typological discussion for the last 25 years in the research tradition that originates in Talmy's later work: In satellite-framed languages, the verb encodes the manner; in verb-framed languages, the verb encodes the path (e.g., Talmy, 1991, 2000). I have specifically chosen telic motion as the target construction in this study for two reasons: (1) this construction has been particularly central in discussions of the typological status of Spanish in expressions of motion events; (2) this choice is a reasonable way to delimit the data sample for this study. Corpus searches for, e.g., the more general constructional environment of directional motion would return enormous amounts of data that must be gone through, assessed and counted manually.

In English, telic motion events may be expressed by a diversity of goal-marking satellites – for instance, prepositional phrases. This can be exemplified by the English goal-marker *to*:

(1) Peter ran to the bathroom

In Spanish, the expression of goal-oriented motion is frequently elaborated by a goal-marking prepositional phrase. The preposition *a* is the best indicator of goal-oriented directional motion:[1]

(2) Pedro se fue a-l baño corr-iendo
    Pedro REFL go.SPS.3SG to-DET bathroom run-GERUND
    'Peter ran to the bathroom'

The next section (Section 2) provides some background for this study. In Sections 3 and 4, respectively, I present the theoretical framework and the applied methodology for a large quantitative corpus study of the typology of Spanish expressions of directional motion. In Section 5, I present and analyze the results. Section 6 is a theoretical discussion of the results. Finally, a conclusion will be drawn, and some perspectives for future research will be outlined. The Appendix provides a complete presentation of the distributional analysis of Spanish motion verbs in a telic construction.

2. Background

In Talmy's pioneering work on language typology, languages are grouped together according to how they lexicalize different conceptual aspects of the motion event (e.g., Talmy, 1985, 1987, 1991, 2000). The following is the classic example used by Talmy in his early work:

(3) a. The bottle floated into the cave   (Talmy, 1985)
    b. la botella entr-ó en la cueva (flot-ando) Spanish
       the bottle enter-PST.3SG in the cave float-GERUND

In his later work, the principal claim is a two-way general typology in which the determination of the language type depends on how the *main event* and the *co-event* are encoded (Talmy, 1991, 2000). Languages are now classified as *verb-framed languages* (V-framed) versus *satellite-framed languages* (S-framed), referring to whether the basic meaning structure (*the framing event* = main event) in

---

[1] For more details on this matter, see the lengthy discussion in Pedersen (2014).

expressions of complex events is encoded in the verb or outside the verb, respectively. In particular, Talmy maintains that, in expressions of directed motion, some languages, such as English, tend to lexicalize the framing event, i.e., the path of motion, in a satellite; whereas the co-event, i.e., the manner of motion, is lexicalized by the verb. Other languages, such as Spanish, tend to lexicalize the framing event by the verb and may express the co-event by adding an adverbial phrase:

(3) a. The bottle floated   into the cave
                      CE   ME
    b. La botella entr-ó   en la cueva (flotando)
       the bottle enter-PST.3SG in the cave   (floating)
                  ME   CE

Since Talmy's early work on typology, expressions of directed motion have been the subject of on-going interest, and Talmy's work has been, and still is, extremely influential in cognitive semantics as well as in other theoretical frameworks (e.g., Jackendoff, 1990, 1997; Levin & Rappaport, 1995; Mateu & Rigau, 2000, 2002). Nevertheless, important typological variation remains unaccounted for, and numerous authors have tried to explain the variation and elaborate the typological patterns from diverse perspectives.

Most importantly, an extensive literature on the subject indicates that some languages do not seem to fit into his binary typology. Recently, the typology was extended to include a third category, i.e., the so-called *equipollently-framed languages*, referring to languages in which path and manner are expressed by equivalent grammatical forms (e.g., Slobin, 2004; Slobin & Hoiting, 1994; Zlatev & Yangklang, 2004). This extension primarily includes languages with serial verb constructions such as Thai, in which both manner and path are simultaneously encoded as main verbs (Beavers et al., 2010).

Moreover, almost every language, to some degree, has to be judged as a mixed type (see, e.g., Aske, 1989; Beavers et al., 2010; Berman & Slobin, 1994; Croft et al., 2010; Gennari et al., 2002; Ibarretxe-Antuñano, 2004a, 2004b, 2009; Martínez Vázquez, 2001; Pedersen, 2009a; Slobin, 1996a, 1996b, 1997, 1998, 2000, 2004, 2006, 2008; Slobin & Hoiting, 1994; Zlatev & Yangklang, 2004, among many others). For instance, Jon Aske's classic article (Aske, 1989) on path predicates in English and Spanish provides an important contribution to an elaboration of Talmy's typology, though it is still adapting the same fundamental typological machinery. His paper focuses on the syntactic-semantic circumstances in Spanish under which it is grammatically correct to express the path of motion outside the main verb. He suggests that the inability of Spanish to express the path of motion in a satellite and the manner in the verb is limited to telic motion events. The reason for this, according to Aske, is that secondary predicates – i.e., complex predicates – are not allowed in Spanish. However, the Spanish example of telic motion in (4) is a counterexample since the manner of motion is encoded by the verb, which is a Germanic feature according to the typology (see the translation):

(4) Vol-aron   a   Mar de Plata   (Spanish – Martínez Vázquez, 2001: 51–52)
    fly-PST.3SG to   Mar de Plata
    'They flew to Mar de Plata'

In fact, it has been shown recently that some manner of motion verbs do occur regularly in Spanish expressions of telic motion (Pedersen, 2014). This usage is also attested for other typologically similar languages, such as Italian, French and Japanese (see Beavers *et al.*, 2010 and references cited there for examples from other languages). Beavers *et al.* (2010) point out that some languages even allow both canonical S- and V-framed constructions. For example, English and Hebrew – the latter is sometimes classified as V-framed; see, e.g., Slobin (2004) – facilitate both canonical encoding types, as shown in the following Hebrew Examples (5) and their English translations:

(5) a. ha-kelev   zaxal   la-meluna.   (Hebrew – Beavers *et al.*, 2010: 361)
       the-dog   crawled   to.the-doghouse
       'The dog crawled into the doghouse.'
    b. ha-kelev   nixnas   la-meluna   bi-zxila.
       the-dog   entered   to.the-doghouse   in-crawlN
       'The dog entered the doghouse crawling.'

Recently, Ibarretxe-Antuñano, building on Slobin's work, has suggested clines of 'path/manner salience' that classify languages along continua between high-path/manner-salient languages and low-path/manner-salient languages (e.g., Ibarretxe-Antuñano, 2004a, 2004b, 2009). In this typological framework, the typological status of a language depends on its degree of path/ground and manner elaboration. Now the typological question is not first and foremost *how* (in which constituent type) languages encode path and manner but *how much* they elaborate these semantic components. Thus, Ibarretxe-Antuñano intends to account for both inter-linguistic and intra-linguistic variation in terms of typological clines of path/manner salience that cross-cut the classical binary classification as well as the more recent tertiary division between verb-framed, satellite-framed, and equipollently-framed languages. An implication of this approach is that, compared to English, for instance, Spanish provides less detailed information about both the manner and the path component. This approach is arguably a more fine-grained elaboration of Talmy's typology than earlier proposals. Nevertheless, in my view, this direction of research, on the one hand, follows too closely the Talmian tradition based on the mapping of universal semantic components (e.g., path and manner) onto clausal constituents. Below, I discuss some problems of this kind of form-meaning pairing. On the other hand, paradoxically, it tends to dissociate too much from the fundamental, and very important, insights in Talmy's original framework, namely, that different language types facilitate different basic encoding options in expressions of directional motion, as well as in other domains of argument structure.[2] Instead, the explanatory focus in Ibarretxe-Antuñano's work is on the possible factors that may explain differences of granularity. Most importantly, as in other approaches – see, e.g., Beavers *et al.* (2010) – she focuses on the linguistic resources (lexicon, morphology, and morpho-syntax) that each language provides for encoding different aspects of the motion event – e.g., manner and path of motion. This issue is particularly interesting when considered in a diachronic perspective since a crucial question is why languages tend to develop certain types of resources. In a recent study, for instance, Fanego (2012) addresses the question why, and under what conditions, manner salience emerges in the history of English motion verbs. Her study confirms Slobin's hypothesis that the increase in linguistic manner-of-motion diversity correlates with, or is a consequence of, satellite-framed typology (Slobin, 2004, 2006).

Summing up, the question of how to deal with the significant amounts of *unpredicted inter- and intra-linguistic variation* in expressions of directional motion is largely unsolved in the Talmian tradition. A symptom of this situation is the serious lack of quantitative empirical underpinning of the current typologies.

3. Theoretical framework

The analyses of this study were conducted within the general framework of a family of usage-based construction grammars (Boas, 2003; Bybee, 1985; Croft, 2001; Goldberg, 2006; Langacker, 1987, 1988; Tomasello, 2003; among others). From a theoretical perspective, constructions are basically understood as non-derived form-meaning pairings of different specificity, stored as the basic elements of users' grammar (e.g., Goldberg, 1995, 2006). Derived form-meaning pairings, however, may also be stored independently as grammatical constructions if they are sufficiently frequent (e.g., Croft, 2001: 28; Goldberg, 2006: 224; Goldberg & Jackendoff, 2004: 533). An important feature of constructions in a usage-based grammar is that the emergence of different types of constructions reflects frequency effects (see,

---

[2]. The availability of the compounding parameter in Parameter Theory (e.g., Snyder, 2001) represents a theoretically completely different but also highly influential typological framework. It offers similar insights into the available encoding options in different language types that may tend to be blurred when too much focus is put on the granularity of expression at the expense of principles of encoding (±compounding).

e.g., Barlow & Kemmer, 2000; Bybee, 2006, 2007). Lexemes, such as the Spanish [casa] / 'house', have a special status as lexical constructions due to their special role as carriers of substantial meaning in every language.[3] More abstract constructions have diagrammatic features in the sense that they have their own schematic meaning. This is most prominently exemplified by *argument structure constructions*, e.g., the English constructions of directional motion: [SUBJ, V, OBL] / 'X moves Y' (Goldberg, 1995). When argument structure is basically organized as a diagram (in the sense of Goldberg's argument structure constructions) with slots filled out by lexical items, I will characterize it as *construction-driven*. If it is basically organized at the lexical level as verb-framing by means of a conceptual valence structure with a lexical (verbal) profile (Langacker, 1987), I will correspondingly characterize it as *verb-driven* (Pedersen, 2013, 2014; cf., e.g., Boas, 2003, 2010).

Notice that the notions *diagrammaticity/schematicity*) and *verb-framing* in this context refers to an organizational device, a procedural option. On the one hand, diagrammaticity/schematicity does not presuppose the identification of a specific, theoretically well-defined schematic construction.[4] We may argue that a diagrammatic feature could be involved in the following expression: *Peter danced to the bathroom*, since the basic meaning of telic motion cannot arguably be predicted/projected by the verb *dance*. But this argument does not commit us to a specific claim about the exact representational format of the expression type that has this feature. On the other hand, our corpus analysis does not at the outset assume a specific theoretical (e.g., constructionist) understanding of the analyzed object. However, we may still want to derive theoretical interpretations from the extracted sample data, which may, e.g., favor an interpretation of involved diagrammaticity/schematicity or verb-framing/projection. In that sense, the present approach is data-driven though the methodology is specifically designed to test typological theories at the same time.[5]

In terms of practical methodology and theoretical assumptions, the implication is that the type of expression that will be used for the corpus analysis should not be defined beforehand as a specific construction type in a theoretical sense. Thus, I will examine 'verbal lexemes in a specific constructional environment of telic motion'. A constructional environment is a syntactic configuration to be used in the corpus analysis, which is not necessarily a construction in a theoretical sense (e.g., a non-derived entrenched form-meaning pairing), but should be seen as a candidate for construction-hood. The advantage of this approach is that we

---

[3] For the same reason, I believe, we should keep the denomination *lexeme* for this particular construction type.

[4] Though the identification of the specific construction type may often be obvious.

[5] See also the discussion in Gries (2010).

can also analyze the lexeme-construction association data with the objective of deriving theoretical interpretations in relation to the role of schematicity and the verb lexeme in the encoding of argument structure.

4. Methodology

The purpose of this corpus study is to explore the relation between the meaning of the motion verb and its potential occurrence in the telic construction.[6] The main task is to identify motion verbs in the telic motion environment, calculate their association measure with respect to the verbal slot in terms of collostructional analysis, and determine their rank (Stefanowitsch & Gries, 2003). The primary goal is to determine the typological prototype and different patterns of variation. Importantly, however, we also want to attest and characterize the type of motion verbs that do not occur very frequently in the telic environment or do not occur at all in this usage. It is important to keep in mind, however, that this kind of analysis is by no means a detailed semantic characterization of motion verbs in Spanish.

The data sample is extracted from searches in Corpus del Español (Davies, 2002), which is a large monolingual corpus available on the Internet. The corpus consists of around 100 million words in approx. 14,000 Spanish texts from the 12th to the 20th centuries.[7] The corpus was converted from raw text files that were received from a number of sources (the list of sources is available on the web page). These texts were imported into the SQL Server. Corpus del Español is an annotated corpus, tagged for lemma and parts of speech. The texts from the 19th and 20th century were tagged and lemmatized by Mark Davies and Douglas Biber using a tagger developed by the latter – a hybrid probabilistic/rule-based tagger (personal communication with Mark Davies).

The present study is concerned only with modern Spanish usage in texts and speech from the 20th century (approx. 20.4 million words). This part of the corpus contains oral as well as written language (interviews and transcripts, newspaper and magazine texts, fiction, and academic texts). Written language is dominant in the corpus, and we have to be aware that written versus oral language may be a factor that we should take into account when we analyze expressions of telic motion.[8]

---

6. Spanish verbs that do not imply motion cannot be attested at all in expressions of directional motion events (Martínez Vázquez, 2001).

7. In some cases, data doublets (relatively few cases) have been found. For this reason (also), it is important to go through the data manually. Corpus del Español can be accessed on the website: http://www.corpusdelespanol.org/.

8. Literature: 25%; Academic texts: 25%; news and magazines: 25%, oral: 25%. We have to take into account that the first three text categories also may include different kinds of oral usage.

I searched for expressions of goal-oriented motion explicitly marked by the goal-marker *a*: intransitive motion verb + *a* + NP. To avoid the exclusion of relevant data by the determination of the search string, I used a very simple search string: [[V] al/a] (= verb lemma + (goal-marker + definite article in masculine) or only goal-marker). Subsequently, I went through the data manually to exclude all occurrences that were not telic motion. That is, only instances of the constructional environment: [V a NP] / 'telic motion' were selected and counted. For the assessment of verbal constraints on the telic construction, it was important not only to consider motion verbs that actually occur in the corpus in this specific constructional environment of telic motion but also the frequency and semantics of those motion verbs that are only attestable in other usages – for instance, *bailar* 'to dance' (motion activity). Therefore, I decided to carry out searches for each motion verb in the corpus, instead of searching for a general pattern that identifies potential instances of the target construction. Thus, the corpus analysis is performed for an inventory of all motion verbs that occur in some usage at least once in the corpus. The inventory of motion verbs (see Appendix) corresponds roughly to the intransitive part of the list of motion verbs in Cifuentes Ferez's paper *The semantics of the English and the Spanish motion verb lexicons* (Cifuentes Ferez, 2010), which I have used as a basic reference. Nevertheless, a few motion verbs that are not included in Cifuentes Ferez's list have been identified in the corpus and added to the verb inventory in the present study.[9]

To account for the frequency of a specific verb in the telic construction in relation to the entire verbal distribution in the corpus, I analyzed the Spanish data as a collostructional phenomenon (Stefanowitsch & Gries, 2003) – that is, as a co-occurrence of a constructional environment of telic motion: [SUBJ V *a* NP] / 'telic motion event' and a specific lexical construction of motion: [verbal lexeme] / 'motion'. Collostructional analysis applies the principles of measuring lexical collocation to the interaction of lexemes and the grammatical constructions associated with them in the internal structure of constructions. I followed the general methodology and procedure outlined in Stefanowitsch & Gries (2003) (the standard approach). The statistical analysis of the interaction between the lexemes and the construction is based on Fischer's Exact Test (FET).[10] As Stefanowitsch & Gries (2003) point out, the most important contribution of this kind of distributional analysis is the relative ordering of the verbs according to their attraction to the construction.

---

9. For instance, the common verb *volver* 'to go/come back' is included in the present study although, surprisingly, it is absent in Cifuentes Ferez's list of motion verbs.

10. Calculations of right-tailed *p*-values were conducted by using a web-based FET calculator: http://www.langsrud.com/fisher.htm.

The usual purpose of ranking lexemes on the basis of this kind of association measure is to identify a type of lexeme (i.e., top-ranked verbs) with the highest association strength with respect to the constructional environment. In addition, I will identify in this study other variation groups by also focusing on lower ranked verbs. The identification of the kind of verbs that are not (or weakly) associated with the construction is an important point of focus as well.

5. Results

I found in total 19,623 tokens of the target construction (telic uses with *a* marker, see Example (2)). In the next sections, different outcomes of the quantitative analysis are summarized and interpreted in terms of verb ranking and verb semantics. A complete verb ranking list is provided in the Appendix. In the tables, the third column indicates the conceptual component(s) (LCC) that, together with the general component 'motion', is lexicalized by the verb:[11]

Lexicalized Conceptual Components (LCC):

- Motion (–)
- Ground (G)
- Figure (F)
- Path (P)
- Manner (M)
- Cause (C)
- Concurrent Result (CR)
- Path + Ground (P-G)
- Manner + Ground (M-G)
- Path + Manner (P-M)
- Figure + Manner (F-M)
- Cause + Manner (C-M)
- Path + Ground + Manner (P-G-M)
- Manner + Concurrent Result (M-CR)

The fourth column 'all uses' represents the total number of occurrences of each verb in all constructional environments in which it occurs. The next column (telic usage) is the frequency of that verb in the constructional environment of telic motion. The sixth column indicates the telic usage in relation to the general

---

[11]. The semantic notions, originated in the Talmian research tradition, are taken from Cifuentes Ferez (2010), whose componential assignments to the verbs are also adopted in most cases. If not, details and explanations will be provided.

frequency of the verb. The seventh column provides the *p*-value of the Fischer Exact test, and the last column is a $\log_{10}$ transformation of that measure (e.g., Stefanowitch & Gries, 2005) that provides a more reader-friendly measure of the verb ranking: a relatively high $\log_{10}$ value corresponds to a relatively high ranking. The FET calculator returns '0' for extremely low *p*-values, which is indicated as '→0' and, correspondingly, as '→infinite' for the $\log_{10}$-transformed value.

The verb ranking is used to identify and characterize variation groups in terms of association strength (with respect to the telic environment) correlated with similarities of verb semantics. The *p*-values are specifically used as an indicator of relative association – hence the typicality of the verb meaning in the verbal slot of this specific constructional environment – and the chosen breaking point of association as a reference point that helps to categorize the data on typological variation in a meaningful way. The breaking point has been determined to be at the significance level of $p < 0.01$, which indicates the assumed critical level of association that separates the verbs whose frequencies qualify for the feature 'associated with the telic construction' from those verbs that are 'not associated with the telic construction'. The breaking point of association is chosen from the standard levels of significance (e.g., 0.05, 0.01 or 0.001). The selected level is not decisive for the identification of the categories of variation; though it may, in principle, have implications for the categorization of a specific verb. In fact, if we changed the breaking point of association from $p < 0.01$ to $p < 0.001$, a verb would have to change category in only one case due to its *p*-value – the manner verb *rodar* 'to roll' would no longer be considered associated with this constructional environment; and, instead of 'available variation', it would be categorized as 'excludable/exceptional' variation (see Table 3 and Appendix).

5.1 General patterns in the data compared to previous research

The typological feature for Spanish identified in Tesnière (1959) and in the Talmian tradition (e.g., Talmy, 1985, 1991, 2000) associates the verb with the conceptual component 'path of motion' in expressions of directional motion. This basic pattern of lexicalization is confirmed by the top-20 verb ranking of lexical association with the verb slot of our specific constructional environment of telic motion, as shown in Table 1:[12]

---

[12] *Marchar(se)* has a telic reading ('to go away/somewhere') as well as an atelic activity reading ('to march'). Only the telic verb meaning has been attested in the telic constructional environment. *Montar(se)* (see complete verb list in Appendix) also has both a telic ('to get on') and an atelic ('to ride') reading. The usage in a telic constructional environment has only been attested with the telic reading of the verb.

Table 1. Verb association with the telic motion construction – the top-20 verb ranking

Rank	Verbs	LCC	All uses	Telic usage	Telicity ratio (%)	FET-value-p	Log^{10}-trans
1	regresar 'to come back'	P	2780	1251	45.00	→0	→infinite
2	acudir 'to go to a specific place'	P	1171	395	33.73	→0	→infinite
3	viajar 'to travel'	(P)-G	1832	512	27.95	→0	→infinite
4	trasladar(se) 'to move from one place to another'	P	1341	335	24.98	→0	→infinite
5	entrar (a/en) 'to enter'[13]	P	6651	1512	22.73	→0	→infinite
6	subir 'to ascend, to go up'	P	3209	614	19.13	→0	→infinite
7	llegar 'to arrive'	P	19639	3439	17.51	→0	→infinite
8	acercar(se) 'to move closer to'	P	4229	721	17.05	→0	→infinite
9	ir(se) 'to go (away) somewhere'	P	56430	4936	8.75	→0	→infinite
10	volver 'to come back'	P	12984	1125	8.66	→0	→infinite
11	salir 'to exit'	P	12402	920	7.42	→0	→infinite
12	venir 'to come'	P	12290	658	5.35	→0	→infinite
13	dirigir(se) 'to head to'	P	4850	369	7.61	3.83e-252	251.42
14	emigrar 'to emigrate'	P-G	350	141	40.29	5.53e-207	206.26
15	arribar '(of a ship) to reach port, to arrive'	P	222	107	48.20	2.56e-168	167.59
16	marchar(se) 'to go (away) somewhere, to march'	P	1149	169	14.71	2.28e-164	163.64
17	retornar 'to return, to go back'	P	450	126	28.00	2.89e-161	160.54
18	aproximar(se) 'to move closer to'	P	491	124	25.25	2.03e-152	151.69
19	caer(se) 'to fall down'	P	5675	253	4.46	1.74e-119	118.76
20	bajar 'to go down'	P	2589	142	5.48	3.46e-79	78.46

In general terms, the lexical meaning of the top-20 verbs implies, as expected, 'path of motion' and not 'manner of motion', which is the typical pattern identified in the literature for Germanic languages. As we may also expect, this specific constructional environment seems to be associated particularly with verb meanings of path of motion that set the scene for a combination with an explicit end point (see the next section). The verb *viajar* 'to travel' is difficult to categorize in terms of semantic components. According to Cifuentes Ferez (2010), it is a manner of motion verb. I believe this is a problematic assessment since the way we move when we travel basically depends on the device of transportation at our disposal. I see *viajar* as displacement over longer distances – typically, far away from a point of reference (e.g., the place of communication) – hence, the ground (G)-component. In addition, this verb is strongly associated with an element of directionality – we refer to an activity that usually implies motion in a specific direction (hence, the

---

[13]. *Entrar* 'to enter' occur with two different goal markers, *a* and *en*, with an almost equal frequency: 769 and 743, respectively. For more details on the use of *a* versus *en*, see Ibarretxe-Antuñano (2003).

P-component in brackets). This associated meaning component seems to license the highly frequent telic usage. Interestingly, the directional component is explicitly encoded in a similar verb such as *emigrar* 'to emigrate' (regarding the associated element of directionality, see also the analysis of verb group B in Section 5.4).

5.2 The construction specific prototype

The classic Talmian typology emphasizes the verbal encoding of the *path component* in Spanish expressions of directional motion; see Sections 2 and 5.1. This is reflected in the fact that the notion of path verbs is frequently used in research papers and textbooks of Spanish linguistics to characterize Spanish expressions of directional motion. However, *path verb* may not be the best denomination for many of the verbs that constitute the prototype in this specific constructional environment, telic motion; e.g., *acudir* 'to go to a specific place' or *llegar* 'to arrive' (see Table 1). At least, it is not a very precise characterization.

The verb ranking identifies those expressions that are highly characteristic and representative of the constructional environment in question and its semantics – a typological prototype. The data confirms the basic encoding pattern of the Talmian typology: the verbal encoding of the *path component*. In addition, the top-20 verb ranking in Table 1 suggests that, for this specific constructional environment of telic motion, the typological prototype for the verb meaning is: *path of motion leading to an end point*. This aspectual component of telicity is part of the very core meaning of the verb (its lexical aspect), which sets the scene for a combination with an explicitly expressed end point by means of the goal marker (*a*). It applies to all the verbs in Table 1 (except *viajar* 'to travel', see the discussion in the previous section) such as *regresar* 'to come back', *acudir* 'go to a place', *trasladar(se)* 'to move to', *venir* 'to come', or *llegar* 'to arrive'. Nevertheless, it does not apply to all types of path verbs that occur in this environment. For instance, path verbs such as *avanzar* 'to move forwards' or *seguir* 'to follow' are basically not telic. Thus, *path of motion leading to an end point* is a more precise denomination of the prototypical verb meaning in this specific constructional environment:

(6) Pedro lleg-ó a su destino
    Pedro arrive-PST.3SG to his destiny
    'Pedro arrived at his destination'

5.3 Typological graduation

Table 2 illustrates how this study provides a graduated assessment of the typological features for the verb occurring in the constructional environment of telic motion. It is meant to illustrate how we can assess the typological variation in terms of association ranking, taking the verb rank as an indication of the graduated typicality of the semantics encoded by the verb. First and foremost, examples of verbs from the main categories of variation are included. Hence, there are evidently gaps in this abbreviated version of the ranking (a complete list is provided in the Appendix). The omitted verbs lexicalize features that are similar in those verbs included in Table 2.

The bolded line – the breaking point of association – separates the verbs whose frequencies qualify for the feature 'associated to the telic construction' at a significance level of $p < 0.01$ from those featured 'not associated to the telic construction'.

The most noteworthy source of variation is the typicality of 'path of motion' versus 'manner of motion', though, evidently, the verbs have additional semantic features that may justify their rank – including some of those semantic components listed in the introduction to Section 5. For instance, as explained in the previous section (5.2), the lexical meaning of the top-ranked verbs – the prototype – tends to be *path of motion leading to an end point*. In the next section (5.4), I will identify and analyze the most significant categories of variation.

The data presented in Table 2 provide clear evidence and confirm, on a quantitative basis, what has been suggested in many studies:[14] that different kinds of user variation do not fit the classic versions of the Talmian typology (Talmy, 1985, 1991, 2000). Most importantly, the association patterns show no clear distinction between the typological features 'path of motion' and 'manner of motion' when we look at a broader excerpt of verbs, including not only the most frequent verbs. For instance, manner of motion verbs in combination with a satellite phrase, a characteristic feature of Germanic languages, may also be acceptable in a Romance language such as Spanish, as the relatively high rankings – safely above the breaking point – of verbs such as *correr* 'to run' indicate. We should also notice that some, even rather frequent, path verbs, such as *cruzar* 'to cross' and *elevarse* 'to move upwards', are not strongly associated with this specific constructional environment; and, in fact, these verbs have a much lower ranking – below the breaking point – than certain manner of motion verbs, such as *correr* and *volar*. Even verbs such as *descender* 'to go down' and *ascender* 'to ascend', which are often chosen in the literature as good examples of typical Spanish path verbs, have a lower ranking than manner verbs such as *correr* and *volar*.[15]

---

14. See, e.g., references in Section 2.

15. It should be emphasized that path verbs such as *descender* and *ascender* may still have a stronger association with the more general constructional environment of directional motion compared to the manner verbs *correr* and *volar*, though this is something that has to be investigated. The data in the present study show that the former verbs are less associated with the more specific telic environment than are the latter ones.

Chapter 5. Spanish constructions of directed motion – a quantitative study

Table 2. Graduated verbal association with the telic motion construction

Rank	Verbs	LCC	All uses	Telic usage	Telicity ratio (%)	FET-value-p	Log^{10}-trans
1	regresar 'to come back'	P	2780	1251	45	→0	→infinite
5	entrar (a/en) 'to enter'	P	6651	1512	22.73	→0	→infinite
7	llegar 'to arrive'	P	19639	3439	17.51	→0	→infinite
9	ir(se) 'to go, to go away'	P	56430	4936	8.75	→0	→infinite
11	salir 'to exit'	P	12402	920	7.42	→0	→infinite
12	venir 'to come'	P	12290	658	5.35	→0	→infinite
18	aproximar(se) 'to move closer to'	P	491	124	25.25	2.03e-152	151.69
20	bajar 'to go down'	P	2589	142	5.48	3.46e-79	78.46
23	correr 'to run'	M	3912	150	3.83	4.57e-63	62.34
24	huir 'to flee'	P-M	1129	88	7.79	2.89e-62	61.54
28	pasar 'to pass, to go through, over, along, beyond'	P	21593	306	1.42	3.61e-32	31.44
29	saltar 'to jump'	M	1233	58	4.70	6.62e-30	29.18
31	volar 'to move through the air, to fly'	M-G	995	46	4.62	9.30e-24	23.03
33	ascender 'to ascend'	P	760	34	4.47	1.48e-17	16.83
38	descender 'to go down'	P	987	27	2.74	1.82e-9	8.74
41	abalanzar(se) 'to rush toward'	P-M	72	6	8.33	9.65e-6	5.02
45	partir 'to leave'	P	5509	58	1.05	0.00075	3.12
49	cruzar 'to cross'	P	1984	20	1.008	0.05	1.30
54	caminar 'to walk'	M	2347	21	0.89	0.12	0.94
60	embarcar(se) 'to go on board'	P-G	257	3	1.17	0.25	0.61
64	desviar(se) 'to divert'	P	423	4	0.95	0.32	0.50
67	deslizar(se) 'to slide'	M	462	4	0.87	0.37	0.43
72	adentrar(se) 'to go into the interior part of'	P	146	1	0.68	0.63	0.20
74	pasear 'to walk for pleasure'	M	764	4	0.52	0.75	0.12
76	elevar(se) 'to move upwards'	P	1532	8	0.52	0.80	0.10
85	flotar 'to float or to move smoothly'	M	883	1	0.11	0.997	0.001
92	avanzar 'to move forwards'	P	2265	2	0.09	0.999996	1.70e-6
93	alejar(se) 'to move far away from'	P	1774	1	0.06	1	0
94	conducir 'to drive'	M	1899	1	0.05	1	0
95	alcanzar 'to reach'	P	5342	10	0.19	1	0
247	bailar 'to dance'	M	1283	0	0	1	0
248	atravesar(se) 'to cross'	P	1324	0	0	1	0

5.4 Qualifiable variation

Variation in usage may be categorized and qualified by means of the verb ranking. Based on the distributional analysis that determines the verb ranks of association with the constructional environment of telic motion, we can identify sets of verbs at given p thresholds of association that share basic semantic (typological) features, e.g., path or manner of motion. These verb sets represent groups of qualified variation with respect to the constructional environment of telic motion.

We can identify directly from the distributional analysis four groups of variation that I will term as follows:

1. The prototype. Threshold $p \approx 0$,
2. Available variation. Threshold $p < 0.01$,
3. Excludable variation. Threshold $p > 0.01$,
4. Unavailable variation. Threshold $p \approx 1$.

5.4.1   The prototype

All the verbs (A) in the first group of variation have the basic semantic feature 'path of motion'; see Section 5.2:

A. The prototype (see Table 1)

(7) Pedro llegó   a   Madrid a las 5
    Pedro arrive-PST.3SG to Madrid at the 5
    'Pedro arrived in Madrid at 5'

5.4.2   Available variation

The second group of variation that emerged from the distributional analysis ('available variation') is characterized by having a p-value that is lower than 1% indicating positive associations with the constructional environment (relatively high rank) but with a lower rank than the constructional prototype, represented by the top 20 verbs. This group of variation consists of two major verb types characterized by the basic semantic features 'path of motion' and 'manner of motion', respectively. Since the path verbs coincide with the prototype with respect to this basic feature, I will focus on the other verb group of 'available variation', namely, the one featured by manner verbs (B):

B. Available manner verbs (see Table 3)

(8) Pedro corr-ió   a   la playa
    Pedro run-PST.3SG   to the beach
    'Pedro ran to the beach'

Association data for this group of variation is extracted in Table 3.

Manner of motion verbs may be roughly subdivided into those whose meaning is somehow associated with directionality – for instance, *running* and *flying* – and those that are not, such as *dancing* or *floating*. The lexical meaning of the former type has, if not an explicit component of 'path of motion' (see column 3), an associated element of directionality; and they are typically used in a goal-oriented context. It is plausible to hypothesize that manner verbs of this type are relatively more accessible in combinations with telic path predicates.[16]

---

[16]. See Pedersen (2014) for more details on Spanish manner of motion verbs in telic usage.

Table 3. Available variation – manner of motion verbs

Rank	Verbs	LCC	All uses	Telic usage	Telicity ratio (%)	FET-value-*p*	Log¹⁰-trans
23	*correr* 'to run'	M	3912	150	3.83	4.57e-63	62.34
24	*huir* 'to flee'	P-M	1129	88	7.79	2.89e-62	61.54
29	*saltar* 'to jump'	M	1233	58	4.70	6.62e-30	29.18
31	*volar* 'to fly'	M-G	995	46	4.62	9.30e-24	23.03
32	*lanzar(se)* 'to throw oneself, to pounce on something/somebody'	M	2548	66	2.59	1.17e-19	18.93
34	*tirar(se)* 'to throw oneself'	M	2017	62	3.07	7.51e-16	15.12
35	*arrojar(se)*	M	824	33	4.00	1.04e-15	14.98
36	*precipitar(se)* 'to fall down from a high place, to run, to hurry to'	P-M	323	21	6.50	1.57e-14	13.80
39	*afluir* 'to flow in/into/to/toward'	P-M	11	4	36.36	6.39e-7	6.19
41	*abalanzar(se)* 'to dash to'	P-M	72	6	8.33	0.000009	5.02
47	*rodar* 'to roll'	M	38	3	7.89	0.002126	2.67

In fact, the lexical meaning of the manner verbs in the B-group, as shown in Table 3, has the co-component 'path of motion' (P) and/or an associated element of directionality that seems to license the telic usage. The same semantic description applies to verbs in the C-group (see below), though the manner verbs in this variation group are very rare and occur with a very low frequency. Thus, manner verbs with an element of path/directionality are expected to be found in the telic usage with a frequency that seems to depend on the salience of the associated directional meaning (see the discussion of the C-group).

5.4.3 Excludable variation

In the third variation group identified by the distributional analysis are excludable variants, which are observable with a very low frequency. They are characterized by having a higher *p*-value than 1%, indicating a relatively weak/no association to the constructional environment in question. This group of variation can profitably be divided into two subgroups, featured by path and manner verbs, respectively.

C. Excludable manner verbs (see Table 4)

Some of the excludable verbs are manner of motion verbs, e.g., *caminar* 'to walk', *deslizar(se)* 'to slide', *andar* 'to walk', *pasear* 'to walk for pleasure':

(9) And-a   a-l   hotel donde yo estoy,...   (Davies, 2002)
    Go-IMP.SG   to-the   hotel where I   be.PRS.1SG
    'Go to the hotel where I'm staying'

(10) ??Camin-ó   a   la   biblioteca
     walk-PST.3SG   to   the library'
     'He walked to the library'

This usage is very infrequent and the verbs are scarcely associated with telic usage (*p*-value > 1%). Most of the verbs in this subgroup have a certain element of associated directionality (as do the verbs in the B-group); but, importantly, the former type seems to have a relatively more salient manner profile as compared to the latter type. The telic usage is observable but very rare and in many cases disputable; see (10).

D. Excludable path-verbs (see Table 4)

A subgroup of path verbs represents another group of excludable variation. This subgroup of path verbs are very weakly associated to the telic environment (*p*-value > 1%) due to their specific semantics. The verbs may have a relatively strong profile of directionality, though most of the verbs may only be observed in this environment in very specific telic contexts:

(11) Avanzó   a-l   semáforo
      Advance-PST.3SG   to-DET   traffic light
      'he moved forward to the traffic light'

The group is very diverse. Some of the verbs have a verb meaning that explicitly includes the end location of a telic motion event: *encumbrar* 'to reach the top of', *embarcar(se)* 'to go on board', *atracar* '(of a ship) to reach port', *adentrarse* 'to go into the interior part of'. It seems that the explicit verbal indication of the final destination in these cases is blocking further elaborative goal marking. This is not quite the same with regard to the rareness of a similar group of telic verbs, e.g., *levantarse* 'to stand up, to raise'. The reason the use of this latter group of telic verbs is blocked in the telic environment – while verbs such as *entrar* 'to enter' or *salir* 'to go out' certainly are not – seems to be that the potential meaningfulness to elaborate on the end location by means of a goal-marker phrase is minimal due to the specific verb meaning, e.g., *levantarse* 'to stand up → to where??'. Some of the verbs express motion in different directions: *esparcir* 'to move in different directions', impeding the indication of a specific end location by means of goal marking. Some of the verbs have an implicated origin in their lexical meaning that seems to impede the telic elaboration: *apartarse* 'to move away from' → *se apartó a...*?? 'he moved away from to...'), *alejarse* 'to move far away from' → *se alejó a...*?? 'he moved far away from to...'). Finally, some excludable verbs have such a high frequency in other constructional environments (e.g., *alcanzar* 'to reach', *seguir* 'to follow') that this very high general frequency in combination with a low frequency of telic usage will downgrade their association to this specific constructional environment to such a degree that users may consider this usage rare and exceptional.

The association data on excludable variation is provided in Table 4. The different verb types are excludable to a different degree, depending on their rank:

Table 4. Excludable variation – path verbs and manner of motion verbs

Rank	Verbs	LCC	All uses	Telic usage	Telicity ratio (%)	FET-value-p	$\log^{10}$-trans
53	*retroceder* 'to go back, to back down'	P	372	5	1.34	0.11	0.97
54	*caminar* 'to walk'	M	2347	21	0.89	0.12	0.94
57	*encumbrar* 'to reach the top of'	P	23	1	4.35	0.14	0.84
60	*embarcar(se)* 'to go on board'	P-G	257	3	1.17	0.25	0.61
63	*atracar* '(of a ship) to reach port'	P	53	1	1.89	0.30	0.52
67	*deslizar(se)* 'to slide'	M	462	4	0.87	0.37	0.43
70	*esparcir(se)* 'to move in different directions'	P	132	1	0.76	0.59	0.23
72	*adentrar(se)* 'to go into the interior part of'	P	146	1	0.68	0.63	0.20
74	*pasear* 'to walk for pleasure'	M	764	4	0.52	0.75	0.12
80	*adelantar(se)* 'to move forwards'	P	779	3	0.39	0.89	0.05
86	*andar* 'to walk'	M	3330	10	0.30	0.999	0.0005
87	*apartar(se)* 'to move away from'	P	1023	1	0.10	0.999	0.00045
92	*avanzar* 'to move forwards'	P	2265	2	0.09	0.999996	1.70e-6
93	*alejar(se)* 'to move far away from'	P	1774	1	0.06	1	0
95	*alcanzar* 'to reach'	P	5342	10	0.19	1	0
96	*seguir* 'to follow'	P	15308	14	0.09	1	0
97	*levantar(se)* 'to stand up, to raise'	P-M	3896	3	0.08	1	0

5.4.4 Unavailable variation

A large group of motion verbs does not occur at all in telic usage. Like the third group, this last variation group that emerged directly from the distributional analysis (unavailable variation, p-value ≈ 1) can be divided into two subgroups of path verbs and manner verbs, respectively.

E. Unavailable path verbs (see Table 5)

This small group of path verbs does not occur in telic usage and show, correspondingly, no association at all to the telic environment (p-value ≈ 1); for instance, *distanciar(se)* 'to move away from', or *dispersar(se)* 'to disperse'. The unavailability in the goal-oriented environment is due to their specific verb semantics (cf. group D):

(12) *Se   distanc-ió   de...   a-l   otro   lado
    REFL distance-PST.3SG   from   to-the   other   side
    'he moved to the other side away from...'

F. Unavailable manner verbs (see Table 5)

Most of the unavailable motion verbs are, however, manner verbs:

(13) *Pedro bail-ó   a-l   baño
     Pedro dance-PST.3SG to-DET toilet
     'Pedro danced to the toilet'

This is a very large group of manner verbs (see Appendix) that show no association at all with the constructional environment of telic motion (*p*-value ≈ 1). This group of manner verbs has no lexicalized element of associated directionality. As an example, we can think about the verb *bailar* 'to dance'. When we dance, we are not intentionally moving in a specific direction the way we are when we run (cf. the manner verbs of group B, Table 3).

Table 5 provides an excerpt of all the verbs that are unavailable for telic usage:

Table 5. Unavailable verbs for telic usage

Rank	Verbs	LCC	All uses	Telic usage	Telicity ratio (%)	FET-value-*p*	Log^{10}-trans
112	*ambular* 'to wander about'	M	9	0	0	1	0
136	*cojear* 'to limp'	M	22	0	0	1	0
138	*pedalear* 'to pedal'	M	24	0	0	1	0
159	*gatear* 'to crawl, to climb like a cat'	M	39	0	0	1	0
168	*reptar* 'to crawl or to move like a reptile'	M	51	0	0	1	0
171	*remar* 'to row, to paddle'	M	53	0	0	1	0
176	*esquiar* 'to ski'	M	58	0	0	1	0
179	*empinar(se)* 'to stand up'	M	63	0	0	1	0
182	*trotar* '(of a person) to trot, to ride a trotting horse'	M	66	0	0	1	0
195	*corretear* 'to run about'	M	79	0	0	1	0
201	*distanciar(se)* 'to move away from'	P	99	0	0	1	0
202	*cabalgar* 'to ride a horse'	M	101	0	0	1	0
204	*enderezar(se)* 'to become straight'	M	120	0	0	1	0
205	*galopar* 'to gallop, to ride a galloping horse'	M	123	0	0	1	0
208	*deambular* 'to walk around'	M	127	0	0	1	0
210	*balancear(se)* 'to swing'	M	152	0	0	1	0
212	*aterrizar* 'to land'	P-G	160	0	0	1	0
216	*vagar* 'to wander'	M	186	0	0	1	0
218	*desfilar* 'to parade, to walk in file'	M	191	0	0	1	0
219	*despegar* 'to take off'	P-G	194	0	0	1	0
222	*dispersar(se)* 'to disperse'	P	241	0	0	1	0
235	*acelerar* 'to speed up, to accelerate'	M	473	0	0	1	0
241	*derivar* 'to drift'	M	890	0	0	1	0
245	*alzar(se)* 'to rise'	P-M	990	0	0	1	0
247	*bailar* 'to dance'	M	1283	0	0	1	0

Table 6 summarizes the results. The relative thickness of the lines separates higher verb ranking from lower verb ranking and, correspondingly, more availability from less availability:

Table 6. Summarized results

Group	Rank	Verbs	LCC	All uses	Telic usage	Telicity ratio (%)	FET-value-p	Log^{10}-trans
A	7	*llegar* 'to arrive'	P	19639	3439	17.51	→0	→infinite
	8	*acercar(se)* 'to move closer to'	P	4229	721	17.05	→0	→infinite
B	23	*correr* 'to run'	M	3912	150	3.83	4.57e-63	62.34
	31	*volar* 'to move through the air, to fly'	M-G	995	46	4.62	9.30e-24	23.03
C	54	*caminar* 'to walk'	M	2347	21	0.894759	0.12	0.93632
	86	*andar* 'to walk'	M	3330	10	0.3003	0.998791	0.00053
D	92	*avanzar* 'to move forwards'	P	2265	2	0.0883	0.999996	1.70e-6
	93	*alejar(se)* 'to move far away from'	P	1774	1	0.0563	1	0
E	201	*distanciar(se)* 'to move away from'	P	99	0	0	1	0
	212	*aterrizar* 'to land'	P-G	160	0	0	1	0
F	216	*vagar* 'to wander'	M	186	0	0	1	0
	247	*bailar* 'to dance'	M	1283	0	0	1	0

In sum, this study has identified and analyzed the following groups of variation with respect to motion verbs in telic usage:

Group A: The prototype – path (endpoint) verbs
Group B: Available manner verbs
Group C: Excludable manner verbs
Group D: Excludable path verbs

Group E: Unavailable path verbs
Group F: Unavailable manner verbs

The semantic analyses of the verb groups A–F in Section 5.4 suggest that the Spanish construction of telic motion is highly constrained by the semantics of the verbal lexeme. When comparing the Examples (7)–(12) with (13) and groups A–E with the large verb group F, it becomes clear that as a minimum condition, a lexical element of associated directionality is required. The verbs in group F have no such element. Furthermore, as evidenced by the excludable/unavailable verbs in the C–E groups, which all have an associated element of directionality, the lexical implication of directionality is necessary but not sufficient. This is so because other elements of verb semantics evidently play a role as well, as discussed in Section 5.4.

Moreover, in the (unavailable) expressions of telic motion with manner verbs (the available B-, the excludable C-, and the unavailable F-group), verbal constraints impose conditions for both the expression of path/telicity (some verbal element of directionality is a minimum condition, cf. F) and the expression of manner (the manner profile cannot be too salient in relation to the associated element of directionality, cf. C). In sum, the verb seems to be a principal constraining factor that has to license the use of the verb in the telic environment. Conversely, the translation of Example (13) (= group F) suggests that the corresponding English construction of telic motion is, first and foremost, constrained by the availability of a schematic argument structure construction of telic motion. In the verbal slot, this skeletal construction is filled relatively freely by a verb that only has to be semantically compatible (cf. Goldberg, 1995): *Pedro danced to the toilet.*

6. Theoretical discussion – Spanish as a verb-framing language

From the usage-based perspective adopted in this article, this situation of substantial and diverse inter- and intra-linguistic variation that conflicts with the prevailing typological assumptions exposes a theoretical weakness of the Talmian research tradition in addition to the methodological challenges. Some fundamental theoretical aspects need to be reconsidered. We have to address the question of whether framing events (= main events) such as 'path of motion', should be considered typological universals. In Talmy's later work (Talmy, 1991, 2000), the main event (ME), e.g., the 'path of motion', is assumed to be a universal framing event with the status of *tertium comparationis* in the typology. From a usage-based perspective, this is a problematic assumption that may not correspond to psychological reality since, according to this view, grammar is structured on the basis of generalizations about usage (e.g., Barlow, 2011; Barlow & Kemmer, 2000; Goldberg, 2006; Langacker, 1987, 1988). It is clear that 'path of motion' is a conceptual universal, and the expression of the path component is, undoubtedly, an essential semantic component that divides the languages into different groups. This is clearly confirmed for the telic motion construction by the Spanish data on this construction in the present study (see Table 1). However, there may be fundamental principles behind these groupings that more adequately – and with deeper insight – capture the cross-linguistic differences and the intra-linguistic variation. For instance, expressions of directional motion cannot always be described successfully in terms of a formal (verb or satellite) mapping on to the 'path of motion' event or another framing event. In fact, in his analysis of (14), Talmy states that the main (framing) event (ME) is the transitive motion event ('X moved Y into Z') and that the supportive co-event (CE) is the causal event ('X kicked Y'):

(14) I kicked the ball into the box   (Talmy, 2000, II, p. 228)
      CE   ME??

However, Talmy's typological model does not work in this case. In accordance with his framework in which English is a satellite-framed language, the framing (main) event (ME), 'I moved the ball into the box', is mapped onto the satellite *into*. To argue that the transitive causal element 'X caused Y to move Z' should be part of the meaning of *into* is implausible. This point is complementary to the one made by Goldberg (1995) in her analysis of the caused motion construction (e.g., *he sneezed the napkin off the table*) in which she claims that the verb meaning cannot account for the basic (caused motion) meaning of the construction. I suggest that, if a generalized typology, as the Talmian typology claims to be, is to account for English expressions of directional motion, the *typological units* must be *constructional units* – including lexical and schematic constructions (Pedersen, 2009a). In such an analysis, the framing event (ME), 'I moved the ball into the box', is mapped onto the schematic form of the caused motion construction ([SUBJ V OBJ OBL]); and the supportive co-event (CE) (= the causal event 'X kicked Y') is mapped onto the verbal lexeme construction ([--Kick--]).

Typological distinctions based on constructional units are often understood as a question of whether specific construction types exist, or do not exist, in one or another language – though generalizations can be made. According to Morimoto (2008), for instance, the alleged ungrammaticality in Spanish of the expression type in (15) is due to the absence of this construction type in Spanish:[17]

(15) *Pedro camin-ó   a   la   biblioteca   (Morimoto, 2008: 288)
       Pedro walk-PST.3SG   to   the library
       'Pedro walked to the library'

Nevertheless, we have seen that not only characteristic Spanish expressions of directed motion, such as (16):

(16) Pedro fue   a   la   biblioteca (camin-ando)
       Pedro move.PST.3SG   to   the library   (walk-GERUND)
       'Pedro walked to the library'

---

17. Morimoto's analysis is based on Aske (1989). According to Aske, the inability of Spanish to express the path of motion in a satellite and the manner in the verb is limited to telic motion events. He argues that secondary predicates (i.e., complex predicates) are not allowed in Spanish.

but also the "Germanic type" – cf. (15) – are substantially attested in the data (see Section 5.4) and mentioned in the literature (see Section 2). That is, examples like (17) in which *correr* is an atelic manner of motion verb are perfectly acceptable in the right context, even though they clearly implicate a goal-directed telic action. Moreover, this usage is relatively frequent:

(17) Corr-ió   a-l   lavabo   (Pedersen, 2013:260)
     run-PST.3SG   to-DET toilet
     'he ran to the toilet'

Thus, the corpus data highlight several difficulties or challenges. First, general statements about the availability of specific expression types such as 'this construction type is not available in language X' may not be conclusive – and are often refutable by means of corpus data (see, e.g., *caminar* 'to walk' in the telic motion construction – cf. Example (15)). Second, there is a somewhat converse risk that we will end up with what we may characterize as extensive amounts of unqualified variation, that is, endless lists of expression types in each language at a very detailed level. The mere observation that an unexpected linguistic phenomenon may still be considered as available in language X when the corpus from which the data has been extracted is big enough may be an unsatisfying insight. In the present study, it has been my intention to try to avoid or, at least, minimize this latter potential flaw in the corpus analysis by qualifying the observed variation: *caminar* 'to walk' and *correr* 'to run' in the telic motion construction represent 'excludable variation' and 'available variation', respectively.

In addition, we should not restrict ourselves to a mere focus on the (un)availability of, for instance, telic expressions in combination with manner of motion verbs. This quantitative study has confirmed the hypothesis suggested in previous studies: only Spanish motion verbs that lexicalize an element of associated directionality may license the construction of telic motion (Pedersen, 2013, 2014; see also Son, 2007). Thus, the constraining role of the Spanish verb lexeme is essential in the construction of telic motion. Conversely, the characteristic role of the schematic construction in English argument structure constructions, including the construction of directional motion, is well-described in some constructionist frameworks (e.g., Goldberg, 1995).

The combination of these insights suggests that the typological differences between English and Spanish expressions of directional motion may be anchored in the role of schematicity as opposed to the constraining role of the verbal lexeme. This is an attractive approach to the typological theory – particularly, because similar patterns in other types of argument structure/semantic domains can be observed (see Pedersen, 2013, and the following Examples (18)–(30)). In the English *way* construction, for instance, none of the lexical items have *per se* a central, organizing role in the encoding of the basic meaning, which is: 'the subject moves somewhere (with difficulty) by creating a path' (e.g., Goldberg, 1995; Jackendoff, 1990). Specifically, the basic meaning is not predictable from the verb meaning *fought*. Instead, a schematic form, a *way* construction, carries its own characteristic meaning, while the verb *fought* specifies the means of carrying out this motion event:

(18) [Peter [fought] his way out of the restaurant]   (Pedersen, 2013:242)
[SUBJi V POSSi *way* OBL] / 'X moving Y by creating a path'
[fought] / 'specification of means'

In Spanish versions of the *way* construction, the basic meaning of 'creating a path' is always predictable and, therefore, projectable from the inherent meaning of the verb – e.g., *abrirse camino para salir…* 'open for himself a way in order to move somewhere':

(19) Pedro se   [abr-ió]   camino ([a codazos])   (Pedersen, 2013:242)
Pedro DAT open-PST.3SG way   (by using elbows)
[SUBJ, DAT, abrir, OBJ] / 'X creates path to move…'
[Adverbial construction] / 'means of motion'

Specifying information about the means of motion may be added as an adverbial construction (*a codazos*). Thus, the Spanish version of the *way* construction, when it comes to how the core argument structure and the specifying information are organized, seems to differ systematically from the English version.

The core meaning of the English ditransitive construction involves transfer between a volitional agent and a willing recipient (Goldberg, 1995):

(20) She gave him a cake (prototype)

(21) Le   dio   una torta
DAT give.PST.3SG a   cake

As we can see in Example (21), Spanish has comparable expressions. However, in prototypical expressions, as in (20)–(21), there are no indications whether the transfer meaning is provided by means of lexical government[18] or in a schematic argument structure construction with transfer meaning, elaborated by the lexical specification. "The confusion" is due to the fact that the transfer meaning of the clause is perfectly attributable to the basic meaning of the trivalent verb both in English and Spanish: 'to give something to someone'. Atypical examples,

---

18. The notion *lexical government* refers to what has been termed *the lexical approach* (see, e.g., Grimshaw, 1990; Levin & Rappaport Hovav, 1995; Pinker, 1989) but also to the compositional principles in cognitive grammar. It refers to encoding devices based on principles of lexical (verbal) projection, subcategorization, and conceptual valence structure with a lexical profile determinant (Langacker, 1987).

conversely, such as (22), taken from Goldberg (1995), indicate that the transfer meaning must be provided by an independent ditransitive argument structure construction and that the activity of baking is specified by the verb. Thus, the main argument for the role of schematicity is that the transfer meaning cannot plausibly be part of the lexical meaning of *bake*:

(22) She baked him a cake   (Goldberg, 1995)

However, in this case, Spanish cannot match the English ditransitive. Spanish has clausal patterns that are similar to the ditransitive, as exemplified in (21), though not in combination with verbs that do not predict the characteristic transfer meaning (Martínez Vázquez, 2003; Pedersen, 2009b).

The same line of argument applies for the resultative argument structure:

(23) He kissed her unconscious   (Goldberg, 1995)

(24) *La   bes-ó   inconsciente
     ACC   kiss-PST.3SG   unconscious
     'her he kissed unconscious'

(25) La   desmay-ó   con   un   beso
     ACC   faint-PST.3SG with   a   kiss
     'her he fainted with a kiss'

Again, Spanish does not allow any expression that is parallel to the English resultative, see (23)–(24), unless the basic resultative meaning is predictable from the verb, as in (25).

In prototypical communicative expressions, such as (26) and (27), there is no indication of whether the communicative argument structure is projected by the verb or whether it is organized in a schematic argument structure construction and specified by the verb. The reason is that the verb meaning overlaps with the overall clausal communicative meaning:

(26) He said yes

(27) Dijo   que   sí
     say.PST.3SG   that   yes

However, expressions with mismatch between the clausal communicative meaning and the verb meaning, such as (28), indicate that the communicative argument structure is not projected by the verb. Instead, it may be the case that the communicative argument structure is organized in a schematic construction and that the communicative act is elaborated by the verb:

(28) He nodded yes

The rationale is in this case that the meaning of communicating something, arguably, is not part of the lexical meaning of nodding. This kind of mismatch between the semantics of the verb and the communicative meaning is very productive in English, as opposed to Spanish, which only allows them sporadically (Martínez Vázquez, 2003):

(29) *Cabece-ó   un   sí
     nodd-PST.3SG   a   yes

Instead, an expression type in which the communicative argument structure is projected by the verb would be a typical Spanish version of (28):

(30) Asint-ió   con   la   cabeza
     consent-PST.3SG   with   the   head
     'he consented with his head'

To sum up, this study gives another perspective on the typological issues. I have suggested a quantitative methodology that allows us to categorize and qualify the variation, distinguishing significant from less significant variation. In particular, this approach offers an improved usage-based understanding of the role of the Spanish motion verb in a specific constructional environment. I have argued that, in Spanish (in general), the constraining role of the verb is essential, while the role of the schematic argument structure construction is different and not predominant as Goldberg (1995, 2006) argues it is in English (cf. the discussion in this section). Based on the corpus data on the construction of telic motion and supported by evidence from other domains of argument structure, I suggest a typological characterization of Spanish that is centered in this cross-linguistic difference.

Importantly, this is not merely a matter of differences between English argument structure and Spanish argument structure. In many typologically-related languages, the verbs are much more restrictive than they are in English in the sense that they only appear in syntactic environments that match their meanings (Goldberg, 2006). Other Romance languages seem to behave like Spanish in this respect – the French version of the *way* construction, for instance, is very similar to the Spanish version with respect to its verbal projection of the argument structure (Pedersen, 2013) – and, importantly, so do non- or less-related languages such as Turkish and Hindi (Narasimhan, 2003). Based on the observation that there are fundamental constraints on Spanish argument structure (highly verb constrained) that we do not find in English argument structure, we may hypothesize that, instead of mapping form and universal meaning components (the Talmian tradition), emphasis should be on the role of *schematic construction* versus *lexical construction*, as the fundamental typological parameter.

In a general perspective, this study suggests that cross-linguistic analyses of the lexicon-construction associations in languages X versus Y may contribute to uncovering the relative importance of the major driving forces in the encoding of argument structure: lexical projection of / constraints on argument structure versus schematic argument structure construction. The data presented supports what I have previously suggested for a broader range of semantic domains (Pedersen, 2013): the encoding of Spanish argument structure seems to be basically verb-driven (as opposed to construction-driven). A characterization of Spanish argument structure as verb-driven is not the same as categorizing Spanish as a verb-framed language in the Talmian research tradition. In the latter descriptive typology, the notion verb-framed refers to the lexical mapping of the verb onto the path of motion or, in general terms, onto a universal framing event. Verb-driven refers to lexical organization and constraints on argument structure as an encoding strategy. In that sense, it suggests a different version of Talmy's characterization of Spanish that has a more far-reaching explanatory potential: Spanish is a *verb-framing* language. This characterization of Spanish explains the variation observed in this study, which diverges from the classic patterns originating in the Talmian tradition.

7. Conclusion and perspectives

In this article, I have analyzed the use of Spanish motion verbs in a constructional environment of telic motion on the basis of large amounts of corpus data. The observed patterns of typological variation have been qualified in terms of verb association with the constructional environment. Six groups of motion verbs have been identified and discussed with respect to their telic usage:

Group A: Prototypical verbs in telic usage
Group B: Available manner verbs in telic usage
Group C: Excludable manner verbs in telic usage
Group D: Excludable path verbs in telic usage
Group E: Unavailable path verbs in telic usage
Group F: Unavailable manner verbs in telic usage

In future research, the constructional environment may be extended to include directional motion in general and not only telic motion. Typological variation can also be measured in other slots of the constructional environment – e.g., the slot of the goal/direction marker. Or the constructional environment may be another semantic domain of argument structure. In general, current proposals of all kinds of typological features can be quantitatively evaluated and typological prototypes and variation may be identified on the basis of measurements of lexical or morphological association with well-defined constructional environments. Importantly, typological variation in other languages can be assessed in exactly the same way. In sum, this study opens up for a whole array of quantitative and innovative typological research.

The assessment of typological patterns of lexicalization in specific constructional environments, as opposed to the usual universal approach, also has limitations. The results of one single study have a limited scope since, in principle, they are only valid for the defined constructional environment. The study has to be complemented by studies in other constructional environments. As a consequence, this kind of usage-based study of typological patterns is by its nature extremely time-consuming.

Cross-linguistic analyses of lexeme-construction associations may lead to a better understanding of the driving forces in the encoding of argument structure. Based on evidence from a broad range of semantic domains and the data on telic motion presented in this paper, I have argued that the encoding of Spanish argument structure seems to be basically verb-driven. Moreover, I have argued that this is not so in Germanic languages, such as English, in which construction-driven encoding of argument structure, according to some CxG grammarians, is fundamental (e.g., Goldberg, 1995, 2006).

The constructionist focus in this article has moved away from the ongoing discussion of what counts as a construction in a theoretical sense. Instead, it is directed to the question of *how* lexemes and schematicity play a role in the organization of argument structure in different languages. I do certainly not claim that the formation of schematic argument structure constructions is not applicable to Spanish. We may hypothesize that schematic argument structure constructions have a different, elaborative role in Spanish when compared to the prominent role they are assigned in Goldberg's work.[19]

I suggest that there should be more emphasis in future studies on the role of schematicity versus lexical constraints as a fundamental typological parameter. This would enable us to make more insightful typological distinctions on the basis of the relative importance of schematic and lexical constraints on the organization of argument structure. From this perspective, we would characterize Spanish as a verb-framing language rather than a verb-framed language (cf. Talmy, 2000). A characterization of Spanish as a verb-framing language would predict the kind of inter- and intra-linguistic variation observed in this study.

---

19. For more details, see Pedersen (2014).

References

Aske, J. (1989). Path predicates in English and Spanish: A closer look. In K. Hall, M. Meacham, & R. Shapiro (Eds.), *Proceedings of the fifteenth annual meeting of the berkeley linguistics society* (pp. 1–14). Berkeley: Berkeley Linguistics Society.

Barlow, M. (2011). Corpus linguistics and theoretical linguistics. *International Journal of Corpus Linguistics*, 16(1), 3–43. doi: 10.1075/ijcl.16.1.02bar

Barlow, M., & Kemmer, S. (Eds.) (2000). *Usage based models of language*. Stanford: CSLI Publications.

Beavers, J., Levin, B., & Shiao Wei, T. (2010). The typology of motion expressions revisited. *Journal of Linguistics*, 46(3), 1–58. doi: 10.1017/S0022226709990272

Berman, R. A., & Slobin, D. I. (1994). *Relating events in narrative: A crosslinguistic developmental study*. Hillsdale, NJ: Erlbaum.

Boas, H. C. (2003). *A constructional approach to resultatives*. Stanford: CSLI Publications.

Boas, H. C. (2010). The syntax–lexicon continuum in construction grammar. A case study of English communication verbs. *Belgian journal of linguistics*, 24(1), 54–82. doi: 10.1075/bjl.24.03boa

Bybee, J. (1985). *Morphology: A study of the relation between meaning and form*. Amsterdam: John Benjamins. doi: 10.1075/tsl.9

Bybee, J. (2006). From usage to grammar: The minds response to repetition. *Language*, 82(4), 711–733. doi: 10.1353/lan.2006.0186

Bybee, J. (2007). *Frequency of use and the organization of language*. Oxford: Oxford University Press. doi: 10.1093/acprof:oso/9780195301571.001.0001

Cifuentes Ferez, P. (2010). The semantics of the English and the Spanish motion verb lexicons. *Review of Cognitive Linguistics*, 8(2), 233–271. doi: 10.1075/rcl.8.2.01cif

Davies, M. (2002). Corpus del Español. Http://www.corpusdelespanol.org

Croft, W. (2001). *Radical construction grammar*. Oxford: Oxford University Press. doi: 10.1093/acprof:oso/9780198299554.001.0001

Croft, W., Barddal, J., Hollmann, W., Sotirova, V., & Taoka, C. (2010). Revising talmy's typological classification of complex event constructions. In H. C. Boas (Ed.), *Contrastive construction grammar* (pp. 201–35). Amsterdam: John Benjamins. doi: 10.1075/cal.10.09cro

Fanego, T. (2012). Motion events in English: The emergence and diachrony of manner salience from old English to late modern English. *Folia linguistica historica*, 33, 29–85.

Gennari, S. P., Sloman, S. A., Malt, B. C., & Fitch, W. T. (2002). Motion events in language and cognition. *Cognition*, 83, 49–79. doi: 10.1016/S0010-0277(01)00166-4

Goldberg, A. E. (1995). *Constructions. A construction grammar approach to argument structure*. Chicago: University of Chicago Press.

Goldberg, A. E. (2006). *Constructions at work. The nature of generalization in language*. Oxford: Oxford University Press.

Goldberg, A. E., & Jackendoff, R. (2004). The English resultative as a family of constructions. *Language*, 80, 532–568. doi: 10.1353/lan.2004.0129

Gries, S. Th. (2010). Corpus linguistics and theoretical linguistics. *A love–hate relationship? Not necessarily... International Journal of Corpus Linguistics*, 15(3), 327–343. doi: 10.1075/ijcl.15.3.02gri

Gries, S. Th. (2012). Frequencies, probabilities, association measures in usage-/exemplar-based linguistics: Some necessary clarifications. *Studies in Language*, 36(3), 477–510. doi: 10.1075/sl.36.3.02gri

Grimshaw, J. (1990). *Argument structure*. Cambridge, MA: MIT Press.
Ibarretxe-Antuñano, I. (2003). Entering in Spanish: Conceptual and semantic properties of *entrar en/a*. *Annual Review of Cognitive Linguistics*, 1, 29–59. doi: 10.1075/arcl.1.03iba
Ibarretxe-Antuñano, I. (2004a). Language typologies in our language use: The case of Basque motion events in adult oral narratives. *Cognitive Linguistics*, 15(3), 317–349. doi: 10.1515/cogl.2004.012
Ibarretxe-Antuñano, I. (2004b). Motion events in Basque narratives. In S. Strömqvist & L. Verhoeven (Eds.), *Relating events in narrative: Typological and contextual perspectives* (pp. 89–111). New Jersey: Lawrence Erlbaum.
Ibarretxe-Antuñano, I. (2009). Path salience in motion events. In J. Guo, E. Lieven, N. Budwig, S. Ervin-Tripp, K. Nakamura, & S. Özçalişkan (Eds.), *Crosslinguistic approaches to the psychology of language: Research in the tradition of Dan Isaac Slobin* (pp. 403–414). New York: Psychology Press.
Jackendoff, R. (1990). *Semantic structures*. Cambridge, MA: MIT Press.
Jackendoff, R. (1997). *The architecture of the language faculty*. Cambridge, MA: MIT Press.
Langacker, R. W. (1987). *Foundations of cognitive grammar*, Vol. I. Stanford, CA: Stanford University Press.
Langacker, R. W. (1988). A usage-based model. In B. Rudzka-Ostyn (Ed.), *Topics in cognitive linguistics* (pp. 127–161). Amsterdam: John Benjamins. doi: 10.1075/cilt.50.06lan
Levin, B., & Rappaport Hovav, M. (1995). *Unaccusativity: At the syntax-lexical semantics interface*. Cambridge, MA: MIT Press.
Masini, F. (2005). Multi-word expressions between syntax and the lexicon: The case of Italian verb-particle constructions. *SKY Journal of Linguistics*, 18, 145–173.
Masini, F. (2008). Verbi sintagmatici e ordine delle parole. In M. Cini (Ed.), *I verbi sintagmatici in italiano e nelle varietà dialettali. Stato dell'arte e prospettive di ricerca*. (Spazi comunicativi – Kommunikative Räume, Vol. 3) (pp. 83–102). Frankfurt am Main: Peter Lang.
Martínez Vázquez, M. (2001). Delimited events in English and Spanish. *Estudios Ingleses de la Universidad Complutense*, 9, 31–59.
Martínez Vázquez, M. (Ed.). (2003). *Gramática de Construcciones. Contrastes entre el inglés y el español*. Universidad de Huelva.
Mateu Fontanals, J. (2000). Path and telicity in idiomatic constructions. A lexical-syntactic approach to the Way-construction. Paper presented at the *2000 ESSLLI Workshop on Paths and Telicity in Event Structure*. University of Birmingham.
Mateu Fontanals, J., & Rigau, G. (2002). A minimalist account of conflation processes: Parametric variation at the lexicon-syntax interface. In D. A. Alexiadou (Ed.), *Theoretical approaches to universals* (pp. 211–236). Amsterdam: John Benjamins. doi: 10.1075/la.49.09mat
Morimoto, Y. (2008). Grammar of "manner of motion" verbs in English and Spanish: between lexicon and syntax. In N. Delbecque & B. Cornillie (Eds.), *Trends in linguistics, studies and monographs: On interpreting construction schemas: From action and motion to transitivity and causality* (pp. 287–305). Berlin: Mouton de Gruyter.
Narasimhan, B. (2003). Motion events and the lexicon: A case study of Hindi. *Lingua*, 113(2), 123–160. doi: 10.1016/S0024-3841(02)00068-2
Pedersen, J. (2009a). The construction of macro-events. A typological perspective. In C. Butler & J.M. Arista (Eds.), *Deconstructing constructions* (pp. 25–62). Amsterdam: John Benjamins. doi: 10.1075/slcs.107.04the

Pedersen, J. (2009b). Lexical and constructional organization of argument structure. A contrastive analysis. In J. Zlatev, M. Andrén, M. Johansson Falck, & C. Lundmark (Eds.), *Studies in language and cognition* (pp. 230–245). Cambridge: Cambridge Scholars Publishing.

Pedersen, J. (2013). The *way*-construction and cross-linguistic variation in syntax. Implications for typological theory. In C. Paradis, J. Hudson, & U. Magnusson (Eds.), *The construal of spatial meaning, windows into conceptual space* (pp. 236–262). Oxford: Oxford University Press. doi:10.1093/acprof:oso/9780199641635.003.0013

Pedersen, J. (2014). Variable type framing in Spanish constructions of directed motion. In H. C. Boas & F. G. García (Eds.), *Romance perspectives on construction grammar* (pp. 269–304). Amsterdam: John Benjamins. doi:10.1075/cal.15.08ped

Pinker, S. (1989). *Learnability and cognition: The acquisition of argument structure*. Cambridge, MA: MIT Press.

Simone, R. (1996). Esistono verbi sintagmatici in italiano? *Cuadernos de Filología Italiana*, 3, 47–61. Servicio de publicaciones UCM.

Slobin, D. I. (1996a). From 'thought and language' to 'thinking for speaking'. In J. J. Gumperz & S. C. Levinson (Eds.), *Rethinking linguistic relativity* (pp. 195–217). Cambridge: Cambridge University Press.

Slobin, D. I. (1996b). Two ways to travel: Verbs of motion in English and Spanish. In M. Shibatani & S. A. Thompson (Eds.), *Grammatical constructions: Their form and meaning* (pp. 195–219). Oxford: Oxford University Press.

Slobin, D. I. (1997). Mind, code, and text. In J. Bybee, J. Haiman, & S. A. Thompson (Eds.), *Essays on language function and language type: Dedicated to T. Givón* (pp. 437–467). Amsterdam: John Benjamins. doi:10.1075/z.82.24slo

Slobin, D. I. (1998). *Coding of motion events in narrative texts*. Departments of Psychology and Linguistics. University of California at Berkeley.

Slobin, D. I. (2000). Verbalized events: A dynamic approach to linguistic relativity and determinism. In S. Niemeier & R. Dirven (Eds.), *Evidence for linguistic relativity* (pp. 107–138). Berlin: Mouton de Gruyter. doi:10.1075/cilt.198.10slo

Slobin, D. I. (2004). The many ways to search for a frog. In S. Strömqvist & L. Verhoeven (Eds.), *Relating events in narrative. Typological and contextual perspectives* (pp. 219–257). Hillsdale, NJ: Lawrence Erlbaum.

Slobin, D. I. (2006). What makes manner of motion salient? Explorations in linguistic typology, discourse, and cognition. In M. Hickmann & S. Robert (Eds.), *Space in languages: Linguistic systems and cognitive categories* (pp. 59–81). Amsterdam: John Benjamins. doi:10.1075/tsl.66.05slo

Slobin, D. I. (2008). Relations between paths of motion and paths of vision: A crosslinguistic and developmental exploration. In V. C. Mueller-Gathercole (Ed.), *Routes to language: Studies in honor of Melissa Bowerman* (pp. 197–221). Manwah, NJ: Lawrence Erlbaum Associates.

Slobin, D. I., & Hoiting, N. (1994). Reference to movement in spoken and signed languages: typological considerations. In S. Gahl, A. Dolbey, & C. Johnson (Eds.), *Proceedings of the twentieth annual meeting of the Berkeley linguistic society* (pp. 487–505). Berkeley: Berkeley Linguistics Society.

Snyder, W. (2001). On the nature of syntactic variation: Evidence from complex predicates and complex word-formation. *Language*, 77(2), 324–342. doi:10.1353/lan.2001.0108

Son, M. (2007). Directionality and resultativity: The cross-linguistic correlation revisited. *Nordlyd: Tromsø Working Papers in Linguistics*, 34(2), 126–164. University of Tromsø, Tromsø, Norway. http://www.ub.uit.no/munin/nordlyd/.

Stefanowitsch, A., & Gries, S. Th. (2003). Collostructions: Investigating the interaction between words and constructions. *International Journal of Corpus Linguistics*, 8(2), 209–243. doi:10.1075/ijcl.8.2.03ste

Stefanowitsch, A., & Gries, S. Th. (2005). Covarying collexemes. *Corpus linguistics and linguistic theory*, 1(1), 1–43. doi:10.1515/cllt.2005.1.1.1

Talmy, L. (1985). Lexicalization patterns: Semantic structure in lexical forms. In T. Shopen (Ed.), *Language typology and syntactic description vol. 3: Grammatical categories and the lexicon* (pp. 57–149). Cambridge: Cambridge University Press.

Talmy, L. (1987). *Lexicalization patterns: Typologies and universals* (Berkeley Cognitive Science Report 47). Berkeley: Cognitive Science Program, University of California.

Talmy, L. (1991). Path to realization: A typology of event conflation. In L. A. Sutton, C. Johnson, & R. Shields (Eds.), *Proceedings of the seventeenth annual Berkeley linguistics society* (pp. 480–519). Berkeley: Berkeley Linguistics Society.

Talmy, L. (2000). *Toward a cognitive semantics*, Vol. 1–2. Cambridge, MA: MIT Press.

Tesnière, L. (1959). *Eléments de syntaxe structurale*. Paris: Klincksieck.

Tomasello, M. (2003). *Constructing a language. A usage-based theory of language acquisition*. Cambridge, MA: Harvard University Press.

Zlatev, J., & Yangklang, P. (2004). A third way to travel: The place of Thai (and other serial verb languages) in motion event typology. In S. Stromqvist & L. Verhoeven (Eds.), *Relating events in narrative: Typological and contextual perspectives* (pp. 159–190). New Jersey: Lawrence Erlbaum.

Appendix: Complete list of verb ranking

Rank	Verbs	LCC	All uses	Telic usage	Telicity ratio (%)	FET-value-p	Log^{10}-trans
1	*regresar* 'to come back'	P	2780	1251	45	→0	→infinite
2	*acudir* 'to go to a specific place'	P	1171	395	33.73	→0	→infinite
3	*viajar* 'to travel'	P-G	1832	512	27.95	→0	→infinite
4	*trasladar(se)* 'to move from one place to another'	P	1341	335	24.98	→0	→infinite
5	*entrar (a/en)* 'to enter'	P	6651	1512	22.73	→0	→infinite
6	*subir* 'to ascend, to go up'	P	3209	614	19.13	→0	→infinite
7	*llegar* 'to arrive'	P	19639	3439	17.51	→0	→infinite
8	*acercar(se)* 'to move closer to'	P	4229	721	17.05	→0	→infinite
9	*ir(se)* 'to go, to go away'	P	56430	4936	8.75	→0	→infinite
10	*volver* 'to come back, to change direction'	P	12984	1125	8.66	→0	→infinite
11	*salir* 'to exit'	P	12402	920	7.42	→0	→infinite

Rank	Verbs	LCC	All uses	Telic usage	Telicity ratio (%)	FET-value-p	$\log^{10}$-trans
12	*venir* 'to come'	P	12290	658	5.35	→0	→infinite
13	*dirigir(se)* 'to head to'	P	4850	369	7.61	3.83e-252	251.42
14	*emigrar* 'to emigrate'	P-G	350	141	40.29	5.53e-207	206.26
15	*arribar* '(of a ship) to reach port, to arrive'	P	222	107	48.20	2.56e-168	167.59
16	*marchar(se)* 'to go, to go away, to march'	P	1149	169	14.71	2.28e-164	163.64
17	*retornar* 'to return, to go back'	P	450	126	28	2.89e-161	160.54
18	*aproximar(se)* 'to move closer to'	P	491	124	25.25	2.03e-152	151.69
19	*caer(se)* 'to fall down'	P	5675	253	4.46	1.74e-119	118.76
20	*bajar* 'to go down'	P	2589	142	5.48	3.46e-79	78.46
21	*mudar(se)* 'to go from one place to another'	P	260	61	23.46	2.43e-75	74.62
22	*sentar(se)* 'to sit down'	P-M	5898	185	3.14	4.79e-64	63.32
23	*correr* 'to run'	M	3912	150	3.83	4.57e-63	62.34
24	*huir* 'to flee'	P-M	1129	88	7.79	2.89e-62	61.54
25	*retirar(se)* 'to retreat'	P	1898	108	5.69	3.23e-62	61.49
26	*arrimar(se)* 'to move closer to'	P	151	45	29.80	4.37e-60	59.36
27	*acceder* 'to gain access into'	P	744	63	8.47	3.00e-47	46.52
28	*pasar* 'to pass, to go through, over, along, beyond'	P	21593	306	1.42	3.61e-32	31.44
29	*saltar* 'to jump'	M	1233	58	4.70	6.62e-30	29.18
30	*penetrar* 'to enter'	P	771	43	5.58	1.85e-25	24.73
31	*volar* 'to move through the air, to fly'	M-G	995	46	4.62	9.30e-24	23.03
32	*lanzar(se)* 'to throw oneself, to pounce on something/somebody'	M	2548	66	2.59	1.17e-19	18.93
33	*ascender* 'to ascend'	P	760	34	4.47	1.48e-17	16.83
34	*tirar(se)* 'to throw oneself'	M	2017	62	3.07	7.51e-16	15.12
35	*arrojar(se)* 'to throw oneself'	M	824	33	4.00	1.04e-15	14.98
36	*precipitar(se)* 'to fall down from a high place, to run, to hurry to'	P-M	323	21	6.50	1.57e-14	13.80
37	*escapar(se)* 'to escape'	P-M	1698	41	2.41	6.93e-12	11.16
38	*descender* 'to go down'	P	987	27	2.74	1.82e-9	8.74
39	*afluir* 'to flow in/into/to/toward'	P-M	11	4	36.36	6.39e-7	6.19
40	*encaramar(se)* 'to move up to the top of'	P	107	7	6.54	8.77e-6	5.06
41	*abalanzar(se)* 'to rush toward'	P-M	72	6	8.33	9.65e-6	5.02
42	*trepar* 'to climb'	P-M	271	10	3.69	1.85e-5	4.73
43	*larger(se)* 'to leave'	P	205	8	3.90	8.48e-5	4.07
44	*acostar(se)* 'to lie down'	P-M	704	15	2.13	1.13e-4	3.95
45	*partir* 'to leave'	P	5509	58	1.05	7.51e-4	3.12
46	*echar(se)* 'to lie down, to move towards'	P-M	2788	34	1.22	8.67e-4	3.06
47	*rodar* 'to roll'	M	38	3	7.89	2.13e-3	2.67

Chapter 5. Spanish constructions of directed motion – a quantitative study   139

Rank	Verbs	LCC	All uses	Telic usage	Telicity ratio (%)	FET-value-p	Log^{10}-trans
48	*refluir* 'to flow (back)'	P-M	3	1	33.33	0.02	1.70
49	*cruzar* 'to cross'	P	1984	20	1.008	0.05	1.30
50	*fluir* 'to flow'	M	502	7	1.39	0.05	1.26
51	*surtir* 'to gush/spurt out'	P-M	63	2	3.17	0.07	1.17
52	*recostar(se)* 'to lean or to lie down'	P-M	251	4	1.59	0.09	1.05
53	*retroceder* 'to go back'	P	372	5	1.34	0.11	0.97
54	*caminar* 'to walk'	M	2347	21	0.89	0.12	0.94
55	*acurrucar(se)* 'to curl up'	M	19	1	5.26	0.12	0.92
56	*confluir* 'to merge (flows, streams)'	P-M	89	2	2.25	0.12	0.92
57	*encumbrar* 'to reach the top of'	P	23	1	4.35	0.14	0.84
58	*tender(se)* 'to stretch, to lie down'	M	1387	13	0.93	0.15	0.84
59	*navegar* 'to navigate'	M	340	4	1.18	0.20	0.71
60	*embarcar(se)* 'to go on board'	P-G	257	3	1.17	0.25	0.61
61	*revolcar(se)* 'to wallow'	M	50	1	2	0.29	0.54
62	*exiliar(se)* 'to exile'	P-G	284	3	1.06	0.30	0.53
63	*atracar* '(of a ship) to reach port'	P	53	1	1.89	0.30	0.52
64	*desviar(se)* 'to divert'	P	423	4	0.95	0.32	0.50
65	*desertar* 'to desert'	P	64	1	1.56	0.35	0.45
66	*virar* '(of a ship) to swerve'	P	67	1	1.49	0.36	0.44
67	*deslizar(se)* 'to slide'	M	462	4	0.87	0.37	0.43
68	*brincar* 'to jump'	M	96	1	1.04	0.48	0.32
69	*remontar* 'to go up'	P	392	3	0.77	0.49	0.31
70	*esparcir(se)* 'to move in different directions'	P	132	1	0.76	0.59	0.23
71	*desplomar(se)* 'to collapse'	P	137	1	0.73	0.60	0.22
72	*adentrar(se)* 'to go into the interior part of'	P	146	1	0.68	0.63	0.20
73	*inclinar(se)* 'to incline'	M	883	5	0.57	0.70	0.15
74	*pasear* 'to walk for pleasure'	M	764	4	0.52	0.75	0.12
75	*transitar* 'to go along a place or way'	G	231	1	0.43	0.79	0.10
76	*elevar(se)* 'to move upwards'	P	1532	8	0.52	0.80	0.10
77	*apresurar(se)* 'to hurry up'	M	274	1	0.36	0.84	0.08
78	*resbalar(se)* 'to slide'	M	285	1	0.35	0.85	0.07
79	*montar(se)* 'get on/onto an animal or into a vehicle, to ride (on horseback)'	M	1353	6	0.44	0.89	0.05
80	*adelantar(se)* 'to move forwards'	P	779	3	0.39	0.89	0.05
81	*sumergir(se)* 'to dive, submerge'	P-M	364	1	0.27	0.91	0.04
82	*posar(se)* 'to alight, land'	P-M	390	1	0.26	0.93	0.03
83	*oscilar* 'to oscillate, to swing'	M	466	1	0.21	0.96	0.02
84	*pisar* 'to tread'	M-F	526	1	0.19	0.97	0.01

Rank	Verbs	LCC	All uses	Telic usage	Telicity ratio (%)	FET-value-p	Log^{10}-trans
85	*flotar* 'to float or to move smoothly'	M	883	1	0.11	0.997	0.001
86	*andar* 'to walk'	M	3330	10	0.30	0.999	0.001
87	*apartar(se)* 'to move away from'	P	1023	1	0.10	0.999	0.0005
88	*extender(se)* 'to stretch',	M	2917	7	0.24	0.99966	0.0002
89	*girar* 'to rotate/spin, to turn, change direction'	M	1233	1	0.08	0.99975	0.0001
90	*mover(se)* 'to move oneself'	–	2986	7	0.23	0.99975	0.0001
91	*arrastar(se)* 'to drag oneself'	M	1265	1	0.08	0.99980	8.8e-05
92	*avanzar* 'to move forwards'	P	2265	2	0.09	0.999996	1.7e-06
93	*alejar(se)* 'to move far away from'	P	1774	1	0.06	1	0
94	*conducir* 'to drive'	M	1899	1	0.05	1	0
95	*alcanzar* 'to reach'	P	5342	10	0.19	1	0
96	*seguir* 'to follow'	P	15308	14	0.09	1	0
97	*levantar(se)* 'to stand up, to raise'	P-M	3896	3	0.08	1	0
98	*cocear* '(of a horse, donkey) to kick'	M-F	1	0	0	1	0
99	*bandear(se)* 'to swing'	M	3	0	0	1	0
100	*desbarrar* 'to slip'	M	3	0	0	1	0
101	*despeñar(se)* 'to fall down from a rock'	P-G	3	0	0	1	0
102	*contonear(se)* 'to swagger'	M	4	0	0	1	0
103	*desembarcar* 'to disembark'	P-G	4	0	0	1	0
104	*jinetear* 'to ride a horse'	M	4	0	0	1	0
105	*caracolear* 'to turn around'	M	5	0	0	1	0
106	*vaguear* 'to roam/wander'	M	5	0	0	1	0
107	*expatriar* 'to exile'	P-G	6	0	0	1	0
108	*callejear* 'to walk around the streets'	M-G	7	0	0	1	0
109	*hormiguear* 'to swarm'	M	7	0	0	1	0
110	*tremolar* 'to flutter'	M	7	0	0	1	0
111	*culebrear* 'to zigzag'	M	8	0	0	1	0
112	*ambular* 'to wander about'	M	9	0	0	1	0
113	*bogar* 'to row/sail'	M	9	0	0	1	0
114	*campanear* 'to swing'	M	9	0	0	1	0
115	*cimbrear(se)* 'to sway'	M	9	0	0	1	0
116	*piafar* 'to paw the ground, to stamp'	M	9	0	0	1	0
117	*pirar(se)* 'to go away (informal)'	P	9	0	0	1	0
118	*pavonear(se)* 'to strut about'	M	10	0	0	1	0
119	*agazapar(se)* 'to crouch'	M	12	0	0	1	0
120	*fondear* 'to move at the bottom of the sea'	G	12	0	0	1	0
121	*renquear* 'to limp'	M	12	0	0	1	0
122	*repatriar* 'to repatriate'	P-G	13	0	0	1	0
123	*boxear* 'to box'	M	15	0	0	1	0

Rank	Verbs	LCC	All uses	Telic usage	Telicity ratio (%)	FET-value-p	Log^{10}-trans
124	*bracear* 'to brace/wrestle'	M	15	0	0	1	0
125	*colear* '(of an animal) to move its tail, to wag'	F	16	0	0	1	0
126	*encabritar(se)* 'to rear up'	M	16	0	0	1	0
127	*taconear* 'to tap shoes with heels'	M	16	0	0	1	0
128	*traquetear* 'to move repeatedly'	M	16	0	0	1	0
129	*vadear* 'to wade, to ford a river'	P-M	18	0	0	1	0
130	*vagabundear* 'to wander'	M	19	0	0	1	0
131	*columpiar(se)* 'to swing'	M	20	0	0	1	0
132	*patrullar* 'to patrol'	M-C	20	0	0	1	0
133	*pilotar* 'to steer/drive/fly'	M	20	0	0	1	0
134	*arbolar* 'to rear (horse)/going steep (aircraft)'	M	21	0	0	1	0
135	*fugar(se)* 'to flee, to run away'	P-M	21	0	0	1	0
136	*cojear* 'to limp'	M	22	0	0	1	0
137	*escabullir(se)* 'to slip away'	P-M	22	0	0	1	0
138	*pedalear* 'to pedal'	M	24	0	0	1	0
139	*recular* 'to back/recoil/walk backwards/back'	P-M	24	0	0	1	0
140	*patinar* 'to skate'	M	25	0	0	1	0
141	*desandar* 'to walk back to a previous path'	P-M	28	0	0	1	0
142	*ladear(se)* 'to slant, to lean, to move away from, to move on the hillside'	M-G	28	0	0	1	0
143	*bambolear(se)* 'to swing/falter'	M	29	0	0	1	0
144	*trastabillar* 'to stumble/stagger'	M	31	0	0	1	0
145	*cejar* 'to back'	P-M	33	0	0	1	0
146	*bailotear*	M	34	0	0	1	0
147	*codear* 'to move your elbow, to nudge'	M-F	34	0	0	1	0
148	*maniobrar* 'to maneuver'	M	34	0	0	1	0
149	*pulular* 'to swarm'	M	35	0	0	1	0
150	*regatear* 'to dribble'	M	35	0	0	1	0
151	*serpentear* 'to slither, to meander'	M	35	0	0	1	0
152	*zambullir(se)* 'to go down into water in a violent way'	M-G-P	36	0	0	1	0
153	*chapotear* 'to move noisily in water/mud'	M-G	38	0	0	1	0
154	*divagar* 'to wander'	M	38	0	0	1	0
155	*retozar* 'to frolic'	M	38	0	0	1	0
156	*rezumar* 'to seep/ooze'	M	38	0	0	1	0
157	*aligerar* 'to hurry up'	M	39	0	0	1	0
158	*campear* 'to graze'	M-G	39	0	0	1	0
159	*gatear* 'to crawl, to climb like a cat'	M	39	0	0	1	0
160	*rotar* 'to rotate'	M	39	0	0	1	0

Rank	Verbs	LCC	All uses	Telic usage	Telicity ratio (%)	FET-value-p	Log^{10}-trans
161	*colisionar* 'to crash'	M-CR	43	0	0	1	0
162	*zarandear(se)* 'bustle about'	M	44	0	0	1	0
163	*bullir* 'to boil, to stir'	M	45	0	0	1	0
164	*bucear* 'to dive, swim down under water'	M-G	49	0	0	1	0
165	*embestir* 'to plunge'	M	49	0	0	1	0
166	*costear* 'to sail along the coast, to move along the edge of'	G	51	0	0	1	0
167	*patalear* 'to stamp one's feet to show anger'	M-F	51	0	0	1	0
168	*reptar* 'to crawl or to move like a reptile'	M	51	0	0	1	0
169	*aletear* 'to flap, to flutter to wriggle'	M-F	52	0	0	1	0
170	*ondular* 'to wave/undulate'	M	52	0	0	1	0
171	*remar* 'to row, to paddle'	M	53	0	0	1	0
172	*cabecear* 'to move or to shake one's head'	M-F	54	0	0	1	0
173	*cerne(i)rse* 'to swing the hips (walking)'	M	55	0	0	1	0
174	*merodear* 'to walk around, to prowl'	M-C	56	0	0	1	0
175	*ondear* 'to undulate, to sway'	M	57	0	0	1	0
176	*esquiar* 'to ski'	M	58	0	0	1	0
177	*reclinar(se)* 'to lean'	M	58	0	0	1	0
178	*menear(se)* 'to move'	M	62	0	0	1	0
179	*empinar(se)* 'to stand up'	P-M	63	0	0	1	0
180	*blandir(se)* 'to swing/stagger'	M	64	0	0	1	0
181	*enroscar(se)* 'to coil'	M	65	0	0	1	0
182	*trotar* '(of a person) to trot, to ride a trotting horse'	M	66	0	0	1	0
183	*fluctuar* 'to fluctuate'	M	69	0	0	1	0
184	*tambalear* 'to stagger'	M	69	0	0	1	0
185	*encorvar(se)* 'to bend, to curve'	M	71	0	0	1	0
186	*escalar* 'to scale, to climb'	M-P	71	0	0	1	0
187	*pisotear* 'to tread repeatedly and violently over something'	M-F	72	0	0	1	0
188	*naufragar* '(of a ship, people in a ship) to sink'	P-M	75	0	0	1	0
189	*torear* 'to fight bulls'	M	75	0	0	1	0
190	*tiritar* 'to shiver, to tremble'	M	76	0	0	1	0
191	*arquear(se)* 'to bend oneself'	M	77	0	0	1	0
192	*titubear* 'to falter'	M	77	0	0	1	0
193	*curvar(se)* 'to curve, bend'	M	78	0	0	1	0
194	*zarpar* '(of a ship) to set off',	M	78	0	0	1	0

Rank	Verbs	LCC	All uses	Telic usage	Telicity ratio (%)	FET-value-p	Log^{10}-trans
195	*corretear* 'to run about'	M	79	0	0	1	0
196	*danzar* 'to dance'	M	80	0	0	1	0
197	*errar* 'to wander about'	M	81	0	0	1	0
198	*atajar* 'taking a short cut'	G	89	0	0	1	0
199	*rastrear* 'to fly at ground level, to track'	M-G/P	95	0	0	1	0
200	*revolotear* 'to fly around, to flutter'	M-G	97	0	0	1	0
201	*distanciar(se)* 'to move away from'	P	99	0	0	1	0
202	*cabalgar* 'to ride a horse'	M	101	0	0	1	0
203	*rebotar* 'to bounce'	M	119	0	0	1	0
204	*enderezar(se)* 'to become straight'	M	120	0	0	1	0
205	*galopar* 'to gallop, to ride a galloping horse'	M	123	0	0	1	0
206	*patear* 'to go on foot around a place, to stamp one's feet showing one is angry'	M-F	125	0	0	1	0
207	*mecer(se)* 'to swing, rock'	M	126	0	0	1	0
208	*deambular* 'to walk around'	M	127	0	0	1	0
209	*enrollar(se)* 'to roll'	M	129	0	0	1	0
210	*balancear(se)* 'to swing'	M	152	0	0	1	0
211	*botar* 'to bounce, rebound'	M	156	0	0	1	0
212	*aterrizar* 'to land'	P-G	160	0	0	1	0
213	*arrodillar(se)* 'to kneel down'	M	167	0	0	1	0
214	*estrellar(se)* 'to crash'	M	170	0	0	1	0
215	*agachar(se)* 'to crouch'	M	176	0	0	1	0
216	*vagar* 'to wander'	M	186	0	0	1	0
217	*rondar* 'to be on patrol, to prowl about'	M–C	188	0	0	1	0
218	*desfilar* 'to parade, to walk in file'	M	191	0	0	1	0
219	*despegar* 'to take off'	P-G	194	0	0	1	0
220	*torcer(se)* 'to turn, to change direction, to bend'	P	202	0	0	1	0
221	*derrumbar(se)* 'to fall down'	P	240	0	0	1	0
222	*dispersar(se)* 'to disperse'	P	241	0	0	1	0
223	*refugiar(se)* 'to flee'	P-G	242	0	0	1	0
224	*vibrar* 'to vibrate'	M	246	0	0	1	0
225	*espantar(se)* 'to run away as a result of being frightened'	M–C	261	0	0	1	0
226	*profundizar* 'to get into'	P	269	0	0	1	0
227	*voltear* 'to turn/roll over'	M	274	0	0	1	0
228	*erguir(se)* 'to straighten, stand up'	P-M	294	0	0	1	0
229	*estremecer(se)* 'to tremble, shiver'	M	301	0	0	1	0
230	*nadar* 'to swim'	M-G	311	0	0	1	0
231	*tropezar* 'to trip'	M	339	0	0	1	0
232	*estirar(se)* 'to stretch out'	M	390	0	0	1	0

Rank	Verbs	LCC	All uses	Telic usage	Telicity ratio (%)	FET-value-p	Log^{10}-trans
233	*planear* '(of a plane, a bird) to glide'	M-G	393	0	0	1	0
234	*chocar* 'to crash'	M-CR	458	0	0	1	0
235	*acelerar* 'to speed up, to accelerate'	M	473	0	0	1	0
236	*asentar(se)* 'to sit down'	P-M	496	0	0	1	0
237	*doblar* 'to turn, to change direction'	P	525	0	0	1	0
238	*temblar* 'to shiver, to tremble'	M	631	0	0	1	0
239	*agitar(se)* 'to shake, to move about'	M	633	0	0	1	0
240	*sacudir(se)* 'to shake oneself'	M	638	0	0	1	0
241	*derivar* 'to drift'	M	890	0	0	1	0
242	*circular* 'go in a circuit'	G	913	0	0	1	0
243	*encerrar(se)* 'to put oneself into an enclosed place'	P	920	0	0	1	0
244	*hundir(se)* 'to collapse, to sink'	P	974	0	0	1	0
245	*alzar(se)* 'to rise'	P	990	0	0	1	0
246	*manejar* 'to handle/drive'	M	1217	0	0	1	0
247	*bailar* 'to dance'	M	1283	0	0	1	0
248	*atravesar(se)* 'to cross'	P	1324	0	0	1	0
249	*rodear* 'to go round'	M	1858	0	0	1	0
	Total			19623			

CHAPTER 6

A corpus-based study of infinitival and sentential complement constructions in Spanish

Jiyoung Yoon and Stefanie Wulff
University of North Texas / University of Florida

This corpus-based study examines Spanish infinitival and sentential complement constructions. 561 infinitival and 795 sentential complements retrieved from the AnCora corpus were subjected to a *Distinctive Collexeme Analysis* (Gries and Stefanowitsch, 2004) that identified the verbs distinctively associated with either complementation. The results suggest that the two are in fact distinct constructions (Goldberg, 1995, 2006): the infinitival construction attracts verbs denoting DESIRE, whereas the sentential construction attracts verbs denoting COMMUNICATION and MENTAL ACTIVITY. The results furthermore lend credence to usage-based constructionist approaches: verbs fall on a continuum of constructional preferences from which consistent semantic groups emerge. We close with a brief discussion of how grammaticalization processes may account for the constructional preferences of specific verbs.

1. Introduction

Spanish infinitival complement constructions as shown in (1) alternate with full sentential complement constructions as shown in (2):

(1) Creíamos$_{V1}$ saber$_{V2}$ acerca de esta historia.
    we thought   know   about this history

(2) Creíamos$_{V1}$ que sabíamos$_{V2}$ acerca de esta historia.
    we thought   that we knew-IND   about this history
    'We thought that we knew about this history'

---

* Part of this research has been supported by the University of North Texas Research and Creativity Enhancement (RCE) Grant and by the Spanish Ministry of Economy and Competitiveness, grant no. FFI2013-43593-P.

The alternation of the near-synonymous sentences (1) and (2) is subject to syntactic and semantic conditions. Infinitival complement constructions require that the main verb (V_1) and the verb in the subordinate clause (V_2) be co-referential; on the contrary, in sentential complement constructions, subjects may either be co-referential as in (2) or not as in (3). The latter is typically observed with verbs of cognition and communication, such as *saber* 'to know,' *afirmar* 'to admit,' and *creer* 'to believe.' Note that in these instances, the V_2 in the sentential complement is in the indicative mood when the V_1 is in the affirmative variant.[1]

(3) Creíamos$_{V1}$ que sabían$_{V2}$ acerca de esta historia.
     we thought   that they knew-IND   about this history
     'We thought that they knew about this history'

Another quasi-alternation is found with verbs of volition (e.g., *preferir* 'to prefer') and emotion (e.g., *lamentar* 'to regret'). In these instances, co-referential subjects are typically restricted to the infinitival complement constructions as in (4). Non-co-referential subjects can again occur in sentential complements, and they are expressed in the subjunctive mood as in (5).

(4) Preferimos hablar con el   amigo de Ana.
     we prefer speak with the friend of Ana
     'We prefer to speak with Ana's friend'

(5) Preferimos que *hablemos /   hables   con el   amigo de Ana.
     we prefer that *we speak-SUBJ / you speak-SUBJ   with the friend of Ana
     'We prefer that *we speak / you speak with Ana's friend'

Since co-referentiality, verb class membership, and mood are intricately intertwined in these (quasi-) alternations, Subirats-Rüggeberg (1987: 30) notes that "in Spanish grammar there is an important tradition wherein the infinitive has always been studied together with sentential complementation."

Most previous work on infinitival complementation is transformational-generative and focuses on English (e.g., Bošković, 1997; Chomsky & Lasnik, 1993; Stowell, 1982). The majority of these studies are concerned with the syntactic structure and the categorical status of infinitival complements. In discussing many types of infinitival constructions in Spanish (which are labeled *reduced constructions*) Moore (1996), for example, argues that infinitival complements are derived from sentential complements. This notion of derivation is prevalent in formalist studies that postulate that one construction is basic and the other is derived, in which the main concern is not whether or not the two constructions exhibit major

---

1. Note: When the main verb is negated, the subjunctive is frequently used:

   No creíamos   que supieran   acera de esta historia.
   no we thought that we knew-SUBJ about this history
   'We thought that we knew about this history'

differences with respect to the type of verbs that occur in them, or what the frequency of a given verb is that occurs in either construction.

Fewer formalist studies consider the role of semantics in complement constructions. For example, Moore (1996) notes that for perception verbs in Spanish like *ver* 'to see,' two different interpretations are possible, depending on the choice of complementation: infinitival complement constructions as in (6a) evoke a direct perception reading whereas sentential complements as in (6b) may also evoke an epistemic reading:

(6) a. Lo   vi   llorar
       him   saw   cry
       'I <u>saw</u> him cry'
    b. Vi   que   el   carro   era   difícil   de   conducir
       I-saw   that the   car   was   difficult of   to drive
       'I <u>thought</u> that the car was difficult to drive'

This idea of an *iconic link* has been explicated in more detail in cognitive-functionalist work such as Givón (1990), who proposes that when there are two events that are conceptually connected, "the stronger the semantic bond is between the two events, the more intimately is the syntactic integration of the two propositions into a single clause" (Givón, 1990: 516). Here, a stronger semantic bond means that there is more event integration in the sense that "[t]he more the two events coded in the main and complement clauses share their referents, the more likely they are to be semantically integrated as a single event; and the less likely is the complement clause to be coded as an independent finite clause" (Givón, 1990: 534). The notion of semantic bond also has something to do with the *strength of intent* such that when an agent displays stronger intent (e.g., [7a] exhibits stronger intent than [7b]), the probability of the event realization increases (Givón, 1990: 535). To give an example, the infinitival and sentential complements of *expect* in (7a) and (7b) imply different semantic interpretations, respectively:

(7) a. I expect you to be done by noon.
    b. I expect that you should be done by noon.
                              (taken from Givón, 1990: 527 [29])

Givón notes that the sentence (7a) with an infinitival complement is interpreted as manipulation while (7b) is interpreted as a prediction. Thus, (7a) can be construed as *I expect you to be done by noon, so get on with it!*, which is not the case for (7b) – adding a command will make the sentence sound pragmatically awkward: *?I expect that you should be done by noon, so get on with it!*. Adding an adverbial phrase like *if everything goes on schedule*, however, is compatible with (7b) because it reinforces the prediction interpretation. Semantically, the strength of intent manifested in manipulation in (7a) is stronger than in prediction in (7b), as the probability of accomplishing the given task is greater in (7a) than in (7b).

Constructionist approaches explicitly endorse the iconic relation between syntax and semantics as stated in Goldberg (1995: 67): "If two constructions are syntactically distinct, they must be semantically or pragmatically distinct" (*Principle of No Synonymy*). Along similar lines, Achard (1998), who examines the alternation of French infinitival and finite complements from a cognitive grammar point of view, argues that the surface form of a linguistic expression (in our case, complementation) reflects a particular cognitive structure and that formal differences between a large variety of constructions reflect semantic/conceptual differences. In other words, form and meaning are interrelated in a way that "in choosing a particular expression or construction, a speaker construes the conceived situation in a certain way, i.e., he selects one particular image (from a range of alternatives) to structure its conceptual content for expressive purposes" (Achard, 1998: 15).

This premise is at the heart of the notion of *construction* in construction grammar. A construction is defined as a pairing of form and meaning (Goldberg, 1995, 2006) that is symbolically linked. The emergence of construction grammar has stipulated some interesting studies on complementation, yet there have been only a few studies that have tackled complementation in Spanish from a constructionist point of view (Gonzálvez-García, 2011a, 2011b; Yoon, 2004, among others). Gonzálvez-García (2011a), for example, identifies three types of 'subjective attributive constructions' (*seem/parecer*-type verbs):

(8) a. small clauses (direct perception):
 Pedro parece (una) buena persona.
 Pedro seems (a) good person
 'Pedro seems a nice person'
 b. non-finite clause (epistemic perception):
 Pedro parece ser (una) buena persona.
 Pedro seems to be (a) good person
 'Pedro seems to be a nice person'
 c. finite (*que* 'that') clause (epistemic perception):
 Parece que Pedro es una buena persona.
 seems that Pedro is a good person
 'It seems that Pedro is a nice person'
 (examples taken from Gonzálvez-García, 2011a: 5)

He proposes that like in English, the choice of a complementation construction is not random but rather mediated by language users' perception of reality. A small clause construction in (8a) implies direct perception of Pedro's condition by the experiencer, whereas (8b) and (8c) are manifestations of an epistemic perception or deduction (in the sense of 'from what I can observe I think that Pedro is...').[2]

---

2. For a more detailed discussion of the family of *subjective-transitive constructions*, which includes the evaluative subjective-transitive construction (e.g., *I found it interesting*), the

Yoon (2004) presents a constructionist analysis of Spanish complement constructions, suggesting that infinitival complements are constructions in the Goldbergian sense, therefore to be distinguished from sentential complement constructions:

(9) a. Juan piensa ser más fuerte.
Juan thinks to be more strong
'Juan intends to be stronger'
b. Juan piensa que él es fuerte.
Juan thinks that he is strong
'Juan thinks that he is strong'

In the infinitival complement in (9a), the verb *pensar* 'to think' is interpreted as implying intentionality while the same verb is construed as a cognition verb in the sentential complement in (9b). Based on examples like these, Yoon (2004) posits two core constructional meanings for infinitival complement constructions in Spanish: (i) a DESIRE-BECOME construction that incorporates a group of volition verbs (i.e., verbs of desideration, intention, and attempt) as in (10), and (ii) an ASSESS-STATE construction involving non-volition verbs, such as emotion, cognition, and declaration as in (11).

(10) DESIRE-BECOME construction:
El joven piensa ser rico en el futuro.
the young thinks be rich in the future
'The young man intends to be rich in the future'

(11) ASSESS-STATE construction:
Reconocemos tener problemas con las máquinas.
we acknowledge have problems with the machines
'(lit.) We acknowledge having problems with the machines'

The central sense posited for the DESIRE-BECOME construction is 'a subject desires/intends to accomplish an action or to achieve a certain state'; the one posited for the ASSESS-STATE construction is 'one assesses and evaluates one's situation or state.' By postulating the existence of infinitival complement constructions with two different meanings, Yoon presents an alternative to positing different senses of individual verbs occurring in infinitival complements.

The present study seeks to elaborate on previous constructionist work on Spanish infinitival and sentential complementation by adopting a more quantitative, corpus-based perspective. More specifically, this study sets out to test whether

declarative subjective-transitive construction (e.g., *They call me arrogant*), the causative-volitive subjective transitive construction (e.g., *She wants her children strong*), and the generic subjective-transitive construction (e.g., *I like my meat rare*), see Gonzálvez-García (2011b).

the more qualitatively-grounded hypotheses about the distinct constructional status of infinitival and sentential complementation constructions stand the scrutiny of a quantitative, statistical assessment that is based on a comprehensive data sample of several hundred attestations of the two patterns under investigation.

2. Methods

2.1 Data

For the present analysis, we extracted data from the Spanish AnCora corpus (version 1.0.1), which contains 500,000 words of journalistic prose. Using an *R*-script, we first identified all sentences in AnCora containing either an infinitival verb form or a complementizer *que* [that].[3] In a second step, we inspected the resulting 10,749 sentences and manually identified true hits of infinitival and sentential complements. True hits of infinitival complements had to contain a conjugated main clause verb followed by an infinitival complement clause verb; sentential complements had to comprise a conjugated main clause verb followed by *que* [that] followed by a conjugated complement clause verb. In both cases, these sequences could be non-contiguous as shown in (12) and (13).

(12) Telefónica declinó ayer comentar el rumor.
Telefónica declined yesterday comment the rumor
'Telefónica declined to comment the rumor yesterday'

(13) […] dijo ayer que las 700 hectáreas del recinto
he-told yesterday that the 700 hectares of the precinct
podrán ser compradas por la Generalitat.
can be purchased by the Generalitat
'He said yesterday that 700 hectares of the precincts can be purchased by the Generalitat' (examples from AnCora)

Also, only instances containing full verbs that potentially alternate between both constructions were considered. In that way, the tendency of a verb to appear with either type of construction (i.e., *association strength* between a verb and a construction or *verb bias*) could be compared fairly, and consequently, some verbs which were never attested in both constructions were excluded (e.g., *escribir* 'to write'

---

3. In the present analysis, we limited the scope to sentences containing single hits of either complementation pattern; instances of multiple coordinated, listed, or embedded infinitival/sentential complementation were excluded.

appears in sentential but not in infinitival complements and was thus excluded from our data). For this purpose, we initially carried out Google and RAE (*Real Academia Española* database) searches to ensure that all verbs in the analysis were attested in either construction at least once. Many verbs in our dataset are prominently featured in the context of complementation in Spanish grammar reference books or and other linguistics resources such as Hernanz (1999); examples include *afirmar* 'to admit, to say,' *considerer* 'to consider,' *confirmar* 'to confirm,' *precisar* 'to need,' *admitir* 'to admit,' and *proponer* 'to propose.' At the same time, our dataset furthermore comprises a range of verbs that some traditional grammarians and/or native speakers of (different dialects of) Spanish may not consider as alternating between the two complementation constructions. Examples here include *explicar* 'to explain,' *anunciar* 'to announce,' *indicar* 'to indicate,' *entender* 'to understand,' *opinar* 'to say,' *subrayar* 'to stress, to emphasize,' *añadir* 'to add,' and *destacar* 'to highlight.' We ensured that all the verbs included in our final dataset were attested in *both* infinitival and full sentential complement constructions at least once in actual usage data. Many verbs that are not often cited as verbs taking infinitival complements in Spanish grammar reference books were actually found to be employed in infinitival complement constructions in online sources such as online newspapers and titles/subtitles of online videos. Some examples of such attestations of verbs occurring in infinitival complements (in addition to their preferred sentential complements) are given in (14) to (16):

(14) Jencarlos Canela *anuncia* estar pronto en el Perú.
Jencarlos Canela announces to be soon in the Peru
'(lit.) Jencarlos Canela announces to be in Peru soon'
(example taken from YouTube, February 2, 2010)

(15) Senadora del PP no *entiende* tener que pagar para
Senator of the PP NEG understands have to pay for
entendernos.
understand-us
'(lit.) Senator of the PP does not understand to have to pay for understanding us'
(example taken from Europa Press, Spain, January 19, 2011)

(16) Internan a mujer que *denuncia* tener un trozo de bisturí
they admit women who reports to have a piece of scalpel
en una mama.
in a breast
'(lit.) They admit a woman who reports to have a piece of scalpel in her breast'
(example taken from www.emol.com [newspaper in Chile], January 27, 2011)

Conversely, a variety of verbs was excluded from the final sample: verbs with an overt direct object as in (17a); 'raising' verbs as in (17b); auxiliary and modal verbs as in (17c); *gustar* 'to be pleasing (to)'-type verbs in which the semantic subject is syntactically coded as an indirect object as in (17d)[4]; and fixed idiomatic sequences as in (17e).

(17) a. Nos ordenaron salir.
us ordered-3PL leave
'They ordered us to leave'
b. El teléfono parece tener problemas.
the phone seems have problems
'The phone seems to have problems'
c. ¿Puedo ayudarte?
can-1SG help-you-ACC
'Can I help you?'
d. Me gusta nadar.
to me likes [i.e., is pleasing] to swim
'I like swimming (Swimming is pleasing to me)'
e. ¿Qué quiere decir esta palabra?
what wants say this word
'What does this word mean?'

The final data sample comprised 561 instances of infinitival complementation, including 65 different matrix clause verb (V_1) lemma types and 275 different complement clause verb (V_2) lemma types; and 795 instances of sentential complementation, including 120 different matrix clause verb (V_1) lemma types and 325 different complement clause verb (V_2) lemma types.

2.2 Distinctive Collexeme Analysis (DCA)

Over that data sample, we ran a Distinctive Collexeme Analysis (DCA). DCA is one member of the family of collostructional analyses developed by Stefan Gries and Anatol Stefanowitsch (Stefanowitsch & Gries, 2003; Gries & Stefanowitsch, 2004). Collostructional analysis measures the association strength between words (typically verbs) and the constructions they occur in. In essence, collostructional analysis is an extension of the notion of collocation (traditionally defined as a

---

4. Just to take a few examples, the *gustar*-type verb in (17d) is a special type of construction in Spanish in which the semantic subject *me* 'to me' appears as a dative while the grammatical subject *nadar* 'to swim' is semantically interpreted as the direct object of the verb. For this structural peculiarity, this verb type was excluded from our dataset.

word-word association) to word-construction associations. DCA is specifically tailored toward identifying verbs that distinguish best between two (or more) closely related or synonymous constructions. In the present study, we use DCA to address the question concerning which main and complement clause verb lemmas, if any, are most distinctively associated with infinitival and sentential complements when directly comparing their frequency of occurrence in these two constructions.

Technically speaking, in order to determine the distinctive association strength between a verb X and two constructions A and B, we need to obtain four frequency values as shown in Table 1: the frequency with which the verb occurs in the two constructions ($n_{X\ in\ A}$ and $n_{X\ in\ B}$), and the frequency with which other verbs occur in these constructions ($n_{\neg X\ in\ A}$ and $n_{\neg X\ in\ B}$, respectively).

Table 1. Frequency values entering a Distinctive Collexeme Analysis of a verb X

	Verb X	Other verbs
Construction A	$n_{X\ in\ A}$	$n_{\neg X\ in\ A}$
Construction B	$n_{X\ in\ B}$	$n_{\neg X\ in\ B}$

For our study, let us take the example of the main clause predicate *querer* ('want'): in our data sample, *querer* occurs 147 times overall, 135 times in the infinitival complement construction and 12 times in a sentential complement construction. Since we know the overall frequencies of infinitival and sentential complement constructions are 561 and 795, respectively, we can deduce that 426 instances of the infinitival construction occur with verbs other than *querer*, and 783 instances of the sentential complementation construction in our data are occupied by verbs other than *querer*. Table 2 provides an overview.

Table 2. Observed frequencies of *querer* in infinitival and sentential complement constructions

	querer	Other verbs	Row totals
Infinitival complement construction	135	426	561
Sentential complement construction	12	783	795
Column totals	147	1,209	1,256

A glance at Table 2 certainly suggests that *querer* strongly prefers to occur in the infinitival complementation construction. In order to assess whether this impression is statistically sound, we need to contrast *querer*'s observed frequencies with the frequencies we would expect if *querer* were distributed randomly across the two constructions; that is, if *querer* did not have any constructional preference at all. For a given cell in the table, these expected frequencies are calculated by multiplying the row with the column total of that cell, and then dividing that number by the overall total. Accordingly, given our overall sample size of 561 infinitival complements and 795 sentential complements, we would expect *querer* to occur only 61 times in the infinitival construction (that is, 561*147/1,256), and 86 times in the sentential complement construction (that is, 795*147/1,256). The expected frequencies are provided in Table 3.

Table 3. Expected frequencies of *querer* in infinitival and sentential complement constructions

	querer	Other verbs	Row totals
Infinitival complement construction	61	500	561
Sentential complement construction	86	709	795
Column totals	147	1,209	1,256

Now we can statistically assess the degree to which the observed frequencies deviate from the expected ones by applying an association measure. We use the Fisher Yates exact *p*-value, and we report it in its logged form for ease of interpretation. $P_{\log}$ values equal to or higher than 1.3 are significant at the 5%-level of significance. To return to our example, *querer* yields a $p_{\log}$-value of 41.448, which means that it is highly distinctively associated with the infinitival complement construction. In collostructional parlance, that renders *querer* a *collexeme* (a blend of *collocate* and *lexeme*) of the infinitival complementation construction, that is, a lexeme significantly distinctive for the infinitival complementation construction (when contrasted with *querer*'s occurrences in the sentential complementation construction, that is – if we contrasted *querer*'s distribution in sentential vs. other constructions, we would likely obtain different results).

For the present study, we used Gries' (2007) *coll.analysis*3.2, an R-script that allows the user to load all their relevant data (in our case, the frequencies with which all attested verbs occurred in either construction, the overall frequency of the infinitival complement construction, and the overall frequency of the sentential complement construction) and that returns (among other things) $p_{\log}$-values for all verbs and information about which of the constructions every given verb is distinctively associated with. We report these results in the following section.

3. Results

Let us first look at the V_1-slot. Table 4 lists all verbs distinctively associated with infinitival complements.

Table 4. Distinctive V$_1$-collexemes of the infinitival complement construction

V$_1$ Lemma	p_{log}
querer ('want')	41.488
intentar ('try')	15.698
decidir ('decide')	12.502
pretender ('intend')	11.304
lograr ('achieve')	11.137
permitir ('allow')	7.987
hacer ('make')	6.597
preferir ('prefer')	3.721
necesitar ('need')	3.079
conseguir ('get')	2.750
desear ('wish')	1.983
acordar ('agree')	1.536

In terms of a general semantic trend, we can see that this construction attracts verbs of desire: *querer* 'want' is the by far the most strongly distinctive verb, followed by *intentar* 'try;' *preferir* 'prefer,' *necesitar* 'need,' and *desear* 'wish' are also among the top distinctive verbs in that semantic category.

When we look at the corresponding results for sentential complements in Table 5, we first of all see that there are more verbs distinctively associated with this construction, but at the same time, none of the verbs as nearly as distinctive as *querer* 'want' is for infinitival complements. At least two general semantic trends become obvious: first, verbs of verbal communication occupy the top ranks (*decir* 'say;' *explicar* 'explain;' *anunciar* 'announce;' etc. A second prominent group is mental activity verbs, including *creer* 'believe,' *recordar* 'remember,' *reconocer* 'recognize,' and *entender* 'understand.'

Table 5. Distinctive V$_1$-collexemes of the sentential complement construction

V$_1$ Lemma	p_{log}	V$_1$ Lemma	p_{log}
creer ('believe')	11.000	indicar ('indicate')	3.032
decir ('say')	8.673	confirmar ('confirm')	2.329
asegurar ('ensure')	8.016	reclamar ('claim')	2.329
explicar ('explain')	8.014	precisar ('need')	2.095
anunciar ('announce')	6.818	admitir ('admit')	1.866
recordar ('remember')	6.372	manifestar ('state/declare')	1.862
afirmar ('state/declare')	6.146	sostener ('support/hold')	1.862
considerar ('consider')	5.629	entender ('understand')	1.628
señalar ('point out')	4.681	argumentar ('argue')	1.395
reconocer ('admit/recognize')	4.209	denunciar ('denounce/report')	1.395
destacar ('highlight')	3.502	opinar ('say')	1.395
añadir ('add')	3.267	subrayar ('stress')	1.395

Let us now turn to the V_2-slot. Looking first at infinitival complements again, we find a quite heterogenous group of verbs here, none of which are particularly distinctive (if only significantly associated) with the construction. Table 6 gives an overview.

Table 6. Distinctive V_2-collexemes of the infinitival complement construction

V_2 Lemma	p_{log}
ganar ('win')	2.400
crear ('create')	1.890
volar ('fly')	1.890
dejar ('leave')	1.617
comentar ('comment')	1.511
constar ('record')	1.511
dotar ('endow')	1.511
echar ('cast')	1.511
realizar ('perform')	1.409
ver ('see')	1.409

In contrast, a more homogenous picture emerges for sentential complements: as Table 7 illustrates, the top distinctive collexemes are light verbs, with *ser* 'be' leading the list, and including *haber* 'there is/are,' *estar* 'be,' and other highly frequent, semantically bleached verbs like *ir* 'go' and *poder* 'be able to.'

Table 7. Distinctive V_2-collexemes of the sentential complement construction

V_2 Lemma	p_{log}
ser ('be')	18.094
haber ('there is/are')	5.012
existir ('exist')	2.612
deber ('owe')	1.897
tratar ('treat')	1.897
ir ('go')	1.860
estar ('be')	1.751
poder ('be able to')	1.421
recibir ('receive')	1.421

4. Discussion

We can summarize the main results obtained from the DCA as follows. With regard to the V_1-slot, the collexemes distinctively associated with the infinitival complement construction lend credence to Yoon's (2004) description of infinitival complement constructions as primarily meaning 'DESIRE-BECOME': the infinitival complement construction is selected when the speaker expresses desires or intention to accomplish an action or to achieve a certain state. More specifically, Yoon (2004) identifies various related senses that can be expressed in the infinitival complement construction, and it is striking to see that, in fact, our analysis identifies significant collexemes instantiating these senses: DESIRE-BECOME (e.g. *querer* 'want,' *preferir* 'prefer,' *desear* 'desire,' *necesitar* 'need'), INTEND-BECOME (e.g. *acordar* 'agree,' *pretender* 'intend,' *decidir* 'decide,' *permitir* 'allow'), and ATTEMPT-BECOME (e.g. *intentar* 'try,' *lograr* 'achieve,' *hacer* 'make,' *conseguir* 'get').

The analysis of the V_2-slot in infinitival complement constructions did not reveal any coherent semantic trends – which could be expected since what a speaker desires or intends to become or achieve is entirely subjective and context-dependent. The particular V_2-collexemes that yielded significance in our data sample, then, are probably best seen as snapshots of the desires and intentions of the writers captured in AnCora (and/or more likely the desires and intentions of people these writers referred to, AnCora being a corpus of journalistic prose).[5]

The V_1-collexemes distinctively associated with the sentential complement construction fall into two semantically coherent groups: verbs of communication and verbs of mental activity.

While the results of the DCA support the *Principle of No Synonymy* such that generally, the two complementation constructions are associated with distinctive semantic verb classes, we can also see that for any given verb, the extent to which it is associated with either the infinitival or the sentential complementation construction is a matter of degree. In other words, we can conceptualize the verbs occurring in both constructions as located on a cline that ranges from verbs like *querer* 'want', which is strongly associated with the infinivital construction, to verbs like *creer* 'believe' that occur in the sentential complementation construction most of the time. The overarching association of the two complementation constructions with differential semantics becomes only obvious once we consider a representative sample of verbs and their individual constructional preferences.

Figure 1 provides a graphical illustration of the picture that emerges once we consider all verbs significantly associated with either complementation construction into consideration at the same time. In this figure, all collexemes distinctively associated with either construction (that is, the verbs listed in Tables 4 and 5) are arranged in increasing order of their preference for the sentential complementation construction. (This was an arbitrary choice: one could as well have arranged them in increasing order of their preference to occur in the infinitival

---

5. It is also noteworthy that in Spanish the infinitival complement construction is highly constrained and in a way predicted by V_1, and much less by V_2 (see Pedersen, this volume).

construction, in which case the figure would have been flip-sided. Also, we only included the distinctive collexemes here for reasons of space – in principle, any verb occurring at least once in one of the two constructions could be plotted in this graph, which would then still display the same overall trend.). Looking at Figure 1, we see that even when we consider only those verbs that, statistically speaking, exhibit a marked preference for either complementation construction, the overall picture that emerges is not one of two distinct groups of verbs, but rather a continuum of preference/dispreference. Moreover, we can see that in terms of semantic verb classes, the verbs most strongly associated with the infinitival construction (mostly in the left third of the graph) can all be categorized into one of the above-mentioned classes of DESIRE verbs (represented in Figure 1 as solid squares); the middle range of verbs that do not exhibit the most marked preferences are COMMUNICATION verbs (represented in Figure 1 as solid circles); and some of the verbs most strongly associated with sentential complements are MENTAL ACTIVITY verbs (here represented as solid triangles).

In accordance with the distribution of the verbs across the two constructions, we find partial semantic overlap between the verbs associated with the sentential complement construction and the ASSESS-STATE construction that Yoon (2004) identifies for infinitival constructions. (18) provides such an example with the verb *creer* 'believe;' other collexemes of the sentential complementation construction that lend themselves to an ASSESS-STATE reading include *recorder* 'remember,' *reconocer* 'admit/recognize,' *confirmer* 'confirm,' and *admitir* 'accept.'

(18) a. infinitival construction:
Cree/Afirma tener un control.
believe/claim-3SG have a control
'S/he believes/claims to have control'
b. sentential construction:
Cree/Afirma que tiene un control.
believe/claim-3SG that have-3SG a control
'S/he believes that s/he has control'

What may motivate this overlap? Within the scope of the present study, we can only venture a hypothesis, to be outlined in the following, that takes as its starting point the fact that in English, the same verbs are most distinctively associated with sentential complements: *think* (typically in the sense of 'believe'), *say*, *know*, and *mean* (Wulff, 2011). What renders these collexemes particularly interesting is the observation, initially made by Thompson and Mulac (1991), that they seem to have been re-analyzed as epistemic markers that may serve a multitude of meta-discoursal functions, such as hedging the information provided in the complement clause. In English, these instances of grammaticalization typically coincide

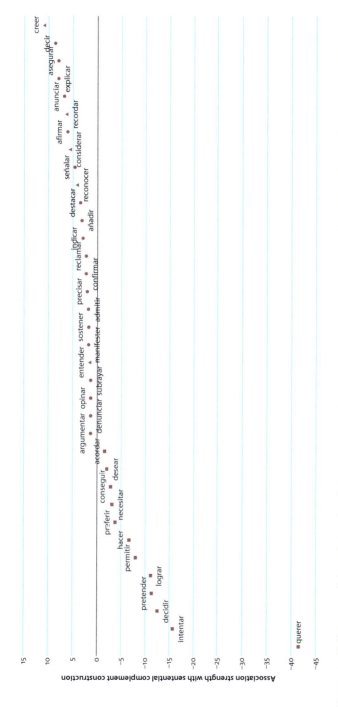

Figure 1. Collexemes of the infinitval and sentential complementation constructions, arranged in order of increasing preference for sentential complementation, and coded for major semantic class

with higher shares of particular pronominal forms in the matrix clause (*I think*; *you know*; *I mean*) as well as frequent omission of the complementizer *that*, which ultimately results in an erosion of main and complement clause.

Although Spanish is often described as a language that does not license omission of the complementizer *que* 'that', it has been noted in literature that a full sentential complement can appear without complementizer in Spanish just like in English. Brovetto (2002) proposes that the Spanish complementizer *que* 'that' may be omitted when the embedded proposition conveys a meaning of uncertainty or an irrealis meaning:

(19) Lamento (que) no estés contenta con tu trabajo.
I-lament (that) not you-be-SUBJ-2PS happy with your job
'I lament (that) you are not happy with your job'
(example taken from Torrego, 198,3 cited in Brovetto, 2002: 34)

(20) Espero (que) se solucionen pronto los problemas
(I)hope (that) SE solve-SUBJ-Pres.-3PS soon the problems
causados por el huracán.
caused by the hurricane
'I hope (that) the problems caused by the hurricane will be solved soon'
(example taken from Brovetto, 2002: 34)

The absence of the complementizer in Spanish typically occurs with verbs of propositional attitude such as the 'suppose' class of verbs (e.g., *suponer* 'suppose', *dudar* 'doubt', *parecer* 'seem'), 'lament' class of verbs (that is, emotion verbs) (e.g., *lamentar* 'lament', *preocuparse* 'be worried', *alegrarse* 'be glad', *sentir* 'be sorry'), and verbs of volition and desire (e.g., *querer* 'want', *desear* 'desire', *esperar* 'hope') (Brovetto, 2002: 33–34). As shown in the Examples (19) and (20), Brovetto (2002) hypothesizes that one can then expect to find the omission of *que* with the verb in the complement clause in subjunctive mood rather than in indicative mood (although the omission may be still possible in some cases) because subjunctive mood is associated with unreality or possibility. Interestingly, she notes that the absence of *que* is not usually possible with verbs of utterance such as *decir* 'say' and also with factive verbs such as *confesar* 'confess', *admitir* 'admit', and *jurar* 'swear' if the embedded clause denotes a realis meaning, but she also mentions that with these types of verbs, the omission can occur if the indicative mood of the embedded clause conveys irrealis meaning in the form of conditional or future tenses as in (21):

(21) Dijo (que) llegaría tarde a la reunión.
he-said (that) he-arrive-IND-Cond. late to the meeting
'He said (that) he would be late to the meeting'
(example taken from Brovetto, 2002: 35)

Now, returning to our results in Table 5, recall that the most distinctive V_1-collexemes of the sentential complement construction were *creer* 'believe, think' followed by *decir* 'say'. Those two verbs indeed seem to conform to Brovetto's (2002) proposal in that they both belong to the class of verbs that supposedly license omission of the complementizer when the embedded clause conveys a possibility or irrealis meaning. As we have mentioned, these verbs along with other verbs in Table 5 are possibly undergoing a grammaticalization process in which the full lexical meaning of the verb is getting attenuated and instead obtains a more subjective meaning as an epistemic marker. One example found in the *Real Academia* database (CREA corpus) illustrates a typical use of *creer* 'believe, think' being used as an epistemic marker:

(22) Es   muy importante, *creo*,   tener como contrapeso   de los
     (it)is very important   I think   have   as   counterbalance of the
     Parlamentos políticos   una   asamblea de culturas europeas.
     parliament   political   a   meeting   of cultures European
     'It is very important, I think, to have a meeting of European cultures as counterbalance of the political parliament.'
     (example taken from CREA: Prensa Española [Madrid], 1997)

In (22), the verb *creo* 'I think' appears without complementizer; even more interestingly, it occurs sentence-medially between pauses, which further corroborates our hypothesis that this verb is undergoing grammaticalization and is used as an epistemic marker (Yoon, 2015). Note that the embedded clause in (22) (i.e., *it is very important to have...*) denotes a meaning of irrealis, thus confirming the semantic condition proposed by Brovetto (2002). More examples in (23) and (24) with *creo* '(I) think' (with an implicit subject) and *yo creo* 'I think' (with an overt subject) show that the syntactic position of this verb is sufficiently flexible to allow it to appear also sentence-initially and sentence-finally. In (23) and (24), we also see another example of the epistemic markers *creo* and *yo creo* occurring as a syntactic unit separated by commas:

(23) Y   yo creo,   estoy convencida que [...] la   labor de de estos
     and I think   I am   convinced   that   the labor of of the these
     hombres, como en el caso de Omar Dengo, estuvo estrechamente
     men,   like in the case of Omar Dengo, was   closely
     ligada en su   origen.
     linked in their   origin
     'And I think, I am convinced that [...] the labor of these men, just like in the case of Omar Dengo, was closely linked to their origin'
     (example taken from CREA, oral data, Costa Rica)

(24) Yo todavía creo   que Liberación va   a ganar las elecciones,
    I still   believe that Liberation goes to win   the elections
    todavía creo.
    still   I believe
    'I still believe that Liberation is going to win the elections, I still believe'
                                    (example taken from CREA, oral data, Costa Rica)

Our second most distinctive V₁-collexeme of the sentential complement construction was *decir* 'to say'. Examples like the ones in (25) and (26) illustrate that *decir* can also be used as an epistemic marker without a complementizer, typically in the form of *yo digo* 'I say'. As with *creo*, the position of the marker appears to be flexible:

(25) [...] si no fuera   por eso, yo digo, hasta simpáticas
         if not be-SUBJ-3SG for this   I   say   even   nice
    serían   las intervenciones, como la   del Senador Andrade
    BE-Cond.-3PL the interventions   like the one of the Senator Andrade
    'If it were not for this, I say, even the interventions (like the one of Senator Andrade) would be nice'   (example taken from CREA, oral data, Mexico)

(26) Y   yo digo, la   responsabilidad del   pri y   del   Gobierno
    and I say   the responsibility of the pri and of the Government
    Federal, es mucha y   muy grave
    Federal is a lot and very serious
    'And I say, the responsibility of the PRI and of the Federal Government is a lot and very serious.'   (example taken from CREA, oral data, Mexico)

In sum, *creo/yo creo* 'I think, I believe' and *yo digo* 'I say,' when being used without a complementizer sentential complement constructions, appear to be semantically bleached and carry out a meta-discoursal function that stands in contrasts with these same verbs occurring in infinitival complement constructions, where they display their (default) full lexical semantics. We are in the process of pursuing this hypothesis further in another study that will be based on a representative data sample including sentential complement constructions with and without the complementizer *que*.

In conclusion, the distinctive collexeme analysis confirms that specific verbs exhibit significant constructional preferences, and these preferences can be accounted for from a construction grammar perspective. At the same time, the distinctive collexeme analysis illustrates that for the most part, a majority of verbs exhibit distributional preferences rather than rigid dichotomies: that is, while they tend to occur more in one construction than the other, they may occur in the other construction as well. This raises the question of what motivates speakers to alternate between the two constructions. Addressing this issue is beyond the scope of the present paper, so we can only speculate that various contextual and processing-related factors must play a role here, including priming effects at the verb and constructional level (for evidence in favor of constructional priming, see Gries & Wulff, 2005, 2009). Clearly, more in-depth corpus-based and experimental studies are needed to fully understand Spanish complementation constructions, and how they compare to complementation constructions in other languages.

References

AnCora: <http://clic.ub.edu/corpus/en/ancora>.
Achard, M. (1998). *Representation of cognitive structures: Syntax and semantics of French sentential complements*. Berlin & New York: Mouton de Gruyter. doi: 10.1515/9783110805956
Bošković, Ž. (1997). *The syntax of nonfinite complementation: An economy approach*. Cambridge, MA: MIT Press.
Brovetto, C. (2002). Spanish clauses without complementizer. In T. Satterfield, C. Tortora, & D. Cresti (Eds.), *Current issues in Romance languages: Selected papers from the 29th Linguistic Symposium on Romance Languages (LSRL)* (pp. 33–46). Amsterdam/Philadelphia: John Benjamins. doi: 10.1075/cilt.220.04bro
Chomsky, N. A., & Lasnik, H. (1993). The theory of principles and parameters. In J. Jacobs, A. von Stechow, W. Sternefeld, & T. Vennemann (Eds.), *Syntax: An international handbook of contemporary research* (pp. 13–127). Cambridge, MA: MIT Press.
Givón, T. (1990). *Syntax: A functional-typological introduction*, Vol. II. Amsterdam/Philadelphia: John Benjamins. doi: 10.1075/z.50
Goldberg, A. E. (1995). *Constructions: A construction grammar approach to argument structure*. Chicago: The University of Chicago Press.
Goldberg, A. E. (2006). *Constructions at work: The nature of generalization in language*. Oxford: Oxford University Press.
Gonzálvez-García, F. (2011a). Looks, appearances and judgements: Towards a unified constructionist analysis of predicative complements in English and Spanish. In P. Guerrero Medina (Ed.), *Morphosyntactic alternations in English: Functional and cognitive perspectives* (pp. 264–293). London: Equinox Publishing Ltd.
Gonzálvez-García, F. (2011b). Metaphor and metonymy do *not* render coercion superfluous: Evidence from the subjective-transitive construction. *Linguistics*, 49(6), 1305–1358. doi: 10.1515/ling.2011.037
Gries, St. Th. (2007). Coll.analysis 3.2. A program for R for Windows 2.x.
Gries, St. Th., & Stefanowitsch, A. (2004). Extending collostructional analysis: A corpus-based perspective on 'alternations'. *International Journal of Corpus Linguistics*, 9(1), 97–129. doi: 10.1075/ijcl.9.1.06gri
Gries, St. Th., & Wulff, S. (2005). Do foreign language learners also have constructions? Evidence from priming, sorting, and corpora. *Annual review of cognitive linguistics*, 3, 182–200. doi: 10.1075/arcl.3.10gri
Gries, St. Th., & Wulff, S. (2009). Psycholinguistic and corpus-linguistic evidence for L2 constructions. *Annual Review of Cognitive Linguistics*, 7, 164–187. doi: 10.1075/arcl.7.07gri

Hernanz, M. L. (1999). El infinitivo. In I. Bosque & V. Demonte (Eds.), *Gramática descriptiva de la lengua española*, Vol. 2 (pp. 2201–2356). Madrid: Espasa Calpe, S.A.

Moore, J. C. (1996). *Reduced constructions in Spanish*. New York/London: Garland.

Pedersen, J. (this volume). Spanish constructions of directed motion – a quantitative study: Typological variation and framing strategy.

Stefanowitsch, A., & Gries, St. Th. (2003). Collostructions: Investigating the interaction between words and constructions. *International Journal of Corpus Linguistics*, 8(2), 209–243. doi: 10.1075/ijcl.8.2.03ste

Subirats-Rüggeberg, C. (1987). *Sentential complementation in Spanish: A lexico-grammatical study of three classes of verbs*. Amsterdam: John Benjamins. doi: 10.1075/lis.14

Stowell, T. (1982). The tense of infinitives. *Linguistic Inquiry*, 13, 561–70.

Thompson, S. A., & Mulac, A. (1991). The discourse conditions for the use of the complementizer that in conversational English. *Journal of Pragmatics*, 15, 237–251. doi: 10.1016/0378-2166(91)90012-M

Wulff, S. (2011). Gradient grammaticalization in English complement constructions. Paper presented at the *Symposium on exploring the boundaries and applications of corpus linguistics 2011*, 15–17 April 2011, The University of Alabama.

Yoon, J. (2004). Infinitival complement constructions in Spanish: A construction grammar approach. In J. Auger, J. C. Clements, & B. Vance (Eds.), *Contemporary approaches to romance linguistics* (pp. 381–397). Amsterdam: John Benjamins. doi: 10.1075/cilt.258.20yoo

Yoon, J. (2015). The grammaticalization of the Spanish complement-taking verb without a complementizer. In María Isabel González-Rey (Ed). *Journal of Social Sciences*. Special issue: Phraseology, Phraseodidactics and Construction Grammar(s), 338–351. doi: 10.3844/jssp.2015.338.351

CHAPTER 7

Sense-based and lexeme-based alternation biases in the Dutch dative alternation

Sarah Bernolet and Timothy Colleman
Ghent University

In semantic studies of argument structure alternations as well as in psycholinguistic studies on syntactic priming, lexical alternation biases are typically measured at the level of the verb lexeme. This study explores the hypothesis that the proper locus of subcategorization probabilities is the verb *sense*. It investigates the effects of lexical polysemy on the subcategorization probabilities of Dutch dative alternating verbs as reflected in frequency data from natural language corpora and from a priming experiment. A sense-based distinctive collexeme analysis on the corpus data indicates that distinct senses of the same verb may indeed display different alternation biases. The response patterns in our priming experiment suggest that language users keep track of verb subcategorization preferences at different levels of schematization.

1. Introduction[1]

Psycholinguistic research has shown convincingly that language users have implicit knowledge of verb subcategorization frequencies (verb biases) and that this knowledge influences their behaviour in the production and processing of language. For instance, in recent research on syntactic priming, priming effects have been shown to be sensitive to the alternation biases of both prime verbs and target verbs – i.e., to the lexical preferences of the test verbs for one of the two (or more) alternating constructions under investigation (see Gries, 2005; Jaeger and Snider, 2007; Bernolet and Hartsuiker, 2010). Similarly, the subcategorizing preferences of individual verbs have been shown to be relevant to the processing of sentences with temporary syntactic ambiguities, the ability to reproduce

---

[1]. The order of the authors is arbitrary. The first author is affiliated with the Department of Experimental Psychology, the second author with the GLIMS research unit of the Department of Linguistics. Thanks go to the editors of the volume and to two anonymous referees for their helpful comments on an earlier version of the article.

sentences correctly, variation in phonetic production, etc. (see, e.g., Trueswell and Kim, 1998; Lombardi and Potter, 1992; Wilson and Garnsey, 2008; Gahl and Garnsey, 2004). In sum, there is an extensive – and growing – body of evidence for the idea that speakers and hearers have access to probabilistic knowledge on verb subcategorization frequencies.

In linguistic studies of argument structure alternations, the concept of lexical alternation bias plays a crucial role, too. Hypotheses about the subtle semantic contrasts between functionally equivalent constructions often refer to observations about the behaviour of individual verbs in the alternation. For a good example from the literature on one of the most well-studied grammatical alternation phenomena, the English dative alternation, it has been observed that verbs of refusal such as *refuse*, *deny*, and *spare* consistently prefer the double object construction over the so-called prepositional dative construction (i.e., the *to*-dative). Goldberg (1992:62), *inter alia*, reports the acceptability contrasts in (1) and (2) below, citing these as evidence for her general semantic hypothesis that the *to*-dative basically denotes 'caused motion' rather than 'caused reception'.

(1) a. She refused Joe a raise.
    b. *She refused a raise to Joe.
(2) a. His mother denied Billy a cake.
    b. *His mother denied a cake to Billy.

More recent corpus-based research has shown that such observations are better rephrased as statistical generalizations: it is not that *refuse* and *deny* are actually *impossible* in the *to*-dative construction, for instance, it is just that they are attested (much) more frequently with double object than with prepositional dative syntax in real language (see Stefanowitsch, 2006; Goldberg, 2011; specifically on *refuse* and *deny* also see Colleman and De Clerck, 2009: 24). Conversely, there are verbs which are (strongly) biased towards the *to*-dative: good examples identified by Gries and Stefanowitsch (2004: 106–107) on the basis of their distinctive collexeme analysis method include *bring*, *take*, and *pass*. Distinctive collexeme analysis (DCA) is a quantitative technique aimed at identifying the lexical items that are significantly biased towards one of two (or more) functionally similar constructions in a given corpus through the statistical evaluation of the observed frequencies of the lexical items in question in each of the alternating constructions in relation to the overall frequencies of the alternating constructions in the corpus. The output are two (or more) ordered lists of so-called *distinctive collexemes*, i.e. of those lexical items which significantly prefer one of the investigated constructions over the other(s). The method has been applied to various grammatical alternations from several languages in recent years, as the lists of strongly biased collexemes resulting from the quantitative test can potentially provide a good insight into the semantic differences between the constructions under investigation. Existing case studies along these lines include Wulff (2006) on the *Go*-V vs. *Go-and*-V constructions, Gilquin (2006) on causative constructions in English, Levshina et al. (2010) on similar constructions in Dutch, Noël and Colleman (2010) on accusative-and-infinitive and nominative-and-infinitive constructions in English and Dutch, Hilpert (2008) on future constructions in various Germanic languages, Lauwers (2010) on near-synonymous complex prepositions in French, Strik Lievers (2011) on adjectives with infinitival vs. finite clause complements in Italian, and Colleman (2009a) on the dative alternation in Dutch. The latter of these studies will be discussed in some detail below.

However, the large majority of such studies do not address issues of *lexical polysemy*: the output of the distinctive collexeme analysis is typically two (or more) ordered lists of verbs, or nouns, or adjectives etc., which do not distinguish between the different *senses* of the lexical items in question. Similarly, in psycholinguistic studies, alternation biases are typically measured at the level of the verbal lexeme, abstracting away from issues of verbal polysemy. While this rather coarse-grained approach has of course produced interesting results in the past (see the references at the onset of this paper), it is somewhat at odds with the intuitively appealing hypothesis that the proper locus of subcategorization probabilities may well be the *verb sense* rather than the verbal lexeme. Roland and Jurafsky (2002: 335–336) posit the *Lemma Argument Probability hypothesis*: each lemma (i.e., each verb sense, their terminology following that of Levelt, 1989) contains a vector of probabilistic expectations for its possible argument frames, and the vectors of different senses of one and the same verb may differ in important respects; a similar proposal is made by Hare, McRae, and Elman (2003, 2004). Gries & Stefanowitsch (2004: 125, footnote 5) themselves note, in relation to the behaviour of the polysemous phrasal verb *have on* ('wear' as well as 'conduct') with regard to particle placement, that "in some cases it might be more precise and rewarding to not just look at the distinctive collexemes of verbs, but of verb *senses*, i.e. verb-sense specific patterns", pointing to work by Roland and Jurafsky and by Hare and colleagues, too. To date, the only two case studies we know of which have implemented this verb-sense specific approach to DCA are Wiechmann (2008) and Gilquin (2010: Ch. 8), both of which will be briefly discussed in subsection 3.2 below.

The present paper explores this issue of sense-based lexical bias in relation to the Dutch dative alternation, i.e. the variation between the double object (DO) construction in (3a) and the prepositional dative (PD) construction with *aan* in (3b). These constructions are discussed in somewhat more detail in Section 2 below, which also includes references to existing investigations of their syntax and semantics.

(3) a. De man heeft zijn broer een boek gegeven / verkocht/
       the man has his brother a book given sold
       beloofd / aangeboden.
       promised offered
       'The man has given/sold/promised/offered his brother a book'
    b. De man heeft een boek aan zijn broer gegeven/
       the man has a book to his brother given
       /verkocht /beloofd/ aangeboden.
       sold promised offered
       'The man has given/sold/offered/promised a book to his brother'

After thus setting the stage, we will turn to an investigation of polysemy effects in the dative alternation. Section 3 will have a closer look at the double object and *aan*-dative frequencies of 15 selected polysemous ditransitive verbs included in the database of Colleman (2009a). We will label these occurrences for verb sense, re-enter the sense-specific frequencies into a DCA, and compare the resulting sense-specific biases to the overall alternation biases of the 15 verbs in question. The findings of this comparison will serve to fine-tune earlier semantic generalizations about the kinds of verbs preferring the double object construction over the *aan*-dative or vice versa. After this, Section 4 takes a somewhat different perspective: it reports on an experimental study on structural priming, focussing on the effects on priming strength of lexeme-based and sense-based lexical biases. The findings suggest that it is best to include *both* kinds of information in experimental designs. Section 5 is the conclusion.

2. The dative alternation in Dutch

As is evident from Example (3a) above, the Dutch double object construction closely resembles the equivalent English construction formally: it is a three-argument construction with a subject and two bare NP objects which, in the prototypical case, encode the agent, recipient, and theme participant of a 'possessional transfer' event, respectively. Semantically, there is a large degree of overlap, too. Just like its English equivalent, the Dutch construction accommodates verbs of giving as well as verbs from a number of other, semantically related verb classes – verbs of future transfer, verbs of permission, verbs of teaching, telling, and showing, verbs of bringing and sending, etc. – so that it can be used to denote a variety of 'caused reception' scenarios (cf. the seminal analysis of the English ditransitive as a polysemous category built around a prototypical 'X causes Y to receive Z' sense in Goldberg, 1995, 2002, 2006). Interesting differences with English include the presence in Dutch of two sets of complex 'dispossession' verbs (with the prefix *ont-* or the particle *af*, e.g. *ontnemen* and *afnemen*, both of which can be glossed 'take away') which can enter into the double object construction and the virtual absence in the present-day (Netherlandic) standard language of double object uses with verbs of creation and obtaining. Further details about the syntax and semantics of the Dutch DO construction are provided in studies such as Van Belle and Van Langendonck (1996), Janssen (1997), Geeraerts (1998), and Colleman (2009b), the latter two of which take an explicitly construction-based perspective.

In the construction in (3b) above, the recipient is marked by the preposition *aan*, which is cognate with English *on* and German *an*, but which is in this context of course relevantly similar to English *to*.[2] In fact, there are *several* three-argument constructions with prepositional objects in Dutch which display a certain degree of semantic overlap with the DO construction: double object uses with verbs of creation and obtaining, to the extent that these are still possible in the present-day language, alternate with a prepositional construction with *voor* 'for' rather than *aan*, double object uses with certain dispossession verbs alternate with a construction with the source preposition *van* 'from' rather than *aan*, etc. – we refer to Van Belle and Van Langendonck (1996) and Colleman and De Clerck (2009) for further details. This being said, the construction with *aan* is undeniably the default prepositional alternative for the Dutch double object construction, on a par with the *to*-dative in English: unlike the other prepositional constructions, it can denote largely the same array of '(projected) caused reception' scenes as the DO construction – see Colleman (2010) for a detailed corpus-based study of the the *aan*-dative's semantic range. Hence, the label "dative alternation" in Dutch refers first and foremost to the variation between the DO construction and the *aan*-dative; in what follows, wherever we use the term prepositional dative (PD) construction, we refer to this construction with *aan*, specifically.

Given the large degree of formal and semantic similarity between the double object constructions of English and Dutch *and* between the *to*-dative and the *aan*-dative, it should not come as a surprise that existing hypotheses about subtle differences in construal between the constructions involved in the Dutch dative alternation revolve around very much the same set of semantic notions often invoked in the linguistic literature about the English alternation: the DO construction and the prepositional dative differ in the degree of emphasis put on the affectedness and/or involvement of the recipient participant (the DO construction according a more central position to this participant than the *aan*-dative), the PD construction highlights the spatial aspects of the denoted 'transfer' scene whereas

---

2. See Colleman and De Clerck (2009), however, for discussion of a number of (minor) semantic differences between the English *to*-dative and the Dutch *aan*-dative that can be traced back to the different basic spatial semantics of *to* vs. *aan*.

the DO construction highlights the possessional aspects, etc. (see, e.g., Schermer-Vermeer, 1991, 2001; Janssen, 1997; Van Belle and Van Langendonck, 1996). Empirical investigations into the semantic relation between the two constructions are scarce, however: the majority of existing studies rely on semantic judgments about constructed minimal sentence pairs and/or introspection-based observations about the constructional preferences of selected (subclasses of) 'transfer' verbs. In contrast to such studies, Colleman (2009a) builds on the results from a distinctive collexeme analysis of the DO and PD frequencies of 252 potentially alternating ditransitive verbs in a 9 million word sample from the newspaper component of the CONDIV corpus of present-day written Dutch (Grondelaers et al., 2000). 58 verbs were found to be significantly biased towards the *aan*-dative at the 0.05 level of statistical confidence, and 73 verbs showed a likewise significant preference for the double object construction. The lists of the 30 most highly distinctive collexemes for each of the two constructions resulting from the test provided the basis for a number of semantic generalizations, some of which will be revisited below.

3. Polysemy effects: A sense-based distinctive collexeme analysis

3.1 Word-sense variation

In a previous joint investigation, Colleman and Bernolet (2012), we compared the findings from the above-mentioned corpus-based investigation to the findings from a series of picture description experiments conducted in the framework of an experimental study on syntactic priming (which was part of Bernolet, 2008).[3] We noticed a striking contrast in the overall proportions of DO and PD occurrences. In the natural language data from CONDIV, the DO construction was found to occur more than twice as frequently as the *aan*-dative, viz. 11,116 double object instances vs. 4949 *aan*-instances, which amounts to 69.2 and 30.8% of relevant occurrences, respectively. The participants in the picture description experiments, however, produced DO datives in slightly over one-fifth of the total number of relevant responses only, viz. 237 (= 21.8%) DOs versus 851 (= 78.2%) PDs (see Colleman and Bernolet, 2012 for further details on both datasets). One of the factors contributing to this noticeable contrast identified in the 2012 article was *word-sense variation*. The pictures used in the experiments all depicted prototypical 'transfer' scenes involving a concrete object being passed from one human participant to another: the participants were instructed to use the verb printed

---

3. *Syntactic* or *structural priming* refers to the tendency of speakers – first demonstrated in Estival (1985) and Bock (1986) – to repeat syntactic structures across otherwise unrelated utterances, i.e. to re-use structures from the (immediately) preceding discourse.

underneath the picture in their description of the scene; see Figure 1 for an example involving the verb *geven* 'give'. Of course, many of the verbs participating in the dative alternation, including *geven*, are polysemous and can denote all kinds of other scenes besides material transfers of possession, too. Whereas, by definition, the pictures used in the experiment trigger the basic 'transfer of possession' sense, the corpus frequencies reported in Colleman (2009a) generalize over *all* the senses of the verbs included in the investigation. In Colleman and Bernolet (2012), we briefly discussed three cases of verbs where such polysemy effects were at least partly responsible for the less-than-complete agreement between the results from the corpus investigation and those from the experimental study.

GEVEN

Figure 1. Example of a target picture for *geven* 'give'. Intended result: *De cowboy geeft de bokser een/de taart* 'The cowboy gives the boxer a/the cake' or *De cowboy geeft een/de taart aan de bokser* 'The cowboy gives a/the cake to the boxer'

The present investigation wants to explore this issue of word sense variation in the dative alternation in somewhat more detail. To this end, we selected 15 polysemous ditransitive verbs included in the database compiled for Colleman (2009a). The selected verbs had to meet a double criterion:

– The dictionary description in the most recent edition (2006) of the *Van Dale Groot Woordenboek der Nederlandse Taal* (henceforth. GVD) distinguishes between at least two different senses;[4]
– These senses occupy different positions along a "concrete-to-figurative" gradient: there is a fairly prototypical 'transfer of possession/control' sense – a sense that can be depicted by pictures of the kind illustrated in Figure 1 – next to one or several more figurative or metaphorical senses.

---

4. There is a single exception: for *ontfutselen*, the dictionary mentions the two senses distinguished in the analysis (viz. '(secretly) take from' and 'fish out of') alright, but groups them under the same sense label.

In case of several figurative senses, only one of these was selected for the investigation. The 15 test verbs are listed in Table 1 below, together with glosses that give a first approximation of the selected senses. Some of these will be discussed in far more detail in subsection 3.3.

Table 1. The 15 ditransitive verbs selected for the investigation and their selected senses

	Sense 1 ("concrete")	Sense 2 ("figurative")
aanreiken	'hand (on), reach'	'suggest'
bezorgen	'deliver, bring'	'cause (with a DO referring to an effect caused in the IO referent)'
brengen	'bring'	'perform (of salutes, songs, tributes, etc.), pay (a visit)'
doorgeven	'pass (on), hand (on)'	'pass on, let know about (of news, information etc.)'
geven	'give'	'direct at (with a deverbal noun as the DO: kisses, blows, kicks, etc.)'
lenen	'lend'	'lend (one's name, one's cooperation, etc.)'
leveren	'supply, deliver (of goods, as part of a transaction)'	'furnish, bring forward, provide (of evidence, information, etc.)'
meegeven	'give with s.o.'	'tell (something construed as a lesson)'
ontfutselen	'(secretly) take from'	'fish out of (of secrets, information, etc.)'
presenteren	'offer (of food, drink, etc.)'	'show, describe (to an audience)'
schenken	'give (as a present)'	'focus on, devote to (of one's attention, one's energy, etc)'
toevertrouwen	'entrust with (of people or valuable goods)'	'confide in, pass on to (of important information)'
verkopen	'sell'	'direct at (with a deverbal noun as the DO: blows, kicks, head butts, etc.)'
voorhouden	'hold out to, show'	'confront with, remonstrate with'
voorstellen	'introduce'	'propose, suggest'

3.2 A sense-based distinctive collexeme analysis

We hand-coded all DO and PD instances of the 15 test verbs included in Colleman's (2009a) database for verb sense and re-entered these sense-specific observed frequencies in the DCA. Care was taken to select verbs with sufficiently distinct senses, which typically select very different kinds of direct object NPs: in case of the "concrete" senses in the middle column of Table 1, the direct object slot is typically filled by an NP referring to concrete objects or, occasionally, people, whereas the "figurative" senses in the right-hand column select a variety of more abstract direct object referents (effects, actions, attributes, ideas, propositions, etc.). This greatly facilitated the semantic coding process; still, several verbs raised issues that had to be solved on an item-by-item basis, often to do with the demarcation between the selected figurative sense and *other* figurative or metaphorical senses. The added DO and PD frequencies of both senses hardly ever add up to the lexeme-based frequencies listed in Colleman (2009a): especially in the case of highly polysemous verbs such as *geven* 'give' or *bezorgen* 'deliver, provide, cause', many instances from CONDIV represent neither of the two senses selected for the investigation (also see below). The results are summarized in Table 2, which lists the lexeme-based as well as the sense-based collostruction strengths; the raw frequencies are mentioned in brackets (observed DO frequency:observed PD frequency). Negative values indicate a preference for the DO construction, positive values indicate a bias towards the PD construction. The measure of collostruction strength used is the log-transformed Fisher exact p-value (cf. Gries, Hampe, and Schönefeld, 2005) and the DCA was done with version 3.0 of the R-script for collostructional analysis developed by Gries (2004). For clarity's sake, it should be added that, for the lexeme-based as well as for the sense-specific DCA's, we used the overall token frequencies of 11,116 double object instances vs. 4,949 *aan*-instances from Colleman's (2009a) database – rather than simply adding up the attested DO and PD frequencies for this random selection of 15 verbs (in the lexeme-based analysis) or 30 verb senses (in the sense-based analysis). This makes sense, as these added frequencies for the near-exhaustive set of 252 potentially alternating verbs included in Colleman (2009a) provide the best approximation of the *total* frequencies of both constructions in the corpus used, and the whole idea of DCA is that it computes which items stand out in displaying a constructional preference that is significantly different from what would be expected on the basis of the *overall* proportions of the constructions at stake. This means that, for the sense-specific DCA, we simply entered 30 items in the analysis (15 selected verbs x 2 selected senses) and computed to what extent the observed distributions of DO and PD frequencies in these 30 cases differed from the expected distributions given an overall 11,116:4,949 proportion. Of course, for a *complete* verb-sense specific DCA of the Dutch dative alternation, we would have to check for *all* potentially alternating verbs whether it may not be more fruitful to distinguish between several senses. Also, ditransitive verbs may well have more than just *two* different senses. As pointed out by an anonymous reviewer, the 15 selected verbs are quite different in this respect. For *aanreiken*, for instance, the added DO and PD frequencies of both senses included in the analysis ('hand on' and 'suggest') equal the overall frequencies that went into the lexeme-based analysis. For *bezorgen*, to give just one example, this is completely different: the 'deliver, bring' and 'cause an effect' senses add up to 162 tokens, which is only 45% of the grand total of 360 *bezorgen* instances in the database. This means that, for *bezorgen*, a complete sense-specific DCA of the Dutch dative alternation would have to include more than two senses.[5] The aim of the present exercise is somewhat more modest than that, however: we only want to illustrate the added value to be gained from including sense-specific frequencies in quantitative investigations of grammatical alternations, on the basis of a limited sample of verbs and senses. As will be shown below, even this rather small sample of test verbs suffices to shed additional light on the semantics of the dative alternation.

Table 2. Overall and sense specific alternation biases (*: $p<.05$, **: $p<.01$)

Verb	Overall bias	Sense 1	Sense 2
aanreiken	−0.83677 (12:2)	−0.95977 (6:0)	−0.27464 (6:2)
bezorgen	−28.4126** (335:25)	0.563741 (47:25)	−14.4423** (90:0)
brengen	43.28592** (61:177)	−1.78702* (16:1)	70.88457** (13:171)
doorgeven	21.88827** (9:61)	1.469655* (1:4)	11.57765** (7:35)
geven	−5.56451** (2461:939)	2.198693** (191:115)	−12.7718** (157:13)
lenen	3.626959** (11:19)	−1.75992* (11:0)	8.701446** (0:17)
leveren	54.55818** (28:162)	19.34166** (20:70)	7.270694** (8:26)
meegeven	−2.44322** (71:15)	−0.20069 (9:4)	−1.38007* (27:5)
ontfutselen	−2.37941** (29:3)	−1.05553 (14:2)	−1.65011* (15:1)
presenteren	2.611731** (14:18)	−0.53409 (9:2)	4.221796** (5:15)
schenken	13.27942** (71:100)	12.97423** (23:57)	7.177966** (16:34)
toevertrouwen	2.534262** (23:24)	2.357015** (1:6)	−0.3097 (20:8)
verkopen	66.26254** (39:204)	79.29087** (12:186)	−2.14544** (23:2)
voorhouden	−14.1203** (88:0)	−0.6398 (4:0)	−10.5814** (66:0)
voorstellen	2.719117** (72:55)	11.14599** (3:28)	−1.02233 (67:21)

---

5. To give an example, another sense of *bezorgen* frequently attested in the newspaper data is the one illustrated in (i) below. In reports of sports matches, but also of elections and political debates, *bezorgen* is often combined with direct objects such as *de zege/de overwinning* 'the victory', *een voorsprong* 'a lead', *de meerderheid* 'the majority', etc., meaning 'win, be the agent or cause of the indirect object referent getting something'. Such uses qualify neither as material 'bring, deliver' neither as the abstract 'cause an effect' sense selected for the investigation.

  (i) Met drie goals bezorgde Gica Popescu Roemenië in groep 8 in zijn eentje
     with 3   goals delivered PN   Romania in group 8 in his one-DIM
     een vlotte 0–3 zege   in Macedonië.
     a   easy 0–3 victory in Macedonia
     'In group 8, Gica Popescu propelled Romania to an easy 0–3 victory away in Macedonia on his own, with three goals.'

In four out of fifteen cases, viz. with *brengen, geven, lenen,* and *verkopen,* one of the senses selected for the investigation displays a significant bias which is qualitatively different from the overall bias of the verbal lexeme, i.e. has the reverse orientation. In seven more cases, viz. with *bezorgen, meegeven, ontfutselen, presenteren, toevertrouwen, voorhouden* and *voorstellen,* there is a somewhat less dramatic contrast, in that one of the two senses does not mirror the lexeme-based bias but is found by the test to behave more neutrally – though, in some of these cases, this may simply be due to a lack of power, as the overall frequencies of the "concrete" senses, especially, tend to be quite low. In sum, the figures reported in Table 2 corroborate the position that different senses of the same verb may display quite different subcategorization preferences.[6] The sense-based information in the two rightmost columns is completely lost in a lexeme-based collexeme analysis which lumps together all occurrences of the investigated verbs regardless of the lexical semantics involved. Subsection 3.3 will discuss a number of cases where these sense-specific biases can shed more light on the semantic relation between the DO and PD constructions. First, however, we will briefly look into the results of two earlier investigations which included sense-based data in a distinctive collexeme analysis.

Wiechmann (2008) addresses the question what kind of lexical subcategorization information is used for the resolution of temporary syntactic ambiguities of the garden path kind. On the basis of frequencies culled from a sample of the British National Corpus, he computed the lemma-based and sense-based alternation biases of 20 English verbs which can take either a nominal or a sentential complement. The sense-based biases – but, relevantly, not the lexeme-based biases[7] – were found to correlate significantly with the reading time latencies in a self-paced reading experiment reported in Hare, McRae, and Elman (2003). This furnishes proof for the hypothesis that the relevant subcategorization information is not to be situated at the level of the verbal lexeme, but at a more fine-grained sense-specific level of lexical organization. Wiechmann does not, however, address issues of constructional semantics: the results of the sense-based collexeme analysis are not used to shed more light on the semantic relation between the constructions

---

6. In fact, an interesting question is to what extent these different subcategorization probabilities contribute to the perception of distinct "senses". We will not dwell on such matters here, however.

7. Wiechmann (2008) labels the overall biases as *form-based* rather than sense-based. This is a somewhat unfortunate label, in our view, as it suggests that a distinction was made between the different *word forms* of a single verb. Gilquin (2010) uses the label *lemma-based*, but that is even more prone to cause confusion, as in psycholinguistics, *lemma* is often used as a synonym for *verb sense*. To avoid such confusion, we will refer to the overall biases which lump together all the distinct senses and all the distinct word forms of a single verb as *lexeme-based* or *verb-based*.

involved. This is different in Gilquin (2010: Ch. 8), which includes sense-based frequencies in a multiple distinctive collexeme analysis of ten different periphrastic causative constructions in English with the specific aim of getting a better view on what distinguishes these constructions semantically. For instance, in a comparison of the [X *get* Y V$_{pp}$] and [X *have* Y V$_{pp}$] constructions, which are often mentioned in the same breath in the linguistic literature on periphrastic causatives, Gilquin shows that the 'deal with, sort out' sense of the verb *do* is the top collexeme of the *get* pattern (as in *I'll never get my bingo done*) whereas the 'clean, tidy, make attractive' sense of the same verb is much more distinctive for the *have* pattern (as in *I'm having my hair done tomorrow*). These lexical preferences – which would have gone completely unnoticed in a lexeme-based analysis – highlight the importance of the frame of effort/difficulty for the former pattern and the frame of professional service for the latter: the distinctive meanings of both patterns are paraphrased as 'to organise an activity in difficult circumstances or under a tight schedule' and 'to commission someone to do something', respectively (Gilquin, 2010: 220). In the same manner, we will discuss a number of cases in the next subsection where the sense-based alternation biases in Table 2 shed additional light on the semantic relation between the Dutch DO construction and the *aan*-dative.

3.3 Sense-based alternation bias and the dative alternation

The rationale behind DCA is that the lists of distinctive collexemes and their association strengths resulting from the quantitative analysis point towards subtle differences in meaning between the (functionally equivalent) constructions under investigation. In a usage-based approach to language which takes speakers' mental representations of the semantics associated with schematic syntactic patterns to be the result of generalizing over encountered instances, each of which involves specific lexical material filling the various slots of the construction (cf. Langacker, 2000; Goldberg, Casenhiser, and Sethuraman, 2004, *inter alia*), it is natural to assume that "the semantics of constructions can usually be read off from the words most strongly attracted to [them]" (Gries, 2006: 136). After all, schematic argument structure constructions such as the double object construction and the prepositional dative are considered to be composed of whole clusters of verb-specific sub-constructions (e.g. [NP *give* NP NP], [NP *hand* NP NP], [NP *sell* NP to NP], etc.), some of which are more central to the superordinate construction's semantics than others by dint of their high relative frequency. However, in such a bottom-up view of constructional semantics, there is nothing that precludes the existence – and relevance to the superordinate construction's semantics – of even lower subschemas, at the level of the verb sense. The results from our sense-based distinctive collexeme analysis corroborate that different senses of one and the same verb may indeed display quite different degrees of association to the constructions involved in a grammatical alternation.

3.3.1 *The "light verb" uses of* geven *and* verkopen

Some of these observed contrasts can help to further pinpoint the semantic differences between the DO construction and the *aan*-dative. The first verb to be discussed in some detail is *geven* 'give', which displays an overall preference for the DO construction. In Colleman and Bernolet (2012), we already pointed out, on the basis of the frequencies in a 1.5 million word sample from CONDIV, that while the use of the *geven* verb to encode prototypical 'transfer of possession' scenes is typically the first one to come to mind, it is definitely not the most frequently attested use in corpora of natural language. The figures from the whole 9 million word newspaper corpus confirm this trend: the basic 'transfer' meaning accounts for 306 of the 3400 ditransitive *geven* instances in the database only (= 9%). A couple of such prototypical instances are given in (4) below.

(4) a. *De president gaf zijn vrouw onlangs voor*
the president gave his wife recently for
Valentijnsdag een hartvormige gouden pin {waarbij
Valentine's.day a heart.shaped golden pin
hij haar bezwoer nooit meer vreemd te gaan}. [Tel][8]
'Recently, the president gave his wife a heart-shaped gold pin for Valentine's Day {swearing never to cheat on her again}'
b. *{Nadat hij met pensioen was gegaan}, gaf hij de banden*
gave he the tapes
aan een advocaat.
to a lawyer
'{After his retirement}, he gave the tapes to a lawyer'

What is striking is that the alternation bias of this basic transfer of possession sense is qualitatively different from the lexeme-based bias: prototypical *geven* is shown in Table 2 to be significantly attracted to the *aan*-dative. This means that the overall DO bias must be due to the strong preferences for the DO construction of a number of extended senses. One of these is the 'direct at' sense in which the combination of *geven* with a deverbal noun such as *een kus* 'a kiss', *een schop* 'a kick', *een slag* 'a blow', etc. has approximately the same meaning as the base verb (e.g. NP *een kus geven* 'give NP a kiss' ~ NP *kussen* 'kiss NP'), see the instances in (5).

---

[8]. All corpus instances are from the newspaper component of the CONDIV corpus, unless otherwise indicated. The labels in brackets refer to the exact newspaper: NRC = *NRC Handelsblad*, Tel = *De Telegraaf*, Lim = *De Limburger*, Sta = *De Standaard*, GvA = *Gazet van Antwerpen*, HBL = *Het Belang van Limburg*.

(5) a. Toen [de man] opstond en dreigend op hem afkwam,
when the man up-stood and threatening up him off-came
gaf de agent hem een flinke duw. [GvA]
gave the officer him a good push
'When the man rose to his feet and threateningly came closer, the officer gave him a hefty shove'

b. Eind jaren zestig gaf VVD-senator Baas een klap
end years 60 gave VVD-senator PN a smack
aan zijn collega Adams van de Boerenpartij. [Vk 05/10/2002][9]
to his colleague PN of the Farmer's.Party
'In the late sixties, Senator Baas of the VVD gave a smack to his colleague Adams of the Farmer's Party'

There is some debate on the status of such "light verb" constructions as sub-constructions of the schematic DO construction. Trousdale (2008) suggests that English equivalents such as *to give s.o. a kiss* or *a beating* are better not analyzed as instantiating the (regular) double object construction, but as representing a different construction dominated by the general "light verb" construction. Goldberg (1995: 149) does analyse them as instantiations of the DO construction, motivated by a metaphor which "involves understanding actions that are intentionally directed at another person as being entities which are transferred to that person". In any event, this particular cluster of *geven* uses displays a marked preference for double object syntax: the collostruction strength listed for Sense 2 of *geven* in Table 2 is −12,7718, making this the second strongest DO collexeme of all the investigated verb senses (second only to the 'cause an effect' sense of *bezorgen*, which will be discussed below). As a further illustration of the considerable strength of this attraction, it can be pointed out that in Colleman's (2009a) lexeme-based DCA, a collostruction strength greater than 12 suffices to qualify among the *ten* most strongly attracted DO collexemes out of 252 investigated alternating verbs. In other words, the 'direct at' sense of *geven* is strongly associated with the DO construction: the *aan*-dative is not impossible, but it will only be reverted to if this strong semantic preference for the DO construction is overruled by other considerations. In (5b) above, for instance, the choice of PD syntax is probably triggered by the considerable difference in length between the theme and recipient object NPs (as well as by the fact that this is an excerpt from a whole article on sporadic acts of

---

9. This instance was not taken from the CONDIV corpus, but from the web archive of another Dutch newspaper, *De Volkskrant* (last accessed 19/01/2012).

violence in the Dutch parliament, so that *een klap* 'a blow, a smack' may be considered to be highly topical).[10]

The preference of these light verb patterns for the DO construction has been observed before, albeit on the basis of introspection, and it has been attributed to the lack of a spatial transfer (i.e. nothing is actually moving towards the recipient) and/or to the strong degree of affectedness of the recipient participant in the denoted events. A semantic account of the Dutch dative alternation which reduces the alternation to an opposition of a 'caused reception' construction on the one hand and a 'spatial transfer' construction on the other is too simple: as will be shown below, there are clusters of uses which definitely do not involve 'caused motion' or 'spatial transfer', and which prefer the *aan*-dative nonetheless. While this does not rule out the possibility that the presence or absence of a path traversed by the direct object referent is a factor in the dative alternation, it does show that [+/− spatial transfer] cannot be the only semantic determinant. Affectedness is definitely an important part of the story, too: it goes without saying that the events described in (5a) and (5b) have a strong effect on the receiving party and – as has been observed by several authors – there is a strong tendency to encode such heavily affected participants as NPs rather than PPs (e.g. Kirsner, Verhagen, and Willemsen, 1987; Janssen, 1997; Schermer-Vermeer, 1991; Van Belle and Van Langendonck, 1996; see Wierzbicka, 1986; Langacker, 1991, and many others, for similar observations on indirect object affectedness in the *English* DO construction). In addition, there is no reason to choose a construction which focuses on the effect on the theme or on the agent-theme relation (see the hypothesis from Colleman, 2009a on the semantics of the *aan*-dative discussed below), as the theme hardly even exists outside of the action.

Another 'transfer' verb that can be used in combination with deverbal nouns to encode an action directed at another person is *verkopen*, the basic meaning of which is 'sell'. Relevant examples of the DO construction and the *aan*-dative, respectively, are shown in (6).[11]

---

10. It should be stressed that while this section focuses on semantic determinants, we do not want to suggest that the dative alternation is driven by such subtle semantic contrasts alone. Other parameters which have been shown to play a role include the discourse-accessibility of theme and recipient, the length of the theme and recipient NPs, syntactic priming effects, etc. See Gries (2003) and Bresnan et al. (2007), among others, for multifactorial quantitative investigations of the (English) alternation.

11. The lexical possibilities are more limited than with *geven*: as a light verb, *verkopen* only combines with 'blow', 'kick', and 'shove' as the direct object. While *een kus verkopen* (to sell a kiss), for instance, is not impossible, the verb will typically be interpreted in its basic 'commercial transaction' sense there: to offer a kiss for sale. Needless to say, in the examples in (6), Xena and the Mapei cycling team are offering nothing for sale.

(6) a. *De slechte god delft het onderspit als Xena*
the evil god digs the under-spade when PN
hem een keiharde trap verkoopt {na een zevenvoudige
him a INT.hard kick sells
salto vanaf een vlaggenstok hoog aan de muur.} [NRC]
'The evil god tastes defeat as Xena administers him a powerful kick {after a septuple somersault from a flag pole high up on the wall.}'

b. *{Amper één dag nadat Tom Steels in volle spurt uit zijn voethaak catapulteerde} verkocht de Mapei-ploeg een forse dreun aan de*
sold the Mapei-team a heavy blow to the
georganiseerde tegenstand. [GvA]
organised opposition
'{Just a single day after Tom Steels slipped out of his pedals in full sprint}, the Mapei team dealt a heavy blow to the organised opposition'

In Colleman's (2009a) lexeme-based DCA, *verkopen* came out as the second strongest *aan*-collexeme overall, the top collexeme being *overlaten* 'leave, pass on' with a distinctiveness score of 69.07. This strong PD-preference of *verkopen* – which, as it happens, is paralleled by English *sell*, see Gries and Stefanowitsch (2004) – is an argument in favour of one of the semantic hypotheses developed in Colleman (2009a), viz. that the *aan*-dative and the DO construction differ in the amount of emphasis put on the (changing) agent-theme relation. In terms of Goldbergian construction grammar, the *aan*-dative contains two constructionally profiled arguments, viz. the agent and the theme, plus an additional non-profiled recipient argument: the construction highlights the agent and theme participants and their interrelation and backgrounds the involvement of the recipient participant. The double object construction, by contrast, gives pride of place to all three participants and their interrelations, as it has three constructionally profiled arguments. Since *verkopen* lexically profiles the seller and the goods – cf. the traditional frame semantic analysis of verbs of buying and selling in Fillmore (1977) – it tallies well with the hypothesized constructional semantics of the *aan*-dative. We refer to Colleman (2009a) for further elaboration. What matters most in the present context, however, is that *verkopen*'s bias towards the *aan*-dative is even larger if the light verb uses – which, just like the equivalent patterns with *geven*, display a strong preference for the DO construction – are discounted: the basic commercial transaction sense of *verkopen* has a collostruction strength of 79.29, which makes it the strongest PD-collexeme overall.

3.3.2 Bezorgen 'cause an effect'

In passing, Colleman (2009a: 609) also notes that the constructional preference of *verkopen* 'sell' in the dative alternation is shared by several other verbs associated with the commercial transaction frame, such as *leveren* 'furnish, deliver' (3rd most distinctive *aan*-collexeme in the lexeme-based DCA out of the 252 verbs entered in the test) and *betalen* 'pay' (12th most distinctive *aan*-collexeme). In this light, the syntactic behaviour of *bezorgen* 'deliver, provide, furnish' may be quite surprising on first sight: unlike semantically related verbs such as *leveren* etc., *bezorgen* displays a strong overall bias towards the DO construction (in fact, it is the 4th strongest DO-collexeme overall according to the lexeme-based analysis in Colleman, 2009a). Even if we take into account the fact that the events of providing denoted by ditransitive *bezorgen* do not necessarily take place in a commercial context, this finding is still surprising: other "general" verbs of providing such as *verstrekken*, *verschaffen* and *bieden* – all three of which can be glossed as 'provide', though *bieden* can also mean 'offer' – are found to significantly prefer the *aan*-dative (e.g. *verstrekken*) or to behave neutrally (e.g. *verschaffen* and *bieden*). The *bezorgen* facts cease to be surprising, however, if we inspect the sense-specific alternation biases in Table 2. The verb is frequently used with a direct object NP referring to an effect caused in the indirect object referent, see the examples in (7), where it is translated as *cause* or plain *give* in English, not as *deliver* or *provide*. Such uses account for 25% of all ditransitive *bezorgen* clauses in the database (90 out of 360). They instantiate another metaphorical extension of the double object construction briefly discussed in Goldberg (1995: 144), which is based on a metaphor that "involves understanding causing an effect in an entity as transferring the effect, construed as an object to that entity".

(7) a. {*In Scandinavische landen is het eten vaak gepekeld.*} *Recepten uit*
      recipes from
   die   landen   bezorgen ons   alleen maar   veel   dorst. [Lim]
   those countries deliver   us   only   but   much thirst
   '{In the Scandinavian countries, the food is often pickled.} Recipes from those countries give us nothing but thirst.'

b. {*[Bommel] is in zeker twintig talen en dialecten vertaald, in 21 landen gepubliceerd*} *en   heeft miljoenen lezers   intens   genoegen*
      and has   millions   readers intense pleasure
   bezorgd. [NRC]
   delivered
   '{Bommel [a profoundly Dutch comic strip, SB&TC] is translated in at least twenty different languages and dialects and published in 21 countries} and it has given millions of readers intense pleasure.'

c. {*Leerkrachten klagen graag over hun stresserend beroep. Maar ze vergeten soms*} *dat zij op hun beurt stress bezorgen aan*
    that they on their turn stress deliver to
duizenden jongeren.
thousands youngs

<http://www.klasse.be/archief/we-verstressen-elkaar/>, last accessed 19/01/2012

'{Teachers like to complain about their stressful profession. But sometimes they forget} that in their turn, they give stress to thousands of young people.'

As shown in (7c), this sense of *bezorgen* is not incompatible with the *aan*-dative. Such instances are rare, however: *bezorgen* 'cause' is strongly biased toward the double object construction; in fact, (7c) is an example retrieved from the Internet as the database did not include a single instance of this kind. In the hierarchical constructional network, [NP [*bezorgen* NP NP['effect']]] is a salient and highly entrenched sub-construction of the DO construction, whereas the [NP [*bezorgen* NP['effect'] *aan* NP]] sub-construction of the *aan*-dative is hardly entrenched. This preference for the DO construction can be related to the same semantic considerations we discussed in relation to the "light verb" patterns with *geven* and *verkopen* above: the indirect object referents in (7) are heavily affected by the denoted event, and there is no change in the agent-theme relation. The basic 'provide, deliver' sense accounts for 20% of the ditransitive *bezorgen* instances (72 out of 360) and behaves much more neutrally, just like other verbs of providing: it displays a slight preference for the *aan*-dative, which is not statistically significant.

3.3.3 The "figurative" senses of *brengen* 'bring' and *lenen* 'lend'

There are two more verbs with a marked contrast between the alternation biases of the distinct senses selected for the investigation, viz. *brengen* 'bring' and *lenen* 'lend'. In contrast to what we have seen with *geven* 'give' and *verkopen* 'sell', it is the figurative senses of these verbs which are strongly biased towards the PD construction, whereas the concrete 'transfer' senses display a preference for the DO construction. These figurative senses are illustrated in (8) and (9) below.[12]

(8) a. [*De vrijwilligers*] *brengen de zieken een bezoekje*
    the volunteers bring the ill a visit
    op de kamer [GvA]
    in the room
    'The volunteers pay the sick a visit in their rooms'

---

12. Again, (9a) is a Web example as there was no such example to be found in the original database.

b. *De Congolese president Kabila brengt deze week een*
the Congolese president PN brings this week a
bezoek aan de paus. [Lim]
visit to the pope
'The Congolese president Kabila pays a visit to the pope this week'

(9) a. {*Puss In Boots, de temperamentvolle kat uit Shrek 2, krijgt zijn eigen film.*}
Antonio Banderas leende het personage zijn stem
PN lent the character his voice
{*en zal dit naar alle waarschijnlijkheid in de spin-off weer gaan doen.*}
<http://www.filmtotaal.nl/artikel.php?id=4228>, last accessed 19/01/2012
'{Puss In Boots, the temperamental cat in *Shrek 2* will get his own film.}
Antonio Banderas lent the character his voice {and will most probably do that again in the spin-off.}'

b. *Actrice Ming Na-Wen ... leende haar stem aan Mulan,*
actress PN lent her voice to Mulan
{*maar voor de liedjes werd een beroep gedaan op Len Salonga.*} [HBL]
'The actress Ming Na-Wen lent her voice to Mulan, but Len Salonga was engaged for the songs'

The preference of these senses for the *aan*-dative warns us against an all too simplistic account of the dative alternation in terms of abstract vs. concrete 'transfer' scenarios: it is sometimes suggested that the DO construction has specialized in the encoding of all kinds of "abstract" events, whereas the *aan*-dative is the default construction for the encoding of "regular" transfers of possession in which the theme traverses a spatiotemporal path from the agent to the recipient (e.g. Kooij, 1975; Ebeling, 2006: 262). The relevant senses of *brengen* and *lenen* clearly denote abstract events in which the theme is definitely *not* moving along a spatiotemporal path; it is not even readily thought of as a separate participant in the event, just as in the case of *een kus/duw/schop/etc. geven* 'give a kiss/shove/kick/...' (also see Kirsner, Verhagen, and Willemsen, 1987 and Schermer-Vermeer, 1991). Why then do these semi-idiomatic *brengen* and *lenen* patterns prefer the *aan*-dative, whereas the *geven* and *verkopen* patterns discussed above prefer the DO construction? The most likely explanation is that it has got something to do with affectedness or the lack thereof: unlike the receiver of, say, a smack to the head, the receiver of a visit is not particularly affected by the event. Note that whereas both instances in (8) feature animate entities which are being paid a visit, the indirect object slot in *een bezoek brengen* 'pay a visit' is often filled by NPs referring to a location, too, which, by definition, cannot be construed as particularly affected (e.g. *Hij bracht een bezoekje aan Amsterdam* 'He paid a visit to Amsterdam'). Similarly, the indirect object in ditransitive *lenen* clauses with a direct object NP from the class *zijn naam/stem/gezicht/medewerking* (i.e. 'lend one's name/voice/face/collaboration') often refers to an inanimate entity, such as a project, a product or a business. An additional factor contributing to the *aan*-preference in the case of these *lenen* patterns may be the possessive determiner of the direct object NP (e.g. in (9b) *Zij leende haar stem* 'She lent her voice'): a plausible formal hypothesis falling out from Colleman's (2009a) account of the *aan*-dative as highlighting the agent-theme relation would be that the use of a possessive pronoun referring back to the subject NP in the determiner slot of the direct object NP triggers the choice for the *aan*-dative construction. We leave this as a matter for future research, however.

To sum up, the sample of 15 test verbs contains several cases in which the corpus data show the distinct senses of one and the same verb to display markedly different alternation biases. The inclusion of sense-based data in a DCA provides information that is lost, or at least obscured, in a lexeme-based investigation, thus offering a finer-grained view on the semantic differences between the constructions at stake. Another question, however, is whether speakers have access to such sense-specific alternation biases – and, if so, whether these are stored *alongside* the overall alternation biases at the lexeme level, or *instead* of them. This question is to be addressed through psycholinguistic experimentation. The next section presents the results of a first experiment on the influence of both kinds of lexical bias on the strength of syntactic priming.

4. Lexeme-based and sense-based alternation bias in syntactic priming

4.1 The experiment

We further investigated the influence of lexeme-based and sense-based lexical biases on syntactic choices in a syntactic priming experiment in which participants alternated between reacting to written picture descriptions and describing target pictures of dative actions. Like in other syntactic priming experiments (see Pickering and Ferreira, 2008 for a review), the picture descriptions served as sentence primes that were used to influence the participants' target descriptions.

Twenty-five undergraduate students (all native speakers of Dutch) from Ghent University participated in our experiment in exchange for course credits. The set with critical stimuli for the participants contained 45 pictures (3 different target pictures for each target verb) showing line drawings of dative actions with one of the 15 test verbs printed beneath. For each of these pictures, five prime sentences were constructed (one for each prime condition): two prime sentences using the DO construction, two primes using the PD construction with *aan* and a baseline prime sentence using an ordinary monotransitive construction. In the DO and PD priming conditions, the verb used in the prime sentence was either identical to the verb that was printed on the corresponding target picture (same verb conditions) or different (different verb conditions). While the prime sentences always used the dative verb in its figurative meaning, the target pictures always depicted the concrete 'transfer' meaning of the verb. The response patterns in the baseline condition were used to assess the participants' general syntactic preference in unprimed conditions, as well as their verb-specific preferences for the individual target verbs. Apart from the critical pictures, non-critical pictures were selected as fillers. The fillers showed pictures of intransitive scenes (e.g., a cowboy weeping). Additionally, 88 pictures were selected for the participant's verification set. These pictures were used for a verification task that was used to mask the real purpose of the experiment.

The prime sentences were presented in five counterbalanced lists. In each of these lists the primes were presented equally often in the five different priming conditions (DO-prime same verb, DO-prime different verb, PD-prime same verb, PD-prime different verb and baseline) and across all participants every target picture was presented equally often in each of the five conditions. Each verb was used three times in each list. For an example, the five prime sentences used in combination with one of the target pictures for *toevertrouwen* (see Figure 2) are listed in (10).

(10) a. *De ballerina verkoopt de lerares een kopstoot.*   DO-diff
the dancer sells the teacher a head-butt
'The dancer gives the teacher a butt of the head.'

b. *De ballerina verkoopt een kopstoot aan de lerares.*   PD-diff
the dancer sells a head-butt to the teacher.
'The dancer gives a butt of the head to the teacher.'

c. *De secretaresse vertrouwt de pater haar geheim toe.*   DO-same
the secretary trusts the monk her secret to.
'The secretary entrusts the monk with her secret.'

d. *De secretaresse vertrouwt haar geheim toe*   PD-same
the secretary trusts her secret to
aan de pater.
to the monk
'The secretary entrusts her secret to the monk.'

e. *De lerares kietelt de pater.*   baseline
the teacher tickles the monk.
'The teacher tickles the monk.'

Across all conditions, the participants produced 239 DO responses (21.2%), 824 PD responses (73.2%) and 62 other responses (5.5%). For the purpose of the present paper, however, we will only analyze the data of the baseline condition and the

TOEVERTROUWEN

Figure 2. Example of a target picture for *toevertrouwen* 'entrust with'. Intended result: *De zuster vertrouwt de pater het kind toe* or *De zuster vertrouwt het kind toe aan de pater* 'The nun entrusts the child to (the care of) the friar'

priming conditions in which a different verb was used in prime and target descriptions (DO-prime different verb and PD-prime different verb). This is because, when the same verb is used in prime and target, the syntactic priming effects may not only be artificially boosted by the verb repetition (cf. Pickering and Branigan, 1998), it is also impossible to disentangle effects of prime and target verb bias. Table 3 presents the response frequencies and percentages of DO datives in the three critical conditions of our experiment.

Table 3. DO and PD responses in the crucial conditions of the priming experiment

	Baseline		DO prime		PD prime	
	DO:PD	% DO datives	DO:PD	% DO datives	DO:PD	% DO datives
aanreiken	2:12	14.3%	6:8	42.9%	2:13	13.3%
bezorgen	5:10	33.3%	6:9	40.0%	5:10	33.3%
brengen	4:10	28.6%	4:8	33.3%	3:8	27.3%
doorgeven	0:14	0.0%	0:14	0.0%	0:15	0.0%
geven	2:12	14.3%	4:11	26.7%	2:13	13.3%
lenen	1:13	7.1%	5:8	38.5%	1:14	6.7%
leveren	1:13	7.1%	1:14	6.7%	3:11	21.4%
meegeven	5:10	33.3%	4:11	26.7%	2:13	13.3%
ontfutselen	2:13	13.3%	5:10	33.3%	2:12	14.3%
presenteren	7:8	46.7%	2:13	13.3%	3:12	20.0%
schenken	4:8	33.3%	7:8	46.7%	7:8	46.7%
toevertrouwen	3:12	20.0%	2:13	13.3%	5:9	35.7%
verkopen	2:12	14.3%	2:12	14.3%	3:12	20.0%
voorhouden	7:4	63.6%	11:2	84.6%	7:4	63.6%
voorstellen	0:15	0.0%	0:15	0.0%	0:12	0.0%

The participants' responses were fit using a mixed logit model (see Jaeger, 2008 for discussion of the use of mixed logit models for categorical data analysis) that predicts the logit-transformed likelihood of a PD-response. We included random intercepts for participants and items (nested under target verb) in the models discussed below (other random effects or interactions did not significantly improve the log-likelihood of the models).

The first model we built investigated to which extent the response patterns in our experiment were influenced by the bias of the target verb. We used the lexeme-based and sense-based alternation biases computed on the basis of the corpus data for this. There is a slight alteration in comparison with the figures reported in Table 2 above, however, in that, following Wiechmann (2008), we used discounted log odds ratios rather than log-transformed Fisher Exact p-values as a measure of association strength – this was done because odds ratios approximate the results of more accurate measures fairly well while being less dependent on sample sizes (cf. Wiechmann, 2008: 454). As the lexeme-based bias and the sense-specific bias of Sense 1 (= the bias of the verb used in its "concrete" sense) of the target verbs were correlated (Pearson's $r = 0.48$), we did not just add both predictors to the model: rather, we regressed the sense-specific verb bias of each target verb against its verb-based bias.[13] The residuals of this regression were then added as a continuous predictor in addition to the sense-specific verb bias of the target verbs. So the fixed factors in our full target verb bias model were as in (11).

(11)   lmer (Response ~ Prime + Specific Target Verb Bias + Residuals Target Verb Bias + Prime : Specific Target Verb Bias + Prime : Residuals Target Verb Bias + Prime : Specific Target Verb Bias : Residuals Target Verb Bias)

Model comparisons using the likelihood ratio test showed, however, that the three-way interaction between Prime, Specific Target Verb Bias and Residuals Target Verb Bias did not significantly improve the fit of the model ($\chi^2(2) = 0.27$, $p > .1$).[14] The same was true for the interaction between Specific Target Bias and Residuals Target Bias ($\chi^2(1) = 0.77$, $p > .1$) and the interaction between Prime and Residuals Target Bias ($\chi^2(2) = 2.03$, $p > .1$). The interaction between Prime and Specific Target Bias, however, *did* significantly improve the fit of our model ($\chi^2(2) = 8.77$, $p < .05$), as did the Residuals of the Target Bias ($\chi^2(1) = 12.83$, $p < .001$).

---

13. All biases were centered to their means before they were used in the analyses. Residuals Target Bias = residuals (lm(scale(Specific Target Bias, scale = F)) ~ scale(General Target Bias, scale = F)).

14. For this model as well as the other models, we started from a full model and performed a stepwise backward elimination of non-significant predictors.

As a next step, we tested a model that investigated the effect of the sense-specific and/or general verb bias of the *prime* verbs on the response patterns, while controlling for effects of target verb bias. Again, we first regressed the specific verb bias of each prime verb (in this case, the bias of Sense 2, the "figurative" sense in Table 2 above) against its verb-based bias, because both biases were highly correlated (Pearson's r = 0.76). The model included the residuals of this regression and the specific verb bias of each prime verb. The fixed factors in our prime verb bias model thus were Prime (BASELINE, DO PRIME, PD PRIME), Specific Prime Verb Bias and Residuals Prime Verb Bias and the interactions between these factors. Specific Target Verb Bias, Residuals Target Verb Bias and the interaction between Prime and Specific Target Verb Bias were added in order to control for effects of target verb bias (see (12) for the fixed factors in the full model).

(12) lmer (Response ~ Prime + Specific Prime Verb Bias + Residuals Prime Verb Bias + Specific Target Verb Bias + Residuals Target Verb Bias + Prime: Specific Prime Verb Bias + Prime: Residuals Prime Verb Bias + Prime: Specific Target Verb Bias + Prime: Specific Prime Verb Bias: Residuals Prime Verb Bias)

Model comparisons showed that Specific Prime Verb Bias and Residuals Prime Verb Bias as well as their interactions with other factors in the model did not at all influence the response patterns or the priming effects observed in our experiment (all p-values > .08). The simplest model for our data was a model that only included Prime, Specific Target Verb Bias, Residuals Target Verb Bias and an interaction between Prime and Specific Target Verb Bias.

Table 4. Summary of the fixed effects in the mixed logit model (N = 675; log-likelihood = -262.5)

Predictor	Coefficient	SE	Wald Z	p
Intercept	2.44	(0.466)	5.25	<.001
Prime DO	−0.54	(0.298)	−1.82	<.07
Prime PD	−0.06	(0.297)	−0.19	>.1
Specific Target Bias	−0.86	(0.333)	−2.57	<.05
Residuals Target Bias	−0.93	(0.237)	−3.92	<.001
Interaction = *Prime DO & Specific Target Bias*	−0.42	(0.408)	−1.02	>.1
Interaction = *Prime PD & Specific Target Bias*	0.78	(0.406)	1.92	<.06

The intercept of our final model, which is summarized in Table 4, represents the log-odds for a PD-response in the baseline condition, for items at the centre of the Specific Target Verb Bias variable. The significant positive intercept (2.44) indicates that there was an overall bias towards PD-datives: for a verb at the centre of the target verb bias variable the chances for a PD-response in the baseline were significantly higher than 50%. The mean proportion of PDs in the baseline was 78%. This percentage decreased to 72% in the DO-condition; in the PD condition the percentage amounted to 78.1%. The effect of DO-priming (6.0%) was marginally significant; the effect of PD-priming was very small (0.1%) and not significant (see Table 4). The responses in the baseline condition were influenced by the specific bias of the target verb and by the residuals of the regression between the lexeme-based and the specific verb bias: the odds for a PD-dative in the baseline condition decreased significantly as the bias towards a DO-dative increased (see Figure 3). This means that the response patterns for each individual verb mirrored the verb biases measured in the corpus data. This effect of target verb bias in the baseline condition left more room for PD-priming for DO-biased verbs, resulting in a marginally significant interaction between Prime and Specific Target Verb Bias. Figure 4, which plots the effects of PD-priming against the specific verb bias of the target verbs, clearly shows negative priming effects on the left hand side of the graph, which increase in strength and become positive effects when the bias towards DO-datives increases.[15]

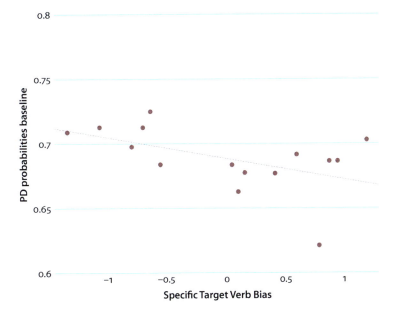

Figure 3. The probabilities of PD responses in the baseline condition plotted against the specific verb bias of the target verbs

---

15. Note that the plots do not show actual data points, but values predicted on the basis of the regression model.

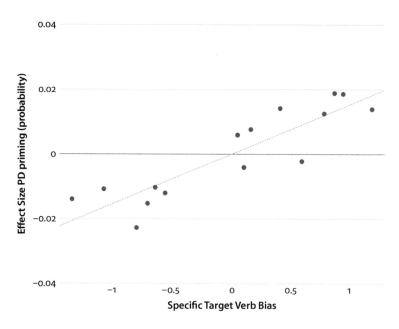

Figure 4. The effects of PD-priming plotted against the specific verb bias of the target verbs

Finally, the finding that specific target verb bias as well as the residuals of the regression between this bias and the general bias of the target verbs were significant predictors in our model might suggest that the lexeme-based bias of the target verbs alone might predict our data equally well as the model reported above. Table 5 summarizes the effects obtained with a model including Prime and General Target Verb Bias and their interactions as fixed factors (as in (13)).

(13)   lmer (Response ~ Prime + General Target Verb Bias + Prime : General Target Verb Bias)

The log-likelihood of the model including the sense-specific verb bias and the residuals is slightly better than the log-likelihood of the model including only the lexeme-based bias of the target verbs (−262.5 vs. −264.4). Both models yield very similar results. Crucially, however, the lexeme-based bias of the target verbs did not interact with the strength of PD-priming. Figure 5 shows that, when the general target verb bias is used as a predictor, there is no clear relationship between target verb bias and the strength of PD priming – though the figure may on first sight suggest something of a trend, note that the slope of the regression line is much flatter than in Figure 4.

Table 5. Summary of the fixed effects in the mixed logit model ($N = 675$; log-likelihood $= -264.4$)

Predictor	Coefficient	SE	Wald Z	p
Intercept	2.41	(0.468)	5.16	<.001
Prime DO	−0.54	(0.294)	−1.83	<.07
Prime PD	−0.05	(0.296)	−0.18	>.1
General Target Bias	−0.97	(0.286)	−3.41	<.001
Interaction = Prime DO & General Target Bias	−0.54	(0.354)	−1.52	>.1
Interaction = Prime PD & General Target Bias	0.36	(0.340)	1.02	>.1

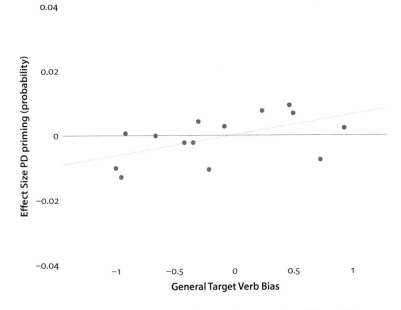

Figure 5. The effects of PD-priming plotted against the general verb bias of the target verbs

4.2 Discussion

The data obtained in our syntactic priming experiment showed stronger priming for DO-datives than for PD-datives, an effect of target verb bias in the baseline condition and an interaction between target verb bias and the strength of PD-priming. So far, the results of our experiment are very similar to the results of the Bernolet & Hartsuiker (2010) study. In their study, however, the effect of target verb bias on the baseline responses and priming effects was obtained when the lexeme-based bias of the target verbs was used in the analyses. When we used this measure in our study, we only obtained an effect in the baseline condition. In addition to the effects of target verb bias, Bernolet and Hartsuiker (2010) also found an effect of prime verb bias on the strength of DO-priming: the strength of DO-priming decreased as the prime verbs became less biased towards a PD-dative and more biased towards a DO-dative. Effects of prime verb bias (the specific verb bias and the residuals of the regression between this bias and the general bias of the prime verbs) were, however, completely absent in our data.

Our failure to find effects of prime verb bias might be due to a lack of power in the current experiment: the Bernolet and Hartsuiker (2010) study included more than twice as many participants (57 vs. 25 in our experiment) and more items in each cell of the design (16 vs. 10). It is also possible, however, that the difference in results is caused by the primes that were used in both studies. In our study, all critical prime sentences used the dative verbs in their "figurative" meanings, while in Bernolet and Hartsuiker's study all primes used the "literal" meaning of the prime verb. Consequently, the concreteness of the theme participants used in the dative primes differs between both studies: our primes contained abstract themes, while the study by Bernolet and Hartsuiker (2010) used concrete themes. In both cases, however, the target pictures depicted actions involving concrete themes that were compatible with the literal meaning of the target verb. It is possible that this mismatch in the meaning of the prime and target verbs and/or the concreteness of the themes involved in the prime and target actions caused weaker priming in our study. It has not yet been investigated whether these factors influence the strength of syntactic priming, but there are some data that speak for this hypothesis. In the domain of word recognition, it has been shown, for example, that associative priming does not occur for word pairs that mismatch in concreteness (Bleasdale, 1987). A syntactic priming study that used primes containing abstract nouns and verbs with multiple senses is Hartsuiker and Kolk (1998), which investigates syntactic priming for Dutch active and passive transitives. Their experiments included prime sentences as *Het lawaai onderbreekt de journalist* [The noise interrupts the journalist] and *De transformator voedt de apparaten* [The transformer feeds the appliances]. The transitive priming effects obtained in their study are much weaker than the priming effects obtained in a study by Bernolet, Hartsuiker, and Pickering (2009) that used more concrete prime sentences in a comparable design (3 vs. 40% priming).

The most important result of our experiment is, however, that, in unprimed conditions, the syntactic choices made by the participants mirrored the sense-specific verb biases that were measured in the corpus data and that the priming effect caused by PD primes interacted with these sense-specific verb biases. Crucially, this interaction offered an explanation for the absence of an overall effect of PD priming in our data: the negative priming effects for PD-biased target verbs cancelled out the positive priming effects for DO-biased target verbs. We admit that, like in other studies investigating syntactic priming for Dutch datives (Bernolet and Hartsuiker, 2010; Hartsuiker et al., 2008), the priming effects observed for PD primes were very small, due to the overall preference for PD datives. By looking at the interaction between the priming effects and the sense-specific bias of the target verbs, however, we were able to demonstrate that DO-biased target verbs offer some "room" for effects of PD priming. The analyses that used the general verb bias of the target verbs as a predictor did not provide this information.

Our results have repercussions for studies investigating effects of verb bias on syntactic priming and for studies on dative priming in general. They do not only indicate that sense-specific verb biases should be used to look at effects of verb bias, they also suggest that the response patterns might differ depending on which verb sense has to be used in the target sentence: in experiments using pictures to elicit target sentences the responses will be heavily influenced by the literal bias of the target verbs; if only the target verb is presented as a stimulus, the influence of the literal target verb bias might be much weaker. The fact that the baseline responses and the effects of PD priming were influenced by the sense-specific verb bias of the target verbs indicates that speakers are sensitive to sense-specific verb biases and that they store this information in memory. Hence, we still believe it should be possible to obtain effects of sense-specific prime verb bias on the strength of syntactic priming. Before we undertake any further attempts to investigate these effects, however, we should investigate whether dative priming is modulated by the abstractness of the themes in the dative prime sentences. If it turns out that dative primes with abstract themes cause weaker overall priming than primes with concrete themes, the chances of finding a sense-specific effect of prime verb bias might be higher if we use the latter kind of primes. It is also possible that priming effects are stronger when prime and target sentences use the same verb sense than when they use different senses. Such a 'sense boost' to dative priming would also point towards sense-contingent verb representations in the mental lexicon.[16]

---

[16]. These issues are further investigated in Bernolet, Colleman, and Hartsuiker (2014), a priming study that was conducted after the present investigation.

5. Conclusion

The results of our sense-based DCA of 15 polysemous verbs which alternate between the Dutch double object construction and the *aan*-dative corroborate that distinct senses of one and the same verb may display widely different alternation biases. We have discussed several cases where this teasing apart of the various senses sheds more light on the behaviour of the investigated verbs in the dative alternation. Of course, this is not to say that interesting polysemy effects will be found in *every* case: some of the verbs selected for the investigation display a markedly consistent alternation bias across their different senses. This is most notably the case for *aanreiken*, *meegeven*, and *ontfutselen*, three verbs which are polysemous between a prototypical 'transfer of possession' sense and a 'communicative transfer' sense (the transfer taking place in the default direction from the subject referent to the indirect object referent in the first two cases, and in the reverse direction with *ontfutselen*). This finding suggests that, if no further semantic factors intervene, the simple distinction between material and communicative transfers does not matter very much for the dative alternation – though, needless to say, this hypothesis needs to be tested against the results of a sense-based DCA including *more* verbs which are polysemous between a 'material transfer' and a 'communicative transfer' meaning before this can be stated with any certainty. In any event, we hope to have illustrated the potential of the systematic inclusion of verb sense distinctions in linguistic studies of argument structure alternations for refining our view of distinctions in constructional semantics. In the second part of the paper, we have reported on an experiment aimed at the investigation of lexeme-based and sense-based bias effects on syntactic priming. Though the results of this experiment were somewhat less conclusive than might have been desirable – we found no effect of the lexeme-based or sense-based biases of *prime* verbs – they still corroborate the position that speakers are sensitive to sense-based verb biases and that they store this information in memory, since we found an interaction between the strength of PD priming and the sense-specific biases of target verbs. The lexeme-based bias of the target verbs, however, was found to be a significant factor in the model, too. In a usage-based perspective, it makes sense that speakers should keep track of verb subcategorization preferences at different levels of schematization, i.e., both at the level of specific verb senses and at the aggregated level of the verbal lexeme. We aim to further explore such matters in future research.

References

Bernolet, Sarah. (2008). *Lexical-syntactic representations in bilingual sentence production*. Unpublished Ph.D. dissertation, Ghent University.

Bernolet, Sarah, Colleman, Timothy, & Hartsuiker, Robert J. (2014). The "sense boost" to dative priming: evidence for sense-specific verb-structure links. *Journal of Memory and Language*, 76, 113–126. doi: 10.1016/j.jml.2014.06.006

Bernolet, Sarah, & Hartsuiker, Robert J. (2010). Does verb bias modulate syntactic priming? *Cognition*, 114, 455–461. doi: 10.1016/j.cognition.2009.11.005

Bernolet, Sarah, Hartsuiker, Robert J., & Pickering, Martin J. (2007). Shared syntactic representations in bilinguals: Evidence for the role of word-order repetition. *Journal of Experimental Psychology: Learning, Memory and Cognition*, 33, 931–949. doi: 10.1037/0278-7393.33.5.931

Bleasdale, Fraser A. (1987). Concreteness-dependent associative priming: Separate lexical organisation for concrete and abstract words. *Journal of Experimental Psychology: Learning, Memory and Cognition*, 13, 582–594. doi: 10.1037/0278-7393.13.4.582

Bock, J. Kathryn. (1986). Syntactic persistence in language production. *Cognitive Psychology*, 18, 355–387. doi: 10.1016/0010-0285(86)90004-6

Bresnan, Joan, Cueni, Anna, Nikitina, Tatiana, & Baayen, Harald R. (2007). Predicting the dative alternation. In G. Boume, I. Kraemer, & J. Zwarts (Eds.), *Cognitive foundations of interpretation* (pp. 69–94). Amsterdam: Royal Netherlands Academy of Science.

Colleman, Timothy. (2009a). Verb disposition in argument structure alternations: A corpus study of the Dutch dative alternation. *Language Sciences*, 31, 593–611. doi: 10.1016/j.langsci.2008.01.001

Colleman, Timothy. (2009b). The semantic range of the Dutch double object construction. A collostructional perspective. *Constructions and Frames*, 1, 190–220. doi: 10.1075/cf.1.2.02col

Colleman, Timothy. (2010). Beyond the dative alternation: The semantics of the Dutch *aan*-dative. In D. Glynn & K. Fischer (Eds.), *Quantitative methods in cognitive semantics: Corpus-driven approaches* (pp. 271–303). Berlin/New York: Mouton de Gruyter.

Colleman, Timothy, & Bernolet, Sarah. (2012). Alternation biases in corpora vs. picture description experiments: DO-biased and PD-biased verbs in the Dutch dative alternation. In D. Divjak & S. Th. Gries (Eds.), *Frequency effects in language representation* (pp. 87–125). Berlin/New York: Mouton de Gruyter.

Colleman, Timothy, & De Clerck, Bernard. (2009). 'Caused motion'? The semantics of the English *to*-dative and the Dutch *aan*-dative. *Cognitive Linguistics*, 20, 5–42. doi: 10.1515/COGL.2009.002

Ebeling, C. L. (2006). *Semiotaxis. Over theoretische en Nederlandse syntaxis* [Semiotaxis. On theoretical and Dutch syntax]. Amsterdam: Amsterdam University Press. doi: 10.5117/9789053568866

Estival, Dominique. (1985). Syntactic priming of the passive in English. *Text*, 5, 7–22.

Fillmore, Charles J. (1977). Topics in lexical semantics. In R. Cole (Ed.), *Current issues in linguistic theory* (pp. 76–138). Bloomington: Indiana University Press.

Gahl, Susanne, & Garnsey, Susan M. (2004). Knowledge of grammar, knowledge of usage: Syntactic probabilities affect pronunciation variation. *Language*, 80, 748–775. doi: 10.1353/lan.2004.0185

Geeraerts, Dirk. (1998). The semantic structure of the indirect object in Dutch. In W. van Langendonck & W. Van Belle (Eds.), *The Dative. Volume II: Theoretical and Contrastive Studies* (pp. 185–210). Amsterdam/: John Benjamins. doi: 10.1075/cagral.3.08gee

Gilquin, Gaëtanelle. (2006). The verb slot in causative constructions. Finding the best fit. *Constructions*, 1–3.
Gilquin, Gaëtanelle. (2010). *Corpus, cognition and causative constructions*. Amsterdam: John Benjamins. doi:10.1075/scl.39
Goldberg, Adele E. (1992). The inherent semantics of argument structure: The case of the English ditransitive. *Cognitive Linguistics*, 3, 37–74. doi:10.1515/cogl.1992.3.1.37
Goldberg, Adele E. (1995). *Constructions: A construction Grammar approach to argument structure*. Chicago: University of Chicago Press.
Goldberg, Adele E. (2002). Surface generalizations: an alternative to alternations. *Cognitive Linguistics*, 13, 327–56.
Goldberg, Adele E. (2006). *Constructions at work: The nature of generalization in language*. Oxford: Oxford University Press.
Goldberg, Adele E. (2011). Corpus evidence of the viability of statistical preemption. *Cognitive Linguistics*, 22, 131–153. doi:10.1515/cogl.2011.006
Goldberg, Adele E., Casenhiser, Devin, & Sethuraman, Nitya. (2004). Learning argument structure generalizations. *Cognitive Linguistics*, 15, 289–316. doi:10.1515/cogl.2004.011
Gries, Stefan Th. (2003). Towards a corpus-based identification of prototypical instances of constructions. *Annual Review of Cognitive Linguistics*, 1, 1–27. doi:10.1075/arcl.1.02gri
Gries, Stefan Th. (2004). *Coll.analysis 3.0. A program for R for Windows*.
Gries, Stefan Th. (2005). Syntactic priming: A corpus-based approach. *Journal of Psycholinguistic Research*, 34, 365–399. doi:10.1007/s10936-005-6139-3
Gries, Stefan Th. (2006). Exploring variability within and between corpora: Some methodological considerations. *Corpora*, 1, 109–151. doi:10.3366/cor.2006.1.2.109
Gries, Stefan Th., Hampe, Beate, & Schönefeld, Doris. (2005). Converging evidence: Bringing together experimental and corpus data on the association of verbs and constructions. *Cognitive Linguistics*, 16, 635–676. doi:10.1515/cogl.2005.16.4.635
Gries, Stefan Th., & Stefanowitsch, Anatol. (2004). Extending collostructional analysis: A corpus-based perspective on "alternations". *International Journal of Corpus Linguistics*, 9, 97–129. doi:10.1075/ijcl.9.1.06gri
Grondelaers, Stefan, Deygers, Katrien, Van Aken, Hilde, Van den Heede, Vicky, & Speelman, Dirk. (2000). Het CONDIV-corpus geschreven Nederlands [The CONDIV corpus of spoken Dutch]. *Nederlandse Taalkunde*, 5, 356–363.
GVD = den Boon, Ton, & Geeraerts, Dirk (Eds.). (2006). *Van Dale Groot Woordenboek van de Nederlandse Taal* [Van Dale Comprehensive Dictionary of the Dutch Language]. 14th, revised edition. Utrecht/Antwerpen: Van Dale Lexicografie.
Hare, Mary, McRae, Ken, & Elman, Jeffrey L. (2003). Sense and structure: meaning as a determinant of verb subcategorization preferences. *Journal of Memory and Language*, 48, 281–303. doi:10.1016/S0749-596X(02)00516-8
Hare, Mary, McRae, Ken, & Elman, Jeffrey L. (2004). Admitting that admitting verb sense into corpus analyses makes sense. *Language and Cognitive Processes*, 19, 181–224. doi:10.1080/01690960344000152
Hartsuiker, Robert J., Bernolet, Sarah, Schoonbaert, Sofie, Speybroek, Sara, & Vanderelst, Dieter. (2008). Syntactic priming persists but the lexical boost decays: Evidence from written and spoken dialogue. *Journal of Memory and Language*, 58, 214–238. doi:10.1016/j.jml.2007.07.003
Hartsuiker, Robert J., & Kolk, H.H.J. (1998). Syntactic persistence in Dutch. *Language and Speech*, 41, 143–184.

Hilpert, Martin. (2008). *Germanic future constructions. A usage-based approach to language change.* Amsterdam: John Benjamins. doi:10.1075/cal.7

Jaeger, T. Florian. (2008). Categorical data analysis: Away from ANOVAs (transformation or not) and towards logit mixed models. *Journal of Memory and Language*, 59, 434–446. doi:10.1016/j.jml.2007.11.007

Jaeger, T. Florian, & Snider, Neal. (2007). Implicit learning and syntactic persistence: Surprisal and cumulativity. *University of Rochester Working Papers in the Language Sciences*, 3, 26–44.

Janssen, Theo. (1997). Giving in Dutch: An intra-lexematical and inter-lexematical description. In J. Newman (Ed.), *The linguistics of giving* (pp. 267–306). Amsterdam: John Benjamins. doi:10.1075/tsl.36.10jan

Kirsner, Robert S., Verhagen, Arie, & Willemsen, Mariëtte. (1987). Over PP's, transitiviteit en het zgn. indirekt objekt [On PPs, transitivity and the so-called indirect object]. *Spektator*, 14, 341–347.

Kooij, J. G. (1975). Diachronic aspects of idiom formation. In A. Kraak (Ed.), *Linguistics in the Netherlands 1972/73* (pp. 122–127). Assen: Van Gorcum.

Langacker, Ronald W. (1991). *Foundations of cognitive grammar. Volume II: Descriptive application.* Stanford: Stanford University Press.

Langacker, Ronald W. (2000). A dynamic usage-based model. In M. Barlow & S. Kemmer (Eds.), *Usage based models of language* (pp. 1–63). Stanford: CSLI Publications.

Lauwers, Peter. (2010). Comment dissocier des locutions prépositives quasi-synonymiques?: Essai d'analyse collostructionnelle. *Revue canadienne de linguistique*, 55, 55–84. doi:10.1353/cjl.0.0066

Levelt, Willem. (1989). *Speaking: From intention to articulation.* Cambridge: MIT Press.

Levshina, Natalia, Geeraerts, Dirk, & Speelman, Dirk. (2010). Changing the world vs. changing the mind: Distinctive collexeme analysis of the causative construction with *doen* in Belgian and Netherlandic Dutch. In F. Gregersen, J. Parrot, & P. Quist (Eds.), *Language variation – european perspectives III. Selected papers from the 5th International Conference on Language Variation in Europe, Copenhagen, June 2009* (pp. 111–123). Amsterdam/Philadelphia: John Benjamins. doi:10.1075/silv.7.09lev

Lombardi, Linda, & Potter, Mary C. (1992). The regeneration of syntax in short-term memory. *Journal of Memory and Language*, 31, 713–733. doi:10.1016/0749-596X(92)90036-W

Noël, Dirk, & Colleman, Timothy. (2010). Believe-type raising-to-object and raising-to-subject verbs in English and Dutch: A contrastive investigation in diachronic construction grammar. *International Journal of Corpus Linguistics*, 15, 157–182. doi:10.1075/ijcl.15.2.02noe

Pickering, Martin J., & Branigan, Holly. (1998). The representation of verbs: Evidence from syntactic priming in language production. *Journal of Memory and Language*, 39, 633–651. doi:10.1006/jmla.1998.2592

Pickering, Martin J., & Ferreira, Victor S. (2008). Structural priming: A critical review. *Psychological Bulletin*, 134, 427–459. doi:10.1037/0033-2909.134.3.427

Roland, Douglas, & Jurafsky, Daniel. (2002). Verb sense and verb subcategorization probabilities. In P. Merlo & S. Stevenson (Eds.), *The Lexical basis of sentence processing: Formal, computational, and experimental issues* (pp. 325–345). Amsterdam/Philadelphia: John Benjamins. doi:10.1075/nlp.4.17rol

Schermer-Vermeer, E. C. (1991). *Substantiële versus formele taalbeschrijving: het indirect object in het Nederlands* [Formal versus substantial language analysis: The indirect object in Dutch]. Amsterdam: Universiteit van Amsterdam.

Schermer-Vermeer, E. C. (2001). Grammatica, lexicon en de dubbel-objectsconstructie in het Nederlands en Engels [Grammar, lexicon and the double object construction in Dutch and English]. *Nederlandse Taalkunde*, 6, 22–37.

Stefanowitsch, Anatol. (2006). Negative evidence and the raw frequency fallacy. *Corpus Linguistics and Linguistic Theory*, 2, 61–77.

Strik Lievers, Francesca. (2011). Constructing judgments: The interaction between adjectives and clausal complements. In M. Kokopka et al. (Eds.), *Grammatik und Korpora 2009. Dritte Internationale Konferenz. Mannheim, 22.4.–24.9.2009* (pp. 287–304). Tübingen: Narr.

Trousdale, Graeme. (2008). Constructions in grammaticalization and lexicalization: Evidence from the history of a composite predicate construction in English. In G. Trousdale & N. Gisborne (Eds.), *Constructional approaches to English grammar* (pp. 33–67). Berlin/New York: Mouton de Gruyter.

Trueswell, John C., & Kim, Albert E. (1998). How to prune a garden path by nipping it in the bud: Fast priming of verb argument structure. *Journal of Memory and Language*, 39, 101–132. doi:10.1006/jmla.1998.2565

Van Belle, William, & Van Langendonck, W. (1996). The indirect object in Dutch. In W. Van Belle & W. Van Langendonck (Eds.), *The dative. Volume 1: Descriptive studies* (pp. 217–250). Amsterdam: John Benjamins. doi:10.1075/cagral.2.10van

Wiechmann, Daniël. (2008). Initial parsing decisions and lexical bias: Corpus evidence from local NP/S-ambiguities. *Cognitive Linguistics*, 19, 439–455. doi:10.1515/COGL.2008.017

Wierzbicka, Anna. (1986). The semantics of 'internal dative' in English. *Quaderni di Semantica*, 7, 121–35.

Wilson, Michael P., & Garnsey, Susan M. (2008). Making simple sentences hard: Verb bias effects in simple direct object sentences. *Journal of Memory and Language*, 60, 368–392. doi:10.1016/j.jml.2008.09.005

Wulff, Stefanie. (2006). *Go–V* vs. *go–and–V* in English: a case of constructional synonymy? In S. Th. Gries & A. Stefanowitsch (Eds.), *Corpora in cognitive linguistics* (pp. 101–125). Berlin/New York: Mouton de Gruyter.

PART III

Multifactorial and multivariate analysis

CHAPTER 8

A multifactorial analysis of *that*/zero alternation
The diachronic development of the zero complementizer with *think, guess* and *understand*

C. Shank, K. Plevoets and J. Van Bogaert
Bangor University / University College Ghent / Ghent University

> This corpus-based study uses a stepwise logistic regression analysis to examine the diachronic development of *that*/zero alternation with three verbs of cognition, viz. *think, guess* and *understand* in both spoken and written corpora from 1560–2012. Eleven structural features which have been claimed in the literature to predict the presence of the zero complementizer form are tested to see if (1) there is indeed a diachronic trend towards more zero use, (2) whether the conditioning factors proposed in the literature indeed predict the zero form, (3) to what extent these factors interact and (4) whether the predictive power of the conditioning factors becomes stronger or weaker over time. The analysis disproves the hypothesis that there has been an overall diachronic development towards more zero use and that the interactions with verb type brings to light differences between verbs in terms of the predictive power of the individual structural features.

1. Introduction

This paper is concerned with the alternation between the complementizer *that* and the zero complementizer in constructions with an object clause, as in (1) and (2).

(1) I think that he is a powerful man. (COCA)
(2) I think they're going to blame him. (COCA)

In previous studies, it has been suggested that this complementation construction has been evolving towards more zero use (Rissanen, 1991; Thompson & Mulac, 1991; Palander-Collin, 1999). The present paper seeks to test this hypothesis by means of a stepwise logistic regression analysis of (n = 9759) tokens of *think, guess* and *understand*, three of the most frequently used complement-taking verbs of cognition, spanning the time period from 1560 to 2012. The literature has put forward a number of conditioning factors promoting the zero form. Our regression model will test whether these features indeed predict the zero form, whether they gain or lose predictive power when combined and what happens to their predictive power over time. Determining the interaction of time with each of the structural conditioning factors, this study adds an innovative diachronic perspective to existing research into zero/*that* alternation by testing the effect of each factor over time on the selection of the zero complementizer.

We start off with a review of the literature dealing with *that*/zero alternation in order to characterize the construction under investigation and to review the factors that have previously been said to condition the use of either *that* or zero complementation. In Section 3 our data and methodology are explained. After presenting our results in Section 4, we offer a conclusion in Section 5.

2. Review of the literature

2.1 *That*/zero alternation and the emergence of discourse formulas and parentheticals

In usage-based approaches to the *that*/zero alternation (Thompson and Mulac, 1991a, 1991b; Aijmer, 1997; Diessel and Tomasello, 2001; Thompson, 2002), frequently occurring subject–verb combinations, e.g. *I think* and *I guess*, are considered to have developed into conventionalized "epistemic phrases" (Thompson and Mulac, 1991a, 1991b) or "discourse formulas" (Torres Cacoullos and Walker, 2009). Torres Cacoullos and Walker (2009) argue that such discourse formulas have reached a high degree of autonomy (see Bybee, 2003, 2006) from their productive complement-taking source construction. The frequency with which the zero complementizer is used is seen as an indication of this increasing autonomy. Following this rationale, Thompson and Mulac (1991b) argue that the absence of *that* points towards the blurring of the distinction between matrix clause and complement clause, i.e. to a reanalysis of this [MATRIX + COMPLEMENT CLAUSE] construction as a monoclausal utterance in which the complement clause makes the "main assertion" (Kearns, 2007a), for which the matrix clause provides an epistemic or evidential "frame" (Thompson, 2002).[1] Thompson and Mulac (1991b) show that the subject–verb collocations with the highest frequency of occurrence

---

1. Bas Aarts (p.c.) has pointed out that syntactically *I think* can never be a clause; it has no syntactic status as it is not a constituent. Therefore, strictly speaking, in a sentence like (1), the matrix clause is the entire sentence starting with *I* and ending in *man*. In the literature, however, the terms "matrix clause" and "main clause" are commonly used to denote the matrix clause

have the greatest tendency to leave out the complementizer *that*. It is exactly these sequences that "are most frequently found as EPAR [epistemic parenthetical] expressions" (Thompson and Mulac, 1991b: 326),[2] which occur in clause-medial or final position with respect to the (erstwhile) complement clause.

(3) We have to kind of mix all this together, *I think*, to send the right message to girls.
(COCA)

These synchronic, frequency-based findings lead Thompson and Mulac (1991b) to propose that *that* complementation (1), zero complementation (2), and parenthetical use (3) embody three degrees or three stages in a process of grammaticalization into epistemic phrases/parentheticals.[3] A study on the use of *I think* in Middle and Early Modern English by Palander-Collin (1999) adds support to the diachronic validity of this grammaticalization path. Her data show an increase in the use of *I think* with the zero complementizer and a concomitant rise in parenthetical use.

Brinton (1996), on the other hand, takes issue with what she calls the "matrix clause hypothesis" and presents an alternative model which posits a paratactic construction with an anaphoric element rather than a complement-taking construction as the historical source construction. Brinton's proposal is consistent with Bolinger (1972: 9), who states that "both constructions, with and without *that*, evolved from a parataxis of independent clauses, but in one of them the demonstrative *that* was added".

(4) Stage I: *They are poisonous. That I think.*
Stage II: *They are poisonous,* {*that I think, I think that/it, as/so I think*}. = 'which I think'
Stage III: *They are poisonous, I think.* OR
They are poisonous, as I think. = 'as far as I think, probably'
Stage IV: *I think, they are poisonous. They are, I think, poisonous.*
(Brinton, 1996: 252)

---

without its complement, i.e. in the case of (1), to refer to *I think*. For the sake of clarity and consistency, this practice will be followed in the current paper.

2. What Thompson and Mulac mean by this is that the bulk of all the "matrix clauses" in their data are tokens of *think* and *guess* and that these same verbs make up the largest share of all parenthetical uses in the corpus, i.e. 85%. This does *not* mean that *think* and *guess* have the highest rates of parenthetical use when all instances of each target verb are aggregated and the share of parenthetical use is calculated for each separate verb. When this method is applied to Thompson and Mulac's data, the respective parenthetical rates of *think* and *guess* are 10% and 29%.

3. For a discussion of the applicability of grammaticalization, pragmaticalization, and lexicalization to this type of construction, see Fischer (2007) and Van Bogaert (2011).

Along similar lines, Fischer (2007) posits two source constructions for present-day parentheticals: what Quirk et al. (1985: 1111) have called subordinate clauses of proportion and the seeming zero-complementation patterns that Gorrell (1895: 396–397; cited in Brinton, 1996: 140 and Fischer, 2007: 103) designates as "simple introductory expressions like the Modern English 'you know'", which stand in a paratactic relationship with the ensuing clause. Fischer (2007: 106) classifies the anaphoric connective element introducing such independent clauses as an adverbial derived from a demonstrative pronoun.

The notion of reanalysis, on which Thompson and Mulac's (1991a, 1991b) account of epistemic parentheticals is based, has been subject to additional criticism. An important point here is the role of zero complementation. Kearns (2007a), for example, does not regard the occurrence of the zero complementizer with epistemic phrases/parentheticals as a diagnostic of the syntactic reanalysis involved in their formation; rather, she accounts for zero complementation in strictly pragmatic terms: it signals a shift in information structure such that the complement clause conveys the main assertion while the matrix clause loses prominence and has a modifier-like use (see also Diessel and Tomasello, 2001; Boye and Harder, 2007). These studies allow for a hybrid analysis in which some occurrences with zero complementation are adverbial in terms of function while syntactically retaining their matrix clause status. A further criticism regarding reanalysis concerns the necessity of *that* omission to the use of *I think* (and similar epistemic phrases) as discourse formulas. Both Kearns (2007a) and Dehé and Wichmann (2010) argue that complement-taking predicates followed by *that*, e.g. *I think that*, may also be analyzed as discourse formulas, the whole sequence having become routinized as a whole. In addition to providing prosodic evidence for this position, Dehé and Wichmann (2010: 65) remark that this view is supported by the historical origins of *that* as a demonstrative pronoun (see the discussion of Brinton, 1996 and Fischer, 2007 above).[4]

In this study, we adopt the matrix clause hypothesis insofar as we aim to test Thompson and Mulac's grammaticalization hypothesis that there is a tendency across time for the zero complementizer to be preferred over the complementizer *that*, i.e. that the verbs under investigation in this study (*think, suppose, believe*) have tended towards higher frequencies of the zero complementizer as conditioned by the factors presented in Section 3. Ascertaining the main effects of these conditioning factors, we determine which ones are good predictors of the zero form. The present study is innovative in approaching the *that*/zero alternation from both a quantitative and a diachronic point of view. While Tagliamonte and

---

4. For more references on the question whether clause-initial occurrences of "parenthetical verbs" should be considered as matrix clauses or as parentheticals, see Kaltenböck (2007: 5-6).

Smith (2005) and Torres Cacoullos and Walker (2009) have performed multifactorial analyses of the synchronic conditioning of *that* and zero complementation, the current paper adds a diachronic dimension along with a parallel analysis of diachronic spoken and written data sets, and investigates, by means of a stepwise regression analysis, whether the zero form is on the increase and how time affects the predictive power of the factors. In addition to interactions with time, this study seeks to lay bare any other significant interactions between factors, notably mode (i.e., spoken versus written data), and to identify any resulting similarities and/or differences between the three verbs of cognition.

2.2 A concise history of the *that*/zero alternation

There is general agreement on the historical development of the complementizer *that* from an Old English neuter demonstrative pronoun (see, for instance, Mitchell, 1985), but the question which of the two complementation patterns, *that* or zero, is older is strictly speaking impossible to answer as both the *that* and the zero complementizer occur in the earliest extant texts (Rissanen, 1991).[5] This renders the notion of "*that*-deletion" or "omission" somewhat problematic. On the other hand, it should be observed that in Old English and throughout most of the Middle English period, occurrences of zero are scant. In Warner's (1982) study of the Wycliffe Sermons, for example, *that* is used 98% of the time. It is not until the Late Middle English period that the zero complementizer gradually takes off (Rissanen, 1991; Palander-Collin, 1999), a trend that continues in Early Modern English. Rissanen (1991) notes a steady increase between the fourteenth and the seventeenth century, but the most dramatic rise in the zero complementizer can be observed in the second half of the sixteenth century and in the early seventeenth century, when its frequency jumps from 40% to 60%. In addition, Rissanen (1991) shows that the zero form is more common in speech-like genres (i.e. trials, comedies, fiction, and sermons) and that its increase is more pronounced with *think* and *know* than with *say* and *tell*. Finegan and Biber (1985), too, find that the zero complementizer is more frequent in the more colloquial genre of the personal letter than in the formal genres of medical writing and sermons.[6] In the

---

5. According to Bolinger (1972), there is a semantic difference between constructions with and without *that* due to a trace of the original demonstrative meaning being retained in present-day uses of explicit *that*. For Yaguchi (2001), too, this demonstrative meaning continues to condition the contemporary function of *that*.

6. This predilection for zero in speech is confirmed in studies of contemporary English (see Tagliamonte and Smith, 2005: 291–293).

eighteenth century, we witness a temporary drop in zero use. Both Rissanen (1991) and Torres Cacoullos and Walker (2009) attribute this change to the prevalence of prescriptivism, which advocated the use of *that* out of a concern with clarity.

2.3 Conditioning factors in the literature[7]

Jespersen puts the variability between *that* and zero down to nothing more than "momentary fancy" (1954: 38, cited in Tagliamonte and Smith, 2005: 290); as will be seen, this is a claim that several scholars have tried to refute through an examination of a wide range of conditioning factors. Some of these factors are of a language-external nature; many are language-internal.

Many previous studies have tried to account for *that*/zero variability from the point of view of register variation (Quirk et al., 1985: 953; Huddleston and Pullum, 2002: 317; see Rohdenburg, 1996 for more references); *that* tends to be regarded as the more formal option while zero is associated with informal registers (see Kaltenböck, 2006: 373-374 for references. For example Kearns (2007b) observes some significant differences across varieties in newspaper prose and attributes these to different degrees of sensitivity to some of the conditioning factors discussed further down in this section.

There is also a wide range of language-internal factors. One semantic factor is discussed in Dor (2005), who notes that the semantic notion of the "truth claim" is crucial to the *that*/zero alternation, in that *that*-clauses denote "propositions" while zero-clauses denote "asserted propositions". Also, particular semantic classes of verbs, notably "epistemic verbs" (Thompson and Mulac, 1991a) or "propositional attitude predicates" (Noonan, 1985; Quirk et al., 1985) turn out to have a stronger preference for zero complementation than other complement-taking verbs, such as utterance or knowledge predicates (Thompson and Mulac, 1991a; Tagliamonte and Smith, 2005; Torres Cacoullos and Walker, 2009).

Importantly, various studies have shown certain high-frequency subject-verb collocations to be strongly associated with zero use (among these are "epistemic verbs" mentioned above). Torres Cacoullos and Walker (2009: 32) therefore hypothesize that the conditioning factors for complementizer choice should be different for these highly frequent "discourse formulas" (viz. *I think, I guess, I remember, I find, I'm sure, I wish*, and *I hope*) than for the (relatively more) productive complement-taking construction, and indeed they find a number of differences in terms of significance and effect size.

---

7. Although the scope of this article is restricted to *that*/zero complementizer alternation in so-called object clauses, some of the studies discussed in this section also deal with subject clauses.

Finally, a wide array of language-internal, structural factors operating on the selection of zero or *that* have been proposed in previous studies, some of which employ statistical methods, of diverse levels of refinement, to ascertain the import of these factors. In the following three sections, the structural conditioning factors favoring the use of zero will be discussed on the basis of the literature. The factors have been divided into three groups depending on whether they concern matrix clause features, complement clause features, or the relationship between the two. At the end of each section, a table provides a summary of the factors discussed. For each factor, we indicate whether previous studies have or have not statistically tested the factor's predictive power, and if so, whether it came out as significant or not.

2.3.1 Matrix clause elements

The subject of the matrix clause has often been said to play a role in the selection of either *that* or zero. In many studies, it is argued that pronouns, particularly *I* or *you* (5), favor the use of zero (Bolinger, 1972; Elsness, 1984; Thompson and Mulac, 1991a; Tagliamonte and Smith, 2005; Torres Cacoullos and Walker, 2009).[8] While it is mostly assumed that the pronouns *I* and *you* in particular promote the use of zero, Torres Cacoullos and Walker (2009: 26) demonstrate that the difference in effect size between pronouns (5a) and full NPs (5b) is greater than that between *I* or *you* versus all other subject types, including full NPs. They conclude that the strong effect attributed specifically to *I* and *you* in Thompson and Mulac (1991a: 242) is due to the inclusion of discourse formulas like *I think* and *I guess* in the data, which Torres Cacoullos and Walker consider separately.

(5) a. but <u>I</u> think a portion of it must have fallen down upon the straw. (OBC)
  b. <u>Some people</u> think that maybe it was a crazy person that stalked Tara. (COCA)

Another matrix clause factor that has received considerable attention is the presence or absence of additional material in the matrix clause. It is believed that matrix clauses containing elements other than a subject and a (simplex) verb are more likely to be followed by *that*. Such elements may be adverbials, negations, or periphrastic forms in the verbal morphology of the matrix clause predicate (Thompson

---

8. In these studies, no distinction is made between declarative and interrogative second person use, although Thompson and Mulac (1991b: 322) indicate that the majority (82%) of their second-person instances of epistemic parentheticals are in the interrogative mood. In the current study, interactions between mood and person as conditioning factors for the selection of *that* or zero are taken into account.

and Mulac, 1991a; Torres Cacoullos and Walker, 2009).[9] For Tagliamonte and Smith (2005: 302), "additional material" is operationalized as "negation, modals, etc.", including adverbials (Tagliamonte p.c.). In Torres Cacoullos and Walker (2009: 26–27), as far as discourse formulas are concerned, adverbial material in the matrix clause is the conditioning factor making the greatest contribution to the selection of *that*. The authors explain that "this is unsurprising, since the presence of a post-subject adverbial ... detracts from (in fact, nullifies) the formulaic nature of the collocation". Distinguishing between single-word (6a) as opposed to phrasal adverbials (6b), and pre-subject (6c) as opposed to post-subject (6d) adverbials in the matrix clause, they find that post-subject adverbials affect both discourse formulas and "productive" constructions while the effect of pre-subject adverbials is restricted to discourse formulas. Phrasal adverbials are different again, promoting the use of *that* only with productive constructions.

(6) a. *I expected maybe that we would be talking about it.*
    b. *At the beginning, we told the guy that we were gonna both-each have our own.*
    c. *Now I find Ø like, even adults use slang words.*
    d. *I totally thought Ø he was a big jerk.*

(Torres Cacoullos and Walker, 2009: 15–16)

As for verbal morphology, the presence of auxiliaries in the matrix clause (7) is also believed to be conducive to the use of *that* (Thompson and Mulac, 1991a: 246; Torres Cacoullos and Walker, 2009: 16). As such, Tagliamonte and Smith (2005) show the simple present to be a significant factor contributing to the use of zero and in Torres Cacoullos and Walker (2009: 27) finite matrix verbs are more favorably disposed towards zero complementation than non-finite forms.[10]

Negation (8), subsumed under "additional material" in Tagliamonte and Smith (2005), is treated as a separate conditioning factor for the use of the complementizer *that* in Thompson and Mulac (1991a: 245), but was found to be not significant. By the same token, the interrogative mood (9) failed to reach significance.

(7) *I would guess that Al Gore will not endorse anyone.* (COCA)

(8) *I don't think they said it was a match.* (COCA)

(9) *Do you think he was talking to the left?* (COCA)

---

9. Although periphrastic verb forms in the matrix clause is generally believed to "reduce the likelihood that the main subject and verb are being used as an epistemic phrase" (Thompson and Mulac, 1991a: 248), both Kearns (2007a) and Van Bogaert (2010) have argued that such modifying use is not restricted to the prototypical first (or second) person simple present form.

10. Tagliamonte and Smith (2005: 25) use the term "present", but in fact "simple present" is meant: "present tense, when there are no additional elements in the matrix verb phrase".

A summary of matrix clause factors is presented in Table 1.

Table 1. Matrix clause factors potentially favoring the zero complementizer

Factor	No statistics	Significant	Not significant
subject = pronoun		Torres Cacoullos and Walker (2009)	
subject = I		Tagliamonte and Smith (2005)	
subject = I or you	Elsness (1984)	Thompson and Mulac (1991b)	Kearns (2007a, 2007b)
absence of matrix-internal elements		Tagliamonte and Smith (2005)	
absence of post-subject adverbials		Thompson and Mulac (1991b) Torres Cacoullos and Walker (2009)	
absence of pre-subject adverbials		Torres Cacoullos and Walker (2009)	
absence of phrasal adverbials		Torres Cacoullos and Walker (2009)	
positive polarity	Finegan and Biber (1985)		Thompson and Mulac (1991b)
declarative mood			Thompson and Mulac (1991b)

2.3.2 *Complement clause elements*

Concerning the subject of the complement clause, it has been suggested that pronominal subjects (10) as opposed to full NPs (11) favor the use of zero (Warner, 1982; Elsness, 1984; Finegan and Biber, 1985; Rissanen, 1991; Thompson and Mulac, 1991a; Rohdenburg, 1996, 1998; Tagliamonte and Smith, 2005; Torres Cacoullos and Walker, 2009)

(10) Bill, I understand <u>you</u> have a special guest with you.   (COCA)

(11) Well, I'm not, because I understand that <u>most of his girlfriends</u> have either been, you know, like the hooker or porn star types.   (COCA)

The high discourse topicality of pronouns has been proposed as an explanatory principle (Thompson and Mulac, 1991a: 248), as well as Rohdenburg's (1996: 151) complexity principle, which states that "in the case of more or less explicit grammatical options the more explicit one(s) will tend to be favored in cognitively more complex environments". While Elsness (1984) regards *I* and *you* as particularly conducive to zero complementation, Torres Cacoullos and Walker's (2009: 28) multivariate study results in the following ordering of subjects from least to most favorable to *that: it/there* < *I* < other pronoun < NP. Elsness (1984) adds that short NPs and NPs with definite or unique reference are more likely to select the zero variant than longer and indefinite NPs. In Kearns (2007a: 494), first and second person subjects (i.e. *I, you* but also *we*) are compared to third person subjects, but identical rates of zero and *that* are found for both data sets. Kearns (2007a: 493, 2007b: 304) also examines the length of the complement clause subject as a possible factor, operationalizing it in terms of a three-way distinction between pronouns, short NPs (one or two words) and long NPs (three or more words). The study reveals significant differences, including one between short and long NPs.

As an additional complexity factor, Rodhenburg (1996: 164) mentions the overall length of the complement clause. He suggests that longer complement clauses tend to favor explicit *that* and in this regard he finds that at least with the verbs *think* and *know*, complement clauses introduced by *that* are "on average much longer than those not explicitly subordinated" (Rohdenburg, 1996: 164).

A summary of complement clause factors is presented in Table 2.

Table 2. Complement clause factors potentially favoring the zero complementizer

Factor	No statistics	Significant	Not significant
subject = pronoun	Warner (1982) Elsness (1984) Finegan and Biber (1985) Rissanen (1991) Rohdenburg (1996, 1998)	Thompson and Mulac (1991b) Tagliamonte and Smith (2005) Torres Cacoullos and Walker (2009)	
subject = *I* or *you*	Elsness (1984)		
subject = *I, you* or *we*			Kearns (2007a, 2007b)
subject = nominative pronoun			Kearns (2007a, 2007b)
short subject	Elsness (1984)	Kearns (2007a, 2007b)	
definite/unique reference	Elsness (1984)		
referential *it*			Kearns (2007a, 2007b)
long complement clause	Rohdenburg (1996)		
intransitive verb		Torres Cacoullos and Walker (2009)	

2.3.3 *The relationship between matrix and complement clause*

Finally, the presence of intervening material between matrix and complement has been widely discussed as a factor favoring the complementizer *that* (Bolinger, 1972; Warner, 1982; Finegan and Biber, 1985; Rissanen, 1991; Rohdenburg, 1996; Tagliamonte and Smith, 2005; Torres Cacoullos and Walker, 2009). Besides potentially leading to ambiguity, which Rohdenburg (1996: 160) regards as a special type of cognitive complexity, the presence of intervening material, as in (12), has been related to a heavier cognitive processing load. In Rohdenburg' (1996: 161) words, "any elements capable of delaying the processing of the object clause and thus the overall sentence structure favor the use of an explicit signal of subordination". Conversely, adjacency of matrix and complement clause is believed to minimize syntactic and cognitive complexity (Torres Cacoullos and Walker, 2009), and thus promote the zero complementizer. In Kearns (2007b), adjacency came out as a key factor responsible for regional differences in zero-complementizer rates, with some varieties being more dependent on adjacency for the licensing of zero than others.

(12) *Well, I'm not, because I understand that most of his girlfriends have either been, you know, I think <u>personally</u> that with time we're going to continue to see positive change.* (COCA)

In Torres Cacoullos and Walker's (2009: 27) study, intervening material – on a par with the complement clause subject – is the factor with the greatest effect on complementizer alternation, at least as regards regular, productive complement-taking verbs; as for high-frequency discourse formulas, the factor with the biggest effect size is the use of matrix clause adverbials (2009: 32–33).

Thompson and Mulac (1991a), Rohdenburg (1996), and Torres Cacoullos and Walker (2009) examine the effect of intervening verbal arguments, as in (13). The factor came out as significant in both Thompson and Mulac (1991a) and Torres Cacoullos and Walker (2009), although in the latter study, the effect is smaller than with other intervening material. As with complement clause subjects, Rohdenburg (1996: 162) points out that pronominal arguments as opposed to full NPs are more amenable to the zero form.

(13) *Within a week, I told <u>him</u> that I'm transgendered, and he was like, you know, what are you talking about?* (COCA)

In Torres Cacoullos and Walker (2009: 7-8), three factors are tested that fall under the explanatory principle of semantic proximity, which predicts the selection of the zero form when the conceptual distance between matrix and complement is minimal.[11] Specifically, subject coreferentiality (14), a factor that was significant in one of Elsness's (1984: 526) text types, cotemporality (15), and harmony of polarity (16), first proposed by Bolinger (1972), are examined, but none of these factors reach significance. Subject coreferentiality is also examined by Kearns (2007a: 493, 2007b: 304), but the factor is not selected as significant.

(14) I think I nodded several times. (COCA)

(15) I parted with my money as I thought it was a very good opening. (OBC)

(16) And I think it will rebound on the Democrats. (COCA)

Table 3 summarizes the factors pertaining to the relationship between matrix and complement clause.

Table 3. Factors pertaining to the relationship between matrix and complement which potentially favor zero

Factor	No statistics	Significant	Not significant
absence of intervening material	Bolinger (1972) Warner (1982) Finegan and Biber (1985) Rissanen (1991) Rohdenburg (1996)	Tagliamonte and Smith (2005) Torres Cacoullos and Walker (2009)	
absence of intervening arguments	Rohdenburg (1996)	Thompson and Mulac (1991b) Torres Cacoullos and Walker (2009)	
subject coreferentiality		Elsness (1984)	Kearns (2007a, 2007b) Torres Cacoullos and Walker (2009)
cotemporality			Torres Cacoullos and Walker (2009)
harmony of polarity	Bolinger (1972)		Torres Cacoullos and Walker (2009)

2.3.4 Non-structural factors

In this final section on factors conditioning the selection of *that* or zero, one last type of non-structural conditioning will be discussed: prosodic realization.

---

11. Conceptual distance needs to be interpreted in terms of Givón's (1980) hierarchy of clause-binding or in terms of the iconic separation of the two clauses (Langacker, 1991; Givón, 1995; Torres Cacoullos and Walker, 2009).

Dehé and Wichmann (2010) argue that there are rhythmic factors constraining the presence or absence of *that*. They point out that the explicit use of *that* may be motivated by a desire to create a more regular stress pattern in which *that* provides an additional unstressed syllable. In (17), *that* results in a regular, dactylic pattern, while in (18), it is required that *that* be *not* realized in order to obtain such regularity. Similarly, *that* may be inserted as an unstressed "buffer" between two stressed syllables in order to avoid a stress clash (Wichmann p.c.). In view of these rhythmic constraints, Dehé and Wichmann (2010: 66) conclude that "the presence or absence of *that* does not affect the way in which we analyze the function of *I verb (that)*". In other words, the absence of *that* is neither a necessary nor a sufficient condition for the use of an *I verb (that)* as a discourse formula.[12]

(17)   - x   -   - x   -   - x
       I think that the problem of faith …

(18)   - - x -   - x - - x   - -
       I believe I'm a bit of a nightmare then

(Dehé and Wichmann, 2010: 66, data from the ICE-GB)[13]

3. Data and methods

Our analysis was based on tokens retrieved from the following spoken and written corpora:

Table 4. Spoken corpora

Sub-period of spoken English	Time span	Corpus	Number of words
Early Modern English (EModE)	1560–1710	*Corpus of English Dialogues (CED)*	980,320
Late Modern English (LModE)	1710–1913	*Old Bailey Corpus (OBC)*	113,253,011
Present-Day English (PDE)	1920–2012	*The British National Corpus – spoken component. (BYU BNC-S). The Corpus of Contemporary American English – spoken component (COCA-S)*	95,341,792

---

12. See also the discussion in Section 2.2 on the role played by the zero complementizer in the reanalysis of matrix clauses into adverbials/parentheticals/discourse formulas.

13. The x's stand for stressed syllables the dashes for unstressed syllables.

Table 5. Written corpora

Sub-period of written English	Time span	Corpus	Number of words
Early Modern English (EModE)	1560–1710	*Innsbruck Corpus of Letters* *CEECS I Corpus (1560 – onward)* *CEECS II Corpus* *Corpus of English Dialogues (CED)* *Corpus of Early Modern English Texts (CMET)* *Lampeter Corpus (Early Modern English portion – up to 1710)*	2,848,314
Late Modern English (LModE)	1710–1920	*Corpus of Late Modern English texts Extended Version* (CLMETEV) *Lampeter Corpus (Early Modern English portion (1710 – onward)*	15,413,159
Present-Day English (PDE)	1850–2009	*The Time Corpus (Time)* *The Corpus of Contemporary American English – written component (COHA)*	500,000,000

The Wordsmith concordance program was used to first to identify the total number of inflected forms of *think* (i.e., *think, thinks, thinking* and *thought*), and *guess* (i.e., *guess, guesses, guessing* and *guessed*) and *understand* (i.e., *understand, understands, understanding* and *understood*) in both the written and spoken corpora from 1560–2012 per period. Results were broken up in smaller 70-year sub-periods, as shown in Tables 6–11. The sub-periods were modeled after those contained in the CLMET corpora (i.e., 1710–1780, 1780–1850, 1850–1920) in order to provide a principled template in which to divide and analyze the other diachronic written and corresponding spoken corpus data utilized in this study. The size, scope, and time periods of the other corpora in this study, especially those outside of 1710–1920, however, did not always correspond (e.g., the Old Baily Corpus ends in 1913 or the BYU-BNC only covers a period from the 1980s to 1993), so some adjustments were necessary but every effort was taken to remain as close to a 70 year period as possible. In addition, following an initial explorative analysis with just the think data, the decision was made to subdivide the first period of 1560–1639 into 1560–1579 and 1580–1639, in order to provide a reference level for the subsequent regression analysis applied to the three verbs discussed in this paper.

For each sub-period, the relative percentage of each inflected verb form per lemma was calculated. These percentages were then applied to the extracted sets (a minimum of (n = 2,000) randomized hits for written data and 1,000 randomized hits for the spoken data) in order to ensure that the extracted sets would be proportionally similar in terms of inflected forms to the larger corpora from which they were taken. This two-step process resulted in the datasets described below for each of the verbs under investigation.

Starting with the verb *think*, we began by extracting (n = 3101) tokens from the spoken English corpora and (n = 6619) tokens from the written English corpora (see Table 5). Randomization was achieved by using the Wordsmith randomization function or by selecting the "randomized sample option" available on the web based corpus resources (i.e., COCA, Time, BYU-BNU, etc). The full set (n = 9,720) of tokens was divided into those containing either a that-clause or a zero-complementizer clause. Those tokens not containing a that or zero form were then discarded. The resulting distributions of these tokens for both the spoken and written data sets are presented in Tables 6 and Table 7.

Table 6. Distribution of *that*-clauses and zero-complementizer clauses from EModE to PDE in spoken English. (n: absolute frequency, N: normalized frequency per million)

	think – spoken corpora			
	think – that		*think* – zero	
Period	n	N	n	N
1560–1579	(n = 8)	92.97	(n = 28)	324.78
1580–1639	(n = 29)	86.37	(n = 116)	345.48
1640–1710	(n = 10)	23.75	(n = 212)	447.47
1710–1780	(n = 22)	45.64	(n = 412)	854.10
1780–1850	(n = 12)	26.09	(n = 439)	938.68
1850–1913	(n = 16)	47.50	(n = 418)	1305.45
1980–1993	(n = 20)	449.18	(n = 142)	3152.25
1990–2012	(n = 22)	471.64	(n = 171)	3139.33
Total	(n = 139)		(n = 1916)	

Table 7. Distribution of *that*-clauses and zero-complementizer clauses from EModE to PDE in written corpora. (n: absolute frequency, N: normalized frequency per million)

	think – written corpora			
	think – that		*think* – zero	
Period	n	N	n	N
1560–1579	(n = 21)	214.00	(n = 17)	173.24
1580–1639	(n = 18)	59.23	(n = 133)	437.65
1640–1710	(n = 65)	174.51	(n = 200)	558.27
1710–1780	(n = 79)	123.19	(n = 290)	535.29
1780–1850	(n = 103)	151.66	(n = 316)	545.23
1850–1920	(n = 101)	175.47	(n = 359)	680.69
1920–1989	(n = 40)	109.44	(n = 204)	561.92
1990–2009	(n = 24)	106.20	(n = 247)	912.90
Total	(n = 451)		(n = 1766)	

A comparison of the diachronic relative frequency patterns of the *that* versus zero forms per million words with the verb *think* indicates that the zero form is clearly the more frequent form from 1560 to 2012, in both spoken and written texts, and this comports with all previous literature on *think* and claims regarding diachronic *that*/zero variation patterns.

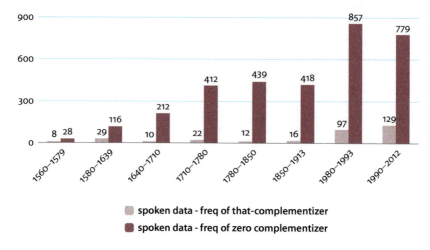

Figure 1. *Think* spoken data – *that* versus zero distribution per million words

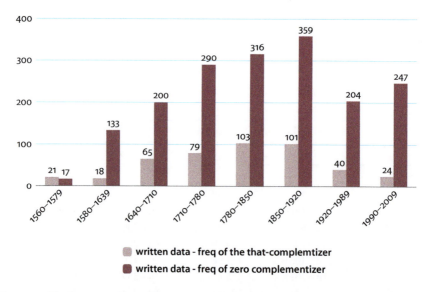

Figure 2. *Think* written data – *that* versus zero distribution per million words

The same extraction process was then performed for the verb *guess*. This yielded (n = 3419) *guess* tokens from the spoken English corpora and (n = 2255) tokens from the written English corpora. The full set (n = 5,674) of tokens was again divided into those containing either a *that*-clause or a zero-complementizer (again, with tokens not containing the *that* or zero form being discarded). The distributions of these tokens for both the spoken and written data sets are presented in Tables 8 and 9.

Table 8. Distribution of *that*-clauses and zero-complementizer clauses from EModE to PDE in spoken English. (n: absolute frequency, N: normalized frequency per million)

	guess – spoken corpora			
	guess – that		*guess* – zero	
Period	n	N	n	N
1640–1780	(n = 2)	1.23	(n = 17)	1.32
1780–1850	(n = 14)	0.30	(n = 23)	0.49
1850–1913	(n = 14)	0.27	(n = 51)	0.97
1960–1993	(n = 4)	7.78	(n = 348)	677.60
1994–2012	(n = 39)	5.84	(n = 538)	108.58
Total	(n = 73)		(n = 977)	

Table 9. Distribution of *that*-clauses and zero-complementizer clauses from EModE to PDE in written corpora. (n: absolute frequency, N: normalized frequency per million)

	guess – written corpora			
	guess – that		*guess* – zero	
Period	n	N	n	N
1580–1780	(n = 15)	1.95	(n = 20)	2.75
1780–1850	(n = 22)	3.80	(n = 38)	6.56
1850–1920	(n = 58)	9.25	(n = 99)	15.79
1920–1989	(n = 93)	10.02	(n = 154)	16.37
1990–2009	(n = 22)	1.67	(n = 312)	41.78
Total	(n = 210)		(n = 623)	

When we compare the diachronic relative frequency patterns of the *that* versus zero forms per million words for the verb *guess*, we find that the frequency of the zero form relative to the *that* complementizer is once again more frequent form in both the spoken and written data sets. The distribution pattern for both types of data is presented below in Figures 3 and 4.

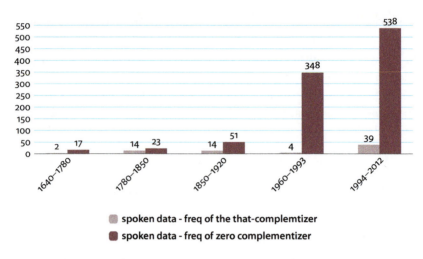

Figure 3. Spoken data – *that* versus zero distribution per million words

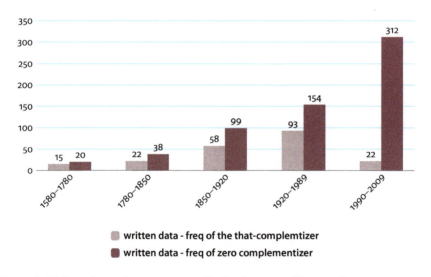

Figure 4. Written data – *that* versus zero distribution per million words

Finally, this process was conducted one last time for the verb *understand*. The extraction yielded (n = 16157) *understand* tokens from spoken English corpora and (n = 6845) tokens from written English corpora. The full set (n = 23,002) of tokens were analyzed and divided into those containing either a *that*-clause or a zero-complementizer. The distributions of these tokens for both the spoken and written data sets are presented in Table 10 and Table 11.

Chapter 8. A multifactorial analysis of *that*/zero alternation 219

Table 10. Distribution of *that*-clauses and zero-complementizer clauses from EModE to PDE in spoken English. (n: absolute frequency, N: normalized frequency per million)

	understand – spoken corpora			
	understand – that		understand – zero	
Period	n	N	n	N
1560–1710	(n = 15)	12.41	(n = 11)	6.31
1710–1780	(n = 106)	8.42	(n = 200)	15.89
1780–1850	(n = 143)	6.48	(n = 303)	13.72
1850–1913	(n = 613)	33.72	(n = 490)	26.96
1960–1993	(n = 94)	19.00	(n = 68)	10.68
1994–2012	(n = 432)	34.83	(n = 163)	15.89
Total	(n = 1403)		(n = 1235)	

Table 11. Distribution of *that*-clauses and zero-complementizer clauses from EModE to PDE in written corpora. (n: absolute frequency, N: normalized frequency per million)

	understand – written corpora			
	understand – that		understand – zero	
Period	n	N	n	N
1580–1710	(n = 147)	74.62	(n = 61)	24.77
1710–1780	(n = 108)	27.45	(n = 38)	9.66
1780–1850	(n = 143)	24.69	(n = 39)	6.73
1850–1920	(n = 252)	40.19	(n = 31)	4.94
1920–1989	(n = 48)	8.76	(n = 11)	2.41
1990–2009	(n = 63)	25.17	(n = 25)	10.33
Total	(n = 761)		(n = 205)	

In contrast to the relatively consistent diachronic ratio of the complementizer to zero form patterns observed with the *think* and *guess* data sets the *understand* data presents an unexpectedly different diachronic picture. The trends for that/zero ratio with understand, in both the spoken and written understand data sets, and are presented below in Figures 5 and 6.

The results, presented above for the (n = 2638) spoken and (n = 966) written *understand* tokens, show that unlike the first two verbs, *understand* is almost always being used more frequently, regardless of the time period, with the *that*-complementizer form. This pattern is reversed between 1710 and 1850 in the spoken data set, and it is reversed again from 1850 to 2012 but this may be simply an idiosyncratic feature of this type of spoken data. The preponderance of *that* is never observed in the parallel written data set; the *that* form remains consistently

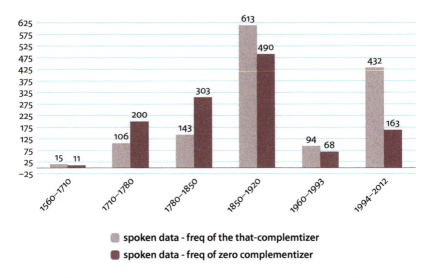

Figure 5. Spoken data *understand – that* versus zero distribution per million words

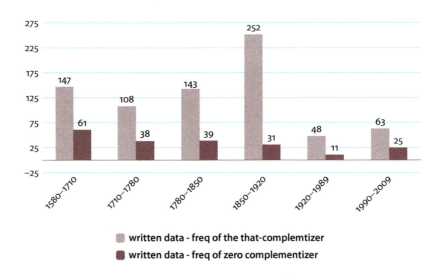

Figure 6. Written data *understand – that* versus zero distribution per million words

more frequent for the 400 plus years covered in our corpus resources. This was an unexpected finding and what consequences it has with regard to the factors predicting the presence of the zero form (if any) remains to be seen. Finally, this finding will be integrated into our regression analysis modelling and thus accounted for in Section 4.0.

The (n = 2,055) spoken and (n = 2,217) written *think* tokens, (n = 1050) spoken and (n = 833) written *guess* tokens, and (n = 2638) spoken and (n = 966) written *understand* tokens which contained either a *that* or zero complementizer clause were coded for 26 features, in separate spread sheets, within four categories: corpus information, matrix clause features, complement clause features and the relationship between matrix and complement. The goal of this coding process was to allow for the identification and subsequent statistical analysis, via a regression analysis, upon the following eleven features which in the literature are said to favour the presence of the zero complementizer. A summary of these structural features are presented below in Table 12.

Table 12. Factors which favour the presence zero-complementizer selected for this study (cf. also Tables 1, 2 & 3)

1. Matrix clause subjects either 'I' or 'You'
2. The absence of extra elements in the matrix clause (viz. auxiliaries, indirect objects, adverbials)
3. The absence of intervening elements between the matrix and complement clause
4. Pronominal subject of the complement clause, co-referential with the matrix clause subject
5. A pronominal subject (versus a NP) in the matrix clause
6. A pronominal subject (versus a NP) in the complement clause.
7. Complement clause subject either 'I' or 'you'
8. The length of the matrix clause subject (pronoun > np-short > np-long)
9. The length of the complement clause subject (pronoun > np-short > np-long)
10. Cotemporality between the matrix and complement clauses
11. Harmony of polarity between the matrix and complement clauses

The corpus information features included information such as the time period of the corpus (e.g., 1710–1780), the inflected form of the token and the full context in which it appeared. The matrix and complement clauses of each extracted token were also coded for the features person, tense, polarity, length of the subject (pronoun / short NP (i.e., 1 to 2 words) / long NP (i.e., 3+ words), and subject coreferentiality. In addition, the presence of additional elements within the matrix clause (elements between the subject and the matrix verb) was also noted along with intervening elements (between the matrix clause and the complement clause) and the location of the intervening elements (either pre-complementizer or post-complementizer and before the complement clause subject).

In addition to the aforementioned categorical coding processes, the data sets for all three verbs were also chronologically reorganized in order to create sufficiently large sample sizes close to or greater than (n = 30) examples per period. This data aggregation procedure was especially important in the early periods (e.g., 1560–1579, 1580–1639 and 1640–1710), where due to the paucity of available data, using every available token and subsequent *that*/zero example still resulted in data-sets that fell below the methodologically desirable threshold of (n > 30) per period. In such cases data from several periods was combined. For example, with the verb *guess*, this process resulted in an initial period spanning from 1640–1780 in the spoken data set and in the written data 1580 to 1780 and with the verb *understand* it created an initial period spanning 1560 to 1710 in the spoken data and 1580–1701 in the written data sets. The verb *think* was however frequent enough per period for this step not to be needed. Once the aggregation process was completed, these data sets, per period, were then sufficiently large to function as reference levels for our subsequent diachronic logistic regression analysis. This process was also employed for the PDE spoken data categories from 1980 to 2012 for all three verbs in order to set up a single 20th century period in which to directly compare and contrast with the written data sets which spanned from 1920–2009.

Once these respective processes were completed, the data was loaded into the statistical program *R*, in order to test the effects of the factors represented in Table 12. This was done by means of a *stepwise logistic regression analysis* (using the function stepAIC in the *R* package MASS).[14] The stepwise selection procedure was both-ways and the minimal model was of course an intercept-only model. The maximal model contained all main effects plus two-way interactions of the factors with period, verb and mode (together with the two-way interactions between period, verb and mode themselves). This necessitated some a priori filtering of the factors. The factor 'I.or.U', for instance, was recoded into two separate factors 'Person' and 'Number', rendering 'I.or.U' itself entirely redundant. Redundancy also applies to the factors 'Mat.Pro.vs. and 'CC.Pro.vs.NP', as the respective factors 'Mat.length' and 'CC.length' contain all the subdivisions of 'it', pronoun, np-short and np-long, and thus capture the important distinctions. The solution was to exclude the redundant factors from the analysis.

The resulting model after stepwise selection contains 11 main effects and 15 interactions (see Table 13), which fits reasonably well: the goodness-of-fit is significant (LLR = 5355.511; df = 57; p-value = 0), the predicted variation (C-score) is 89.3%, but the explained variation (Nagelkerke-R^2) is only 54.2%. This shows that our model still has potential for improvement.

The model diagnostics show a sound model: only 3.5% of the standardized residuals are outside of the range between −2 and 2, and none of the dfbeta's (i.e. the influence of each observation on the coefficients of the effects) fall outside of −1 and 1. In addition, we implemented the procedure in Agresti (2013: 221–224) to dichotomize the fitted probabilities for the *that* zero alternation for comparison

---

[14]. The general outline of this methodology was suggested to us by Stefan Th. Gries, for which we wish to express our gratitude.

with the observed probabilities. This yields a classification accuracy of 84.6%. The significance of this result was finally tested against two baseline models: one that would always predict the most frequent form, and one that would guess an outcome randomly. In both cases, the classification accuracy was highly significant (close to 0). In sum, these diagnostics show that our model is appropriate.

Table 13 gives the ANOVA-table with type III LLR tests. It can be seen that the three strongest predictors are (in decreasing order) the interaction between verb and period, the main effect of length of the complement clause subject ('CC.length'), and the main effect of matrix internal elements ('mat.int'). Only the main effect of cotemporality ('CC.T.co.ref') is not significant, but its interaction with period is border-significant. The interpretation in the next section will discuss all effects. This will be done by means of effect plots (obtained with the *R* package effects).

Table 13. ANOVA-table with type III LLR tests

	Df	Deviance	AIC	LRT	Pr(Chi)
<none>		8143.4	8259.4		
Verb	2	8149.7	8261.7	6.284	0.0431921
mat.int	1	8220.1	8334.1	76.701	< 2.2e-16
Person	2	8162.0	8274.0	18.534	9.45e-02
Interv	1	8181.2	8295.2	37.736	8.10e-07
CC.length	3	8228.6	8338.6	85.187	< 2.2e-16
TYPE	1	8184.1	8298.1	40.698	1.78e-07
Tense	3	8158.4	8268.4	14.951	0.0018590
Number	1	8152.3	8266.3	8.857	0.0029196
Mat.length	2	8154.5	8266.5	11.097	0.0038937
Period	1	8167.5	8281.5	24.063	9.33e-04
CC.T.co.ref	1	8144.4	8258.4	0.930	0.3347531
Verb:Person	4	8153.4	8261.4	9.989	0.0406096
Verb:tense	6	8195.2	8299.2	51.779	2.07e-06
interv:TYPE	1	8168.2	8282.2	24.806	6.34e-04
TYPE:tense	3	8151.7	8261.7	8.232	0.0414572
Verb:period	2	8238.6	8350.6	95.191	< 2.2e-16
TYPE:period	1	8185.4	8299.4	41.989	9.18e-08
CC.length:period	3	8169.1	8279.1	25.675	1.12e-02
tense:period	3	8164.3	8274.3	20.879	0.0001115
Verb:TYPE	2	8153.6	8265.6	10.203	0.0060890
interv:period	1	8148.6	8262.6	5.211	0.0224387
Verb:Number	2	8149.5	8261.5	6.031	0.0490240
Person:TYPE	2	8149.1	8261.1	5.713	0.0574741
Verb:mat.int	2	8148.6	8260.6	5.221	0.0734856
Verb:CC.length	6	8157.0	8261.0	13.535	0.0352890
period:CC.T.co.ref	1	8146.5	8260.5	3.032	0.0816159

4. Results

In this section, we present the results from the stepwise regression analysis on eleven factors that have been argued in the literature to predict the presence of the zero complementizer form with verbs of cognition such as *think*, *guess* and *understand* (see Section 2.3). Because of the complex structure of our model (with sixteen interactions), this will be done by means of graphical visualization in effect plots that were obtained with the R package effects. The main factors under consideration are the main effects of verb, period, and mode (i.e. spoken versus written), the absence of matrix-internal elements, the absence of intervening elements between the matrix and complement clause, the length of the complement clause subject, matrix clause person, matrix clause number, matrix clause tense, coreferentiality of person between the matrix and complement clause subjects, and harmony of polarity between the matrix and complement clauses.

In 4.1, we discuss the five statistically significant interactions with verb, v viz. interactions with matrix internal elements, length of the complement clause subject, person, number and tense. In 4.2, we show that the following interactions with mode are statistically significant: the absence of intervening elements between the matrix and complement clauses, person and tense. The final set of interactions, presented in 4.3, offers a diachronic account of conditioning factors for zero use. The analysis shows that there are significant changes across time in the extent to which verb, length of the complement clause subject, person, and harmony of polarity predict the use of zero.

4.1 Verb type

A 'panchronic' model aggregating all time periods was used to examine the interaction of the factor 'verb' with other factors as predictors of the zero complementizer form. This allows us to gauge to what extent the main effects observed above are verb-specific. The significant factors are presented below in Figures 7–11.

In Figure 7 we see that the absence of intervening elements in the matrix clause is a strong predictor for the zero form for all three verbs; for each individual verb, the value for zero complementation is significantly higher in the left panel (absence of intervening elements) than in the right panel (intervening material is present). However, due to scarcity of data (there were only 219 occurrences of *guess* with intervening material in comparison to more than 1000 for the other 5 effects) we get a larger confidence interval for *guess* with intervening material. Therefore, some caution is warranted when interpreting this data point. With that proviso, we can say that while the difference in zero use with *think* and *guess* without intervening material is minimal, *guess* has a considerably lower rate of zero than *think* when intervening material is present. Comparing all three verbs, intervening material has the strongest effect on *guess*; the difference in zero use between presence and absence is the greatest for this verb. We also observe that for *understand*; zero rates are much lower overall; there is only a 50% chance of the zero form being used when there is no intervening material compared to values of over 90 and 80 per cent respectively for *think* and *guess*. When *understand* occurs with intervening material, its zero rate is lower than 30%.

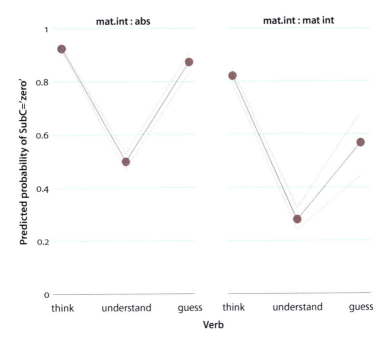

Figure 7. Verb: matrix-internal elements

In Figure 7 we see that the absence of matrix internal elements is significant for all three verbs, with the proviso that there were so few occurrences of *guess* with matrix-internal elements that the confidence interval for this data point is so large that we cannot make any reliable claims about the effect of the present factor on this verb. Comparing the zero rates of the three verbs in the left panel, i.e. when there are no matrix-internal elements, we observe a strong conditioning effect for *think* and *guess*, but a very weak effect for *understand*; when a matrix clause with *understand* contains additional elements, the chances of getting zero or *that* are split 50-50. The results also reveal that the presence of matrix internal elements is predictive for the *that*-complementizer form for *understand*.

The analysis of the effect of the length of the complement clause subject reveals additional differences between these three verbs. The results presented in Figure 8 show that *it* and other pronouns as complement clause subjects have largely the same predictive effects for both *think* and *guess*; however, as the weight of the complement clause subject increases *guess* has a lower likelihood of using the zero form relative to *think*. In addition, the analysis reveals that the length of the complement clause subject has a much lower predictive effect overall for the verb *understand*; an np-long complement clause subject with *think* is still more predictive of the zero-form than *it* is for the verb *understand*. In fact, *it* is the only *understand* data point with a +50% value. All other subject types predict the *that* form with *understand*.

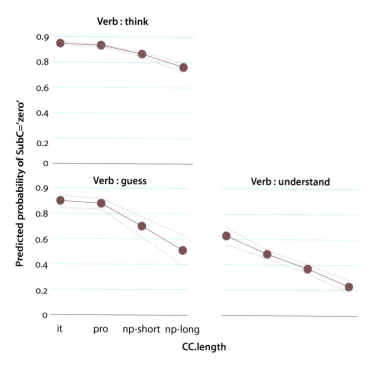

Figure 8. Verb: complement clause length

This variation across verbs is also seen when we look at the remaining categories of person, number and tense. In Figure 9 below we see the results for the effect of person across all three verbs.

The results presented Figure 9 indicate that the verbs *think* and *understand* parallel the previous findings regarding person in that (a) the overall predictive effect is much stronger for *think* relative to *understand* and (b) that P1 > P2 > P3 in terms for both verbs in terms of serving as a predictor for the presence of the zero form. Furthermore, with the verb *guess* only the result for 1st person is reliable while the 2nd and 3rd person forms are shown to be unreliable predictors due to large confidence intervals.

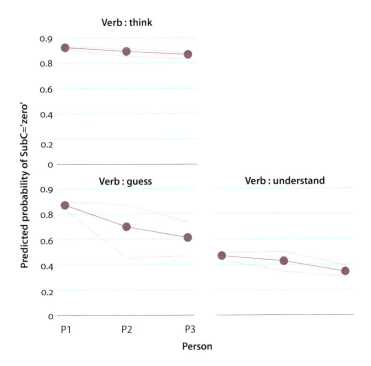

Figure 9. Verb: person

The analysis of number once again confirms the outsider status of *understand*. The predictive power of singular matrix clause subjects is stronger for *think* and *guess* than it is for *understand*. Since the zero form occurs less often with *understand* than with *think* or *guess* overall (see Figures 5 and 6), zero rates for both singular and plural *understand* are lower than those of the other two verbs. The plot in Figure 10 also indicates that the differences in complementizer use between singular and plural subjects are minimal for all three verbs; the locations of the data points in the two panels do not shift much. In fact, only the difference between singular and plural *think* is significant. In addition, we also see that much like our initial analysis of the main effects, the singular form more strongly predicts the zero form with *think* and to a lesser degree with *guess*, while *understand* is more likely to be used with *that* regardless of number.

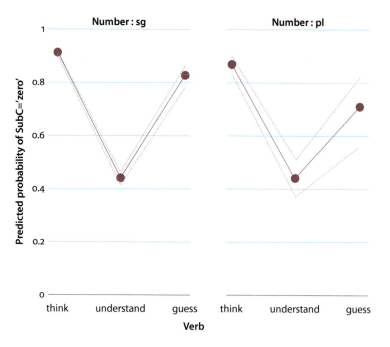

Figure 10. Verb: number

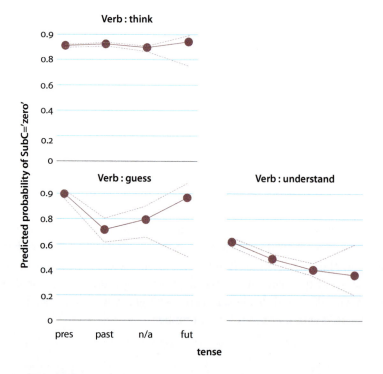

Figure 11. Verb: tense

The final factor to be discussed in this section is the effect of tense on each of the verbs. Although the main effect for tense was not significant, the interaction of this factor with verb type is. The analysis of tense indicates that the future tense is an unreliable factor across all three verbs and that there are no significant differences in zero rate between past, present and n/a tense forms with *think*. Furthermore, the results for all tense values of *guess* except present are unreliable due to large confidence intervals. Finally, Figure 11 shows that all tense forms of *understand* are predictive of the *that* complementizer.

4.2 Mode (spoken versus written data)

Our analysis revealed that the effect of interaction between the factor mode and a number of other factors is significant. We will now compare the extent to which these factors predict the use of the zero form in the spoken and written modes. Once again a stepwise regression procedure was used to examine the effect of the factors presented in Table 13 relative to the mode (i.e., spoken versus written language). This model is also panchronic, i.e. all periods are conflated. Recall that although there was a significant difference between the spoken and written modes in terms of the probability with which zero is used, the main effect of mode on complementizer use was not that strong. In this section, we will see that mode plays a more important role in the zero/*that* alternation than one would expect on the basis of the main effects analysis; the strength of various other factors depends heavily on mode, i.e. some factors may be better predictors of the zero form in one mode as opposed to the other.

In Figure 12 we see that there is little difference with the verbs *think* and *guess* with respect to mode as a predictor for the zero form. The situation is different for *understand*, however. While in the spoken mode, *understand* has a 50% chance of being used with the zero form, there is in fact a greater likelihood of *that* when *understand* is used in the written mode.

Figure 13 allows us to compare the conditioning effect of intervening elements between matrix clause and complement clause in the spoken and written modes. Recall that absence of intervening elements was a very good predictor overall. The interaction confirms this earlier finding; in both panels we observe a dramatic difference in complementizer use between presence and absence of intervening material. A notable difference, however, resides in the conditioning effect of the absence of intervening material in the written mode. When there is intervening material in the written mode, we are much less likely to get the zero form than in the spoken mode, so much so that the explicit complementizer *that* in fact becomes more likely; the zero rate drops to 0.2. It may be that writers are more led by the complexity principle than speakers and feel the need to insert *that* to make clause boundaries clearer when intervening material risks impairing clarity.

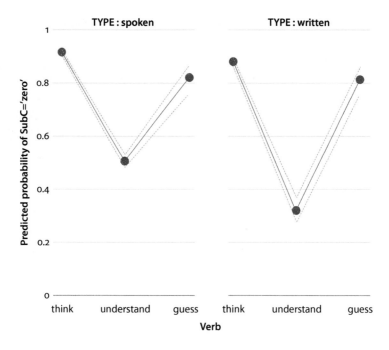

Figure 12. Mode: verb

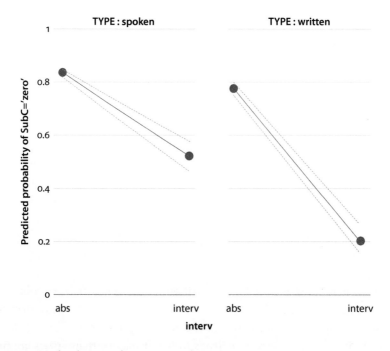

Figure 13. Mode: absence of intervening elements

In Figure 14, we examine the effect of person in the two modes. The plot reveals that in both the spoken and written modes the 1st person subject predicts more zero use; however, in both cases the 2nd person subjects are not significant. We also see that the 1st person subject form is a stronger predictor in the spoken versus the written data and that compared to the spoken mode, 3rd person subjects in written data are less likely to be used with zero complementation.

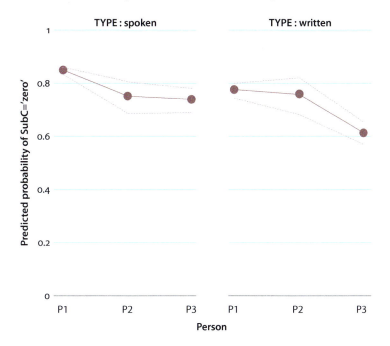

Figure 14. Mode: person

The final factor that we will examine in this section is the effect of tense as a predictor of the zero form relative to mode. The analysis of tense, presented above, again follows the pattern established in the preceding discussions of the main effect of tense and its interaction with verb type; in both the spoken and written data, the future form, again due to the sparseness of data, results in large confidence intervals and therefore, we cannot make any claims about the effect of the future on zero use in spoken versus written data. In addition, Figure 15 reveals that the past, present and n/a forms are not significantly different from one another in the spoken data but they are in the written data. We can thus conceive the following predictive cline for the zero form: n/a > past > pres.

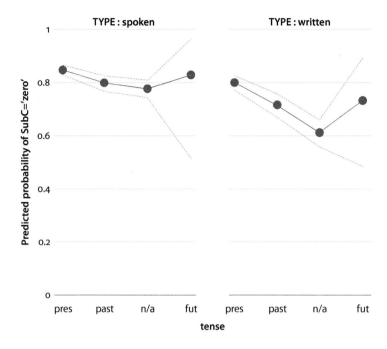

Figure 15. Mode: tense

4.3 Period

We now will turn to the final stage of our analysis and look at the effect of the structural factors across the eight time periods. Thus, in the following sections, we adopt a diachronic approach, discussing the interactions with period that came out as significant. The interaction effects with period were significant with the following factors: verb, mode, absence of intervening elements, complement clause length, cotemporality between the matrix and complement clause and tense. This final step in the analysis offers a diachronic perspective; it shows whether the import of a given factor becomes stronger or weaker over time.

Figure 16 shows the diachronic development of the zero form for each of the three verbs and it reveals a great deal of variation between them with respect to *that*/zero alternation. The verb *think* starts out with a high rate of zero relative to the *that* form and exhibits a gradual loss of the zero form (relative to *that*) over time. *Guess* on the other hand shows a strong and constant increase in the ratio of the zero from over time, starting out below 0.5 and culminating in value comparable to that seen with *think* in PDE. *Understand,* by contrast, is characterized by a dramatic drop in zero use. It drops below 0.5 in period 6 and in the most recent time period it barely reaches 0.3. Thus, while *understand* used to have a strong

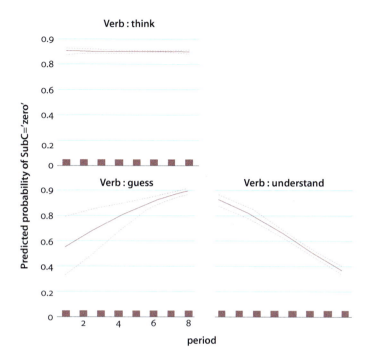

Figure 16. Period: verb

preference for the zero form, in more recent years it has come to prefer the explicit complementizer *that*. This shows that there is no homogeneous zero/*that* alternation trend and that interactions with verb type are highly relevant. Also, it opens up perspectives for future research on the basis of a larger number of verb types.

An analysis of the effect of mode over time shows that in the earliest periods the zero form was far more prevalent in the spoken data relative to the written data but over time, as the zero form has gone down in the spoken mode and increased in the written mode, in PDE the two modes are at the same predictive level. As Figure 17 shows, the endpoints in PDE for both modes are almost identical which suggests that nowadays mode, in and of itself, is no longer a good or a significant predictor of the zero form with these verbs anymore.

An analysis of the diachronic effect of the absence of intervening elements between the matrix and complement clauses produces a result which confirms what has been argued in the literature on *that*/zero variation, namely that the absence of intervening elements is a strong predictor of the zero form. The results show that this trend is decreasing over time; however, it still remains quite robust relative to the presence of intervening elements. The values in the right panel suggest that intervening elements predict the explicit *that*-complementizer throughout all periods, although the effect gets weaker, but these findings cannot be ascertained due to large confidence intervals.

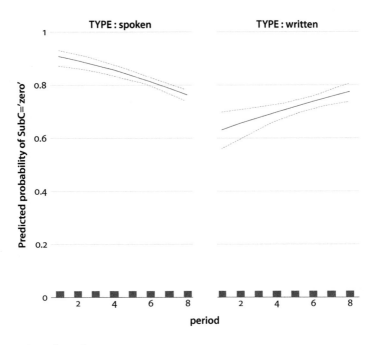

Figure 17. Period: mode

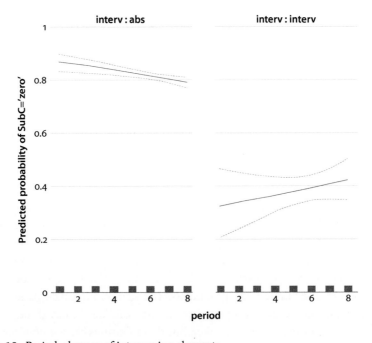

Figure 18. Period: absence of intervening elements

In Figure 19 the analysis of the effect of the length of the complement clause subject over time shows a clear division between *it* and other pronouns versus NPs in that the former two have been and still remain the stronger predictors of the zero form while the latter (i.e., NPs) are actually increasing in their own respective predictive abilities of the zero form but they have yet to reach the level of *it* or other pronouns. Furthermore, an examination of the start and endpoint for *it* and other pronouns shows that they are higher compared to NPs at any stage of their development and that '*it* and other pronouns remain the stronger predictive factors in PDE with the current set of verbs.

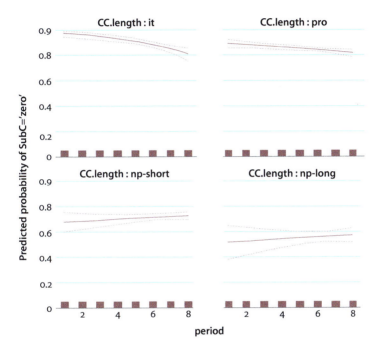

Figure 19. Period: complement clause length

A diachronic analysis of the effect of cotemporality between the matrix and complement clause reveals yet another interesting pattern in that (a) the difference between cotemporal and non-cotemporal tense forms is only marginally significant (b) both have become less associated with the zero form over time. Figure 20 shows that the predictive power of the non-cotemporal patterns decreases faster than that of the cotemporal patterns. The net result is that the effect of this interaction is significant and that at least in PDE the non-cotemporal pattern, as indicated in the literature, is now a slightly better predictor of the *that* form vis-à-vis its cotemporal counterpart.

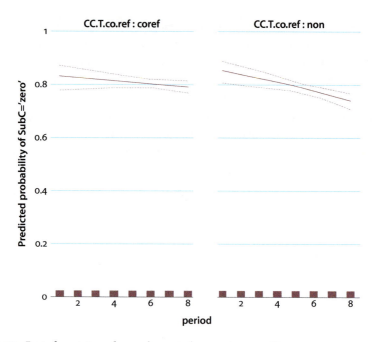

Figure 20. Period: matrix and complement clause cotemporality

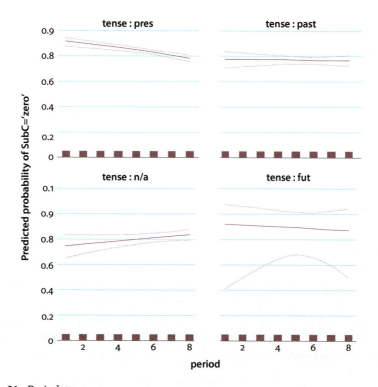

Figure 21. Period: tense

The final significant effect over time to be discussed in this section is the interaction between tense and period. Figure 21 shows that while present tense is gradually decreasing in predictive effect over time for the zero form its endpoint is largely equal to that of the past tense form regardless of time. This suggests that n there is very little predictive difference between the present and past tense forms. Finally, the future form is also shown to be diachronically problematic and the effects are too uncertain to be of any value for the current discussion.

5. Conclusion

This study has shown that, contrary to claims and speculation in the literature to the effect that there has been an overall diachronic tendency towards more zero complementizer use at the expense of *that*-complementation, the aggregate values for *think, guess* and *understand* show a steady *decrease* in zero complementation. In fact, two of the three most frequent complement-taking mental verbs in present-day English, viz. *think* and *understand*, exhibit a diachronic decrease in zero use and a concomitant *increase* in *that* use. *Guess* is the only verb exhibiting a diachronic increase in zero use.

The rigorous methodological approach developed and utilized in this study, and the attention given to ensuring sufficiently large and representative sample sizes when possible from each period has also highlighted the fundamental problems seen in previous work on this topic which have often relied heavily upon descriptive statistical processes. As evidenced by our initial presentation of findings in Section 3.0, reliance of descriptive statistics (often presented in the literature in conjunction with Chi-square analysis) can unintentionally obscure important multicollinear interactions between factors or variable and/or not reveal the stability or robustness of diachronic trend-lines or patterns. From a descriptive perspective it would appear that the zero form for *think* is robust or at least remaining consistent over time and thus one could reasonable infer that the factors which have been proposed to facilitate the zero-form are either equally predictive or also remain significant over time. It is only when a methodology such as the one used in this study is applied that the true significance of the various factors becomes apparent along with diachronic robustness of predicted or expected trends and/or patterns vis-à-vis a dependent variable such as the presence of the zero-complementizer.

In addition to invalidating the long-standing assumption that complement-taking verbs have diachronically developed towards higher levels of zero complementation, this study also highlights the need to differentiate between individual verbs when examining complementation patterns. It became apparent; firstly, that only one verb examined in this study, viz. *guess*, exhibits the aforementioned diachronic increase in zero use. There is a very slight decrease in zero use with *think* over time and *understand*, though starting out with a preference for the zero form, gradually shifts to being a *that*-favouring verb.

Second, the extent to which the factors mentioned in the literature actually predict zero use may differ from verb to verb, as the interactions with verb type suggest. A striking finding in this regard is the effect of matrix internal elements. A strong predictor overall, lack of matrix internal elements is an especially good conditioning factor with *understand* and *guess*; *understand* actually favours the *that* form when matrix-internal elements are present and *guess* exhibits the largest difference in zero rate as conditioned by this factor.

This study has shown that the effect of conditioning factors is also dependent on mode. Again, intervening material was a case in point. Its predictive power is much stronger in the written mode than in the spoken mode; when intervening material is present in the written mode *that* is favoured. Also, mode is a much more powerful predictor for *understand* than for the other two verbs; in the written mode, the zero rate with *understand* drops to below 30% as compared to over 50% in the spoken mode.

With regard to perspectives for future research, the results of the current study call for a methodologically similar analysis with a larger set of verb types as this may reveal additional differences in the way zero/*that* alternation has evolved with each individual verb and as well as shedding more light on how the effect of a conditioning factor may differ from verb to verb.

An additional avenue for future research consists in looking beyond familiar local conditioning factors that are of a strictly structural nature. Priming effects, as in Jaeger and Snider's (2008) study of the syntactic persistence of complementation patterns, and prosodic information (cf. Dehé &Wichmann, 2010) could be incorporated into the logistic regression model. One drawback to the study of prosody and its effect on zero/*that* use from a diachronic point of view is the absence of audio recordings of older corpus data. This shortcoming could be remedied by reconstructing the natural rhythmic patterns of the data on the basis of current knowledge about prosody.

References

Agresti, Alan. (2013). *Categorical data analysis*. Hoboken: Wiley.
Aijmer, Karin. (1997). *I think* – an English modal particle. In T. Swan & O. J. Westwik (Eds.), *Modality in germanic languages: Historical and comparative perspectives* (pp. 1–47). Berlin: Mouton de Gruyter. doi: 10.1515/9783110889932.1
Bolinger, Dwight. (1972). *That's that*. The Hague: Mouton.

Boye, Kasper & Harder, Peter. (2007). Complement-taking predicates: Usage and linguistic structure. *Studies in Language*, 31(3), 569–606. doi: 10.1075/sl.31.3.03boy

Brinton, Laurel J. (1996). *Pragmatic markers in English: Grammaticalization and discourse functions*. Berlin: Mouton de Gruyter. doi: 10.1515/9783110907582

Bybee, Joan L. (2003). Mechanisms of change in grammaticalization: The role of frequency. In B. D. Joseph & R. D. Janda (Eds.), *The handbook of historical linguistics* (pp. 602–623). Oxford: Blackwell. doi: 10.1002/9780470756393.ch19

Bybee, Joan L. (2006). From usage to grammar: The mind's response to repetition. *Language*, 82(4), 711–734. doi: 10.1353/lan.2006.0186

Dehé, Nicole, & Wichmann, Anne. (2010). Sentence-initial *I think (that)* and *I believe (that)*: Prosodic evidence for uses as main clause, comment clause and discourse marker. *Studies in Language*, 34(1), 36–74. doi: 10.1075/sl.34.1.02deh

Diessel, Holger, & Tomasello, Michael. (2001). The acquisition of finite complement clauses in English: A corpus-based analysis. *Cognitive Linguistics*, 12(2), 97–141. doi: 10.1515/cogl.12.2.97

Dor, Daniel. (2005). Toward a semantic account of *that*-deletion in English. *Linguistics*, 43(2), 345–382. doi: 10.1515/ling.2005.43.2.345

Elsness, J. (1984). *That* or zero? A look at the choice of object clause connective in a corpus of American English. *English Studies*, 65, 519–533. doi: 10.1080/00138388408598357

Finegan, Edward, & Biber, Douglas. (1985). *That* and zero complementizers in late modern English: Exploring ARCHER from 1650–1990. In B. Aarts & C. F. Meyer (Eds.), *The verb in contemporary English* (pp. 241–257). Cambridge: Cambridge University Press.

Fischer, Olga. (2007). The development of English parentheticals: A case of grammaticalization? In S. D. Smit, J. Hüttner, G. Kaltenböck, & U. Lutzky (Eds.), *Tracing english through time. Explorations in language variation* (pp. 99–114). Vienna: Braumüller.

Givón, Talmy. (1980). The binding hierarchy and the typology of complements. *Studies in Language*, 4(3), 333–377. doi: 10.1075/sl.4.3.03giv

Givón, Talmy. (1995). Isomorphism in the grammatical code. In R. Simone (Ed.), *Iconicity in syntax* (pp. 47–76). Amsterdam: John Benjamins. doi: 10.1075/cilt.110.07giv

Gorrell, J. H. (1895). Indirect discourse in Anglo-Saxon. *PMLA*, 10, 342–485. doi: 10.2307/456122

Huddleston, Rodney, & Pullum, Geoffrey K. (2002). *The cambridge grammar of the english language*. Cambridge: Cambridge University Press.

Jaeger, Florian T., & Snider, Neal. (2008). Implicit learning and syntactic persistence: surprisal and cumulativity. In B. C. Love, K. McRae, & V. N. Sloutsky (Eds.), *Proceedings of the cognitive science society conference* (pp. 1061–1066). Washington, DC.

Kaltenböck, Gunther. (2006). '... That is the question': Complementizer omission in extraposed that-clauses. *English Language and Linguistics*, 10(2), 371–396. doi: 10.1017/S1360674306001961

Kaltenböck, Gunther. (2007). Position, prosody and scope: The case of English comment clauses. *Vienna English Working Papers*, 16(1), 3–38.

Kearns, Kate. (2007a). Epistemic verbs and zero complementizer. *English Language and Linguistics*, 11(3), 475–505 doi: 10.1017/S1360674307002353

Kearns, Kate. (2007b). Regional variation in the syntactic distribution of null finite complementizer. *Language Variation and Change*, 19, 295–336. doi: 10.1017/S0954394507000117

Langacker, Ronald W. (1991). *Foundations of cognitive grammar. Vol II: Descriptive application*. Stanford CA: Stanford University Press.

Mitchell, Bruce. (1985). *Old english syntax*. Oxford: Clarendon Press.
doi: 10.1093/acprof:oso/9780198119357.001.0001

Noonan, Michael. (1985). Complementation. In T. Shopen (Ed.), *Language typology and syntactic description. Volume II: Complex constructions* (pp. 42–140). Cambridge: Cambridge University Press.

Palander-Collin, Minna. (1999). *Grammaticalization and social embedding: I THINK and METHINKS in Middle and Early Modern English*. Helsinki: Société Néophilologique.

Quirk, Randolph, Greenbaum, Sidney, Leech, Geoffrey, & Svartvik, Jan ([1985] 1997). *A comprehensive grammar of the English language*. London: Longman.

Rissanen, Matti. (1991). On the history of that zero in object clause links in English. In K. Aijmer & B. Altenberg (Eds.), *English corpus linguistics: Studies in honour of Jan Svartvik* (pp. 272–289). London: Longman.

Rohdenburg, Günter. (1996). Cognitive complexity and increased grammatical explicitness in English. *Cognitive Linguistics*, 7(2), 149–182. doi: 10.1515/cogl.1996.7.2.149

Tagliamonte, Sali, & Smith, Jennifer. (2005). *No momentary fancy!* The zero 'complementizer' in english dialects. *English Language and Linguistics*, 9(2), 289–309.
doi: 10.1017/S1360674305001644

Thompson, Sandra A. (2002). "Object complements" and conversation: Towards a realistic account. *Studies in Language*, 26(1), 125–164. doi: 10.1075/sl.26.1.05tho

Thompson, Sandra A., & Mulac, Anthony. (1991a). The discourse conditions for the use of the complementizer that in conversational English. *Journal of Pragmatics*, 15, 237–251.
doi: 10.1016/0378-2166(91)90012-M

Thompson, Sandra A., & Mulac, Anthony. (1991b). A quantitative perspective on the grammaticalization of epistemic parentheticals in English. In E. C. Traugott & B. Heine (Eds.), *Approaches to grammaticalization* (pp. 313–339). Amsterdam: John Benjamins.
doi: 10.1075/tsl.19.2.16tho

Torres Cacoullos, Rena, & Walker, James A. (2009). On the persistence of grammar in discourse formulas: A variationist study of *that*. *Linguistics*, 47(1), 1–43. doi: 10.1515/LING.2009.001

Van Bogaert, Julie. (2010). A constructional taxonomy of *I think* and related expressions: Accounting for the variability of complement-taking mental predicates. *English Language and Linguistics*, 14(3), 399–427. doi: 10.1017/S1360674310000134

Van Bogaert, Julie. (2011). *I think* and other complement-taking mental predicates: A case of and for constructional grammaticalization. *Linguistics*, 49(2), 295–332.

Warner, Anthony R. (1982). *Complementation in middle English and the methodology of historical syntax*. London: Croom Helm.

Yaguchi, Michiko. (2001). The function of the non-deictic that in English. *Journal of Pragmatics*, 33(7), 1125–1155. doi: 10.1016/S0378-2166(00)00045-X

CHAPTER 9

A geometric exemplar-based model of semantic structure
The Dutch causative construction with *laten**

Natalia Levshina
F.R.S. – FNRS, Université catholique de Louvain

This paper addresses an under-investigated issue of the structure of constructional meaning, presenting an innovative corpus-based bottom-up approach, which represents the semantic similarities between exemplars of a construction with the help of Multidimensional Scaling. The study explores the main semantic dimensions and senses of the Dutch causative construction with the auxiliary *laten* 'let'. The quantitative analyses of 731 corpus examples, which were coded for 35 various contextual variables, show that the constructional semantics is organized as a doughnut, with an empty centre and extensive periphery. The main senses, which are represented by clusters of similar exemplars, are not discrete, but represent a continuum. These findings are contrasted with previous accounts, which assumed a discrete prototype-based structure of the meaning.

1. Introduction: Different models of semantic structure

Construction Grammar treats constructions as pairings of form and meaning. In order to describe the semantics of a construction, or to explain and predict its variation and change, it is important to know how the meaning is organized. While it is commonly accepted both in psychology and linguistics that natural language categories have fuzzy boundaries, from the intercategorial point of view, and degrees of category membership, from the intracategorial point of view (see Geeraerts, 2010: 183–192), greater specifics of structure have not been investigated

---

* A significant part of this research was implemented at the University of Leuven as a part of my PhD project under the supervision of Dirk Geeraerts and Dirk Speelman. The project was financially supported by a grant from the Research Foundation – Flanders (FWO). I also thank the anonymous reviewer for valuable comments and suggestions. All remaining mistakes and imperfections, of course, are solely mine.

very thoroughly. Although many semanticists rely unquestioningly on traditional century-old lexicographic practices, today, with the advances of empirical quantitative approaches to semantics and constructions, we have sufficient data and a broad range of tools to test our hypotheses about semantic structures.

In Cognitive Semantics and Cognitive Construction Grammar, there have been a number of suggestions about how meaning can be organized. These suggestions differ with regard to two major distinctions, which are described below.

1. Distinct senses vs. semantic dimensions. Most semantic studies follow the traditional lexicographic practice, describing related but distinct senses. Some of the best-known examples are studies of the semantics of the preposition *over*; e.g. Brugman (1983), Lakoff (1987), Tyler and Evans (2001). These studies differ in many respects, which are beyond the scope of this article, but most of them propose a number of distinct senses, which are frequently represented as nodes in a radial polysemy network: for instance, the sense formulated as 'on the other-side-of', e.g. *The village is just over the river*, and the 'above-and-beyond' sense, e.g. *The arrow flew over the target* (Tyler and Evans, 2001).

An alternative to this approach is Geeraerts' (1998) theoretical justification and Colleman's (e.g. 2009) corpus-based implementation of a multidimensional approach to semantics. Extensions from the basic sense are organized along several dimensions of variation. For instance, there is variation in the Dutch ditransitive construction with regard to the direction of transfer (i.e., causing to receive vs. causing to lose), as exemplified by the ditransitive predicates *geven* 'give' and *ontnemen* 'take away (from)', respectively (Colleman, 2009). Another dimension is the polarity of transfer, i.e. whether or not the transfer takes place. The examples are, again, the predicate *geven* 'give' (successful transfer) and the verb *weigeren* 'refuse', which denotes unsuccessful transfer (*ibid.*).

In fact, despite their differences, these two approaches are closer than it might at first seem. On the one hand, some authors who describe distinct senses do not always exclude a continuum between these senses, at least on a theoretical level (e.g., Brugman, 1983). This continuity can be regarded as a manifestation of dimensionality. On the other hand, the multidimensional approach can lead to discrete senses if the dimensions are of a categorical nature; e.g., the above-mentioned direction of transfer has only two possible values. A list of all possible combinations of such binary values would therefore be a list of discrete senses.

2. Presence vs. absence of the central sense or exemplar. The overwhelming majority of studies in Cognitive Linguistics and Cognitive Construction Grammar assume the existence of a basic sense (primary sense, central sense, prototype, protoscene, etc.), the other meanings being extensions from the prototype. For instance, Goldberg (1995), in her analysis of the English ditransitive construction,

treats the actual physical transfer (e.g., *I gave him the book*) as the basic sense, and transfer of information (e.g., *She told me the news*) as a metaphorical extension from the basic sense. Yet, in some cases it is difficult to find the semantic centre. An example is the subject-auxiliary inversion (SAI) construction in Goldberg (2006: Ch. 8). She shows that the category is organized in a family resemblance fashion, with different senses sharing some of the functional features of the construction, but no central element sharing all of these features (Goldberg, 2006: 176). However, such an analysis is more of an exception than a rule.

If these distinctions are combined, it becomes possible to distinguish four extreme types of semantic models. These four types are represented schematically in Figure 1. Type A (discrete senses plus the core sense) is the most popular in Cognitive Semantics, whereas Type D (no discrete senses, no core sense) has not yet been proposed, to the best of my knowledge. Type B with the empty centre is probably the most similar to Goldberg's (2006) analysis of the SAI construction. Type C is modelled as continuous dimensions with a core – periphery distinction.

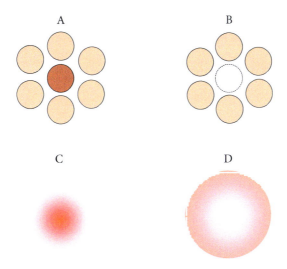

Figure 1. Different types of semantic structures: A – distinct senses with the central sense; B – distinct senses without a directly expressed central sense; C – a continuous structure with the central sense; D – a continuous structure without a central sense. Colour intensity corresponds to semantic centrality

In my opinion, this predominance of the model with distinct senses and the single prototype in the Cognitive Semantic studies should be taken critically. In Prototype Theory of categorization (e.g., Rosch, 1975; Rosch and Mervis, 1975), prototypes are commonly understood as abstract combinations of the most typical features shared by all members of the category. These combinations may be represented by any specific category member, which is normally regarded as the most representative member of the category (e.g. a robin is a highly representative member of the category BIRD). It has been shown that the more prototypical members are more easily learned, identified and reproduced in various kinds of experimental tasks than the less prototypical ones (cf. Murphy, 2002). Still, a prototypical member that has all the characteristic properties of the category does not necessarily exist; it can be only an abstract representation at the intensional level, without any extensional counterpart.[1]

The idea of distinct senses is equally problematic. In studies of concrete categories (e.g. BIRD or FURNITURE), it is relatively easy to come up with a list of subcategories, such as sparrows, swallows and swans, or chairs, tables and sofas, respectively. As one moves to more abstract words and constructions, a classification of the instances into usages or senses becomes increasingly difficult. One of the main problems is the level of granularity and detail (Tyler and Evans, 2001). In principle, there exist an unlimited number of strategies, from the radical splitter, when every exemplar is treated separately, to the ultra lumper, when the category is described as a whole, with most researchers finding themselves somewhere along the continuum in between.[2] For instance, Brugman (1983) suggests several image schemata for the covering sense, including the full coverage sense (*She spread the cloth over the table*) and the multiplex trajector and incomplete coverage sense (*The bushes are scattered over the field*), whereas Tyler and Evans (2001) mention only covering, as a single sense. Another obvious problem is the boundary between closely related senses. In sum, describing discrete senses involves quite a few difficult decisions.

However, the dimensional model is not always an easy solution, either. There may arise problems with establishing whether any two dimensions are distinct, or whether they instead represent a single underlying conceptual dimension. For instance, the enabling use of the ditransitive construction (*Mary offered John a glass of wine*) and the benefactive meaning (*John cooked Mary a risotto*) can be seen as two separate dimensions, or as one superordinate dimension: 'X causes Y to receive Z'.

---

1. In her later works (e.g., Rosch, 1978), Rosch is even more cautious about the use of the word 'prototype'. It is only a convenient shortcut to refer to the prototypicality effects, and it should not be interpreted as the mental representation of the category.

2. The influential Exemplar Theory (e.g., Medin and Schaffer, 1978) assumes that the general representation of a category as a prototype is not relevant. The radically exemplar-based view has been criticized by Goldberg (2006), who dedicated this entire volume to proving that speakers can learn and store generalizations above the level of the specific occurrences; however, there is evidence of the relevance of the exemplars when understood as low-level schemata (e.g., Bybee and Eddington, 2006; Zeschel, 2010). These findings do not contradict each other from the non-reductionist usage-based perspective, which assumes the co-existence of different levels of abstraction in the speaker's knowledge of constructions.

In the present study, all these issues are regarded as empirical questions, which have to be answered for each particular construction in question. I propose a quantitative corpus-based methodology that can be applied to model semantic structures. This method can be used to establish the dimensions and senses, as well as the centre and periphery of a category in a bottom-up fashion. I demonstrate how the method works using a case study of the Dutch causative construction with *laten* 'let'; in a previous study (Stukker, 2005), this category was modelled with the Type A model, with a prototype and distinct extensions. This study tests these assumptions empirically.

The paper is organized as follows. Section 2 introduces the main results of previous research in the semantics of *laten*. Next, I present the data and an innovative multivariate method of representing the semantic structure. Section 4 reports the results of the statistical analyses, and Section 5 concludes with a general discussion.

2. The Dutch causative construction with *laten*

The Dutch construction with *laten* is a periphrastic causative. In many languages, this is a special type of construction that combines the causing and caused events in one causative chain. The causing event is expressed by a Causative Auxiliary (such as *make*, *cause*, *have* or *get*, in English) and is highly schematic. Consider (1), an example with the auxiliary *laten* in the past form (*liet*). The causing event (i.e., what the general did) is unspecified, although one can guess that the general probably gave his army orders. The caused event (i.e., the effect of the general's actions) is that the army destroyed the city. This action is expressed by the Effected Predicate *vernielen* 'destroy', a bare infinitive.

(1) *De generaal liet het leger de stad vernielen.*
 the general let the army the city destroy
 CAUSER AUX. CAUSEE AFFECTEE EFFECTED
  PRED.   PRED.
 'The general ordered the army to destroy the city'

In addition, the construction includes several nominal slots:

- the Causer, who performs the roles of the initiator and/or the responsible entity (the general in the above-mentioned example);
- the Causee, who carries out the caused event expressed by the Effected Predicate (the army);
- the Affectee, the end point in the causation chain (the city), available only in the case of transitive Effected Predicates.[3]

---

3. I follow Verhagen and Kemmer (1997) in naming the main constructional slots.

The periphrastic causative with *laten* is quite frequent and semantically broad. Although etymologically related to the English *let*, which expresses nowadays only enablement and permission, the Dutch *laten* followed by the infinitive has been used to express the semantics of both letting and coercion from the earliest attested examples (van der Horst, 1998). Note that in Talmy's theory of force dynamics (Talmy, 2000: Ch. 7; the terminology has been adjusted to the purposes of the present paper), letting involves a Causer who fails, deliberately or not, to override the Causee's intrinsic tendency towards rest or motion. As a result, the Causee is maximally autonomous in bringing about the effected event. In contrast, causation *per se* means that the stronger Causer overrides the intrinsic tendency of the Causee towards rest or motion. The contemporary *laten*, like its German cognate *lassen*, expresses both force-dynamic situations. In fact, there are many cases for which the difference between the two is neutralized. Compare the letting context in (2a) with an ambiguous sentence in (2b) and a coercive one in (2c). These examples suggest that the letting – coercion distinction is not encoded, but rather inferred with a higher or lower probability.

(2) a. *De politie liet de dader ontsnappen.*
   the police let the criminal escape
   'The police let the criminal escape.'
b. *Hij liet iedereen zijn roman lezen.*
   he let everybody his novel read
   'He had/let everyone read his novel.'
c. *De trainer liet de spelers loopoefeningen doen.*
   the coach let the players run-exercises do
   'The coach had the players do running exercises.'

This broad and abstract meaning of the construction with *laten* can be interpreted as that of indirect causation (Kemmer and Verhagen, 1994). Indirect causation is observed when "it is recognized that some other force besides the initiator is the most immediate source of energy in the effected event" (Verhagen and Kemmer, 1997: 67). Its opposite is so-called direct causation, i.e. when "there is no intervening energy source 'downstream' from the initiator: if the energy is put in, the effect is the inevitable result" (Verhagen and Kemmer, 1997: 70). Direct causation is covered by the construction with *doen* 'do', and the very infrequent and lexically restricted *aan het V maken (brengen)* 'bring to V'.

As Verhagen and Kemmer (1997) demonstrate, indirectness of causation is closely associated with the particular configurations of the semantic classes of the Causer and the Causee. Thus, if both the Causer and the Causee are animate, one can expect the causation to be indirect because a human being – disregarding the possibility of telepathy – cannot affect another mind directly (Verhagen and Kemmer, 1997: 71). This type of causation is often labelled as inducive causation, e.g. (3a). In the case of volitional causation, with an animate Causer and an inanimate Causee, a human being can also influence the world indirectly, e.g. with the help of automation, as in (3b), or by using natural forces, such as gravity (3c).

(3) a. *De trainer liet de spelers loopoefeningen doen.*
 the coach let the players run-exercises do
 'The coach had the players do running exercises.'
 b. *De machinist liet de motoren draaien.*
 the engine-driver let the engines run
 'The engine driver had/let/left the engines run/running.'
 c. *Hij liet de water weglopen.*
 he let the water away-run
 'He let the water drain out.'

In addition to inducive and volitional causation, Verhagen and Kemmer (1997), followed by Stukker (2005), also speak about so-called physical and affective causation. The former involves an inanimate Causer and Causee, as in (4), and the latter contains an inanimate Causer but an animate sentient Causee, as in (5). However, these two uses are less frequent than inducive and volitional causation.

(4) *De bommenwerpers laten hun dodelijke lading vallen.*
 the bombers let their deadly cargo fall
 'The bombers drop their deadly cargo'
(5) *Het laat ons het beste verhopen.*
 it lets us the best hope-for
 'It makes/allows us (to) hope for the best'

Note that Talmy's use of the term *inducive causation*, or *caused agency* (e.g., Talmy, 2000: Section 5.6) is somewhat different from the operationalization in Verhagen and Kemmer (1997) and Stukker (2005). Talmy's inducive causation involves intentionality, or volitionality of the Causee's actions. For Verhagen *et al.*, inducive causation is defined with the help of the semantic classes of the Causer and the Causee (both are animate entities). It is thus a more coarse-grained operationalization, although in most cases, e.g. (3a), the two interpretations overlap. The difference between the definitions can be seen in the following examples:

(6) *Smoke getting in its eyes made the squirrel leave its tree.*
(7) *He let me know when he returned to New York.*

The Example (6) would be, according to Talmy, a case of inducive causation because the Causee (the squirrel) left the tree intentionally. In the operationalization proposed by Verhagen, Kemmer and Stukker, this context could be interpreted as affective causation because of the inanimate Causer (i.e., the fact of smoke getting in the squirrel's eyes). In contrast, in (7) the Causee (*me*) is only a recipient of information, rather than an intentionally acting participant, so the causation would not be inducive according to Talmy's interpretation. For Verhagen *et al.*, the sentence would be an example of inducive causation, because both the Causer and the Causee are animate sentient beings. In this paper I will try to take into account both Talmy's more direct conceptual interpretation and the approximation used by Verhagen, Kemmer and Stukker.

According to Stukker (2005), inducive causation – a combination of an animate Causer and a sentient Causee – is the semasiological prototype of the *laten* construction. The other senses (volitional, physical and affective causation) are extensions from this sense. Thus, Stukker (2005) assumes the semantic structure of Type A, with the inducive causation in the centre and the other causation types on the periphery. In the following subsections, I test and refine Stukker's hypothesis with the help of an innovative technique, which allows for the representation of constructional exemplars in a low-dimensional space. The data and approach are presented in the following section.

3. The exemplar space of *laten*: Data and method

The approach presented here was developed in Levshina (2011). It allows for the representation of the exemplar space of constructions as a low-dimensional semantic map, which can display both the dimensions of semantic variation and the senses as clusters of similar exemplars. It is important to mention that the exemplars are most commonly understood in psychology as unique instances (see discussion in Murphy, 2002: 58–60), e.g. every time a stimulus is presented to subjects in an experiment. In the present study, exemplars are regarded as occurrences of the construction in a corpus. Exemplars of the other use of the word (e.g. Bybee and Eddington, 2006) – i.e. fully or partly lexically specified constructions – are treated here as low-level abstractions. The following subsections describe the steps of the analysis.

3.1 Selection and preparation of the data

I used data from three popular registers:

- the fundamental register of spontaneous face-to-face conversations: data from the Corpus of Spoken Dutch (Oostdijk, 2002);

- the newspaper register: data from Twente News Corpus (Ordelman *et al.*, 2007) and Leuven News Corpus (constructed at the Quantitative Lexicology and Variational Linguistics research unit of the University of Leuven);
- the online communication register: postings from several Belgian and Dutch online discussion groups (the Usenet) collected by Tom Ruette (University of Leuven).

All three subcorpora contained samples of Dutch spoken in both the Netherlands and in Flanders, the Dutch-speaking part of Belgium. Since previous studies (Levshina, 2011) have shown that there is no substantial conceptual variation in the semantics of *laten* in the three registers and the two countries, the variational aspect is ignored here. For this study I created a sample of 731 occurrences of the causative *laten*, randomly selected from the above-mentioned subcorpora. The exemplars were then coded manually for 35 contextual variables. These variables can be subdivided into several groups:

- the variables related to the nominal slot fillers (i.e., the Causer, the Causee and the Affectee, if available): the semantic class, syntactic expression, part of speech, grammatical person, number and definiteness;
- specific features of the Causee: volitionality, as well as whether the participant undergoes or causes a change;
- the variables describing the relationships between the main participants: relationships of coreferentiality and possession;
- the features of the Effected Predicate: transitivity (in a broad sense, including ditransitivity, copula functions, etc.), and the type of prepositional complements. The semantics of the caused event was also considered, both in the literal and metaphorical sense (if applicable). The specific lemmata of the predicates were also considered as a separate variable, because many of them occurred several times;
- the variables related to different modifiers: polarity (i.e. the presence of negation), adverbial modifiers and modal verbs modifying the auxiliary;
- the syntactic function of the construction;
- the more general properties of the clauses and sentences where the construction was found, such as the mood and tense of the clause, the syntactic type of the clause (main, relative, adverbial, etc.) and the communicative type of the sentence.

This list of variables represents all possible contextual variables that could be described at an acceptable level of objectivity, with the help of linguistic markers or simple tests. This comprehensive approach is similar to the one used in Gries' (2006) corpus-based analysis of the verb *run*, which also involved a large number of heterogeneous variables. Although many of these variables are associated, this redundancy of linguistic cues is natural when we learn a new word or construction.

In some observations the relevant information was missing. In this case, I had either to rely on the context (e.g. the semantic class of implicit Causees), or, if the contextual clues were insufficient, to code the feature as 'Not Applicable' (e.g. the grammatical properties of the missing Affectee).

3.2 Multivariate analyses of the sample

The matrix with the individual exemplars (731 rows) coded for the categorical variables (35 columns) was used as the input for a series of statistical analyses in R (R Development Core Team, 2011). With the help of Gower's distance (Gower, 1971) – a universal distance metric for numeric and categorical variables – I created a matrix of distances between the exemplars. An example of a distance matrix is a chart of distances between cities. The distances are defined on the basis of the shared semantic features: the more features two observations share, the smaller the distance between them. The exemplars with the same features have a distance of 0. If one or both exemplars in a pair contained a missing value, the corresponding feature was disregarded in the calculation of the distance between the exemplars.

Next, this distance matrix was represented spatially with the help of Multidimensional Scaling (MDS). In this study I used the SMACOF algorithm developed by de Leeuw and Mair (2009; see also Borg and Groenen, 1997: Ch. 8). Both metric and non-metric solutions were tested, and the representations were nearly identical. In the following subsection, the metric solution is reported. This MDS map serves as a visualization of the differences and similarities between the exemplars of the construction, and can be treated as a semantic or conceptual map of semantic categories. One can evaluate the general structure of the category, interpret the main dimensions and explore the different clusters or senses. Since the exemplars with the same values will have the same coordinates on the map, it may also be useful to represent the semantic structure in a density map, which shows how densely different semantic regions on the map are populated by the exemplars. I used a 2D kernel density estimator in the package MASS (Venables and Ripley, 2002) to create such a map.

4. The results of the quantitative analyses

The map in Figure 2 shows the two-dimensional solution for the data discussed in the previous section. The stress of the solution was only 9%, which means that more than 90% of the variation was captured by the map. The subsequent dimensions (3, 4 and 5) did not add more than 5% of the variation and are difficult to interpret, so they will not be discussed in this paper.

Looking at Figure 2, the semantics of the *laten* construction has a somewhat irregular doughnut-like structure, with a relatively empty centre and broad periphery. This indicates that there is no central sense, which would be equidistant from all others. There is no evidence of discrete senses, although there are a few very fuzzy clusters. Before describing these clusters, it is necessary to check if the solution reveals any conceptual dimensions, which I did using two complementary methods. The first was intuitive and visual. For each variable, I created a map with all exemplars represented as different symbols corresponding to the values of the variable. An example is shown in Figure 3. The variable describes the semantics of the caused event, which can be mental (as in *Ik liet hem weten dat...* 'I let him know that...'), physical (*Ik liet hem mijn huis schilderen* 'I had him paint my house') and social (*Ik liet hem zijn verhaal doen* 'I let/had him tell his story'). The mental caused events are mostly in the bottom-left part of the map, and the social events are predominantly in the upper-right part, intermingled with the physical caused events.

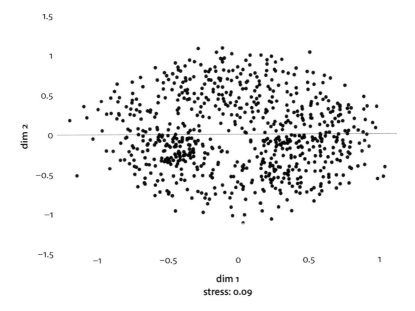

Figure 2. The exemplar space of *laten*

The second approach was quantitative and was applied only to the horizontal and vertical dimensions established by the MDS algorithm. For every variable, I carried out two simple linear regression analyses and ANOVAs; the coordinates of the points on the horizontal and vertical dimensions were set as the response, and the

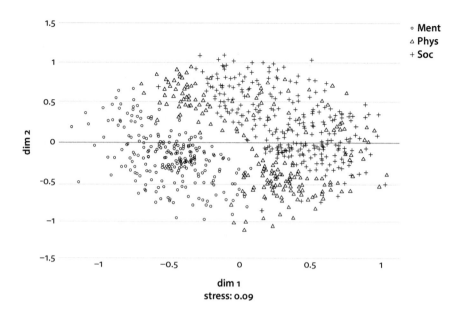

Figure 3. Distribution of the semantic domain of the caused events in the exemplar space of *laten*

variable was set as the predictor.[4] Next, I compared the explained variance statistics (R^2 and F-score) of the variables to see which ones best explained the position of the exemplars. The results can be found in the Appendix.

Both approaches showed very similar results. The horizontal dimension mainly corresponds to the distinction between mental and non-mental caused events: the ANOVA F-score for the semantics of the caused event (in the case of figurative expressions, the figurative meaning was coded) was 476.1 on 2 and 716 d.f., $p < 0.001$; the explained variance R^2 was 0.57. The F-score and R^2 were the highest observed scores for Dimension 1 (see the numbers in bold in the Appendix. Compare the Example (8) of a mental caused event from the extreme left of the map (*ontmoedigen* 'discourage'), and the Example (9) of a physical caused event from the extreme right (*rijden* 'ride, drive'):

(8) Laat u niet ontmoedigen en zet uw bijdragen voor deze
    let you not discourage and set your contributions for this
    nieuwsgroep gewoon voort!
    newsgroup as usual forward
    'Don't let yourself be discouraged and continue contributing to this newsgroup as usual!'

---

4. Except for the Effected Predicate lemmata, which had too many hapax legomena for a meaningful analysis.

(9) 's avonds   willen ze   geen bussen meer laten rijden.
    in-the-evening want they no   buses   more let   ride
    'They want to cancel buses in the evening'

The vertical dimension is associated the most strongly with intentionality, or volitionality of the Causee's actions: unintentional at the bottom, intentional at the top, and with a few ambiguous cases in the middle. The F-statistic was 325.1 on 2 and 728 d.f. with $p < 0.001$, and R^2 was 0.47 (again, these were the largest values for Dimension 2, as can be seen from the table in the Appendix). Intentionality is followed by the role of the Causee (i.e. the Causee undergoes a change – there is no change – the Causee causes a change): $F = 191.9$ on 2 and 727 d.f. with $p < 0.001$, $R^2 = 0.34$. Both features imply a distinction between the patient-like and the relatively agentive autonomous Causees. Compare (10), where the implicit Causee is the food that is being prepared, and (11), an exemplar with an agentive implicit Causee, someone who has the power to exclude a redundant holder. The exemplars are located in the extreme bottom and top areas of the map, respectively.

(10) ... heel even   laten roerbakken heel even   en   klaar.
        very briefly let   stir-fry   very briefly and ready
        'Just a little bit, let (it) stir-fry just a little bit, and it's ready.'

(11) Is   er   een   reden   voor   om   4   volmachthouders   te
     is   there a   reason for   in-order   4   authorized-holders to
     hebben? Waarom die   andere drie   niet   laten   schrappen?
     have   why   those   other   three   not   let   drop
     'Is there any reason for having 4 authorized holders? Why not have the other three dropped?'

These two variables – intentionality and the semantic role of the Causee – correspond closely to Verhagen and Kemmer's (1997) distinction between direct and indirect causation, which was discussed in Section 2. The map shows that this distinction is really a continuum, and that the exemplars of *laten* have different values along this continuum.

One can also see in Figure 3 that the mental caused events are located, on average, a little lower than the physical and social ones. The mental caused events represented by *laten* involve, on average, less control by the Causee, because most of these events refer to perception and knowing, as in the collocations *laten weten* 'let know, inform' and *laten zien* 'let see, show', which will be discussed below.

However, if one examines the distribution of the variables more closely, one can find additional semantic dimensions. The most important one is transitivity of the Effected Predicate, which cuts the map diagonally, as shown in Figure 4. Most intransitives are located in the bottom right of the map, while the transitives populate the upper left. Transitivity of the Effected Predicate and the number of participants were discussed in detail in Kemmer and Verhagen (1994), who write that intransitive causative constructions, which contain only two participants (i.e., the Causer and the Causee) are similar to simple transitive clauses, which also contain two participants (prototypically, the Agent and the Patient); transitive causative constructions, which contain three participants (i.e., the Causer, the Causee and the Affectee) are similar to ditransitive clauses, which also have three participants (i.e., the Agent, the Recipient and the Theme). In the two-participant constructions, causative or not, the second entity (i.e., the Causee in a causative construction or the direct object of a transitive predicate) is the affected one; in contrast, in the three-participant constructions, the second participant (i.e., the Causee in a causative construction or the indirect object of a ditransitive predicate) is less affected and more peripheral. Thus, the degree of affectedness, or patientivity of the Causee is greater in intransitive causative constructions than in transitive causatives, and the degree of the Causee's autonomy is smaller. For illustration, compare two above-mentioned examples: (10), which contains a patient-like Causee, has an intransitive Effected Predicate, whereas (11), which has a relatively agentive implicit Causee, is an example of the transitive *laten* construction.

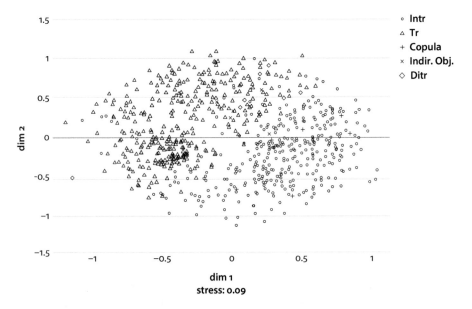

Figure 4. Distribution of the Effected Predicate transitivity patterns in the exemplar space of *laten*

This is exactly the picture that one can see in the maps. Most of the intransitive Effected Predicates (see bottom right) co-occur with the patient-like Causees (see bottom), whereas the majority of the transitive Effected Predicates (see upper left) are combined with the agentive autonomous Causees (see top). Although this is in line with Kemmer and Verhagen's interpretation, these two dimensions – transitivity of the Effected Predicate and affectedness vs. autonomy of the Causee – do not fully coincide. There are quite a few transitive Effected Predicates in the bottom left part of the map, which involve less agentive Causees, as in (12):

(12) *Ik liet een vriendin een song horen.*
I let a friend-FEM a song hear
'I let a friend hear a song'

At the same time, some intransitive Effected Predicates in the upper-right part of the map are quite autonomous entities. Consider (13):

(13) *… daarom lieten we rechtsback Bryssinck almaar mee*
that's why let we right-back Bryssinck continuously with
oprukken.
advance
'That's why we had the right back Bryssinck push up all the time, too'

Next, let us examine the clusters of the exemplars, which may represent the constructional senses. Looking at the map, one can see three main regions, although these are not very distinct. The density plot in Figure 5 gives a clearer picture of the structure. The contour lines delineate the regions with different densities of the exemplars, revealing two regions with very high density. A closer look reveals that the one on the left is populated mostly by instances of *laten weten* 'let know, inform', as in (14), and by the exemplars of *laten zien* 'let see, show' and some other mental caused event constructions, as in (15), repeated here for the sake of convenience:

(14) *Berlusconi liet gisteren weten de functie van Ruggiero*
Berlusconi let yesterday know the function of Ruggiero
voor zeker zes maanden waar te zullen nemen.
for sure six months true to shall take
'Berlusconi said yesterday that he will fill in the function of Ruggiero for at least six months'

(15) *Ik liet een vriendin een song horen.*
I let a friend a song hear
'I let a friend hear a song.'

The densely populated area in the non-mental caused event part also contains some frequent fixed expressions, e.g. *(links) laten liggen* 'ignore' and *laten vallen* 'drop, abandon', and although this region is less lexically homogeneous than the region with mental caused events, most of these exemplars are conceptually similar. They represent metaphorical expressions with the sense of leaving, abandoning or missing an opportunity. For instance, see (16).

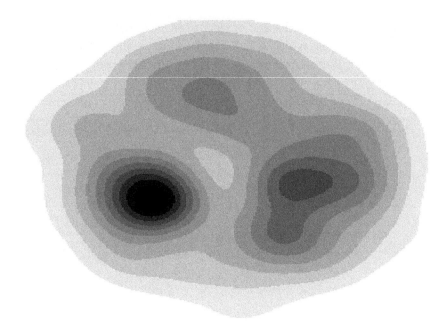

Figure 5. A density map of the causative construction with *laten*, based on the coordinates of the individual exemplars (see the previous maps)

(16) *AS Roma liet gisteren de kans liggen om naast*
AS Roma let yesterday the chance lie in-order near
Inter aan de leiding te komen.
Inter to the leadership to come
'A.S. Roma missed the chance to become a leader next to Inter yesterday.'

The area at the top of the semantic map with medium density corresponds to transitive Effected Predicates and to maximally autonomous, usually implicit Causees. Examples from this region commonly convey the sense of delegated causation, e.g. service encounters (17) or administrative interaction (18):

(17) *De makkelijkste manier van beleggen is om het*
the easiest way of investing is in-order it
iemand anders te laten doen.
someone else to let do
'The easiest way to invest is to have someone else do it'

(18) *Daarom vroeg het aan het parket om*
that's-why asked it to the public-prosecutor in-order
het complex opnieuw te laten onderzoeken.
the complex again to let search
'That's why they asked the public prosecutor to have the complex searched again'

On the periphery of this region, mostly in the upper left, there are a few examples of middle voice events (e.g. Davidse and Heyvaert, 2003) with coreferential Causers and Affectees, as in (19):

(19) *Het cultuur laat zich niet makkelijk exporteren.*
the culture lets itself not easily export
'The culture cannot be exported easily'

The Causers in contexts like (17) and (19) are to a certain degree affected by the effected event: They are either the beneficiaries of the delegated causation, as in (17), or the semantic objects of the action denoted by the Effected Predicate in the reflexive constructions, as in (19). As this area of the map involves agentive Causees, it thus also contains non-agentive Causers. This inverse correlation between the agentivity of the Causer and of the Causee is logical: As the causation becomes more indirect, the impact of the Causee increases, and the role of the Causer as the main driving force becomes less prominent.

Because these semantic regions are not distinct, one should also explore the transitional zones between them. First, the transitional zone between delegated causation and the abandonment sense is exemplified by (20), which is about a football club selling a player. This is an intransitive construction with a relatively autonomous Causee:

(20) *FC Utrecht weigerde evenwel de door de eigen fans*
FC Utrecht refused as-well the by the own fans
geadoreerde cultheld te laten gaan.
adored cult-hero to let go
'FC Utrecht also refused to sell the cult hero, adored by his own fans'

Between the abandonment cluster and the cluster with *laten weten* and similar expressions, there are a few hybrid metaphorical examples regarding the abandonment of mental states conceptualized as physical objects:

(21) *De directeuren hebben hun vooroordelen blijkbaar schielijk*
The directors have their prejudices apparently suddenly
laten varen.
let sail
'Apparently, the directors have suddenly abandoned their prejudices'

Finally, between the giving-information cluster and the region with delegated causation are a few reflexive constructions that resemble the above-mentioned middle-voice contexts. The Causer yields to or resists a negative mental influence, as in (22), repeated here for the sake of convenience:

(22) *Laat u niet ontmoedigen en zet uw bijdragen voor deze*
let you not discourage and set your contributions for this
nieuwsgroep gewoon voort!
newsgroup as-usual forward
'Don't let yourself be discouraged and continue contributing to this newsgroup as usual!'

This brief examination of the exemplar space shows that the continuum between the main senses that appears on the map can be also interpreted in semantic terms, and the relationships between the semantic regions are those of family resemblance.

After the analysis of the exemplar space of *laten* presented in this section, it is time to address the main question of this study: What is the semantic structure of the construction really like? The first important issue is whether the category is organized along dimensions, or whether it represents a set of distinct senses. The graphical representations in Figures 2 to 5 suggest that both types are involved. On the one hand, there is a clear continuum along the two main dimensions – the semantic domain of the caused event and the indirectness of causation. However, the exemplars are not distributed homogeneously along the dimensions, instead forming clusters, albeit very fuzzy ones.

It is important to mention that the distinctiveness of a cluster correlates positively with the frequency of the lexicalized expressions that it contains. Recalling that the most autonomous cluster is that with the collocations *laten weten* and *laten zien*, according to Bybee (2010: Ch. 3), highly entrenched lexically specific constructions are reproduced by speakers without invoking the general schema of *laten*. This results in a shortcut routine, which is an important source of linguistic change. As the routine becomes more entrenched, the link of the cluster with the general schema may be lost, and an independent construction with its own peculiar functions will be formed. The method presented in this article can be useful in capturing such frequency effects and in predicting the future development of such constructions.

The other question posed at the beginning of this paper is whether any central sense, such as inducive causation, exists. The graphical representations in this section indicate a lack of any sense that is sufficiently frequent to be the origin of most other senses. In fact, inducive causation, in Talmy's terms, corresponds to intentionality of the Causee, which constitutes a dimension, as opposed to a regular cluster. As far as the approximation by Verhagen, Kemmer and Stukker is concerned, most exemplars with animate Causers and Causees are located in two very distinct regions: the delegated causation region at the top of the map and the cluster with mental Effected Predicates (*zien* 'see', *weten* 'know', etc.). These two rather different senses are difficult to interpret as a single starting point for the other extensions.

5. Conclusions

To conclude, the analysis presented in this paper largely supports the Geeraerts-Colleman multidimensional model of semantics, which focuses on the dimensions of semantic variation, rather than on specific discrete senses; however, the map also displays some fuzzy clusters, which can be interpreted as the main senses of the Dutch causative construction with *laten*. Further, no clear conceptual centre that could serve as a prototype, protoscene, etc. was found. The exemplars of *laten* are connected in a family-resemblance fashion, without an explicit central subschema. Needless to say, the results of this corpus-based analysis need support from other types of evidence. For instance, it is necessary to know to what extent the distances between the exemplars reflect their perceived similarity in the speakers' minds – this information could be collected from similarity judgments or sorting tasks.

From a more general perspective, the study demonstrates that some assumptions about the semantic structure – such as the existence of distinct senses and prototypes – should not be taken for granted. In each specific case, researchers should rely on empirical evidence, rather than on intuitions about the units of semantic analysis and the relationships between them. Although the notion of prototype may be useful for teaching and learning purposes (e.g., Lindstromberg, 2010), a prototypical structure should not be assumed *a priori*. This awareness is especially important for the emergent area of empirical constructional semantics.

References

Borg, I., & Groenen, P. (1997). *Modern multidimensional scaling: Theory and applications*. New York: Springer. doi:10.1007/978-1-4757-2711-1

Brugman, C. M. (1983). *The story of over*. Bloomington: Indiana University.

Bybee, J. L. (2010). *Language, usage and cognition*. Cambridge: Cambridge University Press. doi:10.1017/CBO9780511750526

Bybee, J. L., & Eddington, D. (2006). A usage-based approach to Spanish verbs of 'becoming'. *Language*, 82(2), 323–355. doi:10.1353/lan.2006.0081

Colleman, T. (2009). The semantic range of the Dutch Double Object Construction. A collostructional perspective. *Constructions and Frames*, 1, 190–221. doi:10.1075/cf.1.2.02col

Davidse, K., & Heyvaert, L. (2003). On the so-called 'middle' construction in English and Dutch. In S. Granger, J. Lerot, & S. Petch-Tyson (Eds.), *Corpus-based approaches to contrastive linguistics and translation studies* (pp. 57–73). Amsterdam: Rodopi.

Geeraerts, D. (1998). The semantic structure of the indirect object in Dutch. In W. van Langendonck & W. Van Belle (Eds.), *The Dative. Vol. 2. Theoretical and constrastive studies* (pp. 185–210). Amsterdam/philadelphia: John Benjamins. doi:10.1075/cagral.3.08gee

Geeraerts, D. (2010). *Theories of lexical semantics*. Oxford: Oxford University Press.

Goldberg, A. E. (1995). *Constructions. A construction grammar approach to argument structure.* Chicago: University of Chicago Press.

Goldberg, A. E. (2006). *Constructions at work: The nature of generalization in language.* Oxford: Oxford University Press.

Gower, J. C. (1971). A general coefficient of similarity and some of its properties, *Biometrics*, 27, 857–874. doi:10.2307/2528823

Gries, S. Th. (2006). Corpus-based methods and cognitive semantics: The many senses of *to run*. In S. Th. Gries & A. Stefanowitsch (Eds.), *Corpora in cognitive linguistics. corpus-based approaches to syntax and lexis* (pp. 57–99). Berlin: Mouton de Gruyter. doi:10.1515/9783110197709

van der Horst, J. M. (1998). Doen in Old and Early Middle Dutch: A comparative approach. In I. Tieken-Boon van Ostade, M. van der Wal, & A. van Leuvensteijn (Eds.), *'Do' in English, Dutch and German. History and present-day variation* (pp. 53–64). Munster: Nodus Publicationen.

Kemmer, S., & Verhagen, A. (1994). The grammar of causatives and the conceptual structure of events. *Cognitive Linguistics*, 5, 115–156. doi:10.1515/cogl.1994.5.2.115

Lakoff, G. (1987). *Women, fire, and dangerous things: What categories reveal about the mind.* Chicago: University of Chicago Press. doi:10.7208/chicago/9780226471013.001.0001

de Leeuw, J., & Mair, P. (2009). Multidimensional scaling using majorization: SMACOF in R. *Journal of Statistical Software* 31(3): 1–30. http://www.jstatsoft.org/v31/i03/. (Last access 17.11.2011)

Levshina, N. (2011). *Doe wat je niet laten kan: A usage-based analysis of the Dutch causative constructions.* Ph.D. dissertation, Katholieke Universiteit Leuven.

Lindstromberg, S. (2010). *English prepositions explained.* Amsterdam/philadelphia: John Benjamins. doi:10.1075/z.157

Medin, D. L., & Schaffer, M. M. (1978). Context theory of classification learning. *Psychological Review*, 85, 207–238. doi:10.1037/0033-295X.85.3.207

Murphy, G. L. (2002). *The big book of concepts.* Cambridge, MA: MIT Press.

Oostdijk, N. H. J. (2002). The design of the Spoken Dutch Corpus. In P. Peters, P. Collins, & A. Smith (Eds.), *New frontiers of corpus research* (pp. 105–112). Amsterdam: Rodopi.

Ordelman, R., de Jong, F., van Hessen, A., & Hondorp, H. (2007). TwNC: A multifaceted Dutch News Corpus. *ELRA Newsletter* 12 (3–4), http://doc.utwente.nl/68090/ (last access 17.11.2011)

R Development Core Team. (2011). *R: A language and environment for statistical computing.* Vienna: R Foundation for Statistical Computing. http://www.R-project.org (last access 17.11.2011)

Rosch, E. (1975). Cognitive representation of semantic categories. *Journal of Experimental Psychology*, 104(3), 192–233. doi:10.1037/0096-3445.104.3.192

Rosch, E. (1978). Principles of categorization. In E. Rosch & B. B. Lloyd (Eds.), *Cognition and categorization* (pp. 27–48). Hillsdale, NJ: Erlbaum.

Rosch, E., & Mervis, C. B. (1975). Family resemblances: Studies in the internal structure of categories. *Cognitive Psychology*, 7, 573–605. doi:10.1016/0010-0285(75)90024-9

Talmy, L. (2000). *Toward a cognitive semantics.* Cambridge, MA: MIT Press.

Tyler, A., & Evans, V. (2001). Reconsidering prepositional polysemy networks: The Case of *Over*. *Language*, 77(4), 724–765. doi:10.1353/lan.2001.0250

Stukker, N. (2005). *Causality marking across levels of language structure.* University of Utrecht dissertation.

Venables, W. N., & Ripley, B. D. (2002). *Modern applied statistics with S*. New York: Springer. doi: 10.1007/978-0-387-21706-2

Verhagen, A., & Kemmer, S. (1997). Interaction and causation: Causative constructions in modern standard Dutch. *Journal of Pragmatics*, 27, 61–82. doi: 10.1016/S0378-2166(96)00003-3

Zeschel, A. (2010). Exemplars and analogy: Semantic extension in constructional networks. In D. Glynn & K. Fischer (Eds.), *Quantitative methods in cognitive semantics: Corpus-driven approaches* (pp. 201–219). Berlin: De Gruyter Mouton.

Appendix

Table 1. ANOVA F-scores and linear regression R^2 (the adjusted version) for 34 variables (the lemmata of effected predicates were excluded). The asterisks and other symbols indicate the level of significance

Variable	Dimension 1 (horizontal)		Dimension 2 (vertical)	
	F-score	R^2 (adjusted)	F-score	R^2 (adjusted)
Causer's Semantics	11.96***	0.09	1.43	0.004
Causer's Syntactic Expression	0.69	0	13.27***	0.03
Causer's Part of Speech	0.03	0	1.29	0
Causer's Definiteness	1.87	0.001	1.3	0
Causer's Person	7.73***	0.02	16.8***	0.04
Causer's Number	12.25***	0.02	12.27***	0.02
Causee's Semantics	32.2***	0.26	61.41***	0.41
Causee's Syntactic Expression	156.5***	0.52	30.77***	0.17
Causee's POS	3.02*	0.01	5.28**	0.03
Causee's Definiteness	1.56	0.001	0.02	0
Causee's Person	23.9***	0.1	11.35***	0.05
Causee's Number	0.01	0	2.55	0.004
Affectee's Semantics	2.02.	0.02	18.9***	0.25
Affectee's Syntactic Expression	9.04**	0.02	123.3***	0.23
Affectee's POS	10.13***	0.05	5.94**	0.03
Affectee's Definiteness	3.94*	0.01	10.16**	0.03
Affectee's Person	5.93**	0.03	0.08	0
Affectee's Number	8.19**	0.02	7.06**	0.02
Causee's Volitionality	10.32***	0.02	325.1***	0.47
Causee's Role (affecting or affected)	112.1***	0.23	191.9***	0.34
Coreferentiality of main participants	48.07***	0.11	63.75***	0.15
Possession relationships between main participants	13.51***	0.05	5.45**	0.02
Effected Predicate Transitivity	136.2***	0.48	38.93***	0.21
Prepositional Complements of the Effected Predicate	1.45	0.01	1.83*	0.01

Variable	Dimension 1 (horizontal)		Dimension 2 (vertical)	
	F-score	R^2 (adjusted)	F-score	R^2 (adjusted)
Caused Event Semantics (if metaphor, literal interpretation)	467.5***	0.57	77.19***	0.18
Caused Event Semantics (if metaphor, figurative interpretation)	476.1***	0.57	69.8***	0.16
Negation	1.03	0	1.34	0.003
Adverbial Modifiers	1.83.	0.01	0.55	0
Modals	2.73*	0.01	0.82	0
Syntactic Function of the construction	8.36***	0.02	0.48	0
Clause Mood	14.79***	0.04	26.56***	0.07
Clause Tense	2.54*	0.01	1.59	0.004
Clause Type	2.29.	0.01	5.8***	0.03
Sentence Type	10.59***	0.03	24.78***	0.06

*** for $p < 0.001$, ** for $0.001 \leq p < 0.01$, * for $0.01 \leq p < 0.05$, '.' for $0.5 \leq p < 0.1$.

Index

A

aan-dative   168–170, 176–184, 194–195
-*ata* nominal   45
Absolute frequency   2, 215, 217, 219
  See also frequency
Abstract noun   44, 50–52, 57–58, 61, 192
Accessibility   84, 179
Accusative   4, 65, 67–68, 70–74, 167
  clitic   70–71
Adposition   11, 19–20, 25–30, 32–33, 35–36
Affectedness   31–32, 76–77, 88, 169, 179, 183, 254–255
Agency   88, 96, 247
Agentivity   77, 89, 96, 99, 257
Ancora corpus   145, 150
Animacy   4, 65, 71, 77, 80, 84, 88–90, 94–95
  hierarchy   88–89
  See also animate
Animate   31, 70–71, 84, 88–90, 183–184, 246–248, 258
  See also animacy
Annotated corpus   112
  See also corpus
ANOVA   197, 223, 251–252, 261
Argument frame   167
Argument structure   2, 4–5, 7, 36, 40–41, 44, 63, 87, 97, 100, 105, 110–112, 126, 128–136, 163, 165–166, 176, 194–196, 198, 260
  alternation   165–166, 194–195
  construction   2, 111, 126, 128–133, 176
  See also argument frame
  See also verbal argument

ARTHUS corpus   4, 77–81, 88
Aske   56–57, 108, 127, 134, 256
ASSESS-STATE construction   149, 158
Association   2, 5, 62, 88, 94, 98, 101, 105–106, 112, 114–116, 118–124, 132–134, 150, 152–154, 157, 159, 176–177, 187, 196
  strength   2, 5, 114–115, 150, 152–153, 159, 176, 187
ATTEMPT-BECOME construction   157
Attraction   2, 4, 113, 178
Auxiliar   6, 14, 18, 36, 152, 208, 221, 241, 243, 245, 249
Available variation   115, 120–121, 123, 128

B

BADIP   4, 70, 77–79, 98
Beavers   27, 36, 108–110, 134
Biber   112, 205, 209–212, 239
Boas   101, 110–111, 134, 136
BYU-BNC   214

C

Causation   66, 99, 245–248, 253, 256–258, 261
  See also direct causation
  See also Dutch causative
  See also indirect causation
  See also periphrastic causative
  See also volitional causation
Causative emotional verb   74, 76
Caused agency   247
  See also caused motion
  See also caused reception
Caused motion   26, 127, 166, 179, 195
  See also caused agency
  See also caused reception

Caused reception   166, 168–169, 179
  See also caused agency
  See also caused motion
Child Directed Speech   41–43, 62
Child language   7, 39, 41–42, 46, 56, 60–61, 63
CHILDES   3, 39, 42, 45, 63
Cifuentes Ferez   113–114, 116, 134
Clitic   70–75, 84–86, 92, 100–101
  See also accusative clitic
  See also dative clitic
CLMET corpora   214
Cluster analysis   2
Co-referential   40, 146, 221
Cognitive complexity   211, 240
Cognitive Grammar   11–12, 16–19, 23, 36–37, 100, 129, 135, 148, 197, 239
  See also cognitive linguistics
  See also cognitive semantics
Cognitive linguistics   1, 3, 6–7, 36–37, 134–135, 163, 195–196, 198, 239–240, 242, 260
  See also Cognitive Grammar
  See also cognitive semantics
Cognitive semantics   37, 108, 137, 195, 242–243, 260–261
  See also Cognitive Grammar
  See also cognitive linguistics
Collexeme   4–5, 137, 145, 152–158, 160–162, 165–167, 170, 172, 175–176, 178, 180–181, 197
Colligation   2
  See also collostruction
Collocation   2, 39, 61, 63, 113, 152, 202, 206, 208, 253, 258

Collostruction 2, 4–5, 7,
    105–106, 112–113, 137, 152,
    154, 163–164, 173, 178, 180,
    195–197, 259
    See also colligation
Communication verb 134, 158
Communicative expression 130
Complement clause 6, 147, 150,
    152–153, 158, 160, 202–204, 207,
    209–212, 221, 223–224, 226,
    229, 232–233, 235–236, 239
    See also complementation
Complementation 5, 145–154,
    157–158, 160, 163–164,
    201–206, 208–209, 224, 231,
    237–238, 240
    in Spanish 148, 151, 164
    See also complement clause
    See also complementizer
Complementizer 6, 150,
    160–164, 201–206, 208–211,
    213, 215–221, 224–225, 227,
    229, 233, 237, 239–240
    See also zero complentizer
Complex predicate 36, 127, 136
Complex verb 3, 12, 26–29, 36
Complexity 2, 209–211, 229, 240
Conceptual constituency 11, 13,
    15–19, 21, 23, 25, 27–35, 37
Conceptual valence structure
    111, 129
Concordance 6, 63, 214
Concrete 5, 44, 48, 50, 52, 56,
    90, 170–173, 175, 182–183, 185,
    187, 192–193, 195, 244
    -to-figurative 17
Conditional probability 2
Conditioning effect 225, 229
    See also conditioning factor
Conditioning factor 6, 201–202,
    204, 206–208, 224, 238
    See also conditioning effect
Constituency 3, 7, 11–19, 21–23,
    25–37, 70, 85, 109–110, 202
Construction 1–7, 11–19, 21–23,
    25–27, 29–37, 39, 41–45, 47,
    49–51, 53–63, 65–69, 71–77,
    79–85, 87–101, 105–137, 139,
    141, 143, 145–170, 173, 175–184,
    194–198, 201–206, 208,
    240–246, 248–251, 254–262
    -driven 5, 111, 132–133

See also construction
    grammar
See also constructional unit
Construction grammar 1–7,
    16, 36–37, 39, 41, 43–44,
    60, 62–63, 77, 100–101, 110,
    134, 136, 148, 162–164, 180,
    196–197, 241–242, 260
    See also construction
Constructional unit 127
Control 66–67, 88, 158, 171,
    188, 253
Coreferentiality 212, 221, 224,
    249, 261
Corpora 2–4, 6–7, 37, 42, 72,
    77–79, 97–99, 149, 163, 165,
    177, 195–196, 198, 201, 213–215,
    217–219, 238, 249, 260
    See also corpus
Corpus 1–7, 11–13, 42, 50, 52,
    60–63, 65, 67, 70–72, 74, 76–
    83, 87–88, 91, 98–101, 105–107,
    111–113, 128, 131–132, 134, 137,
    145, 147, 149–151, 153, 155, 157,
    160–161, 163–166, 169–171,
    173, 175, 177–178, 184, 187,
    189, 192, 195–198, 201, 203,
    213–215, 220–221, 238–242,
    245, 248–249, 259–261
    See also corpora
    See also annotated corpus
Corpus del Español 4, 112, 134
Cotemporality 212, 221, 223,
    232, 235–236
Croft 16, 36, 41, 62, 88, 99, 108,
    110, 134

D

Data aggregation procedure 221
Data-driven 111
Dative 4–5, 65, 67–68, 70–74,
    79, 84, 101, 152, 165–171,
    173–174, 176–186, 188–189,
    191–195, 198, 259
    See also Dutch dative
    See also prepositional dative
Dative clitic 70, 74
    See also clitic
Davies 112
DCA 152–153, 156–157, 166–168,
    172–174, 176, 178, 180–181,
    184, 194

See also Distinctive
    Collexeme Analysis
Density map 250, 256
Derivation 45–46, 63, 146
DESIRE verbs 158
    See also DESIRE-BECOME
    construction
DESIRE-BECOME construction
    149
    See also DESIRE verbs
Diachronic 3, 6, 110, 197, 201–
    205, 214, 216–217, 219, 222,
    224, 232–233, 235, 237–238
Diagrammatic feature 111
    See also diagrammaticity
Diagrammaticity 111
    See also diagrammatic feature
Direct causation 246, 253
    See also causation
Direct object 12, 14–15, 25–27,
    32–33, 35, 42–44, 52, 66,
    70–76, 78, 97, 152, 172–174,
    179, 181–184, 194–195,
    197–198, 221, 254, 259
    See also Double object
    See also Indirect object
    See also Object
Directional motion 105–107,
    110–112, 115, 117–118,
    126–128, 132
    See also directionality
Directionality 116–117, 120–122,
    124–126, 128, 137
    See also directional motion
Discourse formula 202, 204,
    206–208, 211, 213, 240
Discourse topicality 209
Distinctive Collexeme Analysis
    5, 145, 152–153, 162, 165–167,
    170, 172, 175–176, 197
    See also DCA
Distributional analysis 107, 113,
    119–121, 123
Ditransitive 5, 97, 129–130, 168,
    170–173, 177, 181–183, 196, 242,
    244, 254
Double object 5, 166–170, 173,
    176, 178, 180–182, 194–195,
    198, 259
    See also direct object
    See also indirect object
    See also object

Index

Dutch causative 6, 241, 245, 259–260
See also causative
Dutch dative 5, 165, 167, 169, 173–174, 179, 193, 195
See also dative
Dutch postposition 3, 11

E
Empathy 77, 88–89, 96, 100
English 3–5, 7, 18, 27, 31, 37, 39, 43, 63, 66, 91, 97, 99, 101, 107–111, 113, 126–131, 133–136, 146, 148, 158, 160, 163–164, 166–169, 175–176, 178–181, 195–198, 203–205, 213–215, 217–219, 237–240, 242, 245–246, 259–260
Epistemic 87, 147–148, 158, 161–162, 202–204, 206–208, 239–240
Event integration 147
Exemplar 6, 54, 134, 241–245, 247–259, 261
Experiencer 3–4, 65–67, 69, 71–77, 79–81, 83–89, 91–94, 96–97, 99, 101, 148

F
Family resemblance 243, 258, 260
Feeling 4, 65, 72, 80–81, 86, 88–89, 92–94, 96–98
Figurative 5, 103, 171–173, 182, 185, 188, 192, 252, 262
First person subject 87
See also person
Fisher Exact 173, 187
Force dynamics 246
Formalist 146–147
French 31, 39, 99, 109, 131, 148, 163, 167
Frequency 2–4, 44, 46–48, 50–51, 54, 60–61, 63, 65–67, 71, 77–78, 80, 83, 85, 92–93, 97–98, 101, 106, 110, 113–116, 118, 121–122, 134, 147, 153–154, 165–166, 168, 170–177, 186, 195, 198, 202–206, 211, 215–217, 219, 239, 258
See also absolute frequency

G
Genre 4, 65, 72, 78–81, 83, 93–95, 97–98, 205
Germanic language 5, 105–106, 116, 118, 133, 167, 238
Givón 36, 76, 84, 89, 100, 136, 147, 163, 212, 239
Goal-oriented 107, 113, 120, 123
Goldberg 3, 5, 7, 16, 33, 36, 41, 53, 63, 97, 100, 110–111, 126–131, 133–134, 145, 148–149, 163, 166, 168, 176, 178, 180–181, 196, 242–244, 260
Gower 250, 260
Grammaticalization 36, 101, 145, 158, 161, 164, 198, 203–204, 239–240
Granularity 2, 110, 244
Gries 1–2, 4–7, 65, 94, 100, 105–106, 111–113, 115, 134, 137, 145, 152, 154, 163–167, 173, 176, 179–180, 195–196, 198, 222, 249, 260
gustar 67, 72–73, 76, 82–83, 101, 152

H
Harmony 212, 221, 224
Hebrew 109
Hindi 131, 135

I
Iconic(ity) 52–53, 147–148, 212, 239
Idiom 39–42, 44, 49–50, 63, 135, 152, 183, 197
Implicit knowledge 165
Indirect causation 246, 253
See also causation
Indirect object 66, 70–72, 74–76, 97, 152, 174, 179, 181–183, 194–195, 197–198, 221, 254, 259
See also direct object
See also double object
See also object
Infinitival complement 5, 145–147, 149–157, 162, 164
See also sentential complement
See also complementation

Inter-linguistic variation 105–106, 110, 126, 133
See also intra-linguistic variation
Interaction 7, 36–37, 42, 72, 113, 137, 164, 187–194, 198, 201–202, 205, 207, 222–224, 229, 231–233, 235, 237–238, 256, 261
Intra-linguistic variation 105–106, 109–110, 126, 133
See also inter-linguistic variation
Intransitive 3, 12–13, 15, 26–29, 35, 54–58, 60, 113, 185, 210, 253–255, 257
See also transitivity
Italian 3–4, 39–43, 45, 47, 49, 51–55, 57, 59–63, 65–71, 73–75, 77–87, 89–94, 96–99, 101, 106, 109, 135–136, 167

J
Japanese 39, 96, 100–101, 109
Judgments 1, 11, 13, 15, 30, 32–33, 35, 170, 198, 259

L
LABLITA corpus 79
Landmark 17, 19–20
Langacker 3, 7, 11, 13, 16–20, 23, 36–37, 89, 100, 110–111, 126, 129, 135, 176, 179, 197, 212, 239
Language acquisition 3, 39, 41–42, 48, 58, 61, 63, 100, 137
Language-internal 206–207
factor 206
Lemma 81–83, 112–113, 152–153, 155–156, 167, 175, 214, 249, 252, 261
Lemma Argument Probability Hypothesis 167
Length 6, 23, 28, 107, 178–179, 210, 221–224, 226, 232, 235
Leuven News Corpus 249
Lexicalization 105, 115, 133, 137, 198, 203
Light verb 3–4, 39, 41–42, 61–63, 156, 177–180, 182

M

Manner salience 109–110, 134
Manner verb 115, 118, 120–121, 123–126, 132
Matrix clause 6, 152, 160, 202–204, 207–209, 211, 213, 221, 224–225, 227, 229
Meaning 5, 16–17, 23, 36, 43–44, 47, 50, 52–56, 60, 66, 68–69, 71, 73, 76, 80–82, 92, 97, 106–107, 110–112, 115–118, 120–122, 127–131, 134, 136, 148–149, 157, 160–161, 174, 176–177, 179, 185, 192, 194, 196, 205, 241–242, 244, 246, 252
Mental activity 5, 96, 145, 155, 157–158
Mental process 66, 80, 86, 96, 98, 100
Mental verb 99, 237
 See also verb of cognition
Metaphorical sense 171, 173, 249
Mode 6, 36–37, 94, 105, 112, 127, 134–135, 174, 187–191, 194, 197, 202–205, 213–215, 217, 219–220, 222–224, 229–234, 238–241, 243–245, 247, 249, 251, 253, 255, 257, 259, 261
Monolingual corpus 11
Motion 3–5, 19–24, 26, 28–29, 31–32, 34–36, 55, 65, 73–74, 76, 88, 93, 96–97, 105–129, 131–137, 139, 141, 143, 146, 149, 160, 164, 166, 179, 195, 246
 event 19–24, 26, 28–29, 31–32, 34, 105–108, 110, 112–113, 122, 127, 129, 134–137
 verb 29, 34–36, 105–107, 109–110, 112–113, 116, 118, 120–121, 123, 125, 128, 131–132, 134, 160
Multi-word unit 39
Multidimensional 2, 6, 241–242, 250, 259–260
Multidimensional Scaling 2, 6, 241, 250, 259–260
Multifactorial 2, 6, 100, 179, 201, 203, 205, 207, 209, 211, 213, 215, 217, 219, 221, 223, 225, 227, 229, 231, 233, 235, 237, 239
Multivariate 2, 210, 245, 250

N

Narasimhan 131, 135
Negation 207–208, 249, 262
Network 16, 41, 55, 61, 182, 242, 260–261
Nominalization 3, 12, 14, 32, 40, 47–48, 74, 92
Noun 5, 18, 21, 23, 25, 40–41, 43–58, 61, 67, 78, 84–85, 89, 91, 98, 100, 151, 155, 167, 172, 177, 179, 184, 192, 204–205, 207, 209–210, 221–222, 226, 235
Number 1, 4, 16, 32, 40, 44, 58, 65–66, 72–74, 77–79, 81–83, 85–87, 92, 94–95, 112, 114, 154, 168–170, 175–177, 202, 206, 213–214, 222–224, 226–229, 233, 242, 244, 249, 252–253, 261

O

Object 3–5, 12, 14–16, 25–27, 31–33, 35, 42–44, 52–55, 61, 65–79, 81, 83–93, 96–97, 99–101, 106, 111–112, 152, 166–170, 172–174, 176, 178–184, 194–195, 197–198, 201, 206, 211, 221, 239–240, 249, 254, 257, 259
 See also direct object
 See also double object
 See also indirect object
Observational data 1
Old Baily Corpus 214
Onomatopoeia 51–52, 58, 61
Oral 4, 18, 70, 74, 77–79, 81, 83–84, 93–95, 99, 112, 135, 161–162, 183, 212, 221, 223, 232, 235–236
 See also spoken
 See also written

P

p-value 113, 115, 120–124, 154, 173, 187–188, 222
Panchronic 224, 229
Parallel analysis 205
Particle 3, 11–14, 106, 135, 167, 169, 238
Passive/passivization 3, 12–16, 30–33, 35–37, 74, 76, 81, 91, 192, 195
Path verb 117–118, 120, 122–123, 125, 132
Period 1, 48, 51, 60, 201, 205, 213–215, 217, 219, 221–224, 229, 232–237
Periphrastic causative 176, 245–246
 See also causation
Person 4, 65, 71–72, 74, 76–77, 80, 84–89, 94–101, 112, 124, 142, 148, 178–179, 183, 205, 207–208, 210–211, 221–224, 226–227, 231, 249, 261
 See also first person subject
Phonological constituent 18, 29–30
Piacere 67, 71–72, 82–83
Pivot schema 39, 41, 60–61
$P_{\log}$ value 154
Polarity 209, 212, 221, 224, 242, 249
Polysemy 62, 165, 167–168, 170–171, 194, 242, 260
Prepositional dative 5, 166–167, 169, 176
 See also dative
Prepositional phrase 12, 23, 27, 29, 34, 37, 70, 75, 107
Prime verb 6, 165, 188, 192–194
Priming 5, 42, 53, 163, 165, 168, 170, 179, 184–186, 188–198, 238
 experiment 5, 165, 184, 186, 191
Principle of No Synonymy 148, 157
Private verb 96
Probabilistic knowledge 166
Processes of feeling 96
Pronominal subject 209, 221
Pronominal syncretism 67
Prosodic realization 212
Prototype/prototypical 2, 6–7, 49, 63, 106, 112, 117–118, 120, 125, 129–130, 132–133, 168, 170–171, 177, 194, 196, 208, 241–245, 248, 254, 259
 sense 6
Psych-verbs 66, 99
Psycholinguistic 5, 163, 165, 167, 175, 184, 196

Q

Quantitative   1–3, 6–7, 45, 80, 84, 98, 100–101, 105–107, 109–111, 113–115, 117–119, 121, 123, 125, 127–129, 131–133, 135, 137, 139, 141, 143, 149–150, 164, 166–167, 174, 176, 179, 195, 204, 240–242, 245, 249–251, 261
Querer   5, 80–82, 153–155, 157, 160

R

Radial category   3, 39, 41, 55, 61
Radial polysemy   242
Regression   2, 6, 81, 94–95, 187–190, 192, 201–202, 205, 214, 220–222, 224, 229, 238, 251, 261
Resultative   22–23, 25, 27, 29, 97, 130, 134
Rhythm   213, 238
Romance language   67, 77, 84, 93, 98–100, 105–106, 118, 131, 163

S

Satellite-framed   106–107, 109–110, 127
Schematic construction   5, 19, 53, 111, 127–128, 130–131
  See also schematicity
Schematicity   105, 111–112, 128, 130, 133
  See also schematic construction
Second person subject   210
Secondary predicate   108, 127
Semantic bond   147
Semantic map   6, 248, 256
Semantic proximity   211
Semantic variation   248, 259
Semantics   6, 13, 16, 18–19, 22, 28, 30–32, 34–35, 37, 39, 43, 45–46, 49, 54, 60, 74, 76, 99–101, 108, 113–115, 117–118, 122–123, 125–126, 131, 134–135, 137, 147–148, 157, 162–163, 167, 169, 174–176, 179–180, 194–196, 198, 241–243, 245–246, 249, 251–252, 259–262

sense   5–6, 30, 32, 42, 45, 49–50, 52, 73, 80, 96, 111, 131–133, 147–149, 157–158, 165, 167–185, 187–197, 241–245, 248–251, 255–260
Sentential complement   5, 145–147, 149–164, 175
  See also complementation
  See also infinitival complement
Slobin   108–110, 134–136
Spanish   1, 3–5, 18, 65–73, 75–87, 89–94, 96–97, 99–101, 105–109, 111–113, 115, 117–121, 123, 125–137, 139, 141, 143, 145–152, 157, 160, 163–164, 259
Spoken   2, 6, 77–79, 98–99, 101, 136, 196, 201, 205, 213–222, 224, 229–234, 238, 248–249, 260
  See also oral
  See also written
Stefanowitsch   4–5, 7, 105–106, 112–113, 137, 145, 152, 163–164, 166–167, 180, 196, 198, 260
Stimulus   4, 65–66, 75–76, 80–81, 88–92, 94–95, 193, 248
Structural ambiguity   14
Structural factor   207, 212, 232
Structural feature   6, 201, 221
Subcategorization   5, 129, 165–167, 175, 194, 196–197
  probability   5, 165, 167, 175, 197
Subject   3–4, 6, 12–13, 15, 23, 25–27, 29, 32–35, 40, 44, 65–67, 69, 71–81, 83–94, 96–97, 99–101, 108, 129, 145–146, 148–149, 152, 157, 161, 163, 168, 184, 194, 197, 202, 204, 206–212, 221, 223–224, 226–227, 231, 235, 243, 248
Syncretism   67–68, 71–72, 74–75, 97

T

Talmy   19, 37, 105–110, 115, 118, 126–127, 132–134, 137, 239, 246–248, 258, 260
Target verb   165, 184–194, 203

Telic motion   4, 23, 105–109, 111–117, 119, 122, 124–128, 131–133
Tense   6, 87, 135, 160, 164, 181, 208, 221, 223–224, 226, 228–229, 231–232, 235–237, 249, 262
Tesnière   115, 137
that/zero   6, 201–207, 209, 211, 213, 215–217, 219, 221–223, 225, 227, 229, 231–233, 235, 237, 239
to-dative   166, 169, 195
Tomasello   41, 49, 61–63, 110, 137, 202, 204, 239
Topicalization   3, 12–16, 30, 33–35
Trajector   17, 19–20, 244
Transfer of possession   171, 177, 194
Transitivity   7, 31, 36–37, 63, 99, 101, 135, 197, 249, 253–255, 261
  See also intransitive
Traversal   20, 23–28
Turkish   62, 131
Twente News Corpus   249
Typology   4, 36–37, 39, 62, 80, 101, 105–112, 115, 117–119, 126–128, 131–137, 163–164, 239–240

U

Unavailable variation   120, 123
understand   6–7, 18, 21, 41, 56, 61, 76–77, 80, 84, 96, 98, 111, 131, 133, 151, 155, 163, 178, 181, 201, 209, 211, 214, 218–222, 224–230, 232–233, 237–238
Universal semantic component   109
Usage-based   1, 5, 36, 39, 41, 48, 61, 63, 97–98, 106, 110, 126, 131, 133, 135, 137, 145, 176, 194, 197, 202, 244, 259–260

V

Variation   30, 40, 93, 97–98, 105–106, 108–110, 112, 114–115, 117–123, 125–126, 128, 131–133, 135–136, 164, 166–167, 169–171, 195, 197, 206, 216, 222, 226, 232–233, 239–242, 248–251, 259–260

Verb-driven 5, 105, 111, 132–133
Verb-framed 105–106, 109, 132–133
Verb-related noun 44–49, 51, 57–58
Verbal argument 211
 See also argument
Verb of cognition 6, 101, 146, 201, 205, 224
 See also mental verb
Verb of communication 157
Verb of feeling 4, 72, 80, 86, 89, 92, 97

Volitional causation 247
 See also causation

W

Way-construction 128–129, 131, 135–136
Wordsmith 214–215
Written 2, 4, 6, 30, 66, 70, 75, 77–79, 81, 94, 112, 170, 184, 196, 201, 205, 213–222, 224, 229–234, 238
 See also oral
 See also spoken

Z

Zero complementizer 6, 160–163, 201–206, 209–211, 213, 216, 218, 220–221, 224, 237, 239
 See also complementation
 See also complentizer
Zero Derived Noun 45–46
Zero form 201–202, 204–205, 211, 215–217, 219–220, 224–227, 229, 231–233, 235, 237–238